THE SHORT-TERM RETIREMENT PROGRAM

Break Out of Your Financial Prison

ROBERT C. FEOL

The Short-Term Retirement Program
Copyright © 2019 Robert C. Feol

Trade Paperback ISBN: 978-1-7340230-0-8
eBook ISBN: 978-1-7340230-2-2

Dark Horse Solutions
PO Box 381373
Germantown, TN 38183

FIRST EDITION

Designed by GKS Creative, Nashville

Publisher's Cataloging-In-Publication Data

(Prepared by The Donohue Group, Inc.)

Names: Feol, Robert C., author.
Title: The Short-Term Retirement Program : break out of your financial prison / Robert C. Feol.
Description: First edition. | Germantown, TN : Dark Horse Solutions, [2019]
Identifiers: ISBN 9781734023008 (trade paperback) | ISBN 9781734023022 (ebook)
Subjects: LCSH: Real estate investment--United States. | Finance, Personal--United States. | Retirement--United States--Planning.
Classification: LCC HD255 .F46 2019 (print) | LCC HD255 (ebook) | DDC 332.63240973--dc23

To Shannon, Robbie, Kerrigan, and Tennessee
I realize my life's purpose when I look in to each of your faces.
And to Al Plumb
For believing.

All the financial calculators in this book were designed by Robert Feol and can be accessed for free by going to ShortTermRetirement.com. While you are there, feel free to ask questions, leave comments, and look around for updated news, investment strategies, and tools designed to help you on your journey to financial freedom.

If you want to take your financial awareness and supercharge it to the next level, Robert Feol offers online courses and private coaching for those looking to implement Short-Term Retirement strategies into their daily life or those who are considering a career change who want to be trained in real estate investing by one of the top real estate minds in the industry. Go to ShortTermRetirement.com/coaching for more information.

If you want to start collecting graded numismatic silver and gold coins, and become part of Robert's and his team's mission to get physical gold and silver into every reader's home each and every month, go to WeeklyGoldReport.com.

Contents

Foreword by Robert Shemin

I first met Robert Feol years ago when I was scheduled to speak to a local real estate group in Memphis, Tennessee. A few weeks before the scheduled appearance, I got a call from this young guy who had a Memphis radio show; he wanted to interview me for my upcoming appearance. While I didn't know who he was before the phone call and subsequent radio interview, I was so impressed AFTER the interview that I went on record saying, without a doubt, his interview was the best radio interview I have had in a long time, and his radio show, while consistently #1 in weekend talk in Memphis, is also, in all likelihood, the best real estate show in the United States, hands down.

It doesn't surprise me then, after reading this hefty manuscript that he has taken his energy, passion for helping others, and not inconsiderable investing experience and parlayed them into the book you now hold in your hands. A veritable tome of investment knowledge, theory, and mathematics, and a primer on why, when you think you are doing everything right, you are actually doing everything wrong. It's a testament to his unique genius, this Short-Term Retirement Program. I have invited him to speak at my seminars, and my students are always remarking what a fascinating speaker and teacher he is. I am glad to call him my friend and need to emphasize that this is an absolute MUST READ for any beginning or advanced real estate investor.

In life, there are leaders and there are followers, but long before those groups show up, there are prophets. Prophets are rare, the stuff of legends.

And when it comes to real estate, Robert Feol is exactly that...legendary.

Robert Shemin
New York Times best-selling author
RobertShemin.com

Prologue

Equity is dead.

Net worth? That's dead too.

Think I'm wrong? Let me offer you a hypothetical proposition. You can, at this very moment, take one of the two following offers. You have five seconds to decide, so choose well. I will offer you your choice of one of the two following things:

1. One million dollars in equity, secured by nine million dollars in real estate holdings. Total value of the real estate portfolio gifted to you is ten million US dollars. If you choose this option, you will INSTANTLY become a millionaire

2. One hundred thousand USD in cash.

Which do you choose?

If you choose anything other than option B, for any reason, you have made a grievous error in judgment. Option A is a—follow me here—***HORRID*** choice. Choice A is simply wrong, and there is no other way of putting it.

Here's why:

If you choose option A, you do, in fact, get a million dollars of an equity stake. You are, at that moment in time, transformed into an instant millionaire. **But the double-edged sword is that the one million dollars in "equity" exists only because the actual fair market value (FMV) of the properties you obtained, in this case ten million dollars, carry nine million dollars in debt against them.** You need to remember that, in addition to "getting" one million dollars in equity, you are also "getting" nine million dollars in real estate debt obligations (loans), ***all*** of which require monthly payments. **Loans that YOU need to repay.** Because that is what equity is—the difference between the amount you OWE on a property and its true fair market value.

The problem with choice A is that most Americans simply don't realize that the idea of being a "millionaire" is an antiquated notion that gets overused and, quite simply put, abused today. **Being a millionaire is meaningless if the label comes with a seemingly endless stream of monthly debt obligations that last for thirty years or more. If being a millionaire means you are saddled in debt and are awake at night wondering how you will repay that debt, quite frankly, you don't WANT to be a millionaire.**

This book is about the simple notion that everything you have been taught about money is WRONG. For example, consider this timeless wisdom we have all been given: you should "buy a house using a thirty-year loan." It will, in theory, appreciate. Then when you "have some equity in the house," refinance the home if you can get a fractionally lower interest rate and "cash out." Use these funds to "improve your house" or "pay cash for a car."

For a short time, you will know what it is like to have money until you realize that you have started the debt cycle all over again. Another thirty years of payments on your house. When does it end?

Answer: it doesn't end. This idea was never designed to make a person wealthy. **It is, by its very nature, designed to *keep you in debt*.**

And yet, tens of millions of Americans are engaged in this futile exercise throughout their lives—this endless cycle of thirty-year loans and loan refinancing—only to find out later in life that they are underwater on their houses and can NEVER PAY THEM OFF because their thirty-year loan refinances extend beyond their expected lifetime.

Truth be told, at that point, these people start to realize that they never really "owned" anything. That they were, quite simply, de facto slaves to the bank.

The only way we can break this cycle is to change our perspective on what matters financially and to begin aligning our financial priorities with a new, effective, and systematic financial plan that carries measurable outcomes and goals that work in OUR financial favor, as opposed to some bloated, corporate, corrupt financial institution's gain.

Traditional real estate investing systems, which are focused on how much equity you are able to build up, are *poison*. Investing systems that rely on students building equity and then equating this to profit and/or wealth is farcical. It is like someone telling a blatant lie. If I told you my students become millionaires because they take over someone's debt obligations and have an equity stake in a house (along with payments), I'd be lying to them. **They *may* have a million-dollar net worth, but they certainly aren't able to live like millionaires.** In fact, I would suggest to you that they would have been better off NOT buying real estate this way in the first place. **And the reason for this is because, at some point, they simply won't be able to service the debt.**

Mathematically, the odds are against them servicing this debt to completion, as I will explain later in this book. The day that happens, the house of cards comes falling down.

Why Does Option B Make Sense?

There are many reasons option B is a far superior option, but I will give you five simple ones

1. One hundred thousand dollars in cash is spendable money in hand.

2. These funds can be used to reduce debt and, in doing so, improve cash flow.

3. These funds can be invested to provide a long-term income stream, through savvy investment in cash flowing real estate purchased significantly below market prices.

4. These funds carry no debt obligations or monthly payments.

5. These funds actually DO improve your net worth and, if invested wisely, can multiply it exponentially.

If you have ever heard the saying "cash is king," you are getting a glimpse of why option B makes so much more sense than option A. Yet many real estate gurus over the past few decades have touted the idea of "zero-down investing." As recently as 2017, I had investors come to me and say, "*If I can't buy for zero down, I am not buying.*" It's an idea that is ingrained in our American collective unconscious that good deals come only if you can get something for nothing.

Let me tell you what happened to these people who bought properties for zero down and pulled cash out from their thirty-year mortgages when banks would allow them to, prior to the 2008 "credit crisis," with very, *VERY* few exceptions: **They lost all their properties to foreclosure, ruined their credit, and spent the cash they never should have had in the first place**. I saw it personally.

Is that the person you want to become? Or is it possible there is something better?

In this book, I am going to teach you a radically different system of buying your primary residence *AND* investing in real estate (should you choose to do so), so radical, in fact, that I use myself. That may not sound strange to you, but it should. **Many real estate "gurus" who have "systems" never actually use the systems they design, and frequently, they don't even own real estate, though they would lead you to believe that they do!**

But I own lots of real estate. Paid off real estate, by the way. I left my teaching position in the Memphis City Schools by investing in real estate. And I use this system, not only because I designed it but also because it WORKS.

And if you do it properly, it will work for you too.

I designed The Short-Term Retirement Program with a really simple idea in mind, the idea that *until we are able to set up a consistent stream of income free of debt obligation sans the ever-present threat of foreclosure, we don't really have anything and will always be at risk.* Everything in life is risky, to be sure, but some things are more risk laden than others. One of the things I think is the most risky is having a single source of income through an employer. Your boss can fire you at any time, for any reason. When that happens, you get to hit the bricks and pray you find a job.

You know what is better than having a boss for most people? **NOT having one** and having multiple streams of income. In my opinion, the best way to do this is through owning free and clear, unencumbered rental real estate. And, if I may add, to own as many homes as possible, free and clear, in the shortest period of time. But even if you don't want to own real estate for investment purposes, that's okay, *because the best thing in the world that can ever happen to you financially is to pay off your primary residence as quickly as you can and never have a mortgage obligation again.*

And I will show you how.

So that is what this book is about. I will show you how to purchase highly discounted real estate and pay it off in as little as three to five years with as little money as possible. Know, however, that doesn't mean "no money down." As a rule, we always want to minimize our cash investiture, but we don't want to seek out a zero-cash transaction. **Paying zero cash down is not the goal; paying houses off in full is the goal**.

And time is of the essence.

I don't have a degree in finance and am not a certified public accountant. I am a former schoolteacher by profession, turned full-time real estate investor by a series of fortuitous circumstances, which, at the time, seemed absolutely disastrous. And I have had the fortune of being given tons of hardships, which tested my resolve, my ability to keep my *word* in situations that were extremely challenging, to say the least. I have been betrayed by some of my closest "friends" whom I had built successful companies with and consulted for men who yearned to use this system I designed only to have their unethical business practices betray them.

Yet the system has stood intact. It has stood up to the challenges of what real estate, life, and dark circumstances had to throw at it, so I know it will work for you too.

You are going to have to change a lot of ideas along the way as I show you how to buy real estate. There are concepts you need to absorb such as how to find motivated sellers who fit our criteria (important), how to negotiate properly (important), and how to find your "pieces of the puzzle" (critical) to make this whole system work. Remember, if you learn the techniques in this book but fail to absorb the principles of fiscal health and responsibility included herein, you are only going to create more problems for yourself in the future.

Real estate investing is truly a double-edged sword. Allow me to show you how to use it the right way, one time, and in doing so, you will never have to worry about money again.

I can give you the fishing pole you need for the financial freedom that not only your family yearns for but also for generations of your family to come.

It can be done.

Robert Feol

Memphis, Tennessee, (July 19, 2011/January 15, 2019)

An Important Note
Regarding Footnotes and Citations
in This Book

It is impossible to understand many of the concepts in this book without additional reading, research, and supporting documentation, especially when such supporting articles will give you evidentiary proof of what I am describing or discussing conceptually.

As much as possible, and within the acceptable limits of what is known as *"fair use"* under International Copyright Law, I have tried to incorporate excerpts from articles that will assist the reader in the additional learning and understanding of fundamental concepts. However, whereas I cannot obtain permission to reprint every article I would like to use in this book, I have instead created website notations, which will steer you to the appropriate websites and the commensurate original, creative works, which will assist you in understanding ideas and concepts discussed within this text.

I take no credit for any of these authors' works and instead am merely guiding the reader to websites or articles I myself have found informative or useful as additional, supplemental reading material for further research and investigation.

Whether you choose to read these or not is solely at your discretion.

Risk Disclaimer

This book is intended for educational purposes only and should NOT be taken as financial advice of any kind. Investing in any asset class, including real estate, carries inherent risk and the potential downside of a total and catastrophic financial loss. By reading this text, you agree to hold the author harmless and acknowledge that all examples and financial strategies in this book are for illustrative purposes only. All people mentioned in this text have had their names changed or are fictitious. Any similarities between real and fictitious people is strictly coincidental. Consult with your financial advisor and tax preparer before embarking in any financial investment journey, including real estate.

Introduction

On Mississippi Highway 302 one night, back somewhere in late July of 2011, a series of circumstances transpired which ended up with me walking, unexpectedly, for miles and miles in a Southerly direction on a lonely highway, in what started as late afternoon, then steadily progressed without reprieve—crepuscule, dusk, evening, night, and deep blackness. Eventually, I saw a light in the distance, and an hour later on foot I arrived at a gas station where I was run out by the manager as a homeless loiterer. Even though I had not been drinking and have never done any drugs, I am sure I looked homeless. So, I sat outside on the sidewalk, in the most oppressive heat I have ever felt. But I knew something was happening when, a short while later, the temperature dropped at least forty degrees. And then, what I can only describe as a series of "events" happened to me—the final event culminating in the most massive, and catastrophic, Mississippi hailstorm crushing in—where I was caught in the middle. I watched as it stopped traffic in all directions. People were running for shelter from their cars, sheltering in their cars, sheltering under bridges, the gas station, sheltering...anywhere.

It reminded me of what people prophetically call "the end times." And there I was, drenched, with no shelter to run to, where in the middle of it I had never felt more alone, more diminutive, more abandoned. Orphaned.

But it was in that moment that—as failingly as I am putting this into words—that "The Download" happened. In that moment the ideas for this book—which had certainly been swirling in my head for years—were unfalteringly cemented. This book had to be written, and there was absolutely no going back. Which was hard to believe, because at that moment, I was soaked like a rat, had been cast out of a gas station like a homeless person, and honestly felt like any hero's journey I had ever embarked on had most certainly come to an end. Yet, in the last moment, down to 1% of my cell phone battery, I was miraculously able to procure a ride from my first real Memphis friend of almost 20 years, Lisa Fairchild, an absolutely brilliant concert pianist, who was willing to head 50 miles south from Memphis to pick me up, somewhere after midnight, somewhere in the Mississippi blackness, even though I was unable to explain to her how I ended up in that particular place, or why.

I am sure I sounded like a total failure in that moment when I called her. Maybe I was. But, on that drive home, so out of my element, something kept reminding me of the Jonah and the Whale story from the bible. I learned later, there is no whale in that story. Jonah was swallowed by a big fish for running away from God's will and desire for action from him.

It stuck with me.

So it was, now in a completely unknown place, I started writing this book. I had some help, if only serendipitous guideposts on the way. A Native American shaman woman, Sister Wolf, was the first interlocutor, whose presence permeated my dreams. One dream of her, in addition to our phone calls and email exchanges, which I am sure she intentionally brought to me, was where I learned the difference between the words "purify" and "sanctify." Most people think the words are synonymous.

The lesson there was the meaning of "sanctify." It means to make holy or sacred, vs. clean or to make pure were not synonyms when I really looked at it.

I struggled with it, with the lesson. How did it, how could it, apply to me?

Trying to explain to my wife was equally difficult. We had just come off a recent business theft where our income went to zero, at the hands of what we had once considered "close friends." While she really worked hard to tell me that she knew I was in a good place, it was pretty hard to explain to her what was going on. Something strange had happened to me that dark Mississippi night. Our finances were in a tenuous place due to the theft, and we were unsure of where we were headed. Family planning was put off. The IRS hit us with a double audit. With the help of the greatest C.P.A. in the world, Jimmy Luke of Titan Financial, we got through. Truth be told, watching Jimmy in action made me feel like I could be an awesome CPA. He let me down by telling me this adage: "Robert, there are three types of people engineers, salespeople, and accountants. You are a salesperson, and you always will be."

So far—though I have tried—I can't seem to prove him wrong.

At one point, after I paid off the Adirondack home I mention in Chapter 1, I went to our Adirondack house for a week. Just by myself. I had heard on a fellow host's radio program about a woman who could allegedly read "The Akashic Record," what is described as "The Book of Life," and, allegedly, past lives. I was going through this transformation, so I called her. We spent an hour on the phone and she was spot on. I am a classic skeptic, but listened guardedly. I won't mention everything she said, but she talked about the book. She told me I was on point and was headed in the right direction, but it was a long road ahead. She seemed right about everything else, too. So, I kept writing. It took seven years.

When I finished the book, I wasn't sure what to do. I knew I had something different. I had coded all the Excel calculators and graphs to try to illustrate, as a teacher with a teaching background, what the student needed to know to start to implement **The Short-Term Retirement Program,** in their own personal life, and with success. It was a lot of work. I called some friends who had written books and was told to consider the sacrifices involved when you give your book copyright to a major publishing firm. They talked, quite frankly, about the tradeoffs—how, once your book goes out of print, under major publishing houses, if for no other reason because your publisher doesn't think it will be a success, that they mothball it and you can never get it back.

I couldn't do that. Not this far into the journey, and not with this text.

Nonetheless, I went to publishers. First, I went to BiggerPockets.com. It has its own real estate publishing arm. I had their founder on the radio a few years back, Joshua Dorkin, a super-intelligent guy. I was hoping that my experience, and the huge volume of transactions I had done, would be a boost for me getting in. Their editor asked for the first chapter and then turned the book down, saying that they had several upcoming books about retiring early with real estate. The fact that **The Short-Term Retirement Program** is, in fact, not about early retirement, but achieving financial freedom for people of any age was an irrelevant fact. A turn-down was a turn-down. I felt embarrassed in front of my staff, who were daily contributors to the site. Somehow, I kept buying houses, selling houses, paying my staff, paying my bills, and paying off my rental homes. The system was working, even as people disparaged it. I refused to let this book die.

Finally, I got accepted by a New York City publisher. I was elated. I felt l had arrived. But with every edit, and every recast of the book from their editorial team, I realized the publisher I had gone with was far less interested in my manuscript than it was with making money from the manuscript. They wanted to sell this book for $50! It was then I knew I had to get this book and this program out in a way that everyone could afford. So I have done that here. This book is the culmination of everything I want to share with you all.

Finally, I found Amy Collins and New Shelves Books. Less of a direct publisher and more of a marketing and literary consultancy, Amy is a genius when it comes to publishing. I was lucky to be one of the few authors they selected, to bring my book to market. Working with them has been eye opening, and was a crucial step to get this book into the form it is now – what you hold in your hands – an affordable, comprehensive manual on real estate investing and finance, designed to help anyone get from where they are now to where they want to be financially, regardless of circumstance.

It has been an honor to be able to write this book. A lot of heart and passion was poured into the project of writing and there wasn't a day where I worked on this book that I didn't pray it gets into the hands of someone who needs it and can benefit greatly from it. In a sea of books on finance and real estate, where you have so many choices, I want to sincerely thank you for picking up this book.

And, if I can do anything to help you on your journey to financial freedom, please don't hesitate to contact me.

PART 1

MONEY AS A MENTAL CONSTRUCT

1

An Interesting Story

How to buy an out-of-state vacation home without using a realtor, finance it without using a bank, and pay it off in full without giving the lender all the money in less than one year.

Before I get into the actual technical aspects of how *The Short-Term Retirement Program* and its fundamental acquisition and pay-down strategies operate, I thought I would give you a brief chapter on how creative real estate investing works. Creative real estate investing is not to be confused with no-money-down real estate investing, while in the past these two terms have been synonymous. Here is a quick comparison of a few types of real estate investing you need to know:

Retail real estate investing—paying full market value for a property, generally using all cash or by getting a bank loan. It requires an appraisal by the lender of record, if getting a loan.

No-money-down real estate investing—purchasing properties by (usually) some combination of non-bank financing, which does not include using an appraisal to determine property value or seeks to avoid using one. This can include taking a property "subject to," which means getting the deed to a home and taking over responsibility for the owner's payments (complicated and risky) or assuming a mortgage (usually not allowed anymore, although once it was allowed on certain mortgages).

Creative real estate investing—using simple forms of negotiation and logic to obtain favorable financing from sellers or banks in distress, which allows us to bypass the need for a loan application and (God forbid) approval process that puts us in a position of being told *no*. We don't like being told *no*, so we solve that issue by taking away the option of giving someone the opportunity to tell us *no*.

Creative real estate investing is what *The Short-Term Retirement Program* is about. It is about understanding motivated sellers and how you can solve their problems by architecting a win-win situation with them. It is a radical, "outside-the-box" thinking approach, which doesn't focus blindly on accumulating property but forces you to understand WHY a property may or (more importantly) may not be a good fit for you.

Buying properties is VERY EASY. Managing properties (including a primary residence with an income-producing unit, which is a core precept of this book) successfully and exiting them profitably is an altogether different story. Real estate can be extremely illiquid.[1]

With that in mind, and knowing that we are focused on using proven, solid techniques for creative real estate acquisitions, let me give you a personal story about a deal I did a few years ago, which illustrates many of these principles.

Pullman Avenue, Old Forge, New York

Growing up, I got to spend my summers in the Adirondack Mountains, an amazing place in upstate New York and my favorite place on Earth. My grandfather had purchased a waterfront cabin on the Fulton chain of lakes, specifically Fourth Lake, in the early 1950s. While I periodically got to visit this cabin with my father on home visits as a child during the summer, my parents divorced at an early age, and **an overwhelming memory I have of my visits to that property were that it was emphasized to me that the cabin was a very, very prized family possession**. So prized, in fact, that it remained to be seen if I or my sister were worthy of inheriting it. (This started when I was about five years old and continued into adulthood.)

The cabin became a huge source of contention between my father and my aunt (the custodians of the property) as the years passed, with my mother (divorced from my father) periodically adding fuel to the seemingly unending fire with various acrimonious comments since it had become a bad memory for her, too. Pleasant childhood memories of visits to the cabin became reminders of the conflict and duress that this material possession had unwittingly brought to so many members of our family, myself and my sister included. **It was almost like the idea of having a cabin in the Adirondack Mountains**

---

1   **Illiquid:** Not readily available, or in the case of a property, hard to move or sell in a timely fashion. For example, if you buy a property with cash and need that cash for some emergency purpose at a later time, generally, unless you can divest yourself of the property, you cannot access your cash. Hence, your cash is illiquid.

was an unattainable dream for common people like me, a dream reserved only for the doctors and lawyers of the world or their really well-behaved children. As time passed and I grew into adulthood, I found that instead of asking permission to stay at the family cottage, I would simply book a week rental in the village close by and then come to the family cabin to visit when I was in town. I did this for a few years, but it got old pretty fast. Finally, around the time I was about to turn thirty-five, I was coming to the conclusion that even though I had spent thirty-five years of my life doing what I was told would make me successful (working since the age of seven, having multiple jobs, getting four degrees, going to school, and getting excellent grades, etc.), I still didn't have much to show for it financially, and that needed to change. I told my wife it was about time we got our own vacation home and put this life issue to bed, so to speak.

   You see, the thing is, you will find that earning your own material things without inheriting them or stealing them from people who cared for you and trusted you is a good and rewarding thing. For me, I wasn't about to wait around another forty years to see if I might have a vacation home deeded to me, along with various other nuclear and non-nuclear family members, at which point we could draw up a "sharing schedule." For some people, this would be a fine arrangement, but I came from a poor, working-class family, and that isn't the legacy I want to leave for my children. I certainly don't want my son growing up with the lesson of *"If you are really nice to your 'allegedly' rich aunts and uncles AND you get lucky, you MIGHT inherit something of value someday."* **I want him to understand, clearly, from his youth, that ONLY hard work and quality education—along with some basic, honest financial principles—are the ticket to life success. I want to be living proof of these lessons I intend to share with him, and to show him that hard work and creative knowledge, when applied together, DO pay off.**

   Besides, a sharing schedule for the family camp would never have worked for me, anyway. It got tiresome to ask if I could come to the family vacation home once a year as it was, so I figured it was high time to start taking my own vacations and get my own place where no one would be my master. Assuming that could happen, permission to take a vacation in an area I loved was simply no longer needed.[2]

   We faced some significant obstacles, however. Primarily was the fact that most properties worth owning in the Adirondacks are priced in the over-500k range, particularly for what we were seeking. As there was simply NO way I had that much cash available, I needed to find a ***very*** motivated seller who was offering seller financing,

---

2   It also occurred to me that if I bought my own vacation home, I might stop feeling bad about myself and the whole experience—that maybe I had a chance to break the cycle of family squabbling over the family cabin.

which can be very hard to come by, if you don't know where to look. Personally, while many colleagues I have tremendous respect for have referred to me as a bona fide "hustler," I have found that years of nonstop work since childhood had burned me out and made me instinctively seek the path of least resistance in any situation, and this project was no exception. So, as you will see, **I took a radically different path, which many of my friends and family members assured me would be a waste of my time and a fool's errand from the start.**

Which Way Is the Crowd Running?

If you wanted to buy an out-of-state vacation home, what would you do first? Of course, you would look on the Internet and go to various realty-related sites in the region, but eventually you would call a realtor. The realtor would see you as a potential client, immediately get you all kinds of forms to sign so he or she can have exclusivity (meaning only he or she can represent you, guaranteeing themselves a commission), and then they would begin to show you listed properties based on your price range and loan approval amount that are currently available on the Multiple Listing Service (MLS).[3]

The fundamental problem with this approach is that realtors are not real estate investors, not even close. Realtors, for lack of a better euphemism, are like robots who know how to find properties on the MLS and bring them to potential buyers. They then cross their fingers and hope the buyer makes a purchase, AND that the deal doesn't fall through, in which case, they will get a 3% commission based on the sale price, less their pre-arranged split with their brokerage firm. This is fine for some super-qualified buyers who have lots of cash or don't mind paying retail (dare I say overpaying?) for a property. In the Feol house, however, frugality rules the day. We do our best not to pay retail, ever. Period. **And the unwritten rule is that you *NEVER* pay retail for a piece of real estate.**[4]

Knowing these facts, if I had called a realtor in Old Forge, New York, to help begin my vacation home search, I would have gotten shown lots of MLS-type properties that required a formal loan, which in turn would require my qualifying through a bank for a loan and bringing a massive down payment to secure the financing. That is, *if* I even found a realtor who was willing to show me properties without requiring me to furnish

---

3   **The Multiple Listing Service** is a data aggregator used by almost every licensed real estate company in the United States. Various software platforms are used, but essentially, it allows realtors to search homes for sale on the MLS. **The problem with this is that they have no access to homes being sold by private sellers or individuals, which is often where the best deals can be found.**

4   Prepare to become frugal.

them with a formal loan approval letter first. **Many will refuse to show properties or work with clients WITHOUT such a letter.** And even if I can afford a monthly payment on a 500k mortgage, that doesn't mean I have, or want to spend, 100k on a 20% down payment and pray for a bank's appraiser to give me a green light.

That is way too much work. Too much hassle. **And as I will teach you, committing to thirty years of debt enslavement is something I am unwilling and simply don't need to do.**

So instead, we took this route.

From *The Adirondack Express*, Tuesday, April 20, 2010

Out-of-state family seeks to rent, lease, or buy waterfront fixer upper on Fulton Chain, 1ˢᵗ–4ᵗʰ lakes, sandy bottom preferred. Looking to take possession by July 1 2010. All homes considered, regardless of condition. Price range of 500k and below. Short-term seller financing[5] a plus, willing to put down considerable down payment plus favorable interest rate. Excellent credit and references. Call 901.258.6944.

Us placing an ad in the local paper doesn't seem that radical, right? Wrong. The phone started to ring *instantly* with motivated sellers. But more importantly, the ad was designed to attract a very specific type of seller. Let's examine the ad line by line and see what it was designed to do:

- *Out-of-state family seeks to rent, lease, or buy waterfront fixer upper on Fulton Chain, 1ˢᵗ–4ᵗʰ lakes.* Being out of state, on the surface, makes us sound naive—not like we are investors, which usually immediately scares people away (they worry that they will get taken advantage of). Plus, the various types of financing indicate that we are flexible on terms, so more potential sellers are willing to call us.

- *Looking to take possession by July 1, 2010.* Indicates we are very serious and are looking for a quick closing to take possession (which we were).

- *All homes considered, regardless of condition.* Brings motivated and distressed sellers whose properties may be suffering from deferred maintenance or from disrepair.

5　**Seller Financing.** When the seller of a property conveys the property in exchange for a deed of trust (note), a promise to repay an agreed-upon sum over a pre-negotiated period of time. Usually used when there is no existing financing on a property, i.e., a family or seller owns a home in the "free and clear."

- *Price range of 500k and below.* Eliminates motivated sellers with higher value properties who may call and waste our time since that is not what we are looking for.

- *Short-term seller financing a plus, willing to put down considerable down payment plus favorable interest rate.* Shows that we are *seriously looking for seller's terms*[6] and lets sellers know that if they need a hard loan, or retail-type exit, we may not be a reliable source to call. Also informs sellers willing to consider owner's terms (which is what we really wanted) to expect a down payment that is considerable and, thus, encourage them to call.

- *Excellent credit and references.* Shows we are reliable payors and they can expect to call references as part of considering selling us a property on owner's terms.

Now, the phone did start to ring instantly, which is what we wanted. **However, not every call was suitable for us.** Many people calling were in a property they didn't want, were underwater on, or that they never used. Since they saw we were willing to pay up to 500k, naturally, they were asking us for this kind of figure.

We immediately got off the phone with these people as we don't overpay for properties, period.

We got lots of other calls, which, for some reason or another, didn't really fit the profile, and discarded these also. **It's important that if you use a newspaper ad to find motivated sellers, you don't give up; everyone, including my family, told me I would NEVER find a camp** that would be in a great location for the price range we were looking for, on owner's terms, and below 100k in price (even though we were willing to pay up to 500k in the right circumstances, we really were not wanting to pay a hard cost of more than 100k).[7]

Then, one day, the phone rang (it always does), and Emily called. Emily, it seemed, had a property she inherited and had been living there with her family for years, but the arduous Adirondack winters were beginning to have a toll on them. They wanted to move to North Carolina, where the pastures were seemingly greener. And so, I let her tell me about the house she had been trying to sell for two years, which went along the lines of the following:

---

6   In obtaining seller financing, you pay the seller directly instead of a bank.
7   There are two basic ways of finding tremendous value in real property—paying far below what a property is worth (**i.e., getting a great PRICE**), or getting terms that are so favorable on a property the price becomes irrelevant (**i.e., getting GREAT TERMS**). **In my personal case with this property (and as is usually the case), we were bargain shopping, looking for both great price AND terms.** In the Feol house, frugality, generally rules the day.

"It's beautiful in the village of Old Forge...there is a bunkhouse in the back...we just want to move and are ready to get out of here...we currently have it listed for 150k but are willing to take less."

Sounded good so far. The bunkhouse in the back was a HUGE bonus since I was planning on trying to find a vacation compound that my extended family could use as well. But some questions still had to be asked, so I came out with the double-barrel question upon which everything else would hinge:

"Emily, if I gave you enough of a down payment, would you be willing to carry the mortgage balance for me if I made you on-time monthly payments?'

Emily answered, *"If you put enough down, we would definitely be willing to consider that."*

I immediately booked a ticket for Shannon and me to go visit the following week. I knew we were definitely on to something here, and my real estate "instinct" was screaming it to me. But now the real work had just begun, as I had three things to do, each of critical importance:

1. Evaluate if the deal was legitimate AND appropriate for what I was looking for.[8]

2. Negotiate and arrange the terms of the deal with the seller directly, trying to score as low of a price as possible with great owner finance terms, and get these into a contract that the seller was willing to sign.

3. Ensure the seller gets to the closing table and signs, and picks up their check as agreed.

Seller Financing: The Holy Grail of Real Estate

The thing about seller financing—and this really is the thing—is that it eliminates the problems traditionally associated with purchasing a home and when used properly, becomes a tool of empowerment to those who are conditioned to believe that, due to cash, credit, or other historical financial circumstances (like a bankruptcy), they will never "qualify" for a home loan. Believe it or not, in the days before the growth of multinational corporate banks, people would frequently buy things using the barter system, as well as by making *installment payments*[9] on an otherwise unaffordable item, which is where one

---

8   Never settle. Period.
9   **Installment payments.** In the case of property sale or transfer using a Land Contract or Contract for Deed, the seller retains the legal title to the property while permitting the buyer to take possession of it for most purposes other than legal ownership. The sale price is typically paid in periodic installments, often with a balloon payment at the end.

makes a specific number of payments to a seller, which at the end of the payment period, after all payments were completed, the new owner would have full and unencumbered possession of whatever they were buying.

In the days of the great Western expansion of the United States, pioneers and settlers bought land heavily from the US government this way. This is how we get the term *land contract*.

But seller financing does more than take the uncooperative and finicky banks out of the real estate purchase equation; it sets up a potentially winning situation for both the buyer and seller without the hassle of government intervention, regulation, or corporate oversight.[10] More specifically, the seller-financed transaction is actually far, far easier than when you get a bank involved. Here is a comparison of bank financing versus seller financing. As you can see, the seller-financed transaction is not only much less of a hassle; it is also more cost friendly to both buyer and seller.

Bank (Industry) Financing	VERSUS	Seller Financing (Owner's terms)
• Requires an appraisal		• No appraisal needed
• Forces you to pay origination and bank fees, popularly known as "junk fees"		• No junk fees or forced origination points need to be paid, unless negotiated in advance and agreed upon by both parties
• Interest is based on prime. A zero percent interest rate would never happen for a home borrower		• Interest rate is fully negotiable. A zero percent interest rate is possible
• Gives you a 30-year amortization as standard repayment schedule, based on your debt-to-income ration (DTI) to determine loan amount		• Amortization (loan repayment schedule) is negotiable and flexible
• Often has an early payoff penalty		• No prepayment penalty
• Loan payoff is firm and inflexible		• Loan payoff can be settled through savvy negotiation, saving you tens of thousands in principal and interest payments

The fact is that this chart so clearly and simply illustrates why seller financing is far superior to bank financing. It is actually a wonder of mine why most people, generally speaking, believe that the bank has all the answers and make it their first stop when they are seeking out a home loan. Remember, the bank's job when (if) making a loan **is**

---

10   While becoming a rapidly antiquated notion, it is this writer's belief that individuals should be able to buy and sell their legally acquired possessions, including real property, without unnecessary corporate or governmental oversight.

to protect their shareholders' interest. This is why they force the borrower to pay for an appraisal (which is meaningless and cannot hope to reflect actual market value 100% of the time[11]), require a survey, flood insurance, escrow, etc. The list goes on. They are worried their loans are going to go bad, and they must protect themselves in every way possible.

And why wouldn't they? The odds of somebody defaulting in a thirty-year window of time on a primary mortgage are significant—certainly far greater than for someone who seeks to pay a property off in five years, right? **So the banks SHOULD be concerned because they are setting up borrowers for failure.**[12] We will get into this more in another chapter, but remember, *banks are FOR-PROFIT organizations,* which make money by lending to you when you take out a thirty-year loan, **and they make a vast amount of money, all things considered, especially when you look at the interest-bearing amortization schedule the bank furnishes you at the loan closing table.** Money, for banks, is EASY to make. Especially when people come begging for thirty-year loans where the front-end interest is serviced predominately for the first fourteen years of the loan's existence, which I will show you in detail in the following chapters.

Searching for Our Adirondack Camp: The Saga Continues

We arrived during the mud season of the Adirondacks, the part of springtime where the snow has melted and snowmobile season is over, but it is too cold and rainy for any seasonal visitors. Being essentially a tourist hamlet, the town basically shuts down, and all the restaurant and inn owners take their Florida vacations. The town was abandoned when we showed up. You KNOW you are in a small town when you arrive at the hotel and there is a note for you with a room key that says "Let yourself in to your room, and we will see you tomorrow." Old Forge is a dreary place during this time, but we were on a mission to find our vacation home, and for me, slay some internal demons. We settled in around 1:00 a.m. with some trepidation, as meeting with Emily the next day was a huge part of the trip, and I knew that we would be:

1. **Looking to see if the property was suitable for us, and**
2. **Negotiating price and terms.**

---

11   We will get to further detail on this later, but when a bank seeks to make a loan on a property and requests an appraisal, **its purpose is solely to determine if the property will appraise for the requested loan value and gives little consideration to its true fair market value.** Hence, the appraisal in and of itself originates from a skewed approach, i.e., proving that the subject property is worthy of its loan amount, which has little relevance to the borrower but major relevance to the bank. The bank's appraisal rarely, if ever, intentionally seeks the ACTUAL FAIR MARKET VALUE of the subject property. Hence, the process is flawed in the bank's favor.

12   In many cases, knowingly—remember the subprime crisis of 2008, where banks made loans on purpose to borrowers they KNEW WOULD DEFAULT? **Those loans were NOT made by accident.**

The next day, around 10:00 a.m., we went to the property. Emily, like so many Northern residents, had spent most of her life getting hammered by the snowfall that drops in record amounts in that part of the world, and her part-time job at the local coffee shop, coupled with her boyfriend's income as a retired vet, wasn't really cutting the mustard in a tourist-based, small-town economy. All things considered, they probably would have been underwater if they hadn't inherited the house from their parents, but even with that blessing, they were looking for a way out.

They explained to me that rumors of good-paying, full-time manufacturing jobs were plentiful in Charlotte, North Carolina, and with some seed money from the sale of the property, they were looking to be on their way there. The problem was the home hadn't been sold even though they had been trying to sell for over two years. Currently, it was on the market for $149,900, but as it needed some repairs, no offers had been forthcoming, and they were really ready to consider alternate options. It was potentially a perfect scenario to utilize some creative real estate investing techniques to truly create a win-win situation.

Inspecting the Property

Many people believe that a home inspection, using a licensed professional, is the only way to have a level of comfort that you are not buying someone else's home problems. However, if I had to hire a home inspector every time I bought a house as a real estate professional, I would have spent almost half a million dollars on home inspections in my career. **A basic working knowledge of housing systems and their inner systems can allow you to not only save money but also to identify potential problems and "hotspots" that can become a potential financial issue for you, over time, should you decide to purchase a property.** Don't get me wrong; when I am buying a primary residence for myself to live in, I *always* will use a home inspector I trust, if only to give myself and my wife peace of mind since we are planning on staying for a long time in the property.

However, when you buy an investment property[13], it is usually understood that you (generally) are planning on performing some renovations to the home. Remember, **buying distressed property often yields the best discount in price off of what would be considered fair market value[14] due to the fact that maintenance and repairs on the property have often been significantly deferred or are nonexistent,** thus creating the "distressed" property condition and requiring you to make repairs anyway.

---

13 Vacation homes also qualify as investment property since you will be using them part-time and, ideally, renting them out for income the rest of the time. Check with your CPA for the tax benefits related to owning a second (vacation) home.

14 Known also as FMV—we use these terms interchangeably in this book.

In the case of the Emily's property, we were less worried about the cosmetic repairs and cleanliness/condition of the home, and we were more focused on figuring out if there were any major structural concerns with the property. **However, even if a property has no structural flaws, there are still some concerns you should ALWAYS be looking for and subsequently asking the seller about.**

Here is a breakdown of the major questions I ask every seller about their property. Interestingly enough, I got this list from my experience working with an investor who used a 1-800 number and television advertising to generate leads on distressed property. These questions would quickly let us know if a lead was worth pursuing or not.

I have given you some detail on each question and why it matters below.

1. *Is there any repair work needed at the home?*
   The seller is painfully aware (most of the time) of what is wrong with a property. Sometimes they are forthcoming about it, and sometimes they will try to hide maintenance issues for fear of scaring away potential buyers. Asking them directly is the first step to identifying trouble spots within a property.

2. *Does the home have central heat and air?*
   If it does, what is the condition of it, and how old is it? Have there been any recent repairs to it or any known issues with any of the units (furnace, coil, or compressor)? These days, central heat and air (known as HVAC) are practically a prerequisite for most tenants looking for a rental property; you almost always want to have it in your primary residence, and certainly in a vacation home, assuming you want to be comfortable or you want your potential vacation renters to be, which is a necessity. Look for old exterior units, rust on AC housing, flames shooting out of the furnace (indicates a cracked heat exchanger), and so on. HVAC systems are VERY costly, and when in doubt, a licensed heating and air technician will tell you what the actual condition is of the units.

3. *What is the condition of the roof?*
   The roof is one of the most costly items a homeowner can be forced to replace. As such, look for multiple layers of shingles, old asbestos shingles with a "sheen" (shining and shrunk back from their original form), missing shingles, or a large prevalence of rotten wood on the cornice and fascia, which can indicate improper runoff due to moisture entrapment. Exposed rotten wood and decking are all points of concern. Inside, roof problems are often indicated by staining (brownish/

yellow in-ceiling sheetrock), mold presence, collapsed sheetrock insulation, or an overall damp feeling in the house due to rainwater entering the home. When a roof has less than five years of serviceable life, plan on replacing it before a bigger problem occurs, such as sheetrock collapse. Try not to, as most people are convinced to do by unscrupulous roofing companies, make an insurance claim when you need a new roof. **Save your insurance claims for large losses like house fires.**[15]

4. *Are there any tax or insurance issues we need to know about?*
   Outstanding tax liens on a property can cloud title and prevent you from buying a property, which can make even looking at a property a huge waste of your time (ask me how I know this). Sometimes, due to insurance claims or environmental factors, a property may be uninsurable. You need to make sure that you ask these questions. Also ask if the property is in a flood zone, then verify with your insurance company if you are seriously considering buying.

5. *Do you have title to the property?*
   Make sure the person who says they can sell the property actually can. Your closing attorney or escrow agent will help ensure that this is the case on your behalf prior to close by doing a title search.

6. *Is there any seller financing available on the property?*
   This is the MOST IMPORTANT real estate investor question you can possibly ask. Any time you can obtain seller financing, you win in many, many ways, as follows:

   a. You don't have to get a bank loan.
   b. You don't have to use your personal cash, assuming you have some available.
   c. You can negotiate your interest rate.
   d. You can negotiate your down payment.
   e. You can negotiate your loan term (amortization schedule).
   f. **You can, at times, settle the mortgage for less than is owed to the lender, if the note holder is willing to discount the loan payoff.**[16] This is, without exception, one of the most powerful creative real estate strategies you can use.

---

15 Managing insurance risk in your real estate portfolio is a critical concern, especially in a weak economy where people are struggling and tend to make more claims. Often, homeowners who are cash poor will make small claims like spoiled food due to a power outage or an air-conditioner theft. Savvy investors understand that insurance is for LARGE LOSSES ONLY. If you make several small claims that you could just cover out of pocket or with sweat equity, you could be canceled and rated as uninsurable, which makes buying real estate impossible.

16 This would NEVER happen with banks. Even with a short sale, you have to default, then pass title to another buyer.

7. *If I pay you all cash and can offer a quick close, what is the least you will take for the property?*

Gets to the point, finds the bottom line. Should always be followed up with, "'Is that the best you can do?" after the seller names a price.[17]

8. *Why are you selling?*

Gives you critical information that may help you gain an edge in negotiations.

We asked Emily these questions and walked around and inspected the home. The largest issues we encountered were that the bunkhouse had no functioning plumbing even though there was a bathroom in it. The bunkhouse also had all kinds of built-in shelving that was makeshift, preventing it from being habitable (essentially the bunkhouse needed a renovation, estimated to be about 5k); and the main house was cluttered and had lots of deferred cleaning, painting, light maintenance, and so on. **In short, it was perfect!** My wife and I discussed privately (outside) if we could make this our vacation home, and we agreed that it had everything we were looking for. However, now we had to make sure the investment opportunity made sense for us, not only in price, but also in terms.

The Negotiation

I have learned the hard way, through countless seller negotiations, that when you are working with a private seller, **the way to buy a property successfully from them is TO ASK WHAT THEY WANT AND LISTEN.**

Again, I repeat:

> When you are working with a private seller, the way to actually buy a property successfully from them is TO ASK WHAT THEY WANT AND THEN LISTEN TO THEM CAREFULLY.

Although many inexperienced investors would try to convince you so, price is not the critical factor in negotiating a property purchase. Price is secondary to, for example, the reason why someone is selling. Perhaps someone has gotten a job transfer and simply cannot afford two mortgage payments. In this case, price is secondary to a question like, "What is your mortgage payoff?" In Emily's case, the home had been on the market for

---

17   I got this from brilliant real estate investor Scott Rister, as much as I would love to take credit for it.

two years, and it was inherited and in the clear, so I knew that the price was negotiable.

However, it was very clear to me that the way I needed to buy the property was to have Emily tell me what she needed.

I sat at the kitchen table with Emily and her family, and my wife was sitting with me. "Emily," I began, "tell me what it is you need. You have been trying to sell the property for two years, unsuccessfully. You want to move to Charlotte as soon as you can. How is it I can help you?"

Emily responded, "We just need $25,000 cash startup money to move to Charlotte. If we can get 25k up front, we would be willing to consider financing the home."

I told Emily I could do that and slid my offer across the table to her. Here it was:

THE OFFER

Property Address: Pullman Avenue, Old Forge, New York

Purchase Price: $90,000[18]

Down Payment: $25,000

Financing: Seller to carry a first-position mortgage of $65,000 for a fully amortized[19] thirty-year period at an interest rate of 6% fixed for the life of the loan.

Prepayment Penalty: None. Buyer can pay off mortgage at any time.

Conditions: Subject to clear and conveyable title. Seller to use their attorney of choice. Buyer to use their attorney of choice. Seller and buyer to each pay their respective closing costs. Closing to be thirty days from contract date. Buyer will put up earnest money of $500 with seller attorney. Buyer to pay for insurance and taxes annually and provide proof to seller.

Emily silently read the offer over. She then looked at me and said firmly, "I NEED AN INTEREST RATE OF 6.5%."

I told her, "Okay, that's fine," and she signed the contract.

With that, we were on our way to purchasing our first vacation home.

---

18   Note the offer price was $59,900 below the asking price. **Never be afraid to make a low offer.**

19   From Wikipedia: *In lending, **amortization** is the distribution of payment into multiple cash flow installments, as determined by an amortization schedule.*

Getting to the Closing Table

Closing the property was uneventful. I wired in 25k cash, as we had agreed, and paid my closing costs; and in exchange, Emily gave me a mortgage for $65,000 on a thirty-year term and the deed to the property. **Keep in mind, in addition to seller financing, I had offered almost 60k less than their asking price, and they had accepted, which is money that gets added to my balance sheet instantly at the closing in the form of equity.**[20] About a month later, my wife and I drove to our new property with an empty moving truck, and my brother-in-law and I proceeded to gut the bunkhouse and trash out both buildings on the property with a sledge-hammer. This was the start to the property being in the condition that it is today, a fully renovated two-building vacation compound that can be used for rental purposes or simply for family recreation. We have had TONS of fun using this property, in all four seasons, and the fact that I own it in the clear (with no mortgage) is one of the greatest real estate accomplishments of my career. **It is truly a sense of satisfaction to know that your family will always have a place to go in an emergency, always have a place to stay if catastrophe strikes, and, more importantly, have a place to spend quality time together.**

For those of you who are mathematical and wondering about the property's total valuation and income performance post sale, here is a breakdown of the deal as it existed at the time of closing:

Pullman—Investor Fundamentals[21]

Property Fundamentals

Purchase price: $90,000

Cash invested, down payment: $25,000

Renovations invested: $7,000

Mortgage amount: $65,000

Fair market value, after total repairs and improvements: $325,000

---

20 Don't get too excited. Remember "Equity is dead"? **The only thing that matters is paid-off, cash-flowing real estate.** But when you have equity from paid-off homes, that isn't a bad thing; it just shouldn't be your primary focus.

21 Assumes property is used as strictly income property, not as a personal vacation home, fifty-two weeks a year.

Gross Potential Income

Potential rental income, summer season, main house (weekly):
 $850/week × 16 weeks = $13,600 annually

Potential rental income, summer season, bunkhouse (weekly):
 $550/week × 16 weeks = $8,800 annually

Potential rental income, winter/snowmobile season (rented seasonally) main house:
 $5,500 for winter

Potential rental income, winter/snowmobile season (rented seasonally) bunkhouse:
 $4,500 for winter

Total aggregate gross income: $32,400

Expenses

Mortgage (twelve months) = $410.84 × 12 = $4,930.08

Annual taxes: $2,100 (County AND School Tax)

Insurance: $1,000/year

Utilities average: $400/month on monthly averaging plan = $4,800

Oil/fuel expense: $2,000 annually

Net annual income: $17,569.82

Return on investment,[22] **annually if used as rental home:** $17,569.82/$32,000 = **54.9%**[23]

Epilogue

Later in the first year that I purchased the Old Forge property, in the beginning of December 2010, I got a call from Emily. Every month, she had called me on the first of the month to see if I had mailed the mortgage payment, which I always had; and every month, she received it. Somehow though, I got a sense that she was calling me less because she was concerned about my ability to pay promptly and more because she was having

---

22   My total investment here was 25k down payment plus 7k in renovation costs, total of 32k to acquire and get online.
23   No vacancy or maintenance factors are calculated here, as I have seen these numbers vary by investor from 0% to 50% annually. **For me, conservatively, a 10% to 15% factor for each would be more than adequate for those of you who need to know your absolute maximum downside risk.** Assuming a total of 30% for both, the revised return on investment would then be 38.4%. Compare that with your stock market returns.

some financial issues in Charlotte and wanted to ensure the money was on the way. We chatted briefly, and then she got to the point of her call: she asked me if I could, for the December payment (the holiday season), send the January payment along with it and, in doing so, pay her the January mortgage payment early.

Earlier in this chapter, I related to you how powerful paying off discounted mortgages can be. I always make a mental note to myself to call any private mortgage holders I am working with every six months or so and see if they are willing to take a lump sum of cash in exchange for a **heavily discounted**[24] note payoff. Usually I do this in letter format (and was planning on doing this with Emily later in the month), but her phone call was timely, so I told her the truth: I had been saving up money to pay the mortgage off early, but the going was slow, and I didn't have the entire loan payoff amount. If, however, she was willing to discount the mortgage, we might be able to solve each other's problem. However, I had nowhere close to $65,000 cash, which was the balance still owed on the thirty-year loan she had given me. She then asked me a critical question:

Well, how much can you pay?'

Now, as you will see in this book, in the world of creative real estate investing, the first person in a price or settlement negotiation to actually name a number is considered to be making a negotiation mistake: they set themselves up for failure by giving their hand away openly, so to speak. **Consider:** If I had 60k in cash and told Emily I had 60k in cash (I didn't have anywhere near that saved up), we would now be haggling on a payoff amount of somewhere between 60k and 65k. In giving her a number, I was setting myself up for failure by limiting the amount of potential discount on the mortgage I could receive, and I wasn't about to do that.

So I countered her question:

"Emily, what is the least amount of cash you are willing to take to settle the mortgage? I have a limited amount of cash in my savings account, and if we can agree on a settlement amount, basically I will be emptying my life savings account and giving it to you."

Instantly, she fired off a number. Before I tell you the number she stated, however, you should know that I tell this story in seminars and speaking engagements worldwide, and it is amazing to me how little people are willing to consider as a discount. **Most seminar attendees, when told this story, guess that I paid the mortgage off for 50k–60k.** Now, maybe it is because we are talking about larger sums of money here, or maybe most people are simply unfamiliar with the idea of debt holders slashing thousands of dollars

---

24 No less than 50% discount, minimum.

from debt instruments owed to them for cash settlements, **but you need to know that this happens ALL THE TIME**. Knowing this can add millions of dollars to your portfolio over time. Big thinking pays off big dividends, especially when you are thinking about BIG MORTGAGE DISCOUNTS.

Emily's number, by the way, was $35,000. The minute she said her price, I instantly knew I was going to pay off my mortgage early, at a HUGE discount. However, I told her (honestly) that I couldn't pay 35k to her because I didn't have that much money in my savings account.

"Well, how much do you have?" she asked. "Twenty-five thousand dollars?"

"Emily, honestly, all I have in my bank account is $22,000." A true statement.[25]

"That'll work," she said flatly. I told her my attorney would draw up the Trust Deed release and I would wire the money when the document was ready.

A week later, I owned the property in the clear, and Emily had been paid off in full for far less than she was actually owed.

So that is the story of how I bought a 325k vacation home from a private seller for roughly 47k, all told, using limited knowledge of creative financing and some basic ideas about how people operate. It is, essentially, a very true story in (and of) my life, a succinct illustration of what this book is about—using unorthodox real estate investing techniques to achieve financial freedom.

The chapter introduction itself explained in advance what I did plainly and truthfully.

> How to buy an out-of-state vacation home without using a realtor, finance it without using a bank, and pay it off in full without giving the lender all the money in less than one year.

Because I did the following things:

1. I bought an out-of-state vacation home without using a realtor, by placing a classified (real estate wanted) ad in the local daily paper of the town I wanted to buy in.

2. I financed it without using a bank by asking for and obtaining favorable seller financing terms.

---

25   Even if I had zero in my bank account and had negotiated a 22k payoff on the house, I could have refinanced with the bank and paid her off anyway. No legitimate bank is going to decline a first-position mortgage on a home for 10% or less of its fair market value, which was the home's value after we improved it, regardless of your credit history or credit score.

3. I paid the property off in full without giving the lender all the money owed to them in less than one year, by negotiating a settlement with the mortgage holder in exchange for a heavily discounted lump sum of cash.[26]

Ironically, while people who meet me and hear this story (and even my family) tell me I am a genius for doing this deal, the truth of the matter is that I knew I would settle the mortgage the day I signed the papers to buy the property. **In my heart, I knew it wasn't a matter of IF but of WHEN.** Maybe that is part of my gut real estate instinct, but most of it is simply playing the percentages in your favor through the empowerment of common knowledge. The majority of people, strictly speaking, would rather have cash than monthly payments, and Emily was no exception. She needed cash, and I solved her problem, saving myself $43,000 in the process through one phone call and some simple legal paperwork my attorney prepared for $150.

The real question is, if I can do this one simple transaction and I can teach you how to do it, how much more successful can you be?

---

26 It's $43,000 to be exact, not including equity through "forced appreciation," which we will discuss.

2

Running the Race

In order to learn how to purchase real estate correctly (with the goal of paying it off as quickly as possible), I must first show you why traditional methods of real estate investing are not only defunct, but also are, by their very nature, designed to keep a borrower in debt far longer than is necessary to pay off a piece of real estate while adding inordinate amounts (and years) of unnecessary interest.

A Very Short Primer on Real-Life Banking and Finance

In Western society, under the fractional reserve banking system,[27] banks (via the complicity of the Federal Reserve) essentially print money as necessary and then lend these monies to the borrowing customer. How does it work? The Federal Reserve, interestingly enough, requires banks to keep 10% of their deposits "in house," and once that is done, any bank can "lend out" the rest, even though that money is not in the bank. (Basically, the bank can lend ten times of what it has on deposit.)[28] Now, while physical money is printed on paper (known as currency) by the US Bureau of Engraving and Printing, this is ordered each year by the Federal Reserve, and the only cost it incurs is the cost of the paper and ink, plus labor, used in the creation process.[29]

However, what is important to know is that if the US government needs to borrow money (which frequently happens due to government insolvency), it is required to go to the Federal Reserve, request to borrow the money, and then—in order to get the money—the US government is forced to trade US treasury bonds (**which carry a promise to pay in the future with interest, and for the purposes of this discussion, let's consider a US treasury note as an item of secure value**) for an equal amount of paper money (**which

---

27   See here: http://www.investopedia.com/terms/f/fractionalreservebanking.asp.
28   Keep in mind the Fed changes the rules periodically and they may be different by the time you read this.
29   Here is a good and simple primer on how the Federal Reserve operates. If you want to kill yourself after reading this, don't. http://theeconomiccollapseblog.com/archives/10-things-that-every-american-should-know-about-the-federal-reserve.

for the purposes of this discussion, we will consider an item of NO value). The Federal Reserve, basically "prints" paper money when it chooses to and trades them to the US government for US treasuries.

For illustrative purposes, let's review how this works with *you* replacing the Fed, and everything else staying the same. Let's call you *Mary the Money Shoppe*.

The Business Relationship of Mary the Money Shoppe and the US Government

The US government recently announced it was no longer using the Federal Reserve to borrow money; instead, it was replacing the Fed with *Mary the Money Shoppe*, effective immediately.

Today, The US government placed its first order to borrow one million US dollars, and Mary the Money Shoppe filled the order quickly. How?

Mary gets the order, then she orders one million dollars in paper notes from the US Bureau of Engraving and Printing. Shortly thereafter, she receives one million dollars in $100 notes. One million dollars in $100 bills is 10,000 notes. Total cost to Mary is $1,430, according to the Fed's stated printing cost per unit of 14.3 cents per $100 currency note, at the time of this writing.[30]

Mary sends the notes to the US government, who sends her in return one million dollars in treasury bonds.[31]

Mary then sells the treasury bonds to a Chinese investor at a slight discount of 5%, and pockets roughly 950k.

"Man, this is a really good deal for me," says Mary. "I make about 950k for every $1,430 spent on paper supplies and ink!"

The Federal Reserve had no comment.

It's actually a brilliant, *if inherently evil,* scam, and it is really quite surprising that congressional leaders fell for it back on December 23, 1913, when the Federal Reserve Act was formally passed.[32]

---

30 http://www.federalreserve.gov/faqs/currency_12771.htm.
31 FYI, this is usually just done electronically.
32 I will spend some time outlining ideas about how the Federal Reserve's (not a federal institution, by the way, but actually a private corporation) existence continues to derail the US economy to its own benefit, but to really get a feel for what is going on, you have to spend some time studying it outside this reading. The policies of the Federal Reserve, and their significant contributions to the instability of the US dollar, are essentially beyond the scope of this book.

Here is a breakdown of how fractional reserve banking works via a short bedtime story.

The Fable of Bob the Banker, Timmy the Teacher, and Fred the Farmer

Today is the opening day of a new community bank, and Bob the Banker opens his doors for the first time. He needs deposits, so he offers a "great" rate on a five-year CD (certificate of deposit) if depositors place their money at his new bank. Fred the Farmer has 100k in cash, and he decides to take advantage of the "special offer" and place it in a five-year bank CD at a 1% annualized interest rate. This way, Fred is guaranteed to get a 1% fixed interest rate return on his money, which is considered to be "safe." Unless he withdraws early at penalty, Fred won't technically "lose" money, although inflation and dollar attrition due to currency devaluation[33] may actually give him quite the snakebite over time, but that is the subject of a different discussion. Fred makes his deposit in a CD and cannot withdraw it without penalty. He lays his money down and parts with it for five years.

Coincidentally, the same day Fred the Farmer made his CD investment at the local community bank, Timmy the Teacher finds out his wife is pregnant and makes a paternal decision to stop renting the apartment he and his now-expecting wife are living in and purchase a house. He already found the perfect house and is ready to purchase it, but he doesn't have the 100k he needs to buy the property (which is what the seller is asking). So he goes to his banker (Bob) and asks Bob the Banker for a loan, which he is subsequently ***approved*** for. Timmy the Teacher gets his funds to purchase his 100k home, which occurs when Bob the Banker takes Fred the Farmer's recently deposited 100k that Bob agreed to pay 1% on (for five years in the bank CD) and lends it to Timmy the Teacher at 7% fixed interest rate for thirty years.

Everyone wins, right? Fred the Farmer gets his guaranteed 1% (now he won't worry about "losing" money in more volatile investments, like stocks); Timmy the Teacher can buy a house he could otherwise not afford and live in it with his pregnant wife; and Bob the Banker makes a 6% yield[34] on 100k simply for safeguarding Frank's money while lending it to Timmy, who he has underwritten via credit, Social Security number, etc.

Everyone wins. There is only one problem here though, and that arises when Timmy's friend comes in an hour later (Timmy of course, called him immediately after he left the bank because he was so happy and told him about his loan approval) and applies for a loan on a house too because HIS WIFE JUST GOT PREGNANT ALSO. Problem is,

---

33 While the Federal Reserve's mission statement is to promote a "stable dollar," their policies do anything but that. Just search online for ***US Dollar Performance Chart Pre and Post 1913*** for details.

34 Known in the banking industry as yield spread. The next time you apply for a loan, ask your mortgage broker what their yield spread is and see how they react.

Bob the Banker only has one 100k deposit so far, and he lent it to Timmy. Hence, Bob is essentially out of funds to lend (unless he gets another bank deposit from another Fred the Farmer type, which he doesn't yet have), and therefore, Timmy's friend is out of luck and cannot get a loan.

Today, however, is a very special day and something wonderful happens: *Bob the Banker makes the loan to Timmy's friend anyway!*

Is it a miracle?

Well, not actually. **Under the fractional reserve banking system, Bob can lend out money in multiple amounts of what he has on deposit, whether or not he actually has the funds.** He just gets more freshly minted money from the Federal Reserve or shows it as an available credit on his books when his borrower signs the loan documents, and this fictitious money can then be lent at interest when he creates a debit into his customer's account from a "loan" he makes![35]

Now that I have told you this fictitious (yet true) bedtime story, answer the following multiple-choice question:

*In the fable of Bob the Banker, Timmy the Teacher, and Fred the Farmer, **where did the greatest swindle occur?***

a. **When Fred the Farmer commits his money for five years at 1% and can no longer withdraw it without a substantial penalty from the bank;**

b. **When Bob the Banker makes Timmy's friend a loan using money he doesn't really have but simply "conjures" out of thin air, courtesy of the Federal Reserve System using fractional banking principles; or**

c. **When Timmy the Teacher gets offered and commits to a thirty-year loan to purchase his house.**

Now, many people would argue and make valid cases for each answer, but the real answer here, of where the greatest swindle occurred (in my opinion), is answer c—**when Timmy the Teacher gets offered and commits to a thirty-year loan to purchase his house.** Don't agree?

Here is why, when Timmy agrees to take the thirty-year loan, he gets involved in the greatest swindle of all.

---

35 For a more complete description of how the Federal Reserve and fractional banking system work to your disadvantage, see https://seekingalpha.com/instablog/25783813-peter-palms/4549696-history-fractional-reserve-banking-became-model-federal-reserve-system-unbroken-record-fraud.

Figure A: Amortization Table of Yearly Interest Paid on a Thirty-Year Loan Versus Principal Reduction on a 100k Real Estate Purchase at 7% Fixed

Yearly aggregate amortization schedule—100k loan at 7% fixed interest rate—monthly payment $665.30				
Payments	Yearly Total Paid	Principal Paid	Interest Paid	Balance Remaining
Year 1 (1–12)	$7,983.63	$1,016.00	$6,968.00	$98,984.19
Year 2 (13–24)	$7,983.63	$1,089.00	$6,894.00	$97,894.95
Year 3 (25–36)	$7,983.63	$1,168.00	$6,816.00	$96,726.96
Year 4 (37–48)	$7,983.63	$1,252.00	$6,731.00	$95,474.55
Year 5 (49–60)	$7,983.63	$1,343.00	$6,641.00	$94,131.59
Year 6 (61–72)	$7,983.63	$1,440.00	$6,544.00	$92,691.55
Year 7 (73–84)	$7,983.63	$1,544.00	$6,439.00	$91,147.41
Year 8 (85–96)	$7,983.63	$1,656.00	$6,328.00	$89,491.65
Year 9 (97–108)	$7,983.63	$1,775.00	$6,208.00	$87,716.19
Year 10 (109–120)	$7,983.63	$1,904.00	$6,080.00	$85,812.38
Year 11 (121–132)	$7,983.63	$2,041.00	$5,942.00	$83,770.95
Year 12 (133–144)	$7,983.63	$2,189.00	$5,795.00	$81,581.94
Year 13 (145–156)	$7,983.63	$2,347.00	$5,636.00	$79,234.69
Year 14 (157–168)	$7,983.63	$2,517.00	$5,467.00	$76,717.75
Year 15 (169–180)	$7,983.63	$2,699.00	$5,285.00	$74,018.87
Year 16 (181–192)	$7,983.63	$2,894.00	$5,090.00	$71,124.88
Year 17 (193–204)	$7,983.63	$3,103.00	$4,880.00	$68,021.68
Year 18 (205–216)	$7,983.63	$3,328.00	$4,656.00	$64,694.16
Year 19 (217–228)	$7,983.63	$3,568.00	$4,416.00	$61,126.09
Year 20 (229–240)	$7,983.63	$3,826.00	$4,158.00	$57,300.08
Year 21 (241–252)	**$7,983.63**	**$4,103.00**	**$3,881.00**	**$53,197.49**
Year 22 (253–264)	$7,983.63	$4,399.00	$3,584.00	$48,798.32
Year 23 (265–276)	$7,983.63	$4,717.00	$3,266.00	$44,081.14
Year 24 (277–288)	$7,983.63	$5,058.00	$2,925.00	$39,022.95
Year 25 (289–300)	$7,983.63	$5,424.00	$2,560.00	$33,599.10
Year 26 (301–312)	$7,983.63	$5,816.00	$2,168.00	$27,783.17
Year 27 (313–324)	$7,983.63	$6,236.00	$1,747.00	$21,546.80
Year 28 (325–336)	$7,983.63	$6,687.00	$1,296.00	$14,859.60
Year 29 (337–348)	$7,983.63	$7,171.00	$813.00	$7,688.98
Year 30 (349–360)	$7,983.63	$7,689.00	$295.00	$0.00
Totals	$239,508.90	$100,000.00	$139,508.90	

I have bolded the pivot point where Timmy the Teacher begins to pay, annually, more principal down than interest. By the way, that begins to happen in YEAR TWENTY-ONE. Which means for twenty years, Timmy makes the majority of his payments as interest to the bank and, for all of those years, barely reduces his principal owed on the loan. Some people would say he is "throwing his money away," and pretty much everyone but the bank would agree. Want to see some other interesting facts? I have highlighted them for you:

i. **Timmy pays, over thirty years, $139,509.90 *in interest alone*.** This DOES NOT include his taxes and insurance, which are in all likelihood escrowed and will increase every twenty-four months or so, increasing Timmy's payment as he is forced to carry the burden of his city's infrastructure and entitlements since he is a property owner (on whose back the majority of metropolitan infrastructure is traditionally laden, via real property taxation).

ii. **In the first twenty years, Timmy pays $116,974 in interest to the bank while having only reduced his principal by $42,699, even though he has paid two-thirds of the loan**. Essentially, he has paid $159,673 over twenty years, and only 43% ($42,699) of this has been principal reduction. The rest has all been bank profit, even though, technically he has already paid off his home's loan amount in full, strictly through interest, to the bank.

iii. **The bank has a lien on Timmy's house for all thirty of those years—meaning, if anything were to happen to Timmy over a thirty-year period and he subsequently missed a single payment, he would be threatened with foreclosure and be at risk of losing his home.**

iv. **Over a period of thirty years, the bank gets paid back 100% of the principal it lent (100k, remember) PLUS $139,509.90 in INTEREST** for a total recoup of $239,509.90 from a loan that was made using *none* of the bank's money.[36]

v. **Timmy is required to make 360 payments** due on the first of every month without exception.

vi. **Timmy is an older guy when (if) he pays off his house, much older.** Thirty years older, to be exact, assuming no refinance.

In short, Timmy was asked to "run the race."

---

[36] **Fractional reserve banking dictates that the bank never truly has enough funds to cover all of the deposits its customers have placed in the bank at any given time**. It assumes that people will never, at any given time, all want their money back. If they did, there would be the dreaded "run" on the bank (think *It's a Wonderful Life* or recent Bank of Cyprus hardships for concrete examples), and **not all depositors would get their money back since it is impossible for the bank to have liquid funds for all the deposits credited on its books versus the loan obligations it chose to originate in multiples of its deposit amounts.** The bank lends its depositors' money at interest and also lends additional funds it does not actually have, which creates the fact that the bank, quite frequently, has loans on the books that materialized from somewhere other than depositors' funds (like thin air). Hence, the house of cards that sees governmental "officials" crying about institutions that are "too big to fail" when they chose to fail in the first place by engaging in such deceptive lending practices.

3

The "Race" Analyzed

When Timmy and his wife sign the bank paperwork and walk out of the bank, they breathe a sigh of relief.

It's done. They have provided a voluminous pile of paperwork needed to secure their home loan and jumped through every imaginable hoop.

They now own their very own house!

The problem is, they actually DON'T own the house. They now are the proud owners of thirty years of obligatory payments, provided with convenient monthly payment coupons. They have traded their freedom for nothing less than a socially accepted and endorsed form of sanctioned slavery. They now are servants of the bank.

For all intents and purposes, lifetime servants.

In American society today, most people (in a twist of great irony) see the bank as Timmy's savior in this case (since it made him a loan, and he wouldn't be able to "afford" a home otherwise[37]), but the bank *isn't* really some type of messianic prophet who provides a gift of home ownership. As a rule, if I need something or want something (say, a house) and someone comes up to me and hands me a worthless piece of paper (for example, a bank check) that I can in turn hand to someone else (the seller of the property, in this instance), which allows me to purchase a home but THEN **obligates me to make actual payments on the worthless piece of paper (for thirty years)**—well, all of a sudden that transaction starts to look and feel a bit...sketchy. Lots of deception and fraud going on there, not the least of which is me committing myself to thirty years of payments on a property at today's prices. Keep in mind, I have also made a (voluntary) thirty-year commitment to pay twenty years of predominantly interest on my biggest monthly expense **since (generally speaking) an American family's largest monthly expense is their housing payment.**[38]

---

37   This isn't true, but an antiquated and indoctrinated concept we have been ingrained to believe. A bank is one of **many** options for home finance and ownership, as well as for other forms of borrowing which are non-real estate related (like student loans).

38   This is a fundamental concept of this book.

"Did I really make a mistake, though? After all, the Joneses are doing it. They 'own'" their house—that huge newly built house in the new, enviable subdivision!

Aren't we supposed to keep up with the Joneses?"

Timmy the Teacher certainly subscribes to this philosophy since he was raised in Western society and is a routine watcher of television that advocates the idea that "bigger truly is better," so let's see what exactly Timmy has gotten himself into. Timmy also, for the record, generates a 50k a year salary and subconsciously believes that his take-home pay is the most amount of money he can ever hope to generate annually.[39]

If Timmy misses a payment, his home is placed in jeopardy, **regardless of the number of payments he has made so far.** When he misses a payment, generally speaking, if he does nothing to cure the default, he is six months[40] away from losing his house permanently. Due to the fully recourse nature of his loan, by the way, he can (potentially) lose everything he has ever worked for. So he knows he has to keep his payments current no matter what happens. He is led to believe that shouldn't be too hard since he only has 360 payments to make. *After he makes a whopping thirty-six payments (roughly amounting to $24,000 in post-tax, take-home dollars, or about 25% of his original purchase price), he still has 90% of his payments remaining* and is only one-tenth of the way through his payment schedule, although it DID take him three years to get there.

I wonder what could possibly go wrong to interrupt Timmy's lifetime payment obligations? Let's speculate.

Timmy could:

- Lose his job and be out of work;
- Be denied unemployment benefits if he were to lose his job;
- Have to support a parent who is ill and make a difficult decision about the allocation of his earnings, putting their health and well-being before his mortgage payment;
- Have another child who adds to his expense load, whether planned or not;
- Get sick with a paralyzing disease;

---

39 Far beyond the scope of this book is the idea of glass salary ceilings: for example, "you went to college to be a teacher, so you will always make a teacher's salary." Without a doubt, this is utter nonsense, but keeps people chained to their vocations regardless of whether they enjoy them or not, for fear of loss. Timmy can replace his $3,000 per month take-home pay (for which he works 50+ hours a week) by buying and paying off 5 homes that generate, after expenses, $600 per month cash flow each. No degree or license is needed.

40 Depending on your state laws, (varies time-wise from state to state) and on varying circumstances.

- Develop a sickness that impedes him from working;

- Live in a county, state, or country where the economy collapses;

- Get a job transfer and be forced to sell the home;

- Live in a country where the currency is getting devalued due to flooding of the market with worthless copies of the currency by banking institutions such as the Federal Reserve;

- Live in a country where he is asked (forced) to make payments on societal obligations whether he wants them or not, like health insurance, welfare, and entitlements through backbreaking federal and municipal (real estate and state) taxation, as well as skyrocketing cost of living expenses such as groceries, health care, and gasoline;

- Have the bank make a mistake and say he hasn't made a house payment when in fact he has, thus forcing him into foreclosure before he can get an attorney (or afford one) to rectify the situation;

- Get some equity in the house after fifteen years and refinance the home, beginning the process over again for thirty MORE years while convincing himself he actually now has some "cash";[41]

- His wife could divorce him (regardless of circumstance), destabilizing the family and affecting his ability to earn, as well as destroying his credit;[42]

- Be affected by eminent domain and forced to sell his house for less than he owes on the home;

- Be adversely affected though the continuous and unceasing increase of property taxes and insurance rates on his homes through his municipality (which are levied on those who elect to have jobs and own homes) to a point where he can no longer afford his payment;

- Have a real estate collapse where his house loses 50% of its value, making him unable to sell his home should the need to move arise (such as a job transfer);[43]

---

41 When he refinances, he has no cash, so to speak. He has the bank give him equitable cash in exchange for thirty more years of payments, at interest. He would have been better off selling the home and taking profit that way, then reinvesting it in a distressed property, which he could live in payment-free. At least in that scenario he is done with making payments.

42 Divorce, historically, is the number-one destroyer of wealth, regardless of circumstance. Wealthy people tend NOT to get divorced for this very reason.

43 Think Detroit, Michigan, post 2008 "economic collapse." The city is now a ghost town, bankrupted and handed to a state trustee for oversight.

☐   Get in a catastrophic car accident; or

☐   Die.

Encouraging, yes? Certainly, a discussion that will perk you up. On a serious note, however, what we see in Timmy's case is that, essentially, the odds are stacked against his success, **if we define success as him actually paying off the house so he can live in it free of a mortgage encumbrance for the rest of his life.** If Timmy *runs the race* for thirty years and *wins,* **he is a statistical anomaly.** Someone who actually succeeds in paying off their home after a thirty-year period is an exception to the rule, a veritable statistical exception since, statistically speaking, the average homeowner moves every five years.[44] Assuming this is a true fact, ***let's see how Timmy's investment in a thirty-year mortgage is handled if he were to sell after five years have elapsed, assuming he follows "average" American trends and needs to move at the end of every sixty-month period.***

Figure B: Amortization Table of Yearly Interest Paid on a Thirty-Year Loan Versus Principal Reduction on a 100k Real Estate Purchase at 7% Fixed—Months 1–60

Yearly aggregate amortization schedule—100k loan at 7% fixed interest rate

Payments	Yearly Total Paid	Principal Paid	Interest Paid	Balance Remaining
Year 1 (1–12)	$7,983.63	$1,016.00	$6,968.00	$98,984.19
Year 2 (13–24)	$7,983.63	$1,089.00	$6,894.00	$97,894.95
Year 3 (25–36)	$7,983.63	$1,168.00	$6,816.00	$96,726.96
Year 4 (37–48)	$7,983.63	$1,252.00	$6,731.00	$95,474.55
Year 5 (49–60)	$7,983.63	$1,343.00	$6,641.00	$94,131.59

Let's assume that Timmy has to sell his property using a realtor, which (typically) consists of paying a 6% realtor commission and also an additional 6% toward the buyer's closing costs to minimize the buyer's out-of-pocket transactional expenses. Let's ***also*** assume that Timmy's house has appreciated 10% in a five-year period (which, at the time of this writing, is unrealistic since people tend to see their homes losing value across America, and this phenomenon is reflected in recessionary trends that frequently occur and repeat in cycles, so if your house isn't currently losing value, don't assume it cannot and won't happen to YOU), AND we will assume that Timmy gets a full priced offer (also

---

44   http://transcripts.cnn.com/TRANSCRIPTS/0108/05/sun.10.html.

unrealistic since people can purchase foreclosed properties in neighborhoods similar to Timmy's at a 30% to 70% discount), but let's give Timmy the benefit of the doubt.

He, against all odds, gets a full-price offer, and it looks like this:

Buyer's purchase offer of Timmy the Teacher's home:

Offer price: $110,000

Less 6% realtor commission: $6,600

Less 6% to buyer's closing costs: $6,600

Less Timmy's closing costs (estimated for attorney fees, escrow fees, title insurance, tax prorations, etc.): $2,000

Net to Timmy: $94,800

Less bank payoff at end of five years: $94,131.59

Aggregate net to Timmy: $668.41

Sooooooooo, what exactly happened? Timmy leaves the attorney's office after the closing and now no longer feels a sense of relief; he feels a sense of ambivalence and a pervasive question in the bottom of his gut that won't stop nagging him:

Where did all my money go?

I can tell you where it went pretty simply—into the bank's pocket.

Refer back to Figure B; how much interest did the bank make annually over the five years the loan was in existence?

$34,050 in interest alone, not counting its principal reduction.

$5,868 in principal paid over a sixty-month period—money it created out of thin air.

Total of $39,918 paid over sixty months by Timmy in post-tax earnings, and only $5,868 was paid back in principal to the bank, the rest being interest to the bank.

What an AMAZING DEAL for the bank. Timmy is required to pay taxes and insurance on a property (to protect the bank's first position interest) the bank finances by creating paper. Timmy goes to his teaching job every day and makes payments faithfully from a substantial post-tax portion of his earned income over a sixty-month period, and IF the property appreciates 10% over a five-year period, Timmy receives, after his closing expenses and concessions, a whopping $668.41. Even though he paid out

$39,918 in payments, not including his property tax and insurance escrow?[45]

Did Timmy really take a 98% loss on his money simply by making on-time payments to the bank on his primary residence for five years?

Timmy was asked to run the race, and he agreed.

When he chose to not see the thirty-year race through to completion, he *lost*.

---

45   Factoring in Timmy's property tax and insurance payments over a five-year period (not including any maintenance or repairs that had to be paid for), Timmy took a TOTAL loss on his money, with money being defined as the funds he invested in the home for the first sixty months, by simply making on-time payments to his mortgage via the bank.

4

The Short-Term Retirement Program

Now, the critics of this book will tell you that Timmy wasn't actually "ripped off" by the bank. They will say things like, "After all, the money he spent did provide him a safe place for him and his family to live," etc., etc. They will also make various superfluous arguments to try to dissuade a reader from the downright scary nature of the establishment economics we are discussing here. They will make arguments and comments such as:

- [ ] Timmy was able to purchase a house he couldn't "otherwise" afford.

- [ ] Timmy did not have to move and could have continued paying down principal over the remaining twenty-five years, enjoying the mild appreciation, which would compound over time.

- [ ] Timmy could have prepaid on his monthly payments and reduced the amount of years he would have to make payments. The standard logic is if he makes an extra payment a year, he reduces his thirty-year mortgage to a twenty-two-year mortgage, so essentially, he has a mortgage that is much closer to twenty years, not thirty.

- [ ] Timmy actually "had something" to show for his money after five years, where if he had rented, he would have simply "thrown" his money away.

- [ ] Timmy made a "responsible" choice since "responsible" people own properties and "less responsible" people rent.

- [ ] The bank charged a "low" interest rate.

- [ ] Timmy's payment was "reasonable."

- [ ] It's better than "paying rent."

In my mind, however, the only thing that I am concerned with is Timmy's financial state after five years.

Is he better off than he was?

Regardless of the argument made in favor of the bank lending Timmy money, no one can argue against one irrefutable fact: Timmy paid out almost 40k in post-tax income on housing payments through his mortgage, and after five years, when he sold the house, recouped only 2% of that money, not counting his tax and insurance payments.[46] Ironically, we never really discussed the closing costs Timmy had to pay out of pocket when he bought the house, which would in theory make for a total loss, but be that as it may, we know Timmy shelled out 40k in payments, then sold the house, and now has one of two options that he would readily identify with regarding his housing situation:

1. Rent a dwelling for him and his family to live in, throwing away his money on rent with nothing to show for it as the years go by, or

2. Start the thirty-year cycle over again and apply for a bank loan and, in doing so, purchase a retail-valued property.

For Timmy, both options, well, kind of suck. Timmy doesn't want to rent, but he also just got burned on owning a home since he has nothing to show for it after making 40k in payments to the bank, even though he did everything that people told him to do. He doesn't realize he got burned, though; he just assumes it was his fault that he needed to sell after five years, whether that was due to job transfer, growing family, or whatever the reason. We all will agree the bank didn't force him, in this case, to sell; so certainly, it isn't the bank's fault.

As for Timmy, it's up to him to figure out what to do. He will probably be okay, whether he rents and places his hard-earned money into a (savvy) landlord's pocket or whether he starts the thirty-year cycle over again with the next Bob the Banker that comes along. Granted, he will have nothing to show for his efforts, even after another five years lapse (*that would be ten years gone by and NOTHING financially to show in terms of his real estate activity*), but he is doing a pretty good job of making everyone else wealthy, and in all probability, he doesn't know any better.

---

46   Critics might argue that Timmy obtained a "no money down" loan, thus making his five-year $668.41 net gain technically an "infinite" return. Naturally, no bank is going to give Timmy a zero-down loan for a primary residence and pay all his closing costs, so understand Timmy borrows 100k for illustrative purposes when he would be required to put down a down payment and pay his closing costs in real life, creating MORE cost and expense and changing the net gain of $668.41 into an actual loss.

We can't help Timmy.

But I can show *you* a better way.

The Thirty-Year Mortgage Swindle

The problem with the thirty-year mortgage, as well as most debt vehicles, is that they reward the note holder while placing an excessive burden of financial and personal responsibility onto the person who is obligated to pay the note. ***This is also compounded by the concept of focusing exclusively on "affordability" of payments as measured monthly versus examining the value of the time obligation those payments carry.***[47] To exacerbate the problem, the person who is paying the note is led to believe that their financial pressure becomes alleviated as the note amortization (the length of the note term, in months or years, that is required to be paid before the payor has satisfied the debt obligation in full) grows longer. The idea is encapsulated in this type of ideology:

"There is no way I can pay off a [insert mortgage amount here] mortgage payment in ten years, but I certainly can afford a thirty-year payment."

This idea is ingrained into our heads—**that payment affordability is based on having a thirty-year loan since the bank is willing to give us a thirty-year loan, and that is simply the longest term the bank will tolerate. Subconsciously, we are led to believe that owning a house happens[48] only when you are in your fifties to sixties and is predicated on working all your life and in doing so making consistent monthly mortgage payments.**

This notion, of course, is false, but since our society revolves around the mythical debt-to-income ratio and credit scores, people tend to purchase properties using a thirty-year payment, which allows them, in their minds, to afford the "most house they can." **This idea, to be clear, is an absolute farce;**[49] however, in reality, affording the "most house you can," mathematically, involves buying your desired homestead **as cheaply as you can, as far under market value as you can, and paying it off as quickly as possible with as**

---

47   This idea is a cornerstone of this book and needs to be understood fully. Assuming I can afford the payment, I can go purchase a 10-million-dollar home if I place it on a 150-year amortization (assuming zero down), but all I have done in that case is condemn myself to several lifetimes of debt service. ***Being able to "afford" the payment, meaning have enough income to make a monthly payment, is secondary in importance to determining a reasonable amount of time I am willing to carry and service that payment before I can realistically retire the debt and in doing so no longer be obligated to the lender.*** An ongoing theme in this book is that it is our explicit goal to retire debt, NOT perpetuate it.

48   With few exceptions. People who own houses in the clear in their twenties and thirties are viewed by most people as unusual exceptions to the norm. Be an exception. ☺

49   The idea of thirty-year loans as the most affordable payment one can have is a red herring meant to deceive you.

low of an interest rate you can possibly obtain unless you pay cash for it. [50]

Enter The Short-Term Retirement Program

So here's the radical idea that financial pundits on television will endlessly want to debate: What if I could give you the same amount of house (think Timmy's 100k house), but for half the price, AND I can have you pay off the house in ten years instead of thirty?

Would you buy it?

Of course, you would. Everyone wants a bargain. And, more importantly, people love having paid-off assets.

But how much are you willing to sacrifice for your "bargain"? How much are you willing to pay in interest to have a paid-off house? If mortgage rates today are 4%, are you willing to pay double the interest rate instead to get your mortgage? What about triple? Would you pay triple the interest rate to get a mortgage on your primary residence if banks are offering one-third of the rate, knowing that paying much higher interest means you actually get a loan to buy (and pay off) your discounted property, regardless of your credit or debt-to-income ratio?

Let's see what happens when we compare a thirty-year mortgage at a "reasonable" interest rate of 7% against shorter-term mortgages with a very "unreasonable" interest rate of 12% (annually)! How much interest is actually paid over the life of each loan? Assume we buy the house next door to Timmy's 100k house, but it happens to be a bank foreclosure, so we pay 50k instead of 100k. In order to see the power of buying at a discount (*aka a bank foreclosure or motivated seller*) and using a far shorter loan period to pay off a property, we have to study the amortization tables and see what exactly is happening every time you stroke a check for a payment.

Figure C: Mortgage Interest Table: Timmy's Original 100k Loan with
a 7% Fixed Interest Rate

Thirty-Year 100k—7% Fixed Monthly PMT $665.30			
Year	Interest	Principal	Balance
1	$6,967.82	$1,015.81	$98,984.19
2	$6,894.39	$1,089.24	$97,894.95
3	$6,815.65	$1,167.98	$96,726.96

---

50   Paying cash assumes you have a lump sum of cash sitting around, not needed for bills or debt service, from your efforts or from an inheritance or lottery winnings. This book is designed for those people who haven't gotten there yet, which is most of us.

Thirty-Year 100k—7% Fixed Monthly PMT $665.30			
Year	Interest	Principal	Balance
4	$6,731.21	$1,252.42	$95,474.55
5	$6,640.67	$1,342.96	$94,131.59
6	$6,543.59	$1,440.04	$92,691.55
7	$6,439.49	$1,544.14	$91,147.41
8	$6,327.87	$1,655.76	$89,491.65
9	$6,208.17	$1,775.46	$87,716.19
10	$6,079.82	$1,903.81	$85,812.38
11	$5,942.20	$2,041.43	$83,770.95
12	$5,794.62	$2,189.01	$81,581.94
13	$5,636.38	$2,347.25	$79,234.69
14	$5,466.69	$2,516.94	$76,717.75
15	$5,284.74	$2,698.89	$74,018.87
16	$5,089.64	$2,893.99	$71,124.88
17	$4,880.44	$3,103.19	$68,021.68
18	$4,656.11	$3,327.52	$64,694.16
19	$4,415.56	$3,568.07	$61,126.09
20	$4,157.62	$3,826.01	$57,300.08
21	$3,881.04	$4,102.59	$53,197.49
22	$3,584.46	$4,399.17	$48,798.32
23	$3,266.45	$4,717.18	$44,081.14
24	$2,925.44	$5,058.19	$39,022.95
25	$2,559.78	$5,423.85	$33,599.10
26	$2,167.69	$5,815.94	$27,783.17
27	$1,747.26	$6,236.37	$21,546.80
28	$1,296.43	$6,687.20	$14,859.60
29	$813.01	$7,170.62	$7,688.98
30	$294.65	$7,688.97	$0.00
Totals	$139,508.89	$100,000.00	

Timmy buys the house at market value using a thirty-year loan product and pays far more for the house in interest than he actually pays for the value of the house. Assuming he keeps the home for a thirty-year period or more, his exit strategy is to sell the home for whatever market value is at the time of sale *(which he hopes is MORE than he paid)*. His dollars depreciate over time, while his taxes and insurance rates increase over a thirty-year period. He has to pay maintenance on the house and keep up the condition of the home based on normal wear and tear. **He pays $239,508.89 over the life of the loan for a house he bought for a purchase price of 100k thirty years earlier.** The bank gets wealthy while Timmy struggles. At times, Timmy wonders *why he doesn't seem to be getting ahead*, but he thinks back on his parents' life, and they struggled also, and he continues to work today, so he assumes his struggling is normal. Timmy believes he is doing the right thing and making the right choices, pursuing the American dream. Nothing interesting to see here, really.

A 12% Mortgage?

We will go down the rabbit hole much deeper shortly, but here is a how a five-year loan stacks up at 12% annually on a 100k payment, interest wise. *FYI, this is for comparison, and I am NOT recommending buying 100k homes on five-year mortgages at 12% interest rates.*[51]

Figure D: Mortgage Interest Table—Timmy's Modified 100k Loan[52] with a 12% Fixed Interest Rate, Paid over a Five-Year Term

Five-Year, 100k—12% Fixed Monthly PMT $2,224.44			
Year	Interest	Principal	Balance
1	$11,164.31	$15,529.02	$84,470.98
2	$9,194.84	$17,498.49	$66,972.48
3	$6,975.60	$19,717.74	$47,254.74
4	$4,474.89	$22,218.44	$25,036.30
5	$1,657.04	$25,036.31	$0.00
Totals	$33,466.68	$100,000.00	

What most people would say when looking at this table is, "What's the big deal? At 12% interest, the buyer pays almost one-third in interest alone. There is nothing to see here. Short-term payoffs don't work. The payments are too high. The average person cannot afford this payment anyway."

But the smart investor understands that **a buyer using a five-year mortgage at 12% interest over a five-year term pays the same amount of interest in YEAR THREE of their**

51 For the record, of course. I am assuming most people understood this without the footnote.
52 All amortization schedules taken courtesy of MortgageCalculator.org. Check my math if you have questions.

five-year payoff that the thirty-year buyer pays in YEAR ONE to the bank, assuming their interest rate is MORE THAN DOUBLE.

In year THREE, the borrower at a 12% interest rate on a five-year loan has paid down HALF of their note yet incurs roughly the same interest penalty that thirty-year borrowers incur on their "low interest note" in YEAR ONE.

"What's the point?" say critics. "No one pays 12% interest. Rates are low right now; of course, you will pay more interest if the interest rate is higher. This book makes no sense. The author is reaching at straws."

Savvy readers understand, however, the point is that **the compound interest algorithm works strictly in the lender's interest.** Time is NOT on your side. *Any interest-bearing instrument is NOT ON YOUR SIDE when you elect (or are forced) to pay it over an inordinately long period of time.*

An interesting aside—when you reduce the amount of payments by five-sixths (for example, a thirty-year loan becomes a five-year loan), most people generally assume their payment would be six times higher. Not surprisingly, a six-times-higher payment than Timmy's fixed payment at 7% would be $3,991.80. **In this comparison, at almost DOUBLE the interest rate, reducing the payment term by 84%,** *Timmy only pays about 3.3 times the payment.*

What does a 7% payment look like on a five-year term? Let's truly compare apples with apples.

Figure E: Mortgage Interest Table—Timmy's Modified 100k Loan with a 7% Fixed Interest Rate Paid over a Five-Year Term

Five-Year 100k, 7% Fixed Monthly PMT $1,980.12			
Year	Interest	Principal	Balance
1	$6,451.64	$17,309.80	$82,690.20
2	$5,200.32	$18,561.12	$64,129.08
3	$3,858.53	$19,902.91	$44,226.17
4	$2,419.75	$21,341.69	$22,884.48
5	$876.96	$22,884.48	$0.00
Totals	$18,807.20	$100,000.00	

Here is the skinny:[53]

---

53   For comparison purposes and reference only.

On Timmy's 100k Thirty-Year Loan at 7%

☐ He pays predominantly interest until year twenty-one, and

☐ The law of averages is against him since most Americans move every five years.

On Timmy's 100k Five-Year Loan at 12%

☐ He pays 3.35 times his thirty-year payment but reduces his time by five-sixths;

☐ Cuts his interest by $106,042.21, which is roughly a 76% interest savings at a 5% higher interest rate; and

☐ In year three, he pays the interest cost thirty-year borrowers incur from years one to twelve, even though the thirty-year loan has a much lower interest rate.

On Timmy's 100k Five-Year Loan at 7%

☐ He pays 2.97 times his thirty-year payment but reduces his time by five-sixths;

☐ Cuts his interest by $120,701.69, which is roughly an 86.6% interest savings using an identical interest rate to his thirty-year loan; and

☐ *He pays less interest in year one than thirty-year borrowers pay in year one, using the same interest rate and mortgage amount.*

Conclusion: Thirty-year mortgages do not work unless one's goal is to stay in debt for an extremely long period of time.

Additional conclusion: A five-year mortgage, in the right circumstances, can change your financial situation for the better in a meaningful and impactful way. For the average borrower, somewhere between a ten-year mortgage and a five-year mortgage can provide the right type of financial instrument for paying off a property and having a significant nest egg of equity as well, when structured properly, with additional income streams.[54]

Meet Me at the Crossroads?

From a metaphorical standpoint, the crossroads is a place where hard, life-changing decisions are made. I know, because I have been there and lived to tell an amazing tale. People tend to find themselves at the crossroads a few times in their life's travels, forced to make hard decisions.

---

54 Assumes you are buying properties properly and at a significant discount from retail as well as using "reasonable" interest rates and repayment terms.

At the (real or metaphorical) crossroads, people get to see what is possible, what currently is, and what could be. They also get a vision of what price they have to pay to get where they want to go. You probably aren't sure if you need (or want) to be here, but when you start to study these amortizations tables, you practically emerge at a financial crossroads of sorts, somewhat involuntarily. And to be quite frank, a lot of people don't want you to be there, studying the simple math that refuses to tell you a lie. Here are a few people who despise your growing "crossroads style" awareness regarding thirty-year loans (and long-term debt instruments) for your review:

Your banker hates you being there. He needs your thirty-year mortgage indebtedness to make his bank profitable.

Your financial "advisor" who "manages" your stock portfolio hates you being there. He needs you to keep sinking your post-tax dollars into the idea of a diversified portfolio of stocks, with risk spread out by investing in broad technical, medical, industrial, and other sectors so he can keep earning commissions. **Buying and paying off real estate won't earn him commissions.** He HATES you buying real estate and, when asked directly, will usually crawfish and tell you "you don't have time to be a landlord." This is a go-to objection for financial advisors against real estate acquisition.

Your boss hates you being there. He needs you to keep working, living paycheck to paycheck, ensconced in debt so he can count on you coming to work every day, dependably, for years.

Colleges and universities HATE young people being there, learning about the power of rapidly amortized real estate and how to put their money to work for *THEM.* These universities and colleges need unsuspecting young people to take out student loans and get an "education" in the hopes that they will wrap themselves in debt for most of their life, paying professors and other highly paid academics their salaries and keeping them comfortable. They need their basketball coaches and football coaches to keep being able to get paid multimillion-dollar salaries to keep their massive sports revenues and NCAA TV contracts coming into the campus, drawing new students and perpetuating the endless debt cycle. The universities need students to believe in the idea that a college degree is a prerequisite to a financially stable life.[55]

---

55   Nothing could be further from the truth. *Paying more than 40k a year for a college degree (times four years) while spending half your time obtaining a "liberal arts" education and taking out student loans to do so is one of the biggest scams our young people can get involved in, and there is NOTHING STABLE about students borrowing far in excess of their ability to repay over their lifetimes.* Why would a (insert profession here, let's say teacher) spend 160k to obtain a four-year teaching degree to earn a 35k per year salary for thirty years, while they pay back student loans for twenty to thirty years. They are committing themselves to a lifetime of indebtedness from the day they get an acceptance letter. **The college myth is a scam.** Why do you think a law was recently passed that made student loans ineligible for bankruptcy? See here: ***http://www.finaid.org/questions/bankruptcy.phtml***

The federal government HATES you being there. They need you to continue to earn your salaried income, obtain your W-2 in January, and file 1040 EZ every year so you can continue to contribute 30% to 40% of your annual income to entitlement spending, Agenda 21, farm subsidies, foreign aid, black market slush projects, and other governmental spending agendas that do nothing to strengthen or bolster the American public or infrastructure.[56] The federal government hates you being able to depreciate real estate or write off mortgage interest. They can't stand it, which is why you periodically hear talk from congressional representatives about eliminating the mortgage interest tax deduction.

Your friends HATE you being here. They are all working and living paycheck to paycheck, financing everything they want today, and hoping the house of cards won't fall down tomorrow. You are becoming financially successful and debt-free by understanding these basic principles, which will force them to question the actions they elect to perform (some say are forced to perform) every day, which is uncomfortable for them.

Credit card companies hate you being here. They need you in debt to continue to make their massive interest on your unresolved credit card balance each month. **Paying cash for everything is bad for them.** Your being able to pay for things because you have cash and not living on credit is even worse. You might close down your credit cards totally![57]

You get my point. **Almost everyone you know, almost everyone you write a check to or pay electronically each month has a vested interest in you NOT obtaining financial freedom**. The first step to financial freedom, in my opinion, is to strategically eliminate your LARGEST expense each month, which is (generally speaking) housing, by paying off your primary residence using a surgically precise tactical approach in doing so. I mean, you are going to make your housing payment each month anyway, presumably, so why wouldn't you make your payment in such a way that it sets you up strategically to retire your housing debt far earlier than you could ever imagine? Think about how your life would benefit each month (and year) if you had no house payment. Would it be better?[58]

Which brings us back to my system. I have found a better way, and I want to share it with you. I will share the details and minutiae with you in later chapters, but if you can grasp the principle I am speaking of, you are well on your first step to financial freedom.

Essentially, I am talking about making your primary residence work for you and, in doing so, making your mortgage work for you. I am talking about, instead of throwing

---

56   Far from being a political book, but if you fall under this category of W-2 earners, you should ask yourself why you give almost half of your income to the federal government without question. People who own lots of real estate don't, legally. Why do you?

57   Dave Ramsey's brilliant works, such as ***Total Money Makeover*** and related books, are prerequisite reading for living a debt-free life and HIGHLY recommended.

58   One hundred percent of people surveyed privately answered YES.

empty mortgage dollars away on thirty-year amortizations to the bank, making your monthly payments COUNT each month by structuring them properly. In doing so, you will be applying the majority of them to principal, with the goal of financial freedom by eliminating debt as quickly as possible.

In a nutshell, we are discussing the concept of financial freedom through savvy acquisition of real estate starting with your primary residence. But first, we need to study the amortization tables.

The Bank Is Scamming You, But You Can Fade the Scam

The bank wants you to take out thirty-year loans, where you pay mostly interest for the first fifteen years. It's that simple. If the bank thinks you are a "strong" borrower, they may offer you a fifteen-year loan. A 100k mortgage on a fifteen-year amortization costs about $200 per month more, on average, when compared to its thirty-year counterpart. *Now I have taught you everything you need to know about thirty-year and fifteen-year loans.*[59] However, for critics of this book, I will encapsulate the most pertinent information needed to understand regarding fifteen-year and thirty-year loans as follows:

Fifteen-Year and Thirty-Year Mortgage Information: Some Facts

1. **Thirty-year loans are the most common real estate debt instrument**. People take these out in the interest of "affordability" but ironically are laden with thirty years of debt service instead. Most of the first twenty years of a loan are spent paying interest before principal, which is a bad deal for the borrower, regardless of interest rate.[60]

2. **Fifteen-year loans cost, per month on average, $200 more than a thirty-year loan.**[61] Most people think fifteen-year loans are unaffordable. **The reason they seem unaffordable is because you are allowed up to (almost) 40% of your take-home pay to service thirty-year loans**. Another $200 per month in a house note makes for slim living for the average person when their banker shows them their payment for a thirty-year loan, which comprises almost 40% of their income. Federal taxes comprise another 30% to 40% of a borrower's income. When you take this into consideration, thirty-year-loan payments seem cheap, comparatively

---

59   The point being fifteen-year notes tend to not be as "unaffordable" as we are taught to think.
60   **IMPORTANT:** Interest rate starts to become irrelevant if most of your payment applies itself to interest first. You are just paying interest. *An aside—interest-only loans are BAD if your goal is to pay off property quickly.*
61   Assumes a 100k loan. If you want to easily figure out what a fifteen-year monthly principal and interest payment costs, take your thirty-year payment and multiply it by 1.51.

speaking, while payment that is $200 more per month seems practically unachievable. Bankers make this idea more palatable by saying the following statement: *"You can always pay it off early...when things get better."*[62]

3. **Most borrowers consider ten-year loans, on a primary residence an impossible debt to service.**

4. **Most borrowers consider the idea of five-year loans on a primary residence, a joke or notion of fantasy.**

5. **Interest rates are secondary to the amount of time one chooses to service a loan until payoff.** The idea of high and low interest rates is arbitrary when factoring in small amortization schedules. A thirty-year loan at 4% fixed costs far more in interest than a five-year loan at 12% fixed, for example.

6. **Banks HATE it when you prepay or pay a loan off early.**[63]

What Do the Amortization Tables Tell Us?

The amortizations tell us lots of things. Primarily, they tell us that loans, which are short term (defined as ten years or less) are really not nearly as profitable for lenders as long-term loans, regardless of the interest rate. *They show us the power of using amortizations, which apply principal FIRST and interest as an afterthought, and how we can go from paying large amounts of interest for endless years to paying off our primary residence in a predefined period of time using some basic financial planning and a fundamental understanding of compound interest.*

In short, they show us basic steps to financial freedom.

Now, critics of this book will seek to undermine these ideas by offering up the idea that debt service for five or seven years on a primary residence is a practical impossibility. (When done correctly, it isn't.) They will then say things like, "Well, if short-term loans are so unprofitable for banks and finance companies, why do auto loans generally take five years or less?"[64]

The answer to that, simply, is that the auto industry creates much more flexible borrowing standards for purchasing vehicles when compared to home loans, and the rapid depreciation of vehicle values (cars rarely go up in value) makes it untenable for

---

62   Evidently, things are bad now when you are trying to get a thirty-year loan? Go figure.
63   Ask yourself, why? Don't they want their money back?
64   They aren't always. Due to rising automotive and inflationary costs, many lenders will take an auto note out as long as twelve years! But those longer loans carry more risk for the lender due to rapid vehicle depreciation.

auto financiers to structure auto loans for long-term payoffs. If cars were financed on fifteen-year loans, for example, their value would drop to almost zero long before the loan was even close to being paid off, putting the lender at risk. This is why cars are financed, generally speaking, on five-year terms.

Finance companies also "win" by providing working capital to the auto makers and dealers by funding the borrowers through the purchase of discounted auto notes. They then charge interest on the note and make money by recouping the full principal owed plus interest paid monthly on the loan over time.

Here's how that play works, assuming the buyer finances most of the vehicle cost, putting down 5k toward the purchase:

American Car Manufacturer Produces Cool Car Model 1A[65]

Total cost of production of car 1A (includes labor and material): 25k

Blue book value of new car: 55k

Sale price at car dealership in an American city: 55k

Down payment from borrower: 5k

Less commissions to dealership from dealer due on sale: 5k

Total gross income to manufacturer: 50k (via borrowed note)

Finance company buys 10% discount five-year note: 50k note for 45k

American car manufacturer sells discount note to finance company: Nets 45k

American car manufacturer recoups 25k production cost and 20k profit: Net 20k, cash to company

Finance company makes money in interest and overlay: Buys 50k note for 45k, makes interest and recoups principal over time, a 5k gain PLUS interest paid on 50k, although only 45k was lent.

Downside risk: Finance company repossesses car and resells if necessary, providing new financing.

---

65   Understand the finance company is making money by purchasing discounted interest-bearing notes secured by underwritten credit reports plus down payments on first position collateral. If you lend me 45k but I have to repay you 50k at interest, you get paid interest on 50k PLUS the 5k principal repayment over time. **This is a highly profitable venture for you as a lender, especially when you can repossess the collateral and resell it in the case of default.** In this study, it's cars, but in the bank's case, it is foreclosing on houses. *The only loser is the borrower.*

THE SHORT-TERM RETIREMENT PROGRAM

The point is, whether it is a car note and subsequent loan that underwrites it or a house note and the subsequent loan that underwrites it, it is in your best interest (assuming you have to borrow money to pay for something like a primary home) pay it off as quickly as possible and, in doing so, pay as little interest as possible.

We May Not Be in Kansas, Toto, But Foreclosures Exist

Timmy the Teacher made several grave mistakes when he went out and found the house of his dreams and paid retail for it with a thirty-year loan, as follows:

> **Timmy the Teacher's Catastrophic Launch Failure: A Short List**
>
> 1. **Timmy fell in love with his house.** He let his emotion get in the way of his clear thinking, and the process was flawed since the time of inception.
>
> 2. **Timmy committed to a thirty-year loan on a home he was in love with**. Timmy wasn't aware of the statistics that indicate that in all probability, for reasons that may or may not be under his control, he will be moving and/or selling in five years or less. As I have demonstrated, this means Timmy is making a minimum five-year commitment to throwing away practically 40% of his monthly income through mortgage interest, taxes, and insurance (and very little principal).
>
> 3. **Because Timmy fell in love with his house, he ended up paying full retail for a property.**
>
> 4. Assuming Timmy moves after five years as previously described, **he takes a total loss on his money.**[66]

But does Timmy have to take a total loss on his money? Let's look at another short list for Timmy—primarily, what he could have done to avoid the predicament he destined himself to be in through disastrous decision making in his pursuit of the American dream.

> ~~Timmy the Teacher's Catastrophic Launch Failure: A Shortlist~~
>
> **Timmy's Winning Techniques Version 1.0: A Shorter List**
>
> 1. Timmy ~~fell in love~~ didn't fall in love with his house. He ~~let his emotion get in the way~~

---

66   Are you paying attention? **A TOTAL LOSS** on his money when using a thirty-year mortgage.

of his clear thinking, didn't do that, and instead ***committed himself to looking for a heavily discounted foreclosed or distressed property in the exact same area where he wants to live.*** As a general rule, he refuses to pay more than 50% of fair market value (taking into account fully repaired fair market value) before repairs on any property, and wants to keep the repairs low cost, and of a cosmetic nature (carpet and paint, some tile, etc.).

Example: Timmy finds a house for 50k that is a foreclosure and he thinks it needs about 5k of work, and it is worth 100k. He will be in the house at 55k all in, **but his PURCHASE PRICE max is 50k (or less), which represents 50% of FMV.**

2. ~~Timmy committed to a thirty-year loan on a home he was in love with.~~ **Timmy, using the Mortgage Affordability Calculator I have provided in this book, will determine the max monthly payment he can afford** and decide if he can afford a five-, seven-, or ten-year mortgage payoff. Keep in mind, if Timmy wants MORE house for his money, he *CAN* have it; he just has to find a better (***read: less expensive***) deal.

3. Assuming Timmy doesn't move five years from now as previously described, he will either have a home paid off or be half way/almost there, depending on the terms of his mortgage. Accounting for the actual fair market value of the home, assuming he buys it and fixes it up, **Timmy's primary residence may just turn out to be the best investment he has ever made, even if he is FORCED to sell in five years, which, statistically speaking, he will need to.**

Let's put Timmy's previous mistakes to the test using these ideas.

How much house can he really "afford"? He was originally planning on obtaining a thirty-year 100k loan and servicing the debt on that.

Let's use that payment as a baseline figure for "affordability."

Timmy's original loan: 100k borrowed

Terms: Thirty-year 100k loan amount

Fixed interest rate: 7%

Monthly payment: $665.30

Now let's pretend that Timmy had the benefit of reading this tome and wanted to make better decisions. He now understands that a thirty-year loan is a snare of debt enslavement, but he (rightly so and understandably) doesn't want to sacrifice his standard of living. Safety is important to him and his now-expecting wife, and he doesn't want to compromise on safety or security, specifically when it comes to the area he chooses to live in.

Good news! *He doesn't have to.*

Timmy uses The **Short-Term Retirement Mortgage Affordability Calculator** to see what his payment options are. He has some decisions to make, specifically regarding the following mortgage-based questions:

Mortgage Affordability Calculator: Payment Input Questions

1. How much does Timmy want his monthly payment to be? *What is the maximum he is willing to pay, per month, for his housing payment?*

2. How long does Timmy want to service the debt? *What is the maximum number of years he wants to have a mortgage?* (Let's, as a rule, say that he can have a mortgage for no more than ten years using my system.)

3. *What is the maximum interest rate Timmy is willing to pay?* Some borrowers who have poor or marginal credit (or recent bankruptcies, divorces, etc.) may not be eligible to qualify for a loan from a bank or mortgage broker. In this case, they can use a private lender, but private lenders tend to charge a far higher rate of interest than an institutional lender, and this has to be accounted for in advance.[67] The borrower has to decide, at the forefront, what interest rate they can tolerate, then use the Mortgage Affordability Calculator to reflect the increased interest rate.

In Timmy's case, and for our discovery, let's assume Timmy's risk parameters using the same payment as his thirty-year loan:

> **Timmy the Teacher: Mortgage Affordability Calculator Parameters**
>
> **Maximum payment amount: $665.30/month**
>
> **Maximum length of loan: Ten years but would prefer as short as possible of a loan term**
>
> **Maximum interest rate: 7%**

---

67 Private lending rates, if not negotiated correctly, can be exorbitantly high and detrimental to the borrower. Thus, interest rate tolerance must be determined in advance. We will discuss private lenders later in this book.

Timmy decides in advance what his loan terms will be as opposed to a banker looking at his tax returns and pay stubs and telling him what the loan terms will be. With Timmy deciding what his loan terms will be, let's look at Timmy's options regarding purchasing power for his primary residence.

STR Mortgage Affordability Calculator		
Inputs	Desired Monthy Payment	Desired Interest Rate
	$665.30	7.00%
Purchasing Power		
	5-Year Payment	$33,598.98
	7-Year Payment	$44,080.97
	10-Year Payment	$57,299.86

What does the mortgage affordability calculator tell us? **In a nutshell, it tells us that Timmy's 100k house dreams are attainable if he accepts the fact that, to live in his desired neighborhood, he will have to REFUSE TO PAY RETAIL and, instead, search earnestly for a foreclosed property or a distressed private seller in the neighborhood where he seeks to live.**[68] What we have demonstrated is that Timmy, using the exact same payment as his thirty-year loan, can (realistically) achieve the same results in one-third of the time if he finds a foreclosure for roughly 57k or less, including repairs. Basically, he needs a 40% discount.

Do people find foreclosed properties for roughly 60% or less of fair market value?

Answer: YES, ALL THE TIME.

They are generally referred to as "real estate investors." And you can be one too.

We will get to searching for properties and strategies for finding discounted properties in another chapter, but since we are focused on eliminating interest payments to the bank (as much as possible), let's see how much interest Timmy saves using a shorter-term, fully amortized mortgage product.

In this case, let's cut Timmy's purchase price in half, keep his interest rate the same, and see how the payments stack up versus the interest saved.

---

68 Essentially, Timmy has to refuse to pay retail and start looking for a "deal." Tactical techniques and strategic applications will be discussed shortly.

Figure F: Mortgage Interest Table—Timmy's Short-Term
Retirement 50k Loan[69] with a 7% Fixed Interest Rate, Paid Over a Ten-Year Term

Ten-year 50k—7% Fixed Monthly PMT $580.54			
Year	Interest	Principal	Balance
1	$3,386.59	$3,579.92	$46,420.08
2	$3,127.80	$3,838.71	$42,581.37
3	$2,850.30	$4,116.21	$38,465.16
4	$2,552.74	$4,413.77	$34,051.39
5	$2,233.67	$4,732.84	$29,318.55
6	$1,891.53	$5,074.98	$24,243.57
7	$1,524.66	$5,441.85	$18,801.72
8	$1,131.27	$5,835.24	$12,966.47
9	$709.43	$6,257.07	$6,709.40
10	$257.11	$6,709.41	$0.00
Totals	$19,665.10	$50,000,00	

Total interest paid: $19.665.10

Versus total interest paid on thirty-year loan at 100k: $139,515.55

Total interest SAVED versus thirty-year loan at 100k: $119,850.45

Hmm, lots of interest saved when you reduce your purchase price by 50% and cut the payments by twenty years. Critics of this book will point out a degree in rocket science is not needed to figure out such a basic premise. Notice also that Timmy's payment is roughly $100 less per month with a significant reduction in loan term or a 67% reduction in time spent servicing the loan by Timmy, to be precise. He avoids spending an additional twenty years of his life servicing his loan and making payments while he watches his neighbors do exactly that.[70]

Let's see how this works using the same loan terms on a seven-year loan.

---

69 All amortization schedules can easily be found using simple mortgage calculators online, or your banker can furnish you with these if you want independent verification of numbers. Check my math if you have questions.

70 It goes without saying that Timmy, once he has eliminated his biggest monthly payment (we assume it is housing), if he reinvests that payment into something else over the following twenty years (say, for example, investment real estate). Timmy has the option—and distinct probability—of becoming a very wealthy man in comparison to his neighbors who threw their money away for an additional twenty years on principal and interest in a vague but punishing attempt to pay off their house.

Figure G: Mortgage Interest Table—Timmy's Short-Term Retirement 50k Loan with a 7% Fixed Interest Rate Paid Over a Seven-Year Term

Seven-Year 50k—7% Fixed Monthly PMT $754.63			
Year	Interest	Principal	Balance
1	$3,318.25	$5,737.36	$44,262.64
2	$2,903.49	$6,152.12	$38,110.52
3	$2,458.75	$6,596.85	$31,513.67
4	$1,981.87	$7,073.74	$24,439.93
5	$1,470.51	$7,585.10	$16,854.83
6	$922.18	$8,133.43	$8,721.40
7	$334.21	$8,721.40	$0.00
Totals	**$13,389.26**	**$50,000.00**	

Total interest paid: $13,389.26

Versus total interest paid on thirty-year loan at 100k: $139,515.55

Total interest SAVED versus thirty-year loan at 100k: $126,126.99

In this case, it gets more interesting, as for an extra $174 per month, the interest savings is even MORE significant, with the time frame of debt service reduced another 30% from a ten-year mortgage. As a fascinating aside, **assuming Timmy purchases a 50k foreclosure as opposed to a 100k retail property in the same neighborhood**, his monthly payment on a seven-year term is roughly $100 per month more than the payment on his 100k thirty-year loan product.

Most people imagine that a five-year loan payoff is an impossibility.

Is it?

Let's take a look (for fun) at what a five-year loan payoff would entail.

Figure H: Mortgage Interest Table—Timmy's 50k Loan at 7% Fixed Five-Year Term

Five-year 50k—7% Fixed Monthly PMT $990.06			
Year	Interest	Principal	Balance
1	$3,225.82	$8,654.90	$41,345.10
2	$2,600.16	$9,280.56	$32,064.54
3	$1,929.27	$9,951.45	$22,113.09
4	$1,209.87	$10,670.85	$11,442.24
5	$438.48	$11,442.24	$0.00
Totals	$9,403.60	$50,000.00	

Total interest paid: $9,403.60

Versus total interest paid on thirty-year loan at 100k: $139,515.55

Total interest SAVED versus thirty-year loan at 100k: $130,111.95

WOW.

Assuming one's goal was to pay as little interest as possible while paying off their house as fast as possible, finding a property at a 50% discount off retail and placing it on a five-year mortgage seems like a great way to start. Keep in mind, while five years to eliminating most people's housing debt permanently seems like an impossibility to most uninformed Americans, the mathematics prove otherwise. Clearly, one can see that a five-year mortgage CAN work, if the home is purchased correctly with agreeable terms for the borrower.

That's right, I said a FIVE-YEAR MORTGAGE.

Open-minded readers of this book are starting to have a moment of clarity.

Critics of the book are starting to regret having thirty-year mortgages and paying full retail for them.[71]

---

71 I am looking forward to a critic of this book telling me that they LOVE their thirty-year mortgage on the house they purchased at full retail, after absorbing the math presented in this book. It is akin to them setting themselves on fire while the world watches them burn.

5

Analysis of Concepts

Before we start to learn the real estate investing techniques necessary to implement the ideas discussed in the last chapter and extrapolate them to your personal wealth portfolio (starting, ideally, with your primary residence), we need a framework of understanding the basics of The Short-Term Retirement Program so you can internalize and then effectively apply these concepts in action.

As such, I would like to introduce a few rules here for us to follow. Remember, the bank doesn't like these ideas, but you will understand why when you see how smartly efficient and effective they are for your pocketbook and, ultimately, your personal net worth.

Here are some basic ideas we need to keep in mind when learning our basic real estate investment strategy:

1. Affordability of thirty-year notes versus affordability of five-year notes.

2. Ability to afford a property of price "x" on a thirty-year note versus choosing to select a property that can, affordably, have the debt retired in five to ten years through fully amortized (not balloon[72]) payments.

3. Paying retail versus buying a foreclosed property, which needs some "sweat equity."

4. Using institutional fixed-rate financing versus private citizen-to-citizen financing, which carries a negotiable interest rate and flexible payment terms.

5. Getting more land for less.

6. Searching for properties in low-tax areas of your desired region.

---

72 Balloon (also known as "demand") payments = where you pay the note holder as if you had a mortgage of thirty years (or something similar), but the note is due in one total payment after a few years. A common example would be a bank's terms of a thirty-year balloon mortgage with a "five-year call," meaning you make payments as if you were paying a thirty-year mortgage, but in month sixty-one, the payment is due in full for the remaining balance, which is essentially the total amount of principal originated on the loan. This is a losing situation for the borrower because he or she is forced to refinance, renegotiate (beg) with the bank, or default.

7. Low interest rate versus high interest rate with rapid repayment schedule.

8. Weighted/perceived value of interest rate versus total time and term of loan repayment.

9. Practicality of properties we choose to purchase in terms of potential income-producing outbuildings, guesthouses, and storage buildings.

10. Environmental sustainability and the ability to essentially "homestead" on your land, providing nutritional resources for your family in the event of a continued rapid increase in commodity prices, global food shortages, or other events that are out of your control, which could interrupt the food supply in your region (never hurts to be prepared!).

11. Choosing to purchase homes from the MLS based on representation by realtors versus seeking out private motivated sellers.

And here are some basic rules we need to follow:

The Short-Term Retirement Program

Ten Basic Starter Rules

1. **Select a mortgage payment you can afford and set term limits BEFORE you go shopping for a home.** Decide what you can comfortably pay each month using the mortgage affordability calculator.[73] Then, instead of using a thirty-year institutional lending basis to determine a loan value that you should be shopping for, use a five-, seven-, or ten-year loan value. Stick to your numbers and don't deviate. Remember, your goal isn't to buy your dream home; it is to eliminate your largest monthly expense (i.e., your housing payment) in order to begin to keep the money you earn, realize a sizable equity nest egg, and use those newly found monthly funds when you DON'T have a mortgage payment to save and invest so you can someday HAVE your dream home, and your dreams, too.

2. **Determine the highest maximum interest rate you are willing to tolerate, before you go shopping.** For example, I generally know that a 12% interest rate (very high, obviously) should usually be enough to encourage private sellers to carry financing for you (I will explain how to get private financing later in the book), but that doesn't necessarily mean you should go out and actively seek private lending at 12% rates. Remember, you ideally want the lowest interest rate

---

73 Use **The Short-Term Retirement Mortgage Affordability Calculator** to determine a mortgage payment that is suitable for you.

possible, which is open to negotiation if you are working with a private seller willing to carry owner financing, and if not, you can always seek out a bank lender if your credit is "good enough for them." In a worst-case scenario, assuming you find an absolutely stellar deal, you can always seek out a private professional lender (such as a "hard money" lender) and should have no problems getting a loan, especially if the home has a strong equity position and is below market value. Remember, when dealing with private sellers and lenders (sometimes banks also), interest rate is always negotiable.

3. **We NEVER pay retail, and neither should YOU.** Real estate is one of the few investment vehicles where a buyer can make a decision to purchase a property at a significant below market discount. This is done in a variety of ways, including buying at foreclosure, purchasing at the courthouse steps, purchasing a foreclosed property that has become a bank REO (real estate owned) property, working with a motivated seller, and so forth. No one can purchase Home Depot stock at a discount; they can only purchase it at market value plus commission, although that price may be considered "cheap" relative to historic highs or lows. *Real estate can, in fact, be purchased at a fraction of fair market value relative to current neighborhood values and certified by a licensed appraiser.* No other investment vehicle allows you such leverage or shopping power. None. Go to your local numismatic coin dealer and try to purchase MS 70 silver coins at a 50% discount. You won't get far, except for being thrown out of the shop.

4. **IMPORTANT! Always search, whenever possible, for additional income-producing units that will offset the total amount you have to pay on the mortgage.** I love single-family homes that have guest houses or additional income units in good areas! They appeal to a very specific kind of renter and, when done properly, will stay rented for years (ask me how I know this). In looking for a primary residence, it is often possible to find a primary residence below market value with an income-producing suite, guest wing, garage apartment, or cottage on the property parcel. **These little units can pay your mortgage AND your utilities if structured properly**. You would be surprised how far you can get ahead financially with an income-producing property and a roommate who pays you rent plus utilities (assuming you are single).

5. **YOU are the buyer, and YOU make the rules.** Real estate is a relatively illiquid investment, and as such, buyers are ALWAYS in demand, no matter

what your realtor tells you.[74] If a seller is uncooperative, take your business elsewhere.

6. **Never fall in love with a house.** *Fall in love with having a house paid off in full instead.*

7. **Depending on your budget, you may have to look at alternative regions to live in.** If home ownership based on paying off your property in five or seven years isn't feasible for you (assuming you follow these rules), there are other areas of opportunity around the USA and in other countries as well. For example, if all you can afford is a 200k house in California and that means you are living in a horrible, unsafe section of the city, maybe the California economy isn't for you. And that is okay. Don't be afraid of leveraging your retirement, government subsidy/Social Security, or pension in non-US-dollar-denominated economies either.[75]

8. **Simple is better than complicated.** If doing a real estate deal will put you in a compromised position of having to do any of the following—service extra debt, additional taxes, city ordinances, deal with problems from the local utility or code enforcement authorities, and so on—PASS ON THE DEAL and move on to the next opportunity. As we continue to see an increase in authoritarian governmental policies, rampant taxation, and sordid bank practices worldwide designed to steal your money from you at any cost (Bank of Cyprus, anyone?) as well as bankrupt municipalities and states due to poor management (think Detroit), you don't want to be in a position to void your freedom because you got locked into a poor real estate decision.

9. **Debt-free is better than having payments.** Your goal, as Dave Ramsey so eloquently states in all his writings and books, should be to be debt free. The best thing you can do for your family is to have no debt and have peace of mind. **Focus on eliminating your debts.** Use real estate to your advantage, and eliminate your housing payment. When choosing between debt and no debt, always choose no debt.

---

74   I'm not slamming licensed realtors here. *I use them all the time and actively seek out their opinions.* However, realtors generally have knowledge of "on market" (read: Multiple Listing Service) types of retail properties, areas, neighborhoods, and trends. Most are completely unfamiliar with the investment or discounted side of the market, which is what this book focuses on.

75   Go to *InternationalLiving.com* for a *must-subscribe-to* magazine that covers this idea monthly and in far more depth than this book. My favorite magazine of all time.

10. **Nothing should be a struggle, if possible.** The goal of these investing techniques, as well as other ideas presented in this book, is to free you from your debt chains. Critics of this book will say that using a ten-year mortgage or less, is in and of itself, a struggle, but when you find a discounted property and determine your maximum payment in advance, all you are doing is empowering yourself to be debt free, making payments on a home, which you were planning to make anyway, just in a far shorter period of time than your banker wants you to. **If something is going to make your life more difficult, pass on it and move on.**

Understanding the ideas recently presented in this book and changing your world views and paradigms, especially when it comes to finances and family financial stability, can be extremely confusing and disorienting, especially since the path to financial freedom I am suggesting goes against, and is the opposite of, what is considered the "traditional" Western investing and "success" mind-set we are inadvertently (or, some would argue, by design) taught from birth. **What you are told will make you wealthy and successful, and what will ACTUALLY make you wealthy and TRULY financially independent are two very, very different things.**

Consider the traditional wisdom we are encouraged through the media to be a pathway to success:

Traditional Financial Wisdom: Some Epic Fallacies

1. **Fallacy:** It is very important to do well in school and get great grades.

    Reality: No one cares about your grades except your teachers and your parents, maybe coaches if you are an NCAA division I star player. If you aren't in school, ask your boss if he or she cares about grades. Truthfully, they are far more concerned about you showing up for work each day. Grades are meaningless when you leave the academic world. When you are thirty-five years old, call your grade school or middle school and ask them to produce your transcript from more than twenty years ago. That's about how much anyone cares about your grades.

2. **Fallacy:** You need a college degree to get a "good" job.

    Reality: With the notable exception of some highly, highly skilled professions that require substantial additional graduate and doctoral-level or postdoctoral-level education (**read:** medical doctors, lawyers, etc.) the true cost of a college education today cannot justify the salary obtained by the employment that requires it.

Example: A schoolteacher in training attends a 50k per year college. When they complete their education, they have 200k in student loans on a twenty-year term. Assuming a 4% repayment interest rate, this would equate to a monthly payment of $1,211.96. Assuming a $35,000 per year starting salary, broken down in to twenty-six pay periods, less 35% for taxes,[76] **the schoolteacher setting out to dedicate their life's purpose to teaching children is going to have to start searching for a second job before they find the first one** since they would only take home $875 every two weeks from their teaching position, or a total take-home monthly salary of $1,750. Essentially, they would have $538.04 left from their main (full-time) job to make ends meet with their utility bill, food, a housing payment, as well as car payment, and so on. *Having this type of student loan encumbrance is clearly and absolutely unsustainable for most entry-level positions.* A college degree is no longer a prerequisite to getting a job or career, and a liberal arts education today is a clear waste of time and money.[77] One is better off NOT going to college and getting vocational education, then learning how to effectively invest their post-tax take-home pay rather than to get a higher-earning salary through a college degree, only to give away 75% of it to student loan payments for twenty years.

3. **Fallacy:** Food prices are rising due to drought and food shortages.

   Reality: The United States has more than enough arable farmland to sustain its current population (at the time of this writing [323.9 million]). The US government actively engages in practices such as paying farmers "farm subsidies" to NOT grow crops and to, instead, keep their fields fallow. *How can there be a food crisis when the US government uses taxpayer dollars to pay famers NOT to grow crops?* Answer: Food prices, supply, and shortages are manipulated for profit by large corporations with the complicity of the US government.[78]

4. **Fallacy:** Energy prices are rising due to an ongoing energy crisis, generally resulting from a lack of oil. Pressures with Russia and in the Middle East add to the tension and to the subsequent cost. OPEC controls major worldwide supply and demand, and the tenuous relationship the United States has with Middle Eastern countries doesn't help, either.

---

76 I'm being generous here; it's usually closer to 50% in most cases.
77 **Highly interesting sidenote**—by eliminating a college degree and taking a minimum-wage job (with no student loans) in this example, the minimum-wage employee generates more take-home pay for themselves than their college-educated brethren with 200k in student loans and a competitively paying entry-level job requiring an undergraduate degree (in most cases).
78 No other logical answer exists.

Reality: There is no oil shortage, nor does the United States suffer from a lack of oil. These prices are manipulated by large oil companies, which lobby heavily in Washington, for their profitable consideration. Oil also, incidentally, is not the only resource we have for energy, as multiple forward-thinking scientists such as Nikola Tesla and Stanley Meyers (with his water-powered car) have demonstrated.[79] Peak oil is also highly suspect and questionable. Also, for fun, you can look at the rolling blackouts caused by Enron throughout the southwest before its corporate implosion to see how energy "shortages" suddenly materialize and are used daily to help manipulate stock and utility prices nationwide by private companies that provide utility services.

5. **Fallacy:** Things are getting more expensive. Prices are going up everywhere, and this is due to a weak US economy resulting from a recession, specifically from the subprime borrowing default of 2008, which was blamed heavily on speculative real estate investors.

   Reality: The Federal Reserve, which issues US currency and orchestrates its subsequent monetary policy, has weakened the US dollar through its attrition and monetary policies since its inception in 1913.[80] Assuming the Federal Reserve is being truthful and is truly dedicated to its publicly stated mission, which is to (quoting here) **"Conduct the nation's monetary policy by influencing money and credit conditions in the economy in pursuit of full employment and stable prices,"**[81] I think it's safe to say one hundred years later, their efforts have been a catastrophic failure.[82]

6. **Fallacy:** Fuel-efficient cars are difficult to achieve due to a variety of factors. There is only so much mileage you can get from a gallon of gasoline.

   Reality: Here is a fascinating study into the suppression of that technology, with resources for you to research independently. It's probably a safe bet that we can, using technology known to today's manufacturers, get a vehicle that can get far more than 15 or 25 mpg[83] or avoids using gasoline at all.[84]

---

79   See http://waterpoweredcar.com/stanmeyer.html for the fascinating details on Stan Meyer's life and sudden and strange death.
80   http://www.forbes.com/2010/11/24/dollar-inflation-federal-reserve-opinions-contributors-lawrence-hunter.html—one of many, many articles on this dollar trend since the inception of the Federal Reserve.
81   http://www.federalreserve.gov/faqs/about_12594.htm.
82   Is it possible, for all of our sake, that you guys can please stop trying? **Whatever you are doing isn't working.**
83   http://beforeitsnews.com/alternative/2013/03/450-mpg-carburetors-suppressed-by-us-government-2590184.html.
84   http://waterpoweredcar.com/inventors.html.

The Short-Term Retirement Program

Basic Strategy

Just like modern-day blackjack players are expected to learn "basic strategy" before they hit the tables at the casino and then apply the knowledge seamlessly in the heat of the cards being dealt, so too do we have to learn Short-Term Retirement "basic strategy" and then learn how to effectively apply it in the heat of doing a real estate deal, ideally for our primary residence. **These ideas should become second nature to you, as we begin to learn how to analyze and find suitable investment opportunities that are candidates for our portfolio.** These are more generalized concepts and ideas versus hard-and-fast rules, but you will get the idea—what to do and not to do when you are buying a property with the intention of paying it off quickly and in doing so alter your financial picture permanently and for the better.

A few general concepts for us to consider are as follows:

1. Affordability of thirty-year notes versus affordability of five-year notes.

2. Ability to afford a property of price "x" on a thirty-year note versus choosing to select a property that can, affordably, have the debt retired in five to seven years through fully amortized (not balloon[85]) payments.

3. Paying retail versus buying a foreclosed property, which needs some "sweat equity".

4. Using institutional fixed-rate financing versus private citizen-to-citizen financing, which carries a negotiable interest rate and flexible payment terms.

5. Getting more land for less.

6. Searching for properties in low-tax areas of your desired region.

7. Practicality of properties we choose to purchase in terms of potential income-producing outbuildings, guesthouses, and storage buildings.

Let's look, in-depth, at each of the ideologies I have given you and then also analyze the simple rules for changing your financial future one idea at a time.

---

85 Balloon (also known as "demand") payments = where you pay the note holder as if you had a mortgage of thirty years (or something similar), but the note is due in one total payment after a few years. A common example would be a bank's terms of a thirty-year balloon mortgage with a fifteen-year call—meaning, you make payments as if you were paying a thirty-year mortgage, but in month sixty-one, the payment is due in full for the remaining balance, which is essentially the total amount of principal originated on the loan. **This is a losing situation for the borrower because he or she is forced to refinance, renegotiate (beg) with the bank, or default.**

1) Affordability of thirty-year notes versus affordability of five-year notes.

As we have seen in the previous amortization tables, what we often think of as an unsustainable payment (meaning less than thirty years) really isn't that much more significant of a payment than its fifteen-year equivalent. This trend also follows when we compare a fifteen-year mortgage payment with a ten-year mortgage payment. Often the difference in being able to actually pay (consistently) a monthly mortgage that is less than a thirty-year term comes from a commitment to limiting the amount of discretionary income we spend on non-mortgage type items, freeing capital to make payments on an aggressive amortization schedule. Very often for the American family, reducing or eliminating one or two non-essential services (like cable television or a land phone, which is often unused) would be enough to make that five-year note suddenly affordable.

The critical idea here is that **post-tax income should be spent and invested in reducing debt and collecting income-producing and appreciating assets** versus purchasing items like expensive vacations, which are often financed by revolving lines of credit, and provide little lasting values beyond the memories and the debt they often bring if financed.[86]

2) Ability to afford a property of price "x" on a thirty-year note versus choosing to select a property that can, affordably, have the debt retired in five to seven years through fully amortized (not balloon[87]) payments.

While this seems similar to the previous concept, I often compare this idea to the way Americans tend to purchase autos. These days, it seems that the auto makers are able to close sales on higher-priced cars that people could otherwise not afford by simply extending the repayment terms. Thus, you have 25k/year earners who are suddenly able to purchase the 80k Escalade, although it may require a twelve-year repayment. The buyer no longer sets a budget based on a time period of repayment; they simply are asked how much do you want your monthly payment to be, and they—after naming their price—are given a repayment term to allow them to "own" the vehicle, even though it will have very little value relative to what they paid for it by the time they have completed their repayment period.

---

86 This idea is brilliantly encapsulated in Robert Kiyosaki's **Rich Dad, Poor Dad** bestselling series. If you have not read these books, you should go to the library or purchase a copy for your knowledge library immediately. Kiyosaki, quite simply, identifies the idea that "*the rich purchase luxuries last, whereas the poor and middle class tend to purchase luxuries first.*" This is a concept that combines discipline with the conjecture and understanding that sacrifices made today will be repaid tenfold in a future time and, therefore, are worth making. Often, this applies to real estate debt, which can produce income to offset mortgage payments which were necessary to acquire the property.

87 See note number 85.

A more intelligent way to purchase a car would be to identify a reasonable period term of time that we can finance a vehicle comfortably, and based on THAT time period, choose a vehicle with a price that matches our tolerance for the monthly payment associated with the specific time period.

Example: *Anandra, a young college graduate with lots of student loan debt and little cash, just got a new job and needs a reliable vehicle, which she currently does not have. She wants to have a $300/month payment (maximum) and needs to buy a new car. She doesn't have the cash, so she goes to a dealer, but before she goes, she decides she wants to buy a car that will be paid off IN FULL in a three-year time period, no more. Assuming she stays within her budget, she would be looking at a car in the 10k range, depending on the interest rate.*

Now, young Anandra may not find what she is looking for if she starts her search for a vehicle at the Mercedes dealership. She may have to roll off to the Kia dealership or settle for a Ford subcompact. But since she needs a source of reliable transportation and is forced to use financing since she is starting out with no capital, **she can do something none of her friends have the knowledge or discipline to do, which is to pay the note off as quickly as possible.** Yes, she may not be as cool as her friend whose dad bought her a Mercedes or her other friend who got the Escalade on a ten-year payment, but she will have her car paid off in full in three years (or less), and *once that monthly note is retired, she can use those funds, instead of making a car payment, toward accumulating other investment assets that produce cash flow.*[88]

Feol's Fundamental Theorem of Coolness. Cars are not cool. *Not working again for the rest of your life, not having a boss to report to, or pursuing your life passions as opposed to some dead-end job you get trapped in due to your poor financial decisions IS cool.* Following your dreams and living your life free of a master is very, very cool. You will probably lose some friends, though.[89]

A Note About Envying Others' Financial Situations. Envy is the downfall of the person who seeks freedom from financial servitude. If you spend your days envying people who you perceive as "having money," you are spending time pursuing a fruitless pursuit that will kill you inside, and worse, you may be envying something that is actually created by your misconceptions and simply is an illusion. First of all, **no one ever really knows someone else's financial situation since all humans are prone to lying,**

---

88   This is the concept of retiring debt service and substituting those monies for investment-based positive cash flow returns. Once you pay the car off, don't go out to dinner an extra time each month. Pretend you still have the car payment, but place it in an investment vehicle that grows monthly or even a vehicle like a self-directed IRA where you can make your annual contribution as a monthly savings plan.

89   Because so few people will be able to identify with you. They will begin to describe you as an urban legend—**the guy or girl who doesn't need to work!**

especially regarding status items like money. Look at social media like Facebook. You would think all your "friends" are high rollers and never run into problems based on their Facebook page! Don't assume that since someone has a nice car and house, they are necessarily wealthy and/or powerful. First, all those items could be financed, which means that all the person you are envying really owns is heavy debt obligations and the need to go to work each day because they MUST, not because they want to. Be wary of envying what you don't understand or have complete knowledge of.

     Secondly, you need to understand that most families spend beyond their means with no rescue plan in sight. It is not uncommon for an executive management position to pay someone 200k a year, but that person actually has 300k of expenditures, forcing them to tap lines of credit and add additional monthly debt obligations to maintain their standard of living. In many cases, at some point, this house of cards will fall, and payments will, ultimately, be missed. **While most American families are adding debt service payments to their financial portfolio, you should be doing the opposite and be removing these payments by paying off the obligation** OR selling it (them, if they are salable, like over-leveraged car). Use the discretionary income you have left over to "snowball" your debt payoff,[90] build a six-month cash reserve, or accumulate cash-producing or appreciating assets. *Remember, each time you pay a bill, it makes other people wealthy.*

     Basically, all you can do is worry about you. If you are not financially independent, make that your primary concern. Who cares about the neighbor who has a new BMW? Make the correct financial decisions over a long enough period of time, and you can drive a Maserati you paid cash for. How about that? And besides, the YOU of tomorrow will thank the YOU of today for making such disciplined decisions.

3) Paying retail versus buying a foreclosed property, which needs some "sweat equity."

Most people don't understand or cannot grasp the types of significant discounts that are available when you are purchasing real estate. This has never been more true than in the wake of the post-2008 USA credit collapse that the people of the United States have been experiencing at the time of this writing. Purchasing properties for discounts of 40% to 90% off of retail are not uncommon! And yet, most families when buying a house, are focused on buying the "most" house they can, stretching their mortgage budget and making sure they find the "perfect" house. I know this because my wife and I did the same thing when we were searching for our primary residence ten years ago. We did find the house that was perfect for us and went ahead and placed the property on

---

90   A Dave Ramsey, syndicated radio show host, term. See his book, ***The Total Money Makeover,*** for further details.

a thirty-year mortgage. Ironically, we don't place investment properties on longer than a seven-year-mortgage term whenever possible, so why did we make an exception to our rule for our private home ten years ago? **We originally felt that it was okay to fall in love with your home, that you need to find the perfect home. However, I learned the hard way, and now I know this NOT TO BE TRUE.** *Location and land* are far more important to purchasing a primary residence than the quality of the property itself, as **you can renovate homes and improve their quality, or even customize properties to your liking, far more cheaply than you can by simply trying to "find" the perfect home and pay full retail for it.** Plus, most American families move every five years, so the house you purchase today is probably not the house of your dreams and should be treated as such.[91]

It is always better to purchase a house with a significant equity position, knowing you can sell it for a significant gain in a few years, than to purchase at the top of the market and hope the market continues to increase. Remember, you may find yourself wanting to move someday, and having a significant financial equity position that you can sell and realize as profit is a huge incentive to assist you in future moves. You can then upgrade properties while your financial position strengthens over time (assuming you use these ideas presented in this book and sound financial principals in general), *as opposed to the possibility of having to downgrade due to financial duress.* We will talk more about purchasing your primary residence later in this book, **but if you can focus on the idea that you should be buying your primary home for value (via foreclosure properties or a private motivated seller) and forcing value appreciation through cosmetic renovation and light construction, you are getting the idea of where you need to be.**

4) Using institutional fixed-rate financing versus private citizen-to-citizen financing, which carries a negotiable interest rate and flexible payment terms.

The traditional concept of purchasing a primary residence (or any real estate, really) involves an individual or family going to a bank and asking for a loan. This potentially puts the borrower in a position of being told *no.*

I don't like being told *no.* And neither should you.

---

91   My wife and I did refinance our primary home on a fifteen-year note at half of the interest rate of our original mortgage. It is the only long-term mortgage we have, and if we could profitably sell it, we would and buy a foreclosed farm instead for a fraction of what we paid for our primary. However, we also recognize that the market will continue to rebound, and our best move is to continue to attack the debt aggressively, then sell strategically and parlay our equity into a paid-off home when the time is right.

Many readers of this book are, at the time of reading this, in a position of NOT being able to purchase a piece of real estate (either for investment purposes or for their primary residence) due to one of the following reasons:

1.   They do not have sufficient cash for a down payment, for whatever reason;

2.   They do not have sufficient credit to qualify for a loan based on the bank's lending standards, for whatever reason (missed payments, bankruptcy, massive debt-to-income ratio); or

3.   The banks they have relationships with are not lending, for whatever reason.

So if you cannot qualify for a loan, you need to rent, correct? If the bank tells you *no*, then no means *no*, and you are simply out of luck, right?

Wrong.

Private lending is the future of the American small community.[92] The truth of the matter is, relinquishing our life savings to massive multinational companies, governments, and conglomerates simply doesn't work because the nature of human greed—coupled with corporate and political interests—creates a lack of accountability for the shareholder or investor. ***Enron, WorldCom, MF Global, Bernie Madoff (the list is endless), all reinforce to us that we cannot trust Wall Street or multinational publicly traded firms and certainly cannot trust the US government's ability to regulate these corporations in the citizens' best interest.*** Lobbyists are paid, and companies pay lobbyists to funnel millions of dollars to get legislation regulated in their (profitable) favor, at the expense of the small guy. Big money talks, and the small guy's money disappears.

And make no mistake about it, *you* are the small guy.

Wall Street and the Banking World HATE YOU

Here is a recent (and perfect) example of why you cannot trust ANY brokerage firm, let alone place ANY of your money there, no matter how "highly regarded" the leadership is. I have edited the article for brevity's sake, but you will get the idea. I have also highlighted critical parts that should give you an idea to pause and reflect on where, exactly, you want YOUR money placed.

---

92   See Chapter 10 for an in-depth analysis of private lending concepts.

MF Global CEO Jon Corzine Quits as Big Bet Fails[93]

By Jonathan Stempel and Christopher Doering

Fri Nov 4, 2011 11:02pm EDT

(Reuters)—Jon Corzine, one of Wall Street's best-known stars, stepped down as MF Global Holdings Ltd.'s chairman and chief executive after his bets on European debt drove the futures brokerage into bankruptcy.

The departure was announced on Friday, hours before conflicting reports surfaced about the whereabouts of $633 million of missing customer money, whose disappearance derailed MF Global's effort this week to quickly sell a variety of assets.

Okay, so what is going on here? I'll tell you what is going on. You have a banking firm with a fiduciary duty to its depositors running a massive scam, aided and abetted by hundreds—if not thousands—of traders and employees, *the scam itself being corroborated by the fact that he (Corzine) was actively lobbying against reforms designed to regulate against the risk of using clients' money to make proprietary trades on behalf of the firm itself, NOT the client (see article).*

Also, what is interesting is that, basically, MF Global gambled their clients' funds on other countries' debts, and lost. This is why the company went bankrupt—because of a risky gamble with its clients' money by using those funds without their express consent or knowledge.

Here is an article that follows up the original, showing that the depth of the depravity is seemingly boundless. With more lies coming to light, mainly, the original estimate of money lost by the company was about half of the actual losses, which at the time of this writing seem to be a minimum of 1.2 billion. I have edited for brevity here, also.

MF Global Trustee Says Shortfall Could Exceed $1.2 Billion[94]

November 21, 2011, *11:26 am*

By MICHAEL J. DE LA MERCED and BEN PROTESS

The amount of customer money missing from the collapsed trading firm MF Global may be more than $1.2 billion—double previous estimates—the trustee dismantling the firm's brokerage unit said on Monday.

---

93   Link here: http://www.reuters.com/article/2011/11/05/us-mfglobal-corzine-idUSTRE7A331A20111105.
94   See: http://dealbook.nytimes.com/2011/11/21/mf-global-trustee-estimates-shortfall-could-be-more-than-1-2-billion/.

Regulators suspect that as investors and customers fled MF Global in the last week of October, the firm used some of the customer money for its own needs—violating Wall Street rules that customers' money be kept separate from the firm's funds. Much of that money may never return.

More than 1.2 billion missing? I wonder what it would be like to have your life savings invested in a company that gambled it away, and now you cannot get it back... Fortunately, I won't have to experience this because watching these other fools lose money has been an easy enough lesson for me: **don't invest with large multinational companies, especially when your assets are backed by worthless paper.**[95]

While Jon Corzine is now spending his days lawyering up and fearing the phone ringing, I ask you this question: do you want to let some massively overpaid, corrupt executives gamble with your life savings while they are living high on the hog?

Is Your Money Safe in the Bank?

This book isn't about the US government being bad or the financial overmasters who control the average person's destiny having a prescribed agenda to enrich themselves at the average person's expense. Granted, both these things may be true, depending on who you ask, but I like to just point out some major media articles of recent note, which are a concrete indicator of what the average person can expect from Wall Street moving forward, assuming past incidents can predict future behavior.

Most stock brokerages have disclaimers telling you that past events do not predict future behavior or guarantee results. To me, watching the bank and politicians in action historically and expecting them to continue to act as they have done is very much a "sure bet."

But don't take my word for it. Let these news items speak for themselves. One thing is for sure, if these news items become a reality for citizens around the world, we will certainly begin to feel differently about the saying, "Your money is safe in the bank."

---

95   *"But, Robert, so many people make so much money in the stock market!"* you say. I totally agree! The problem is that those people are not YOU or ANYONE you know. Name three of your closest friends who made enough money to retire from investing in the stock market? Exactly my point. Unless you and your friends are in the 1% of 1%, you are not in all likelihood generating ZIP CODE-altering revenue but probably doing an excellent job of paying commissions to your broker while worrying about the arrival of your quarterly statements.

Bank "Emergencies" Mean Your Account Will Dwindle (Some Articles for Further Reading)

Bank of Cyprus executes depositor bail-in[96]

Savers in the Bank of Cyprus took a hit on Sunday as 37.5pc of their uninsured deposits were converted to equity as part of the island's €10bn (£8.4bn) rescue deal.

The so-called "bail-in" forces savers to foot the bill for the recapitalization of Cyprus' biggest bank, after it was hit by massive losses from its exposure to debt-crippled Greece.

Bank of Cyprus said it had converted 37.5pc of deposits exceeding €100,000 into "class A" shares, with an additional 22.5pc held as a buffer for possible conversion in the future. Another 30pc would be temporarily frozen and held as deposits, the bank said.

* * *

New G20 Rules: Cyprus-style Bail-ins to Hit Depositors AND Pensioners[97]

Bail-in in Plain English

The Financial Stability Board (FSB) that now regulates banking globally began as a group of G7 finance ministers and central bank governors organized in a merely advisory capacity after the Asian crisis of the late 1990s. Although not official, its mandates effectively acquired the force of law after the 2008 crisis, when the G20 leaders were brought together to endorse its rules. **This ritual now happens annually, with the G20 leaders rubberstamping rules aimed at maintaining the stability of the private banking system, usually at public expense.**

According to an International Monetary Fund paper titled "From Bail-out to Bail-in: Mandatory Debt Restructuring of Systemic Financial Institutions":

> **[B]ail-in...is a statutory power of a resolution authority (as opposed to contractual arrangements, such as contingent capital requirements) to restructure the liabilities of a distressed financial institution by writing down its unsecured debt and/or converting it to equity. The statutory bail-in power is intended to achieve a prompt recapitalization and restructuring of the distressed institution.**

69

The language is a bit obscure, but here are some points to note:

☐ What was formerly called a "bankruptcy" is now a "resolution proceeding." The bank's insolvency is "resolved" by the neat trick of turning its liabilities into capital. Insolvent TBTF banks are to be "promptly recapitalized" with their "unsecured debt" so that they can go on with business as usual.

☐ **"Unsecured debt" includes deposits, the largest class of unsecured debt of any bank.**[98] **The insolvent bank is to be made solvent by turning our money into their equity**—bank stock that could become worthless on the market or be tied up for years in resolution proceedings.

☐ The power is statutory. Cyprus-style confiscations are to become the law.

☐ Rather than having their assets sold off and closing their doors, as happens to lesser bankrupt businesses in a capitalist economy, "zombie" banks are to be kept alive and open for business at all costs, and the costs are again to be borne by us.

Cyprus-Style Wealth Confiscation Is Now Starting to Happen All Over the Globe[99]

The precedent that was set in Cyprus is being used as a template for establishing bail-in procedures in New Zealand, Canada, and all over Europe. It is only a matter of time before we see this exact same type of thing happen in the United States as well. **From now on, anyone who keeps a large amount of money in any single bank account or retirement fund is being incredibly foolish.**

New Zealand

The New Zealand government has been discussing implementing a "bail-in" system to deal with any future major bank failures. The following comes from a New Zealand news source...

---

98 Notice here that deposits are considered bank "debt," as opposed to actual asset holdings. Assets, in the form of currency (among other things), were physically taken to the bank and deposited. Yet the banks consider these physical assets "debt" that can be defaulted on if deemed necessary by decision-making bank employees or government officials.

99 http://www.globalresearch.ca/cyprus-style-wealth-confiscation-is-now-starting-to-happen-all-over-the-globe/5351565

The National Government are pushing a Cyprus-style solution to bank failure in New Zealand which will see **small depositors lose some of their savings to fund big bank bailouts**, the Green Party said today.

Open Bank Resolution (OBR) is Finance Minister Bill English's favored option dealing with a major bank failure. **If a bank fails under OBR, all depositors will have their savings reduced overnight to fund the bank's bail out.**

"The Reserve Bank is in the final stages of implementing a system of managing bank failure called Open Bank Resolution. The scheme will put all bank depositors on the hook for bailing out their bank.

"Depositors will overnight have their savings shaved by the amount needed to keep the bank afloat."

* * *

The Cyprus Bank "Bail-In" Is Another Crony Bankster Scam[100]

A new strategy has been unveiled around the world, with the first test run in Cyprus. Despite early denials, the "bail-in" strategy for insolvent banks has already become official policy throughout Europe and internationally as well.

Here's what it looked like in Cyprus:

All insured deposits (individuals and legal entities) up to €100.000 have, as of 26 March 2013, been transferred from Laiki Bank to the Bank of Cyprus. In addition, the entire amount of deposits belonging to financial institutions, the government, municipalities, municipal councils and other public entities, insurance companies, charities, schools, educational institutions, and deposits belonging to JCC Payment Systems Ltd have been transferred to the Bank of Cyprus.

All other deposits exceeding €100.000 remain in the "bad" Laiki Bank.

Did you get that? Financial institutions (e.g., German banks and central banks including the Bundesbank) get full repayment, along with government entities, while everyone else gets to eat sand.

* * *

---

100 http://www.forbes.com/sites/nathanlewis/2013/05/03/the-cyprus-bank-bail-in-is-another-crony-bankster-scam/

Well, maybe just holding cash in the banks is a safer bet than investing in securities of firms like MF Global. Isn't it? I mean, the banks are safe and FDIC insured, right? Even if there are bank losses, should you have your cash deposited in an FDIC-insured bank account, you will get your money back, won't you?

* * *

Peter Schiff: The FDIC Has Huge Shortfall In Insuring Deposits[101]

"This episode (Cyprus) also puts into starker focus the inadequacy of deposit insurance. By offering the illusion of systemic safety in bank deposits, government guarantees encourage recklessness by banks and depositors. They provide the same incentives that federal flood insurance does in convincing homeowners to build on flood zones. Consumer choice and risk aversion are powerful forces that could bring needed discipline to banking. The FDIC in the U.S. is in the same situation as insurance giant AIG before the crash of 2008."

"While **the FDIC currently has about $25 billion available** to bail out failing banks in the event of isolated events (**mainly held in U.S. treasuries that would need to be sold**), it insures more than $10 trillion in deposits**. Clearly it lacks the resources to cover major losses in a systemic failure. **A failure of just one of the nation's forty largest banks could swamp the resources of the FDIC.**"

* * *

Everywhere you turn, if you peel back the layers of the onion, it seems like the fractional reserve banking system simply doesn't work. At its greatest essence, it is a catastrophic failure, a sham foisted on an unsuspecting, trusting (and uneducated) public.

Is there a better way? If there is, we can be certain it DOESN'T involve putting your money, or your trust, in banks, Wall Street, or big government.

---

101 http://livinginabubbleblog.wordpress.com/2013/04/24/peter-schiff-the-fdic-has-huge-shortfall-in-insuring-deposits/.

5) Getting more land for less—making your real estate acquisition one that can help sustain and nourish your family while making you wealthy.

Land is becoming, and will continue to be, a very precious and scarce resource. Being able to grow your own food will become an increasingly valuable commodity and investment resource in the future, along with having access to independent fresh water on your property.

One time, I heard a story about a guy who allegedly had contact with an extraterrestrial being. The being remarked to him that it was somewhat amazing (in a bad way) and truly unsustainable that 1% of the Earth's population, statistically, is engaged in food production for the other 99%, and that this creates a situation where people could very easily starve if the precipitous supply chain was disrupted. The "being" continued to remark that most people have no idea how to produce food for their families today.

Whether the story is true or not is really irrelevant, because the thought process behind it is pretty sound and applies to you at this moment. **Do you take for granted the food you buy at the grocery store and think that it will be there tomorrow?** Do you take for granted the water that comes out of your tap?

We all do.

But changing our financial thinking paradigm also dictates that we look at the resources required for daily life and plan for the future should an unforeseen event take place, which could possibly make those resources scarce for some period of time. Taking into account the size of the land on a property you are considering for purchase and its potential resources that are available to your family should be a critical issue on your mind.

Think I am joking? George Soros has a sudden interest in US and South American farmland. So maybe you should pay attention, too.

Here is an article that can give you a glimpse into just how valuable the magnate investor thinks simple farmland is.

Why Is George Soros Selling Gold and Buying Farmland?[102]

Sunday, August 14, 2011 by Mike Adams, the Health Ranger Editor of NaturalNews.com

(NaturalNews) Food prices are skyrocketing all across the globe, and there's no end in sight. The United Nations says food inflation is currently at 30% a year, and the fast-eroding value of the dollar is causing food prices

---

102   Taken from: http://www.naturalnews.com/033319_food_prices_farmland.html.

to appear even higher (in contrast to a weakening currency). **As the dollar drops in value due to run away money printing at the Federal Reserve, the cost to import foods from other nations looks to double in just the next two years—and possibly every two years thereafter.**

That's probably why investors around the globe are flocking to farmland as the new growth industry. "Investors are pouring into farmland in the U.S. and parts of Europe, Latin America and Africa as global food prices soar," reports Bloomberg magazine (http://www.bloomberg.com/news/2011-...). "A fund controlled by George Soros, the billionaire hedge-fund manager, owns 23.4 percent of South American farmland venture Adecoagro SA."

Just because investors are interested in farmland doesn't mean that you have to rush out and buy a farm instead of a primary residence. Just making sure your home (we are talking primary residence here) is on a minimum of an acre can make massive differences in your ability to be self-sustaining. Seeds don't cost much and, other than a time investment, reward you with a multitude of bounties, beyond food even, in the form of fresh air, exercise, and so on.

But in addition to that, did you know an acre of land can provide enough farmed food to feed a family of four?

If you have not read **The Backyard Homestead** by Carleen Madigan, I recommend you do so immediately.[103] This book will change the way you think about fresh food and how you can make small gardening efforts to product massive gains in terms of fresh, nutritious food on the land you own, which is also of excellent quality.

More on Food—The Cornerstone of Your Existence

Over the years, my wife and I have developed a shared love of cooking and fine food. Obviously, there is a difference between a hamburger at your local fast-food restaurant and a prime steak at the finest steakhouse in town, although in theory, both food items have their base stemming from the same animal. My wife and I, along the way, have also developed a sense of shared frugality, i.e., a desire to eat steakhouse-style meals at fast-food prices. Can it be done?

As we explored this idea, we began to notice, as have so many Americans today, that basic foodstuff staples like milk and bread can vary significantly in price, depending on

---

103 http://www.amazon.com/Backyard-Homestead-Produce-food-quarter/dp/1603421386.

how these items were produced. The way they were produced often share a similar trend: If foods were produced by smaller farms or organic-type producers, then the prices would be proportionately higher than their mass produced (nonorganic) corporately monopolized counterpart. For some reason, eating healthy has become very expensive and, at times, against the law. My wife and I continued to ask the question, Why?

Food Wars, Farm Wars, and the Eradication of the Local Food Producer

As we began to study what was really going on, we discovered that major corporate monopolistic companies are, with the collusion of big government and the FDA, working actively to derail the small farmer's ability to produce heritage-style, nongenetically modified crops. The extent of this was staggering, given the fact that we are all told that genetically modified crops are "safe." But they aren't safe, and studies seem to prove this.[104] Worse, legal wrangling by major corporations like Monsanto are working to derail and bankrupt small farms through baseless litigation for copyright infringement.

Here is one example, taken from OrganicConsumers.com.[105]

Down on the Farm

The June 1, 2004 issue of Playboy *tells how one long-time Indiana farmer, Troy Roush, once big on biotech was wrongly accused of saving seed. The legal fight cost him $390,000 in lawyers' fees.* **Since then he has begun to see the way the system is devastating traditional farming. "Genetically modified crops are destroying the social fabric of our rural communities" he says, "Roush probably couldn't go back to conventional crops even if he could find good conventional seed; once Monsanto's DNA is in your field it's almost impossible to get it out.** *And with the corporate DNA police abroad in the land, farmers can't afford to take a chance. So, it looks as though there's no turning back from a future in which Monsanto and a handful of other companies own the genetic building blocks of the world's food supply.*

The war on food—YOUR food—is real. It is beyond the scope of this book to discuss the intricacies of why war is being waged against the American people in the form of food

---

104 http://www.organic-systems.org/journal/92/JOS_Volume-9_Number-2_Nov_2014-Swanson-et-al.pdf; http://farmwars.info/?p=13753.
105 https://www.organicconsumers.org/news/monsantos-global-war-farmers.

modification, but nonetheless, it is real, and it affects YOU. Ensuring survivability and sustainability of your family by looking at land in addition to, or as part of, your primary residence purchase is a wise and prudent decision indeed.

6) Searching for properties in low-tax areas of your desired region.

Paying real estate tax is an onerous and demoralizing burden. In Memphis, Tennessee, where I live, we have the highest property tax rates in the State of Tennessee. If I leave the county where Memphis is located and travel a few miles down the road, my property tax burdens go down by 60% to 90%.

People who have their property tax impounded (escrowed) with their mortgage payment, or have W-2 income where their taxes are withheld through payroll deduction, are somewhat anesthetized to the pain of paying taxes[106] **due to the nature of the withholding by third-party companies (employer, mortgage company, etc.)** When you have to write checks each year for property tax or to the IRS, however, and then you see that money disappear from your account and go out the window to ineffective social programs, municipal programs, and never-ending wars, well, you start to think about downsizing your tax burden. We will talk about taxes later, but a great general meditation on tax burden is that **IT IS NOT YOUR JOB TO CARRY THE BURDEN OF GOVERNMENT'S WASTEFUL SPENDING ON YOUR SHOULDERS OR THE SHOULDERS OF YOUR FAMILY.**

Every dollar you do NOT throw away to big government is a dollar you can save for a rainy day, a dollar NOT thrown away; and over time, these dollars add up. You have to be wary of your local municipality using you as a tax resource. It is like the "one ring" in J. R. R. Tolkien's masterpiece *The Fellowship of the Ring*. The ring wants to get back to its master, the same way your local government would really like you to buy a house without considering the consequences of a large tax burden. **The local municipalities are DYING to put taxpayers on the tax rolls.**

It is YOUR job to avoid taking on onerous and cumbersome tax burdens.

You can do this in a variety of ways, as follows:

1. Do not buy a property with a high tax burden;

2. Always contest your tax assessment and fight to lower your tax burden;

3. Buy in a different municipality with a lower tax rate;

---

106 This doesn't make it any better, of course.

4. Figure out and take advantage of any tax incentives being offered in your municipality; and/or

5. Get creative.

Remember, once you purchase a house, your municipality will try every two years to make your tax burden go UP under pain of you losing the home. **You cannot escape a municipal property tax burden as a homeowner, as the city you live in can legally**[107] **seize your property and resell it if you do not pay.** Unconstitutional legislation has been passed (and been argued over in courts for decades) to insure this can happen to you.

Personally, I am of the opinion that taxation, in all forms, is unconstitutional and illegal. But since you and I cannot fight city hall, and trying to change a corrupt system (yes, your city officials are probably corrupt too) where people have a vested monetary interest in NOT seeing systemic change puts you in a position to be forced to choose a lesser evil, in this case, being smart about your property tax burden and keeping it as low as possible whenever you can.

Sometimes, slaying the dragon is as simple as not living in the same land where the dragon resides, if you get my meaning.

7) Practicality of properties we choose to purchase in terms of potential income-producing outbuildings, guesthouses, and storage buildings.

Land, outbuildings, barns, "man caves," guest homes, barn living quarters—all of these carry value to a homeowner in several different ways. Having these accoutrements on your property, when cared for properly and aesthetically pleasing, can bring tremendous value if and when you choose to resell a property someday down the road. Consider a beat-up old barn. If you invested a few thousand dollars into that barn and turned it into a nice, fresh building, that would add great value to potential homeowners who are horse lovers, and you can charge a premium for your home should you choose to sell it because of this somewhat unique feature.

Secondly, and more importantly, however, is the fact that **ACCESSORY BUILDINGS ON YOUR PROPERTY CAN BE USED FOR INCOME-PRODUCING PURPOSES.**

Let me say this again, clearly:

ACCESSORY BUILDINGS ON YOUR PROPERTY CAN BE USED FOR INCOME-PRODUCING PURPOSES.

---

107   I (and many) would argue, unconstitutionally.

Part of The Short-Term Retirement Program's fundamental strategy is that, **when we choose not to acquire and service thirty-year loans** in an effort to actually pay off and own something, we may face a larger payment on a far shorter and more aggressive mortgage.

And you know what? It's okay if we get someone to "help" us.

That person could be in the form of someone who will rent living quarters on your property or a family member who wants to live near you. You can offer them far cheaper living costs than if they live by themselves or with a roommate looking for a safe space—the list is endless. But the point is, wherever you can add income-producing property to your primary residence, you can shave YEARS off your mortgage. Years.

Remember, interest rates are NOT your enemy; TIME is your enemy.

People confuse interest rates with things that are actually important, like if you should even be buying the house you are buying, whether you can afford it, and what the REAL cost of home ownership is when you factor in your tax burden and the amount of interest you will be paying. It's funny—I mean, really funny—**that people will sit and shop for a quarter-point reduction on an interest rate lender to lender, then pay retail for a house and put it on a thirty-year mortgage when, next door, a foreclosed house that is "ugly" on the surface but has a guest apartment is half the price, and you could pay it off in seven or ten years** using the income from the accessory unit.

This kind of lack of financial understanding permeates the American economy. And YOU have to become an "outside-the-box" thinker to get on board with this because, quite frankly, none of your family or friends will understand you once you start to get your own Short-Term Retirement Program in place.

Here is a chart of how your thirty-year mortgage friends think versus the way you should be thinking.

Thought Process—You Versus Your Thirty-Year Mortgage Friends Who Live Paycheck to Paycheck		
	Your Thirty-Year Mortgage Friends	**You (After Reading This Book)**
On Thirty-Year Notes	They're awesome.	They are the worst debt instrument imaginable.
	It's the cheapest payment I can afford.	It's the most expensive payment that keeps me saddled in debt for most of my lifetime.

On Tenants	Do you REALLY want tenants?	Yes, I need them to pay my mortgage for me.
	Tenants will destroy your house!	Not if I screen them properly.
On Landlording	I had a cousin whose girlfriend knew a guy who owned a crack house, which blew up.	I will avoid renting to people on crack.
	You must *LOVE* fixing toilets	No, but I have a number for a good plumber.
	What will you do if you have to evict a tenant?	Evict them.
On Roommates	I had a roommate in college; she smelled.	They are living in separate residential quarters, so I don't have to worry about smelling them.
	What if they set your house on fire?	I will collect a large insurance payout.
On Paying Off Your Home in Ten Years or Less	That will never happen.	Watch me.
On Refinancing	I just refinanced my ten-year note for one-fourth point less! My payment is $28 less per month! I had been paying that higher interest rate for seven years!	I have three years left on my ten-year note, and you just restarted at thirty years AGAIN, for $27 less monthly. Was it worth it?
	You really have three years left on your note?	YES, thirty-six payments, but you have 360.

Remember, whatever the way the crowd is running, GO THE OPPOSITE DIRECTION.

That's a fundamental premise of these financial ideas—that everything you have been taught is WRONG.

Whenever you service a thirty-year loan by yourself, statistically, you are taking about 40% of your take-home pay to do it. Why do this when you can have others pay this for you? To not take advantage of these sound financial strategies is foolish, at best. By applying a discretionary eye and a fundamental knowledge of how income-producing property works to the process of purchasing your primary residence, paying a discounted price on it, and structuring it for an effective and aggressive mortgage repayment, you can do something that most other people will NEVER do—pay your house off in a short period of time using other people's money.

Let me ask you again, would your life be better if your primary residence was paid off in full?

I know the answer.

Now let me show you how.

6

A Roadmap to Solving Your Wealth Problems

The idea for The Short-Term Retirement Program came to me one day when I was sitting in an incredibly boring meeting with a real estate team I used to consult for. I was basically surrounded by inept salespeople, who were trying to figure out how to sell more investment properties each month, as in the wake of 2008, the mortgage market had basically collapsed, and what banks were not declaring bankruptcy after finding themselves insolvent were certainly not clamoring to make risk-based loans to real estate investors. The problem was, I wasn't interested in selling houses for the sake of "selling more houses"—your average real estate investor who does so ends up in a proverbial catch-22, cannibalizing their client, who—at some point—run out of cash or credit with which they can buy properties, thereby forcing the real estate investor to seek out new clients and creating more work (and selling—yuck).

Additionally, I had seen what happened when thirty-year loans were made to investors of marginal skill and capacity, and what happened in that situation was, once they had a tenant vacate an investment property they owned, they would struggle and miss payments until they either found a new tenant who paid each month or simply lost the house to foreclosure, whichever came first (usually losing the house). Therefore, I wanted to develop a way that people could actually purchase investment property so that they could be set up to "win,"[108] instead of destroy their financial picture. But to explain to you how I designed the program and why it can work for you, first I have to describe to you how many investors were buying properties using freely available bank financing (at the time) and setting themselves up for failure through the infamous "zero down" investing strategy.

---

108 All real estate investing is risky. The risk factor comes into play when you expect people other than yourself (like tenants) to make payments on time. When this happens, usually everything is fine, but when it doesn't and an investor does not have the cash resources to make their monthly obligations is when the trouble starts.

The "Zero Down" Strategy—a Surprisingly Effective Plan to Go Bankrupt

Between the years of 2005 and 2008, clients would come to Memphis, Tennessee, (where I live) to take advantage of Memphis's discounted property offerings. Banks were making loans very liberally at that time, and investors were taking advantage of these open lending policies by using a program that took advantage of certain lending practices—**mainly, that it costs significantly more to buy a house when you are NOT on title than when you ARE on title.**[109] Simply put, if you owned a house, you could refinance it quite easily and with much more relaxed lending standards, as opposed to if you wanted to buy a house, where you had to come up with a significant down payment.

Here's how it worked, in comparison format:

Purchase Money Financing (NOT ON TITLE) VS	Refinance Mortgage (ON TITLE)
• 20% down payment	• *No down payment needed*
• Must appraise for purchase price	• *Can make loan based*
• Cannot pull cash out of an equity position in property	• Cannot pull cash out of an equity position in property
• Requires a full appraisal	• Requires a full appraisal
• Extensive underwriting process requiring specific credit scores	• Extensive underwriting process requiring specific credit scores
• Can have up to 10 loans	• Can have up to 10 loans

As you can see, if you *owned* a house, it was much easier to get a refinanced mortgage than if you had to purchase a property outright. You could get a property for zero down, literally—no money out of pocket, and you could even pull cash out at the closing table—meaning, it was possible to walk into a closing office, sign the requisite paperwork, and walk out with title to a house AND a check for 30k.

Who wouldn't want to do that?

---

109   If you are NOT on title, you need to buy a house with a purchase money mortgage, i.e., 20% down. If you are ON title, you own a house—any type of loan you get from a bank in that situation is known as a "rate and term refinance," where you get an appraisal and are lent a percentage of the homes appraised value. Refinances are ALWAYS easier than purchase mortgages.

Knowing that refinances were preferable to purchase money mortgages, it became a "chicken or the egg" question—how can someone get on title to an investment home to take advantage of the favorable refinance mortgage terms, even if they didn't have the funds necessary to purchase the property outright?

Was this an unsolvable problem?

Enter the Concept of Private Lending

Private lending is a really simple concept, although the financial gurus would love to persuade people that it is really quite complicated and, therefore, unobtainable. Here is a fundamental breakdown of how private lending works and why it makes sense for you to get a handle on the process needed to obtain some private capital and put it to use on your behalf.

Example: Private Lending Made Easy

YOUR GRANDMOTHER places 50k in a five-year bank CD at 2%, getting a "fantastic" return. As of November 2019, most banks are offering 1.25%.

Five years elapse, and she mentions to you that she is thinking of placing the 50k back into another five-year bank CD since her five-year CD is about to mature.

YOU ask her to lend you the 50k instead to buy your primary residence at 7%, and you will repay her in full, with an interest rate of 7% fixed, with monthly payments made to her over a seven-year period where, once you are done making payments, she will have been repaid in full. The loan will be secured by real estate worth 100k since you are buying the house at a significant discount. If you were to die, she would be able to sell the home for 100k, giving her a significant capital gain as well as the interest you paid her before you got hit by a bus (or whatever). **In fact, you tell her that her WORST-CASE SCENARIO (which is where you stop paying) is actually her BEST-CASE SCENARIO because she can sell the house for full market value and will have already recouped some of her principal, plus interest, each month when you make your monthly installment payment to her.**

Your grandmother then makes the loan to you while getting a significantly higher interest rate; you purchase the house at a significant discount; and your grandmother and you have created a symbiotic relationship where EVERYBODY wins.

Just make sure you pay your grandmother on time each month. Don't stiff your grandmother (or any lender, for that matter)!

When seven years is up, I guarantee she will be interested in lending you more money... for an investment property maybe?

Who needs a bank.

Although this will be detailed in a later chapter, *I really do believe that private, citizen-to-citizen lending—vis-à-vis the interconnected borrowing and lending between people who know and respect each other—will provide the future foundation of the United States economy* when the house of cards created by the Federal Reserve, devious and complicit bankers, and our politicians comes falling down. People will be scrambling because our economy will drastically change—once we come to the realization that our dollars are actually WORTHLESS.

It's kind of like the locavore movement, the food and cooking movement which encourages people to purchase locally grown food within a fifty-mile radius of where they live, and in doing so support the local economy and the local food producers. The idea of working with each other within the framework of your local community, whether from an agricultural standpoint or a financial one, really makes sense.

And in a nutshell, private lending, like buying food locally, just makes sense.

It's convenient and allows us to place ourselves in a position to be told *yes*, as opposed to the banks that are looking for excuses to say *no*. And when you work with private lenders, you are able to negotiate ALL your terms, including interest rates, repayment time, and so forth. I have negotiated interest rates of ZERO before in my real estate journeys. Anything is possible versus the banks where most of the time your lender has no idea what they are doing, let alone how to make a loan.

Private lenders are individuals who want to lend money against real estate, and you can negotiate with them, but it is up to YOU to find them, then establish a relationship with them, which allows you to move forward financially. There is another type of private lender in your town you can use, however, but they are far less flexible than your average private lender; they are known as "hard money lenders."

Hard Money Lenders: What Are They?

Hard money lenders are private lenders who make loans on real estate at significantly higher interest rates than banks are willing to lend and do so for very short periods of time (usually less than a year, often less than six months). The reason hard money lenders make money, however, is because they are (frequently) willing to lend 100% of the purchase price of a property, including money for repairs if necessary, assuming the total price of the home plus repairs is far below market value. **If someone uses a hard money lender's funds to buy a house, they can then take title to the property and immediately refinance to pay off the hard money lender, minimizing the amount of cash they have invested in the process.**

Here is a simple example of how this works:

123 Maple Street, the Hard Money/Refinance Equation

James finds a foreclosed investment property he can buy for 40k. It needs 10k in repairs and will appraise for 100k. However, James, like everyone else, does exactly what he has been told to do by his parents (who were, and still are, broke), his friends (who were, and still are, broke), his siblings (ditto), and not coincidentally, he finds himself completely broke. He wants to buy this property but has no money. How does he do it?

Step 1: Find a hard money lender and determine how much money you need.

James goes to a hard money lender and tells him he needs 40k to purchase his property, 10k to fix it up, and 1k in closing costs. The hard money lender will charge him a fee of 4k also (a 10% origination fee or "points"), which of course James does NOT have, so the hard money lender conveniently allows James to roll in his hard money cost, so basically, **the lender makes a loan of 51k, but James owes him 55k** (51k lent plus the 4k charge that needs to be paid back, for a total loan value of 55k, which needs to be repaid). **Basically, James borrows 51k but owes 55k.** James goes to the closing office and signs the paperwork and walks out with a check for 10k (*to be used for his repair/renovation money. Remember, the house cost 40k. James has 1k in closing costs and he borrowed 51k, which gave him a 10k "overage" from the loan for repairs.*)

James repairs the house and gets it into appraisable condition.

Step 2: Get qualified with a mortgage broker and apply for a mortgage refinance on the property.

James goes to his local Bank of America and gets a preapproval letter, and the bank orders an appraisal. Bank of America, like all banks, charges a variety of nonsense fees that are pure profit centers (often referred to as "junk fees") to James, who again, does not have the money (because he is broke). James is relieved, however, when his mortgage lender lets him know that the bank is willing to "conveniently" roll the costs into the total loan amount, alleviating the need for James to come up with any money out of his pocket whatsoever. It's a good thing too since he is broke.

Step 3: Bite your nails while the appraisal is being performed, and pray it comes in high.

A long time ago, it almost seemed like the mortgage lenders could basically just tell the appraiser what value was needed on a loan, and the appraiser would "get it done"— meaning, they would make sure that the property came in at a value necessary to get the loan actually completed.[110] Nowadays, fortunately, there are standards to keep lenders and appraisers away from each other and at "arm's length," which protects the interests of both buyers AND sellers. James' house, in this case, appraises for 100k.

Step 4: Decide how much cash you want to pull out.

James gets the good news—his property appraised at 100k! He only owes 55k to the hard money lender, but the mortgage lender tells him that his closing costs are an additional 5k (the bank's fees, attorney and closing fee, *tax prorations,*[111] etc.), so his loan amount will be 60k. **Sixty thousand dollars, that is, UNLESS he wants to pull some CASH OUT!** In fact, the bank will lend up to 75% of the total value of the home, which means he can get a loan of 75k (max), pay off the 60k owed in his bank closing costs and the hard money lender (whom he owes 55k to), and then get a check for 15k in his hand at the closing. Well, James has never had 15k in his hand, let alone $1,500, so naturally, he opts to get the 15k cash out.

James refinances the house, pulls out 15k, and here is how his monthly debt service looks:

Figure I: Mortgage Breakdown with Escrow: James's 75k Loan with
a 7% Fixed Interest Rate Paid over a Thirty-Year Term

James' mortgage—thirty years fixed at 7%

Loan amount: 75k

Monthly principal and interest payment: $498.98

Taxes and insurance: $250

Total monthly debt service: $748.98

Rent for home (approximate): $850

Total monthly positive cash flow: $101.02/month

Now, for the average financially inexperienced person, this entire transaction seems like an awesome deal. Someone looking at this would say to themselves, "WOW! I bought

---

110 Highly illegal! This is the reason many appraisers and mortgage lenders go to prison for bank fraud.

111 Tax prorations—the amount of taxes owed on a property at the time of a closing. Most municipalities charge an annualized tax payment for the "privilege" of owning property, but since people buy properties 365 days a year and not just on the day the tax bills are due citywide, closing offices (attorneys or escrow offices, depending on the state) will assess how much is owed in tax at the time of the closing and make the seller and buyer both pay their fair share of the total tax owed.

a house for nothing down, have 25k in equity, make $101.02/month to have it, and got 'paid' 15k just to do the deal! HOW GREAT!"

Now listen closely to me.

The problem with this thinking is multifold, as follows:

☐ **First, as stated in the first line of this book, equity is, for all intents and purposes, "dead."** Having 25k in equity is meaningless unless you can get a home buyer to cash you out with minimal to no expenses TODAY. If James tries to sell his appraised house for 100k, assuming he gets a full-price offer, he will have to pay up to 6% in seller concessions (about 6k to the buyer to help defray their closing costs) as well as a 6% commission (another 6k to realtors, assuming he uses one) so James' 100k equity position is now reduced to 88k (of which he owes 75k, to the bank), **and this assumes that James gets a full-price offer, which is unlikely.** The point is, his 25k equity position is meaningless and will most likely get swallowed up in price negotiation, fees, commissions, and closing costs.

☐ **Secondly, James isn't getting paid $101.02 per month to buy the house; he is technically LOSING money if you allot for a vacancy and maintenance factor based on the monthly rent.** Assuming your vacancy AND maintenance factors are each 10%, which adds up to a 20% reduction from $850, which is $170 a month reduction. **So, in reality, assuming James wants to use the home as a rental, he is actually LOSING ALMOST $70/month when you take into account his overall occupancy rate and the fact that things will, in fact, break over time assuming normal wear and tear.** And most experienced real estate investors will tell you that a total vacancy and maintenance factor of 20% is *very low* compared to "real-life rates," which can be as much as even 50%!

In summary, James got hypnotized by the idea of a "no money down" purchase and became hyponotized by the possibility of a $15,000 payday, which was nothing more than liquid cash from the proceeds of a long-term loan. **There was no actual "profit" realized.**[112]

James, statistically speaking, in all likelihood, will lose this house to foreclosure over time. Why? Within months (if not weeks), the 15k he "pulled out" would be spent on some non-essential (like a boat or car) while James was forced to service a losing investment

---

112 Pulling "cash out" of a bank loan is simply you generating more long-term interest-bearing debt for yourself, plus adding extra principal on your original loan cost, which requires repayment also.

for thirty years, of which the first fourteen years saw little reduction in principal. Do you think he could hold on for thirty years while losing almost $70 per month? Keep in mind, $70 is what he loses BEFORE a major repair like a new water tank, which could be an additional (and periodic) $1,000 surprise.

Would you?

And people wonder why so many homes were lost in 2008 to foreclosure.

You see, James is the perfect example of why it is foolish to try to get into the world of investing before one actually has a fundamental understanding of WHY it is so hard for the average person to get out of the cycle of living paycheck to paycheck.

In order to consider the prospect of becoming financially free, one FIRST must come to understand the factors arrayed against them as they begin the journey to financial independence. Part of this has to do with understanding taxation, and part of it has to do with learning how to use other people's money to YOUR advantage.

Understanding how and why you ended up in the financial place you are currently in will be a very helpful study also.

A Better Way, a New Day

I have worked on building wealth all my life, and most if it was spent the HARD way—earning income through an employer (remember, I was a teacher), which is of course subject to all kinds of taxes, notably the three most common ones, which are federal (income) tax, state (income) tax, and Social Security tax. A good, basic, wealth-building rule to remember is that **IT IS VERY DIFFICULT TO BECOME WEALTHY WHEN YOU GIVE AWAY HALF OF YOUR PAYCHECK INVOLUNTARILY TO TAXES EVERY TWO WEEKS FOR YOUR ENTIRE LIFE.**

Now, the IRS tax system is allegedly "voluntary,"[113] and **in NO way am I advocating NOT paying taxes**. I URGE you to comply with all of your obligations to federal, state, and local authorities to satisfy your obligations regarding taxable income and taxable events every year without exception. However, what I have found is that wealthy people seem to actually spend time trying to decipher the tax code and use this knowledge to help limit the amount of tax liability they owe each year. **In doing so, they are able to keep more of their take-home income.**

Are they doing something totally legal? *Yes.*

Are they smarter than the average person? *No.*

Can you do this too? *Yes.*

---

113 Voluntary up until the time you don't pay, then you go to prison involuntarily.

What about all the television pundits who engage in political discourse, suggesting that if hardworking Americans try to minimize their tax liability, they are antigovernment or "un-American"? The people who intimate, quite loudly, that it is the responsibility of every American to pay their "fair share"[114] of tax?

Here are a few famous tax quotes for you:

> [T]here is nothing wrong with a strategy to avoid the payment of taxes. The Internal Revenue Code doesn't prevent that.
> —Judge William H. Rehnquist *[Chief Justice, Supreme Court of the United States]*

> Avoidance of taxes is not a criminal offense. Any attempt to reduce, avoid, minimize, or alleviate taxes by legitimate means is permissible. The distinction between evasion and avoidance is fine yet definite. One who avoids tax does not conceal or misrepresent. He shapes events to reduce or eliminate tax liability and upon the happening of the events, makes a complete disclosure.

> Evasion, on the other hand, involves deceit, subterfuge, camouflage, concealment, some attempt to color or obscure events, or making things seem other than what they are.
> —Internal Revenue Service

> When I was a young tax associate, a tax partner told me that there were about 20 pages in the Internal Revenue Code and about 50 pages of Treasury Regulations that boiled down to one sentence: "If you are in the real estate business, and if you have a good tax lawyer and a good accountant, you don't pay taxes."
> —Jeffery L. Yablon

> Anyone may arrange his affairs so that his taxes shall be as low as possible; he is not bound to choose that pattern which best pays the treasury. There is not even a patriotic duty to increase one's taxes.

> Over and over again the courts have said that there is nothing sinister in so arranging affairs as to keep taxes as low as possible. Everyone does it, rich and poor alike and all do right, for nobody owes any public duty to pay more than the law demands.
> —Judge Learned Hand

---

114 Whatever this means? An ambiguous phrase at best.

So the point is, there is nothing legally or morally wrong to understanding the tax code and minimizing your tax liability in a legal way. **Now that you understand (primarily) that giving away half your paycheck is technically bad (for wealth-building purposes), and that you are not obligated to do so (or any less of a patriotic citizen) by understanding the tax code properly[115] and using that to your advantage, let's talk about building wealth.**

I have worked, as stated at the beginning of this section, on building wealth (and trying to understand how to do so from people far wealthier than I) all my life. People can become wealthy in a variety of ways, but for me, it boils down to two really simple ones when considering the idea of entrepreneurship in the United States at the time of this writing.

DISCLAIMER: I am more focused on business-building ideas here and the idea of entrepreneurship versus winning the lottery, being drafted by the NBA, etc. Those are statistically improbable events that do not apply to the average person and are, hence, unworthy of consideration here.

Two Simple Ways to Get Wealthy

1. **Buy a successful business, build a business, or invent/sell a successful product.** Ideally, whether this business is profitable or not, convince powerful people to take your business public through an initial public offering (IPO). The day you ring the bell at the New York Stock Exchange trading floor, you are rich. The investors cash you out, and they may or may not make money in the casino that is Wall Street.[116]

2. **Get other people to pay your bills for you.**

Let's focus on Number 2.

When people pay my bills for me, it helps me do a variety of things, as follows:

1. **When they pay my bills, I don't have to pay them out of my pocket.**

2. **When other people pay my bills, I can keep the money I earned instead of paying bills.**

---

115 As stated previously, a good CPA or tax attorney is critical here for proper guidance. This book is NOT designed to give tax advice, and any discussion on tax is for educational and informational purposes only.

116 Social media in various forms are a great example of this. Many forms of social media have gone public, but the stock prices plunge when investors realize there is no value and the IPO was based on popular interest and "hype" versus actual earnings. See here: http://www.breitbart.com/tech/2016/01/15/twtr-lol-twitter-stock-plunges-again-down-another-5/.

3. **If I structure my bills properly, I can eliminate them permanently from my life in a reasonable amount of time and have people continue to pay me instead of my bills.**

Number 3, if it hasn't piqued your curiosity yet, is where your financial freedom lies. It is where your bill-free future is hidden, and I will now reveal it to you.

Let's read it again:

If I structure my bills properly, I can eliminate them permanently from my life in a reasonable amount of time and have people continue to pay me instead of my bills.

I am sure the question on your mind is, "How do I get others to pay my bills?"
Let's find out.

Learning How to Become a Master of Your Monthly Expenses versus a Slave

In most cases, no monthly bill happens by accident. A contract, a binding agreement, a credit application, a visit to the sales office where paperwork is transacted: these things happen vountarily, and YOU were involved. As much as you wish you hadn't, you made these bills happen. You CHOSE to acquire these monthly obligations through purchases.

And now you probably are swimming in debt.

The good news is, you can pay off your debts and have a debt-free life. But before we discuss that, we have to talk about what I refer to as "bill structuring." **The fundamental premise of bill structuring is that every time you are facing making a purchase, you have to consider the long-term consequences of the purchase and how it impacts your future financial life.**[117] Some purchases are short-term and inevitable, for example, buying gas or a gallon of milk at the grocery store. These things (generally) trade at market value, and you need them on a daily or weekly basis. And other than cutting a coupon or trying to buy organic versus nonorganic, there really is not much to consider there.

On the other hand, however, you also have purchases that can become recurring monthly (or longer) term obligations, and this is where our attention to bill structuring lies. Once entered into, these (generally speaking) are difficult to exit without paying large sums of money or incurring a financial penalty.

---

117 This is a small price to pay to become wealthy over time.

Examples of these are mortgages, rental contracts, phone contracts, cable television contracts, utility service agreements, car leases or purchases, credit applications for lines of credit or credit cards, etc.

The key question is to ask yourself if you really need what you are considering buying. Or do you simply want it? **Again, if the goal is to become financially free, it goes without saying that it is a prerequisite that you live below your means and defer most of your income FIRST to eliminating debt, and SECONDLY, to reinvesting your leftover funds each month into acquiring tangible assets.**[118] Asking yourself these basic questions will help you get into and develop a habit of going through this mental process before "signing on the dotted line" and potentially making a catastrophic mistake.

Bill Structuring: Basic Questions to Ask Before Making a Significant Purchase

1. Do I need it?

2. Do I want it?

3. How badly do I need or want it?

4. Can it be tabled for another time? Do I need it RIGHT NOW?

5. If I have to get it, can I get it more cheaply at another vendor or retailer?

6. Can I negotiate the price?

7. Can I structure the bill so it goes away permanently in a reasonable period of time, or is this a lifelong bill?

8. Are the terms negotiable to be favorable to me?

Now, the key here is to begin to think of long-term bills, either in the form of recurring monthly contract payments or long-term debt payoffs, as TOXIC. **It really is not in your best interest, financially speaking, to spend years of your life trying to pay something off simply because you either bought an item you didn't need, or acquired something that depreciated significantly once you bought (think new vehicles), where you are forced to pay each year for unnecessary largesse, or got involved in an undesirable debt instrument, which traps you into payments for decades (think thirty-year mortgage) and is expensive and onerous to divest yourself from.**

---

118   Wealth experts like Dave Ramsey and Suze Orman continue to drive these points home in their books and media appearances: wealthy people tend, in general, to live below their means.

Today's family seeking financial freedom simply has to become more savvy than our forefathers seventy-five years ago, who did not face adversarial market factors such as massive inflation, Wall Street manipulation, or blatant dollar engineering by the Federal Reserve. **To summarize, one must consider carefully before signing any long-term debt contract or recurring monthly obligation and do their best to avoid long-term debt whenever possible.** Asking yourself these questions will help you to determine if you really need something. A good rule to remember is when you sign a long-term debt contract, plan on servicing it until it is paid off.[119] If the idea of having that for "x" months or years seems too long, then you probably are paying too much or buying something you don't need.

Bill Structuring: Questions to Ask Before Making a Significant Purchase [Some Thoughts]

1. **Do I need it?** Do I need what I am considering purchasing? Why do I need it? Is it because I made a mistake doing something else and now I am paying for it? Should I have learned something in the past from my mistakes? How badly do I need it? Can it wait?

2. **Do I want it**? Do I just want this item, am I craving the item? Do I want something that may not be necessary for me at this time, for example, if I have iPhone model X and now they just released iPhone model 11, do I really need to keep up with the Joneses at retail price? Would the money I am thinking of spending be better off in my savings account for a future emergency or investment? Can I wait and maybe the price will go down over time, as most retail items do?

3. **How badly do I need or want it?** Is it an emergency, or can I exercise restraint?

4. **Can it be "tabled"[120] for another time?** Do I need it RIGHT NOW? Is this something I may need but I can put off the purchase for later down the road when prices may have dropped or it might go on sale?

5. **If I have to get it, can I get it more cheaply at another vendor or retailer**? Have I invested any time in looking at pricing of this item from other vendors, either brick-and-mortar places or online? Have I found something cheaper online that another vendor will price match? An off-brand, perhaps? Is there a better item with more value for me at a less expensive price?

---

119 Meaning, assume you are stuck with it. If you buy the house with a thirty-year mortgage, plan on having it for thirty years. Do you want it that long? If not, get a different loan term. That is the type of thinking I am discussing here.
120 Meaning, put off.

6. **Can I negotiate the price?** Am I in a position to speak with someone in charge and ask them for a price reduction or discount? Did I just miss a sale, or is there a sale coming up, which I may be unaware of but they know about, which will help influence my decision to make a purchase or restrain from buying?

7. **Can I structure the bill so it goes away permanently in a reasonable period of time, or is this a lifelong bill?** What are the repayment terms? If someone offers me a five-year repayment plan, can I get a better deal through a shorter repayment term with similar pricing?[121]

8. **Are the terms negotiable to be favorable to me?** Are there any incentives via discounts or financing I need to be aware of?

The point of this discourse is simply this: *For most people, their monthly bills match or exceed their monthly income.* This is what is keeping you from being wealthy, and until you rectify the situation, you will continue to encounter financial struggles. You have to begin by eliminating your monthly bills, and when you start doing this, you will begin to see that there is, in fact, a "light" at the end of the tunnel.

Eliminating Your Monthly Bills and Encouraging Others to Pay Your Bills

My personal wealth has been built through the monthly rental payments of others.[122] **That is my secret, and now you have it.** The key for me was the realization that even though I had a good job when I was a school teacher for the Memphis City School District and I went to my job faithfully each day, my bills were higher than my monthly take-home pay, and here was the real kicker: **NO MATTER HOW HARD I WORKED OR HOW GOOD I WAS AT MY JOB, MY PAY NEVER INCREASED.** The nature of my job in the working class defined for me the fact that unless I pursued a different strategy, I would never be financially free. It was impossible, assuming I made no changes and spent my life doing the same thing each year. But I had already been given the answer to this unfortunate problem years before by my mother, even though I hadn't realized it at that time.

---

121 **Time, like money, is a resource that deserves careful consideration when considering any purchase.** For example, you can finance a car for twenty years, but even with a lower payment, you would still be paying off the vehicle far longer than its actual serviceable life, creating a *negative equity* situation. This is why people don't finance vehicles for twenty years. If you require a twenty-year loan on the vehicle you want, you are paying too much or in the wrong vehicle price range!

122 Understand the tenants paid my mortgages off first while I continued to work, then when the mortgages on my investment properties were retired (paid off), I got to keep the monthly rent payments after I paid the taxes, insurance, and maintenance costs that arise. I still work to this day, but the focus is on growing my business versus earning a paycheck.

An Inspirational Story

When I was twenty-one, I finished college at Syracuse University and began working in the Utica City School District, while coaching high school volleyball for a small rural town named Canastota in upstate New York. These combined jobs netted me a grand total of 22k per year, which was not enough to pay my monthly expenses, so when I *wasn't* working my full-time job, I had to go to my (second) full-time job, waiting tables at a restaurant known as The Ground Round six shifts a week, hustling for cash tips.

I do not miss those days.

The caveat was, New York State at that time required licensed educators (of which I was one) to get—or at the very minimum BEGIN—work on their master's degree within five years of their first job or else they would be forefeit their teaching license and be unemployable. So at the end of my second year teaching in Utica, I had received an offer from the ***National Technical Institute for the Deaf*** in Rochester, New York, to join their master of science in education program for the deaf. Becoming fluent in sign language was a goal of mine, and now I had the chance to do it on a full scholarship and get my master's degree at the same time,[123] so these goals all fell together nicely and allowed me to stay in good standing with New York State's pretty rigorous laws on educational compliance. There was only one problem, though—**I had worked for two years at two full-time jobs, and I was (still) absolutely broke.**[124]

My mother lived in Rochester, and I was born there and went to high school there, so moving back was something I was looking forward to except for the fact that since I had left the house at seventeen years old, I was NOT planning on moving back in with my mom. My mom had, however, found a home for sale for me, and it was a discounted estate property[125] where they were asking about 30k below market value. My mom's idea was, I could use an FHA loan[126] to buy the property, get the seller to pay most of my closing costs (did I mention I was broke?), and have a three-bedroom property near the college I was going to be attending for two years.

This all sounded great except for one issue: my rent where I lived when I taught in Utica was $475 per month, but my new mortgage payment would be $750 per month, and I would have no job since I was in school full time.

---

123 While avoiding student loan debt, always desirable.

124 Does this sound familiar to you?

125 Property that is to be liquidated after the death of its owner as an asset of their estate settlement. Usually requires approval from a judge assuming the estate is in probate.

126 FHA = Federal Housing Authority—a low-cost 3% down payment federally subsidized loan for first-time homebuyers.

My mom, however, had the answer: "Rent out two rooms for $375 each per month and your mortgage is paid."

Suddenly the lightbulb went on.

Property Analysis—1680 East River Road

This estate home was located on the Genesee River, close to two popular Rochester, New York, colleges—the **Rochester Institute of Technology** and the **University of Rochester.** The close proximity to colleges and the interstate allowed me to access qualified graduate student tenants who were willing to pay a premium for non-dorm living in a safe and quiet suburban setting. The minute I placed an ad in the paper offering "Rooms for Rent," my phone rang off the hook.[127] With careful tenant screening, I was able to pay my mortgage faithfully for two years from the rent the tenants produced and, in doing so, live for free while building and developing home equity, which resulted from me buying the estate home far below market value.[128]

1680 East River Road Property Breakdown

Home fair market value at time of purchase [1998]: 100k

My purchase price: $69,900

Loan amount: $69,964

Interest rate: 7.5%

Monthly mortgage payment: $750 (includes $490 P & I[129] payment and taxes/insurance rolled into the escrow payment)

Loan term: 30 years

Bedrooms in home: 3

Rent per bedroom: $375 plus 1/3 of utility cost.

---

127 Hard to believe there once was a time newspaper advertising was highly effective.

128 Remember I was using a thirty-year note on my first home, so the equity came from my below-market home-purchase value, NOT the tenants paying rent. –The tenants simply serviced my loan [Again, recall that a thirty-year note has predominantly interest payments for many years upfront], while I pocketed money from my other endeavors, including overnight work at a local children's center and my graduate assistantship pay, which came later.

129 P & I = **P**rincipal and **I**nterest.

Rental Information

Bedroom number 1: Rented for two years by Hyun Jae Do, a doctoral student in mathematics from Seoul, South Korea, attending the Rochester Institute of Technology. Paid each month, stayed for two years. Became a a great friend.

Bedroom number 2: Rented to Bernie, an electrical engineer for Harris Communications who paid faithfully every month. As an aside, Bernie was almost thirty and had never kissed a girl but attended my fingerstyle guitar concerts trying to make out with my girlfriend while I was performing, which was quickly quashed. Awkward!

Bedroom number 3: Myself and my German shepherd Tala. Did not pay rent, but we did pay 1/3 of the utility bill.

Total rent collected monthly: $750

Total mortgage cost to me monthly: 0

Average utility bill monthly: $150

Total utility cost to me monthly: $50

Monthly living and housing costs minus food expenses: $50

Property exit strategy: Upon completion of the master's program at the **National Technical Institute for the Deaf** in 2000, I was offered a graduate scholarship at the **University of Memphis**, in Memphis, Tennessee, which included full tuition plus a monthly stipend if I taught classical guitar at the university.

Upon accepting the Memphis scholarship, I immediately listed the property, knowing I was moving to Memphis and sold the home (all tenants were given notice and vacated upon the sale being completed) for 90k, which was slightly below market but facilitated a rapid sale. **After the closing costs and associated expenses, I netted a 13k profit—a monstrous sum for a twenty-five-year-old kid who had not paid a mortgage payment for the previous two years because the tenants paid it for me.**

I used part of the 13k to eliminate some credit card debt from my school expenses and reinvested the balance of the equity into the purchase of a multifamily home in Rochester on a street named Inglewood Terrace, which would provide me with monthly income while I lived in Memphis.[130] Again, I made sure to purchase the home from a distressed seller and buy far below market value.

---

130   Notice a critical factor here. **The profit realized from the sale was used to reduce debt and acquire more property, not go on a spending spree**. If you follow this method, someday you will be able to have what you want, but patience and deferred gratification are key factors.

I had never considered the possibility that I could buy a house and rent out rooms to pay the mortgage. All my life, I watched my mom struggle to raise two kids and make her mortgage payment, and my father, whom I saw very little of, rented the same apartment in a low-income housing project for the rest of his life after my parents divorced in 1977. He had never discussed with me or even mentioned the idea of home ownership, let alone how to become financially free. My mother, on the other hand, really didn't have time to consider these things because she was perpetually exhausted working three jobs simply to make ends meet.

Serendipitously, however, my mom had given me the key I needed to get my life on a financially different path. She encouraged me to buy a house and rent two rooms out, which paid my mortgage. This allowed me to keep a far larger percentage of my take-home pay from my overnight full-time job at the local children's center, where I was a crisis counselor, as well as my graduate assistantship, which helped me stay out of debt while servicing my bills.[131]

The most important idea planted in me from this experience was that *if* you can think creatively about other people's needs and find a way to service those needs, you just might be able to get people to pay your bills for you. College housing is always in demand, and most students as they pass into their upper collegiate years do not want or cannot afford to be involved in the high-cost student housing wheel.[132] My mother had shown me a way that I could, for a small investment and commitment to servicing a mortgage (I would have to pay living expenses anyway, whether I rented an apartment or owned), eliminate my monthly housing cost and most of my utiliy cost. **TO BE CLEAR, THIS HAS BEEN A WEALTH-BUILDING PRINCIPLE I HAVE USED, AND CONTINUE TO USE, THROUGHOUT MY ENTIRE ADULT LIFE.** Quite simply, **having people pay your bills for you, starting with your biggest monthly expense (housing) only strengthens you each month as you embark on your journey to financial freedom.** And quite frankly, one of two things will generally happen: you either complete the journey and control your own financial destiny having achieved financial freedom, **or you don't complete it,[133] and you are OWNED by money (or lack thereof) your entire life with your lack of financial control being (dangerously) passed to your children, to repeat ad infinitum.**

---

131 **Which, sadly, were significant at age twenty-three.** I had almost 80k in student loan debt from my undergraduate work at Syracuse University, as well as car loans, credit cards, etc.

132 Another for-profit endeavor by your friendly university. Compare dorm and "meal plan" food costs to renting off campus and food costs, and you will find that **most of the time, your costs are far lower off campus**. This is why most freshman and sophomores are REQUIRED to live on campus.

133 Most people don't, can't, or won't. This is represented by the infamous 1% of the world controlling the majority of wealth.

Do you want that to happen? Are you currently engaged in living out a financial struggle because you were never taught how to escape a poverty-stricken financial prison and are now forced to work paycheck to paycheck, wondering when it will get better?[134]

Now is the time to make changes.

The Legacy of John O'Williams—The Greatest Landlord in the History of Mankind

When I was a lowly undergraduate student at Syracuse University, constantly being told by my professors across three majors[135] what an insignificant speck I was compared to them and the rest of the universe, I found myself needing housing as my junior year of college was about to begin. Three female friends of mine asked me to join them as a fourth roommate to share rental costs and housing expenses for the duration of the academic year; having waited until the last minute (and having friends to share expenses with, which would ease all our financial burdens), I was certainly amenable to the idea. The problem was, however, we had waited so long to begin our housing search that most of the off-campus housing was filled up, and the few houses that were still available off campus were total slums. I mean, really low-rent places that we walked into and out of within fifteen seconds, which simply were not suitable for most forms of human habitation. We were getting desperate.

One day, as we sunk deeper into despair, one of my potential roommates said she had found a four-bedroom apartment for rent close to the university. She had driven by it and stated that it looked really well maintained and had set up an appointment to look at it. We all confirmed the time and set off for what we anticipated to be another bust showing.

To our amazement, however, we were met by the landlord, a middle-aged stout man in overalls by the name of John O'Williams. To this day, I remember his opening statement, which was probably the greatest sales line in the history of rental property.[136] After we introduced ourselves, he looked us in the eye and made the following, extremely smooth declaration:

"Everything works around here, including the landlord."

Too stunned to know what to say, we viewed the house, and it was ***perfect*** for us—new carpet, hardwood floors in the bedrooms, lots of parking for four cars (so cute), and a great, safe area. We asked about renting the whole house, but the landlord informed us

---

134 This may sound harsh, but for many people, this is the daily reality of their existence. I was there once too, as were my parents, so I obviously am speaking from experience.
135 I triple majored at Syracuse.
136 I cheekily continue to use this line when renting my properties.

that the only unit available was the bottom floor, which had four bedrooms. The upstairs had an identical floor plan with a separate utility meter but had already been reserved for the year by another group of (coincidentally) four students.[137]

The Big Question

After viewing the property and especially compared to the dives we had looked at previously, we were practically ready to sign. **We asked the big question, "How much was the rent?"** We had been looking at rents of $750 to $850 per month at that time. And then time stopped when the landlord told us how much the unit cost to rent. He made the following statement, forever emblazoned in my entrepreneurial mind:

> **It is ONLY $415 MONTHLY…PER BEDROOM. And everyone is on a separate lease, with a master lease in place for all four people.**

Now there is so much critical information in this guy's statement that I probably should leave a blank page here to let it sink in. At that time, I hadn't realized how powerful, profitable, or efficient an operation this guy was running, because (a) I was an ignorant nineteen-year-old kid, and (b) I had no knowledge of real estate or entrepreneurship. Maybe that was why he wore overalls and tried to look like a farmer, because he didn't want anyone to know that he was obviously a **multi-millionaire**.

But the real meat and potatoes here are the two perspectievs I have now, one as a student at the time and the one I carry today, looking in retrospect, as a real estate investor with deep experience, at what John O'Williams was doing with such quiet savvy. I will give you both.

Undergraduate Student Perspective, ca. 1995: WOW! Only $415 per room, per month? I can afford that with my student loan refund! And the place is so cute! I wonder if I can get him down to $400 per month?[138]

My Perspective Now: This guy was the greatest landlord of ALL TIME. When other people were renting similar homes on the same street for $750/month, he was subdividing his buildings into two separate living units and renting them BY THE ROOM, for a MASSIVE profit increase.[139] The financials on the house that we rented

---

137 The type of property is known as a two-family or duplex—meaning, two separately metered living quarters under one roof on one legally zoned parcel of property.

138 I got him down to $405 per month, per room. Not a great discount, but I felt pretty cool in front of my roommates "negotiating." *I didn't realize, obviously, that it was ME who was being taken!*

139 You can't do this in every town, and I am sure he had some zoning restrictions to comply with. My guess is he bought houses that were existing duplexes and added four bedrooms per unit for maximum rental income per unit.

(remember this is one home, about 2,000 total square feet, split into two living quarters) looked like this:

Our downstairs unit—four bedrooms × $405 each (monthly): $1,620 per month.

Upstairs unit (four other college students)—four bedrooms × $415 each (monthly): $1,660 per month.

John O'Williams' gross monthly income from our building: $3,280 per month.

Again, keep in mind, identical houses on the street were renting for $800 per month.[140]

By the way, did I tell you that John O'Williams told me in passing he owned thirty-two of these buildings that he had paid off, in the "clear," in the same neighborhood?

That would make his MONTHLY income at the time as follows, assuming our building's revenue was normal and customary[141] for him:

32 buildings × $3,280/month: $104,960 per month.

Annual gross [passive] income: $1,259,520 per YEAR.

Do you think John O'Williams went to a day job or worked his entire life in the hopes of receiving a small pension? Not likely.

John O'Williams was a big thinker, who acquired assets quietly and humbly and improved them to generate income that was far above the normal market rates because he was CREATIVE and CLEVER; and most importantly, **he thought outside the box while providing answers for a need that was highly in demand** (i.e., safe college housing). He let his tenants pay off his houses rapidly so he could enjoy his life with a massive stream of monthly passive income and, presumably, no debt.[142]

You can do this too. **Remember, John O' William was able to create a $1.2 million gross annual income from only thirty-two houses.** How much more can you do with this knowledge?

Learning from These Examples versus the Hard Way

The reason I share these examples with you is because seeing how a property can generate income like my first East River Road property or learning how John O'Williams amassed a massive fortune with just thirty-two homes can really give you perspective on how importantly, and how easily, with some ingenuity, you can get other people to pay your bills for you. **When you have other people pay your bills, you become wealthy.**

---

140 Homes like the one we rented were probably selling in the 80k range at that time.

141 Remember this was 1995, and historically, rents DOUBLE every fourteen years, on average.

142 Keep in mind, I am speculating on some of this as the guy did not disclose his entire financial statement to me, nor did I ask. Unless he had some drug or gambling problem, **him being debt-free with that type of income and small holdings is very likely.**

And these bills do not have to be real estate mortgages. I have had people pay things off for me from mortgages to cars, boats, snowmobiles, lawn mowers, laptops, and so on. **The key lies, of course, in bill structuring**—accepting monthly bills or obligations solely under the condition that you will have them for a limited time, whenever possible, and engineering ways to get them paid off quickly through the efforts of others versus yourself and just your take-home paycheck.

Accepting recurring billing obligations or indebtedness contracts with no exit strategy except to pay it off someday when you get the money (or) can "afford to" is a game for **financial losers.**

Bill Structuring—Daily Examples

Becoming financially free is really more of a mind-set versus how many houses, ounces of gold, silver, shares of stocks, etc., you own. **Assets matter, to be certain, but you are never going to acquire them if you first don't learn to adopt a mind-set to protect and defend your available capital, at all times, from those who seek to take it from you, either by force or by deceit.**[143] As I stated before, every time I make a purchase, I really try to think about the nature of the purchase and ask myself the basic bill-structuring questions:[144] Do I want it versus need it? Can I afford it? etc. And if I decide I need to buy it, I focus heavily on the minimum level of cost to me I am forced to incur. Quite simply, how inexpensively can I get it?[145]

---

143 Author Bill Bonner discusses this idea, and the idea of the **Deep State**—the idea that the government, through taxation and other policies, exist to coerce a constant flow of wealth from you (the citizen) to them. An interesting read, though some would consider such a read conspiratorial. See here: http://members.bonnerandpartners.com/ the-war-on-the-credit-cycle/.
144 See page 84 for reference.
145 This is frugality, and it is a smart and proactive mind-set—vs. being "cheap," i.e., you buy a girl dinner and insist on taking home her leftovers, so you can have a free lunch tomorrow, stealing ketchup packets, etc... You get the idea.

A Few Basic Examples of Bill Structuring in Motion

Example 1: My Backyard Playset For My Children[146]

$6,500   versus   **$450**

My wife has many tremendous qualities, but one that sticks out is her gentle way of pointing out—to me as a parent—when it is time for us to do something appropriate for our children. In this case, she had been taking our son and daughter to the park on an almost daily basis, and she commented to me how nice (and convenient) it would be for us to "finally" get our children a backyard playset. I got the message, and when she planned to go to South Carolina to visit family with the kids, I saw an opportunity for a big surprise.

Easily done, right? Just go out and buy one.

Wrong.

First, I don't want to spend a great deal of time giving you a primer on children's backyard playsets, so let's just say this: **ASSEMBLY REQUIRED**. Assembly can jack the cost of the playset to almost twice the price of the materials in the package alone and can take DAYS, not just hours, depending on worker availability and the delivery schedule.

Secondly, if your wife leaves on a Friday and plans to return on a Sunday afternoon, you are not simply just going out and buying a backyard playset at the eleventh hour, Friday afternoon before her return. The reality is you have to plan for the playset's purchase, delivery, assembly, and that is assuming the package is intact.

Naturally, I waited until the eleventh hour. And there our story begins.

---

146   Was $1,499 at the time I bought (list price), $1,199 at the time of this writing on Walmart.com. See here: http://www.walmart.com/ ip/49225460?wmlspartner=wlpa&adid=22222222227036851096&wl0=&wl1=g&wl2=c&wl3=58506253658&wl4=&wl5=pla&wl6=91206187298&veh=sem

102

So when my wife's car leaves the driveway Friday morning, you can imagine that I am immediately on the phone, looking for a children's playset, only to find out the items I just shared with you in the above paragraph are quite true, mainly, that these playsets are extremely difficult to find, generally not kept in stock, and need to be special ordered. When it comes to delivery of any playset, if you are lucky enough to find any in stock, delivery is most likely a week away. Not to mention the assembly charge, if you want assembly. As one salesman on the phone told me, "You can do it yourself, but it might take a week or two."

A week or two? I barely had a day or two. And I had to do something fast.

The good thing about having a real estate brokerage is you get to work with some very smart people. One of the smartest people I have worked with, not to mention the most faithful,[147] is my good friend Patrick Burleson.

Now, Patrick is about ten years older than me and is an "older" parent, so he shared with me his own adventures in trying to obtain a children's playset. He gave me the name of a local company, which I called promptly and was basically told the playset I was looking for—with swings, a slide, and a climbable "clubhouse"—was going to run $6,500 to $11,000[148] installed. Also, there was a two-week delay on ordering parts, etc. I called several other places that also specialized in outdoor recreation and found the same thing—pricewise and timeline wise, we were looking at significant expense and delay.

Perhaps it is a gift, or perhaps it is just many years of being forced to shop for the lowest and best pricing, but intrinsically, I tend to be able to know what something should cost me from a wholesale perspective. I find this happens frequently in the world of construction, where I will budget, say, $15,000 for a rehab and some contractors give me a price of 32k. Yet by shopping contractors and comparing prices, I am generally able to get the quality and price of what I want done on a construction job, usually within my allotted budget. But shopping and comparing prices are critical in this endeavor.

When it came to the impending deadline of trying to get a playset in my backyard in the next forty-eight hours for my children, as inexpensively as possible, these lessons from construction and real estate were in no way lost on me—calling "playground specialists" was not getting me any traction, so it was time to call the manager at the local Toys "R" Us.

I explained my situation. I told him that I was looking to take immediate possession of a children's playset, and I didn't mind an open-box item as long as the parts were intact. **He said he knew there were some unsold playsets that were NOT on display that the store**

---

147 Faithful, honest friends are few and far between. If you are lucky enough to find them, *cherish* them.
148 You heard that right, up to 11k.

was looking to "get rid of" and that he would call me back. When he called back fifteen minutes later, he told me he had a Thunder Ridge playset that they normally sold for $1,599 unassembled, but he would give it to me for $450 if I would come pick it up within the hour.

Keep in mind, equivalent playsets from retail stores are selling for $6,500 to $11,000. So to get a playset for only $450 was obviously a stellar deal. I called my handyman, told him to go pick it up, and take two workers over to my house and start setting it up.

After twenty-four hours and $200 in labor, the playset stood gleaming in the midday sun, and my mission had been accomplished twenty-four hours before my wife and kids came home. The smile on my son's face reassured me that I had gotten him and his sister something they needed and wanted badly, but in doing so, **I realized that I had done what 99% of people will not do—refuse to pay retail and invest a small amount of time instead into talking to decision makers and seeing if I can solve a problem they have (in this case, unsold and umarketed inventory) while solving mine** (needing to buy at 10% of market value). And the best part, of course, is that if I had paid $6,500, I would be out $6,500; but since I paid $650, I still had another $5,850 to "play" with, assuming, of couse, I had budgeted $6,500 in the first place.

This is a simple principle I refer to as "resource management." That is, everyone has a limited and finite amount of resources (in this case, financial resources, like cash, are what we are discussing), but how *MUCH* of a resource you have is really secondary to *HOW WELL YOU UTILIZE THE RESOURCE EFFECTIVELY*. **In my case, just because I needed to buy a $6,500 item didn't mean I needed to pay $6,500 for it.**

Meditate on that.[149]

Example 2: My Son's Train Tower Birthday Present

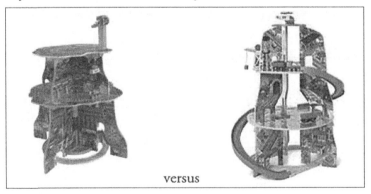

versus

$224.99 $50

149   Some people have no idea what I just said. Do you?

I try to operate in all cash. What that means is while I do not carry large amounts of cash with me at any given time (for safety reasons), I only go out and purchase items with available funds, which are cash assets—i.e., I pay my mortgage with cash, buy groceries with cash, etc. Cash is not necessarily "currency" (green paper); it exists in lots of forms (like a check). But the point is, I do not use credit to pay my bills. **If I cannot afford something, I don't buy it.**

Now, admittedly, this is antithetical to the "American Way." I have had bankers, and other "comrades in debt" tell me that the American economy operates in debt, and this is, in essence, necessary for the economy to "grow" and "function." Maybe that makes them sleep better at night, but in my opinion, nothing could be further from the truth. **A debt-based economy operates only to keep its sovereign citizens in debt and slaves to its rulers**. A debt-free economy is a STRONG economy.

The greatest thing about operating in cash is that it makes you "feel the pain" of your wallet emptying when you make purchases. Suddenly, when you are not using a credit card and have only $200 in your wallet, buying a few videogames at $59.98 seems pretty hefty if you have no food in the house and just as suddenly you are forced to make a choice, a PAINFUL choice. Do you buy the games and forgo eating, or do you do the sensible thing, even if it means your weekend is a bit more boring and you can't play with your friends who bought games on their credit card?[150]

Using cash versus credit makes you feel the true nature of money, its *temporary* nature and the constant demand you face in servicing your living needs with the limited resources that you are allotted. In essence, **it forces you to understand that while credit card companies would prefer to have you feel otherwise, money is a precious and limited resource, and spending it improperly or suboptimally carries drastic and dramatic long-term consequences, which can affect you greatly.**

So when I have to buy something, I use cash, and it hurts. Buying a birthday present for my son "hurts" even more because, as a parent, I refuse to spoil my child, and by setting a budget for his birthday presents (say $200, including necessities, which are part of his birthday, like clothing and shoes), any room for toys or playthings is, admittedly, slim. But naturally, I want to get him some cool things he would, of course, love.[151]

Of course, we work on drawing a fine line between giving our child essentials and giving him playthings. Playthings are given sparsely, and we try to limit indulgent pursuits like television and Internet screen time for him and all our children. As any parent knows,

---

150   You can eat, though, which tackles a basic survival necessity.
151   Keep in mind, we are talking about a three-year-old at the time of this writing.

spoiling your child can lead to trouble, and the Bible[152] is quite clear on this. But when my wife asked me to go buy a toy she thought (and was spot on) would be ideal for our son, I ran into some financial issues, not the least of which was I had allotted $200 for my son's birthday, including essentials (clothing), plus the birthday party costs and party favors.

Basically, she told me to get a Thomas the Tank Engine train tower, which at Toys "R" Us, at the time, was selling for $225.

Now if I had purchased this, I would have been $25 short and blown the birthday budget. The item, given the cash in my wallet, was unaffordable.

Looking Inside the Box

I stared at the box and picked it up. It was light for $225. I instantly sensed something was amiss and that the item was tremendously overpriced (in my opinion). **Now, for the record, I have had this ability for my whole life to look at things and instantly sense their intrinsic value, and I cannot explain it, but it comes in especially handily when I am looking at real estate.** BBC TV had a tremendously popular show called *Lovejoy*,[153] which was a story about an antique expert who also had this ability, so I don't feel alone here in this unique but acquirable ability. The point being, my wife asked me to buy a toy, which I found to be highly overpriced, and at the very least, out of our budget; but she and I both knew our son would love it.

What to do?

As I walked the Thomas the Train aisle at the toy store, I felt a great sense of unease. I didn't want to buy something that would put us over budget.[154] Now it wasn't that I was stressing about spending $25 more; rather, it was an ongoing sense of frugality that was, essentially, preventing me from directly purchasing the item.

So I went through the usual cost-cutting routine. I asked to see the manager, who offered me 20% off. That still left me paying about $180 for the item—again, way too much. I asked about price matching and other available discounts, but it turned out that the company's policy was if you got a discount (say, 20%), you were ineligible for other discounts, and no price matching was available offering a lower price anyway.

So I walked around with a sense of unease, a true quandary. I just didn't feel right spending $180 on a toy. Was there an alternative?

---

152 **To be clear, I find the Bible and Christianity a great and wisdom-filled resource for daily living.** I also find great and useful wisdom in other philosophies like Asian, Far-Eastern, and Buddhist thought. While these statements may be politically "incorrect," the value in these writings is of no less value to those seeking a positive and rewarding path of daily living. Don't be afraid to seek wisdom from your wiser ancestors who came before you.

153 https://en.wikipedia.org/wiki/Lovejoy.

154 Extremely basic wealth-building principle—stick to your budget!

Fate interceded almost immediately when I walked back toward the train aisle. On the endcap of the train aisle, there was an Imaginarium train tower in a sealed box. The tower was three stories high, just like the Thomas train tower. However, the Imaginarium tower offered many more amenities versus the Thomas playset, like three vehicles (instead of one); awesome-looking downhill ramps that connected to the levels (versus none, a major web complaint about the Thomas set); a movable crane; PLUS a helicopter! The best part was the playset was being offered for $74.99— about 30% of the price of the Thomas equivalent!

This was a ***great*** deal comparatively speaking, but I remembered that the manager had stated that they would price-match Internet prices. **So I hefted the box up to the cashier and asked them to price match the tower with online equivalents, and the lowest came back at $50!** In summary, they charged me $50, and in return, I got a toy that was BETTER than the one I was going to get, for 22 percent of the price, brand-new. Then I paid for his party and was ALSO able to buy him some Bristle Blocks, which we wouldn't have otherwise gotten! I stretched the $200 in my wallet farther than I could have hoped for by applying basic cost-saving principles, **and it was worth every penny spent**.

Takeaway Lessons

☐ Always look for alternative equivalents in products you want to purchase, which may cost less or be of higher quality or both.

☐ Always ask for price matching.

☐ Always look for discounts on items you want to acquire before you pay. Asking for one at checkout never hurts and will reward you frequently. If you feel nervous asking, just say, *"I was looking at this item, but the price seems overly high to me. Can you offer me a discount, or do you know if any are available?"*

Example 3: Basic Real Estate Investing Principle—Buy One Rental House, Get One Free

Buy this >   Get this FREE >

The difference between saving money on an item at a toy store versus saving money on a piece of investment real estate is that the numbers are so much larger in the world of real estate that the discounts you can obtain are almost life changing. You can fund your retirement solely by generating equity positions through real estate negotiations with motivated sellers and realizing that equity as cash if you immediately resell.[155] And while this book is really more focused on basic finance principles through real estate and how to gain control of your monthly cash flow by paying off your primary residence, **we certainly cannot ignore the greatest treasure trove of wealth that exists for the average American citizen—investment real estate**.

Recall my story in Chapter 1, where I settled a 65k mortgage indebtedness for 22k in cash. Also, remember that when I give seminars and lectures on this topic and ask attendees how much of a discount they think I received, they generally think it is somewhere between 5k and 10k (meaning I paid 55k–60k to settle the debt versus 22k). This gross margin of difference in the inexperienced investor's mind versus mine illustrates why this book is so important for you as a reader: **You have to learn to grow your financial mind-set and think BIG if you want to become financially free**. And when working on buying investment property, you need to expect BIG discounts, or else buying a property incorrectly can put you back into the "hamster wheel," so to speak, servicing unnecessary debt for inordinately long periods of time.

Discerning Motivated versus Unmotivated Sellers: The "One" Question

The most important question you can ask a seller is, "Why are you selling?"

I will say this again.

The most important question you can ask a seller is, "Why are you selling?"

When you ask a seller this, it gives you insight into what the seller's circumstances are and provides a clue to see if they are motivated to sell and, in doing so, provide you with a significant discount or not.

Truly Motivated Sellers Will Give Reasons Like This:

- Death in family
- Behind on payments
- Behind on property taxes
- Home has deferred maintenance or damage and seller does not have cash or desire to "fix" the problems

---

155 This is a strategy we will explore more deeply in **The Short-Term Retirement Program Volume II: Wholesaling.**

- ☐ Job relocation/transfer
- ☐ Divorce
- ☐ Spouse death, parent death
- ☐ Sick family member

These people have legitimate issues that make selling their home a priority, and usually due to the nature of time in their lives, they may be willing to offer significant discounts.

These people, quite simply, **NEED to sell.**

In the world of investment real estate, there are two types of sellers—those who WANT to sell and those who NEED to sell. *We only want to work with sellers who NEED to sell.* And it is easy to identify sellers who WANT to sell versus those who NEED to sell by their language.

A common "want to sell" conversation looks like this:

> **You:** Mr. Seller, how much are you asking for the property?
>
> **Unmotivated (*want to sell*) seller:** Well, just MAKE ME AN OFFER!

You see, this is the most unproductive conversation a seller and buyer can have. The seller refuses to name his or her price, leaving the buyer to shoot darts at random price targets, then the seller rejects them and maintains control of the negotiation while, generally, ridiculing the buyer.

If you are ever faced with this scenario, use this language instead:

> **You:** Mr. Seller, how much are you asking for the property?
>
> **Unmotivated (want to sell) seller:** Well, just MAKE ME AN OFFER!
>
> **You:** Mr. Seller, I appreciate that sentiment, but we simply don't make blind offers, as our time is very limited, and I know yours is too. *If I pay you ALL CASH and can close QUICKLY, what is the least you will take for the property?*

At this point, the seller either identifies his bottom line or doesn't, and either way, you know if there is an opportunity or not. Learn to ascertain whether a seller is a "want to sell "-or "need to sell"-type seller.

Then make sure to remember that it is critical to ascertain WHY the seller is selling. *Don't forget to do this!*

The Day the Bank Became a Motivated Seller

So it was, I found myself facing this situation: Regions Bank had a realtor who brought me an investment home at 3727 Rhea Street in Memphis. As I went and looked at it, I asked the realtor the most important question you can ask a seller.

Do you remember what it is?

> **Me (to realtor):** Why is the bank selling this?[156]
>
> **Realtor:** The bank just took back two properties from an investor who went under. They are trying to get them off the books before the end of the month.
>
> **Me (casually feigning disinterest):** Oh, there is a second one available?
>
> **Realtor:** Yes, right around the corner. Would you like me to show you it?
>
> **Me (acting cavalier):** Well, only if you think the bank would take a significant discount if I took both, as these houses tend to be not in the greatest of shape.[157]
>
> **Realtor:** I'm pretty sure they would.

Now, I have the information I need and a catalyst for getting a significant discount (buying both homes). I went and looked at the other property at 3851 Guernsey, and it was also a buy, as was the first house, assuming I was able to negotiate a heavily discounted price. The bank was asking something in the ballpark of 40k per home, but I negotiated them down to $46,500 for both, or a unit price of $23,250 per house. Also, for those of you interested in the fair market value of the homes, the home at 3727 Rhea appraised for 72k at the time we purchased it.

Buy One House, Get One Free?

I wasn't in a position to keep both houses at the time, and since we were building our small brokerage at the time and needed cash, I structured the sale slightly differently, which I will detail to you momentarily.

---

156 Keep in mind, I KNOW why the bank is selling: they obviously foreclosed on the property. But I wanted to know more detail and the circumstances surrounding the foreclosure.

157 Always stress to the seller or seller agent how terrible the home's condition is, regardless of its condition, when negotiating.

However, here is how I would structure it today and would recommend you do this as well to maximize your profitability. **This is how you buy one house while getting the other one free at the same closing table.**

How to Structure a Double Bank Purchase to Get a Free Property at No Cost

Property A: 3727 Rhea, a three-bedroom two-bath home, which will rent for $850/month. Appraised for 72k, purchase price $23,250. Home needs about 10k in work to get it "rent ready."

Property B: 3851 Guernsey, a two-bedroom one-bath home that will rent for $650, needs minor paint and flooring work plus central heat and air.

Step 0 (very important): ENSURE YOU HAVE A SIGNED CONTRACT WITH THE BANK TO BUY BOTH PROPERTIES AND THE TITLE WORK IS CLEAN.[158] Remember, my purchase price for both homes was $46,500.

Step 1: *Presell Property A* (3727 Rhea—as is, no renovation) for $50,000 to an investor looking for a discounted property in a strong rental area. Obtain a contract and earnest money from them, and get it to your closing attorney or escrow company, which is also handling your purchase of both properties from the bank seller.

Step 2: Set the closing date for your sale of Property A on the same day as your purchase date of both properties from the bank seller.

Step 3: On the closing day, ensure your buyer comes prior to the closing time of your bank purchase. For example, if the bank is closing at 2:00 p.m., have your buyer come at 1:00 p.m. Your buyer brings in their 50k and then signs papers to buy Property A (3727 Rhea).

Step 4: With the 50k generated from the sale of Property A, you fund your purchase of both Property A and Property B, satisfying your obligation to the bank seller. Property A is then titled to your buyer who paid 50k. **Property B comes to you in the clear, as your sale of Property A funded your purchase price to the bank seller on both Property A and Property B, and you have now paid for both homes.** You also get a check for $3,500 back because your cost basis was $46,500 for both homes and you sold Property A for 50k, creating a small cash overage—just about enough to get the repairs done on Property B, giving you a "free and clear" property that will rent for $650/month, and since it is worth about 50k at fair market value, and you owe nothing on it, you also improve your net worth by about 50k.[159]

---

158 Your closing attorney or escrow company will do the title search for you and ensure the titles are deliverable and that you get title insurance. **Always get title insurance!**

159 I am not including closing costs in this simple scenario, which run about 1k each per house.

How Did I Structure It?

Here is how I actually structured this deal at that time. I sold Property A for $39,900 and rehabbed the house for a client of mine, generating 10k in cash in the process, which I used for overhead and operational expenses (which we needed at that time). I then borrowed 26k on Property B from a private lender to pay the bank's cost and placed the home on a four-year payoff, inserting it into my long-term portfolio and having the tenant pay it off in full. I now own that home in the clear thanks to the tenant who made the forty-eight payments on the home for me.[160]

Paying Off Two Houses in ONE DAY? (Plus a Student Loan)[161]

The beauty of using the system I am teaching is that, when used correctly, financial discipline occurs on a daily basis. You begin to find yourself putting off unnecessary purchases to keep money in your accounts, ideally for a rainy day, and, of course, to make sure you are able to service your debts without going into "crisis mode."

Fast-forward down the line, though, and when you use my investing system to acquire rental property, specifically using short amortizations to pay the houses off quickly, something really amazing happens each month, independently of you really, well, *doing* anything. And that is, tenants pay off your debts for you. **Now, using thirty-year loans would make this process almost unthinkable and certainly less rewarding. However, when you place homes on ten-year, seven-year, five-year, or even three-year payoffs, suddenly you find your net worth increasing each month and your capital base rising also.** This is another idea of **bill structuring** but on a more powerful and advanced level—**having tenants pay off high-value assets for you, like homes, can make you and generations of your family to come permanently wealthy.**

It doesn't happen overnight, to be sure. And paying off your first house will always (seem) to take the longest. However, if you stay the course and apply these financial principles in a daily exercise of discipline, you may find yourself having a day like the one I had February 14, 2016, **where I paid off TWO RENTAL HOMES AND A STUDENT LOAN IN ONE DAY.**

Now to be clear, most people will never pay off one home in their entire lifetime, let alone two houses in one day. But you can't argue with the mathematics involved.

---

160 **But the way I told you to structure this deal was a far superior way to do it**, so make sure you follow that blueprint instead.

161 Happened February 14, 2016.

Quite simply, when you pay more principal than interest each month, you not only reduce your principal balance *but also more importantly, you reduce the amount of principal that is subject to interest-bearing cost by the lender the following month.*[162] In a nutshell, reduce your principal significantly each month, and your subsequent monthly payment will reduce even MORE principal, creating a snowball effect of MASSIVE debt reduction. The best part? The money didn't even come from your pocket; it came from a tenant's paycheck.

In my case, I would have never been able to pay off my student loans in 2015 and 2016 (which I did) had I been on the "standard" repayment plan for my more-than-85k student loans from my undergraduate and graduate educations. That "plan," if you could call it that, would have taken me into 2039 to get the payoffs done. Instead, I used rental cash overages from my properties to pay down and reduce principal on my student loans each month until the balance was (finally!) low enough that I could write one check to pay it off. **Notably, the student loans were paid off by my tenants,**[163] **as were the two housing loans I retired on that day**. And as I have stated, if I can do this, you most certainly can too!

How would your life change if you paid off your student loans and two rental houses in one day?

An interesting aside—the bank teller who processed my mortgage payoffs on the two properties asked me if I was going to go home and open a bottle of bubbly to celebrate. He clearly thought this was a momentous day for me and was probably the first time he had ever seen someone do this. But while paying off debts is an accomplishment, when you make it your lifestyle and a central focus of your life (i.e., living frugally and not overborrowing), retiring debts is just another day in a normal work week, realizing the goals I had planned and worked on for years when I bought the properties below market value and financed them using favorable private financing relationships. I told the banker he was my last stop *before I went BACK to the office and worked on buying MORE property!*

---

162 This is an example of how compound interest works in your favor versus the bank's favor. The bank's mortgage "algorithm" in a thirty-year loan, for example, applies most of the monthly payment to interest FIRST, which is calculated on the principal balance owed. When the principal payment is reduced so little each month on a thirty-year loan, the following month, the bank gets another HUGE interest payment, with you, of course, having a nominal reduction in your balance, and the cycle continues for years. **This is why it takes so long to pay off thirty-year loans and why short amortizations and pre-paying principal to reduce your principal balance, whenever possible, helps you "turn the tables" in your financial favor**. Minimum payments are bad! Always consider all loan terms carefully before you sign yourself into a loan of any kind.

163 In the interest of full disclosure, I did have about 5k of my student loans forgiven by the government because I taught for five years in a Title I school.

Debt: The Sworn Enemy

These ideas don't really matter unless you are focused on the greatest goal, which is to pay off your debt permanently and forever. Sure, saving money on purchases is great, but if you do not work actively and daily on reducing your long-term and short-term debts, you are simply tabling the problem to be addressed at another time, paying monthly or weekly interest along the way on each revolving debt or line of credit you have. And make no doubt about it, **this interest charged to you on each bill you receive is money that comes directly from YOUR paycheck** and goes into someone else's pocket, never for you to see it again. **Remember, when you pay interest on ANY BILL, that money achieves NOTHING for you, except servicing an obligation to the lender, who holds power over you.** You could just as well flush that exact amount of money down the toilet as it achieves the same effect.

Think about that.

And it is extremely difficult to become financially independent this way, repeating this endless cycle of applying your take-home pay to payments, which are predominately interest only, on a daily basis. Yet the majority of Americans do this exact thing each and every day blindly, wallowing in untenable debt, wasting their lives away as they stumble to the financial slaughter.

It is my mission to keep you from doing so. In this chapter, I have reviewed many financial principles, from cost-effective shopping strategies to showing you how effective landlords think, in an effort to give you a fresh and motivating perspective on how vibrantly your life can change if you absorb the concepts I am sharing with you. We haven't even gotten to the best part yet, which is working actively to pay off your primary residence in a few short years.

The lessons in this chapter are clear:

- Debt is the enemy and should be avoided at all costs, whenever possible.
- Frugality should be a part of your daily existence.
- The truly financially free live well below their means each and every day.
- Is this the day your life **finally** changes?

PART 2

PUTTING THE PROGRAM TO WORK: FORENSIC REAL ESTATE INVESTING IN ACTION

7

Let's Play a Different Game

The first part of this book was dedicated to giving you a primer on some of the trickery involved with what has become the most stereotypical "common sense" financial wisdom within the American psyche. I have also tried to give you a small sampling of real estate deals, frugality examples, and cost-saving strategies that will have, hopefully, started the wheels in your head turning, getting you to think about how you can apply these ideas to your own financial life each and every day and **TRULY begin an earnest journey to financial freedom.**

Remember, it is not by chance that the majority of the world's wealth belongs to a mere 1% fraction of the global population. Naturally, when the 1%, whether simply by accident or nefarious design, gives the other 99% of the population losing financial strategies,[164] **one can imagine that it is easy to stay, for lack of a better term, NOT wealthy**.

Consider Timmy the Teacher, once again, buying his first home.

Let's assume Timmy makes $3,000 per month after taxes.

Timmy goes to the banker and asks for a loan. Using Timmy's previous tax returns, Bob the Banker says that Timmy can use about 40% of his take-home pay as a housing payment, or $1,200 per month, which is assumed to include all appropriate expenses like taxes and insurance. Timmy goes out and buys his house and now has a $1,200-per-month payment for the next thirty years. In Part 1, we identified that almost 100% of Timmy's housing payment is going to interest. The math and amortization tables demonstrated this easily.

Now let's use a Robert Feol analogy. We will call it *Feol's Theorem on Interest Payments to a Lender* and define it as follows:

---

164   Like buying and holding stocks, for example, while insiders and banks engage in front running and insider trading.

Feol's Theorem of Interest Payments to a Lender: If we are forced to make a monthly payment to a lender, which is comprised of 90% or more in interest alone (in each payment), **we are using a loan amortization, which is effectively throwing our money away, as we have little or no traction in reducing our principal owed.** Assuming this payment represents a significant percentage of our fixed take-home income, we have obligated ourselves to debt slavery for the term of the loan because our ability to use our "take-home pay"[165] for other investments and expenses is drastically reduced for the life of the loan, and most of our daily life is dedicated to working for the same amount of fixed income.

To wit: Taking a thirty-year loan is akin to become a financially indebted slave to a lender.

We saw countless examples of this in the first part of the book. **Why pay 100k for a house on a thirty-year term when you can buy the house next door, a foreclosure, for half the price and pay it off on a ten-year term? Why use a thirty-year note at full retail when you can find a distressed seller who is willing to carry owner financing for you, regardless of your credit standing, that you can potentially settle for a significantly smaller lump sum of cash later on down the road?**

Essentially, to become financially independent begins with making a conscious decision to eliminate, once and for all, your biggest payment—your housing payment.

Refusing to accept a thirty-year loan is the first, critical part of this.

Adapting to and learning the real estate techniques necessary to find the property you are seeking that will aid you on your journey to financial freedom is another endeavor entirely.

Forensic Real Estate Investing

Let's get one thing straight. Buying and aggressively paying off your primary residence using techniques outlined in The Short-Term Retirement Program is one thing, but becoming a full-fledged, full-time real estate investor is quite another. **This book is NOT designed to make you a full-time real estate investor. Being a real estate investor is VERY risky and requires a VERY specific skillset, which cannot be learned simply from reading.** It carries tons of volatility and is extremely CASH INTENSIVE.

I understand that there are many programs, infomercials, and late-night television

---

165 This is the money in your paycheck after taxes, Social Security obligations, and other deductions are used, **the actual money that YOU get to pay expenses with from your job.**

commercials that advocate miraculous "no money down" strategies for new and inexperienced investors, and I admittedly own many of these. However, there is a category of people who make their living by SELLING BOOKS AND COURSES TO YOU, and many of them will lie, alter truth, fabricate data, and so on to show you that making money in real estate is very easy.

IT ISN'T.

For example, pretend you buy a house with no money down by getting a distressed seller who cannot make their mortgage payments to sign over to you the deed of their house (known as taking a house "subject to"). Then you rent the house and make the obligatory housing payment the seller couldn't make to their bank. Everything is going well until the tenant calls you and the furnace goes out. You call an HVAC contractor, who comes out and tells you it will cost $7,500 for a new furnace system. You simply don't have the money, as you were told in your course that you could buy real estate with no money down.[166] Then, the tenant moves out because they have no heat. After this, due to a freezing cold spell, the pipes burst and the house is flooded, but this is not covered by insurance since you have no water backup or flood insurance on your policy. So what happens? You lose the house and get sued by the owner for negligence as they go into foreclosure, which you promised them wouldn't happen.

And by the way, you made zero dollars.

Does that sound like the "no money down" type of real estate investing experience you were promised when you bought the course on TV? Of course not, but that is the reality of what happens when an illiquid and inexperienced real estate investor tries to get into the real estate investing game. **Making money safely in real estate is done slowly, over a great deal of time, reinvesting small gains into homes until they are paid off.**

The goal of this book is to show you how to eliminate your biggest monthly expense by paying off your primary residence. However, to do so, you will need a command of some solid but basic real estate investing techniques.

Just remember, focusing on finding a home that will eliminate your mortgage payment in full after a few short years is a great and very tenable goal to have. Trying to build a paid-off real estate empire is beyond the scope of this book.

How Many Times Will You Move?

In my house, my wife and I play a game called "how many more times will I move before I die?" And basically, the game is as follows: I am only moving "x" number of times more

---

166   They neglected to tell you in the course that you DO need cash for the upkeep of the property!

before I die, so I want to make it count. Essentially, if I am even going to consider moving into a new home, the property needs to have ALL my desired factors, AND it needs to be significantly discounted. This makes it very hard to identify an ideal property for us, and so we have stayed in the same place for over a decade. **The flip side is, we have watched many of our friends and colleagues go from house to house every two or three years, increasing in size and price each time and taking on massive thirty-year jumbo mortgages, which they will never pay off.** Meanwhile, we make our mortgage payments count, which will allow us to move when and if we find our "dream home," by building equity through aggressive mortgage payoffs and biding our time until we are ready to "strike" on the right dream home.

Part of you finding a home that you can pay off using the principles of The Short-Term Retirement Program is playing this game, deciding that your next home (or maybe the one you are in now, if it makes sense financially) is one where you are willing to STAY UNTIL IT IS PAID OFF and even beyond.

You see, trading up houses every few years paying retail while using a thirty-year lending product is a losing financial strategy.

Here is why:

☐ **Every time you move houses, unless you are planning on holding your existing house for rental purposes, you lose money.** Why? Remember our analysis of amortization schedules? Assuming a thirty-year loan, no one has any real equity after a few years of having a primary residence (assuming they are making their minimum payments), unless they put down a massive down payment[167] or there has been some market event that has created (unlikely) significant appreciation. Even in our "Timmy the Teacher" example, the property appreciates 10% over a five-year period, which as most property owners will tell you is a fairly big assumption. So, assuming someone owns a house for three or four years, they generally will have NO increase in home value and NO decrease in principal owed on a thirty-year note,[168] which is a terrible combination if your goal is to improve your financial picture and the development of your net worth using your home's equity as a major contributing factor.

☐ **The transactional costs of moving alone place you more deeply in debt than you were before you move.** Consider a family that has a 100k home (like

---

167 Very unlikely for the average working family, which is why we have FHA loans and similar low out-of-pocket cost-lending products. Remember, the average American does not even have $500 in a savings account for emergencies.
168 Again, while throwing away almost 40% of their post-tax take-home pay.

Timmy). They sell it after a few years and make nothing (*any equity they have pays out to realtors and seller concessions*), and then they buy a 200k home. Between the closing costs, down payment, loan fees, and costs of moving (plus ancillary items like utility transfer, cable installation, and so on), even if they are allowed to "roll" their closing costs and similar items into a loan, those are still monies that the family owes and will take thirty years to pay back.[169] Indebtedness is indebtedness, and this family just doubled theirs, incurring fees and raising their loan balance along the way, which is exactly what NOT to do, assuming your goal is financial freedom through debt elimination.

☐ **When people change residences, they generally spend disposable funds[170] on improving that residence, whether through furniture, cosmetic, or carpentry upgrades, and so on. This is all money that becomes unrecoverable and is essentially "thrown away."** The furniture becomes used and depreciates; upgrades generally will not improve the value of a home beyond its fair market value, which the family paid for up front (generally speaking[171])—i.e., you repaint the interior of a home, but that does not improve value, though it costs money. You spend 20k to upgrade a kitchen, but if you paid 200k at market value for your house and all other similar-sized homes are worth 200k, your 20k upgrade is lost through market attrition; that is, if you were to sell in a short time frame, and home values did not increase, other than your personal pleasure in your upgraded kitchen, you are not going to sell your house for 220k if all other market comps place your house at 200k—assuming all other homes have upgraded or similar-quality kitchens also.[172]

☐ Upgrading neighborhoods generally means keeping up with the Joneses, who have new cars, whose kids go to private schools, who all entertain by throwing huge parties for the neighbors, and the implied idea is you should be too.

☐ Taxes, insurance, utility, and maintenance costs also increase when you are trading up homes.

☐ **Keep in mind this important fact: Most American families borrow the**

---

169 Again, remember, no progress is made on reducing principal balances for many years if you have a thirty-year note. Consult the amortization schedules described in Section 1 for details.
170 Or borrow using credit, which needs to be repaid
171 **Most families, statistically, buy only primary residences at retail, using thirty-year loans.** This is the most common way of purchasing a primary residence.
172 Which demonstrates, of course, that you overpaid for a house that did NOT have an upgraded kitchen, assuming you paid 200k in this example knowing it needed a kitchen upgrade of 20k. Better strategy—offer/pay 180k, or even LESS!

money to do this because they are unable to afford it on their own and COULD NOT DO IT OTHERWISE.

The matrix is unveiled in that last line: ***Most American families borrow the money to do this because they are unable to afford it on their own and COULD NOT DO IT OTHERWISE.*** They have to borrow money from a banker to live this dream, or else they would be unable to.

Is that the life you want to live, one based on a house of cards that could come tumbling down at any time? **To live a simple veneer of success while true happiness, prosperity, and financial freedom slip from your grasp as you drown in unsustainable debt service?**

I can show you a better way, and it won't take thirty years to do it. But you might have to accept that the Joneses will be "cooler" than you, perhaps for a short time.[173]

Pledging Your Future Earnings: An Uncomfortable Reality

Every time you sign an installment contract on a loan or mortgage, you are, in essence, pledging your future earnings. That is, a portion of your monthly paycheck **for part of your lifetime**. Think about it; **when you sign the thirty-year loan papers, in your mind, you are resigning yourself to having thirty years of payments**. When you execute on the dotted line at the auto dealership, you generally are accepting five to seven years of monthly car payments.

For the average person, a paycheck to paycheck worker, this is basically an allotted percentage of your monthly take-home pay. For example, *if you take home $2,000 per USD a month, and you sign on a home loan for $800 per month, you are basically agreeing to give away 40% of your take-home income to predominantly bank interest for the next thirty years*.

Credit card debt without an exit plan is even WORSE. You are agreeing to pay for an item on a line of credit that allows you to accumulate items, services, miscellaneous charges (both one time and recurring), without a defined time period with which you are pledging your income. *You can make the minimum payment (which the companies want you to do, all of which is interest and fees) and NEVER get out of debt.* It is a losing proposition, especially when banks make money out of thin air and you pay them back with post-tax dollars.

---

173 At least, that is, until they become insolvent and lose everything. Remember the "credit crisis" of 2008?

> The next time you think about signing on a contractually binding dotted line, ask yourself or a close friend if the item you are purchasing is worth pledging "x" percent of your paycheck toward for the next "y" years (or decades). If the answer is *no*, maybe it is time to reconsider. Or better yet, get someone to pay for that purchase for you from *their* paycheck and in doing so keep your income intact.☺[174]

Wealth Building—Some Common Misconceptions

Many people think the key to being financially free is to become rich through luck or great fortune. And while most people have varying definitions of "rich," the average paycheck-to-paycheck worker tends to summarize it in one of the following ways:

1. Making six figures;

2. Winning the lottery (this can, in fact, make you rich, if only for a short time);

3. Getting a sports contract (NBA, NFL, MLB, NHL, etc.);

4. Getting an inheritance of varying sizes; or

5. Getting lucky in the stock market.

Certainly, numbers 2–5 can, in theory, be a path to great wealth. Yet the world is littered with sports stars and lottery winners who are bankrupt, destitute, commit suicide, are murdered, or have encountered other terrible and devastating tragedies. Some without money simply look at the fallen stars as having simply made bad choices, though they had great fortune. Others see the money as "a corrupting influence." **And while these both may be true or have some degree of truth, the reality is almost all of these people had no idea how to handle such sums of money, invest it properly, and/or tell their entourage "no."** And by the way, number one on that list (making six figures as earned income,[175] generally thought of as 100kish) is NOT a guaranteed path to wealth.

The realistic probability of the average person getting any of the above five paths to wealth is so low, from a statistical standpoint, it is really not worth considering. For example, planning your retirement based on winning the lottery is obviously

---

174 I'm talking about owning income-producing assets, which give you receivables, NOT stealing or other criminal measures.

175 Remember, earned income is the least likely path to wealth because of the massive tax burden placed on those who choose to work and, in doing so, are subjected to varying taxes like federal tax, state tax, and Social Security tax.

nonsensical. Investing your entire savings on a "hot stock tip" is also a sure path to insolvency.[176] One has to be smart about building wealth, and understanding it is not an overnight process. However, with daily discipline, it does not take long to see you making such large financial gains; you are surpassing everyone you know and, soon enough, becoming debt-free *after* the revolving monthly bills of your life are permanently eliminated.

Three Things to Remember

1. **Earned income is the least desirable type of income, as it is subject to a variety of taxes *AND* you have to trade your (limited) time to receive it.** In the United States, you generally take home half of what your actual gross paycheck is.[177] This is favorable for the government in that you are taxed on your gross earned salary, but you never really see that full income; it is an illusion.

2. **Any type of debt, except extremely well-purchased (meaning heavily discounted) real estate or asset-based debt,[178] is bad** and needs to be eliminated as a part of your financial freedom plan.

3. **Your goal should be to minimize the number of envelopes that come to your mailbox, assuming that most of your mail is filled with monthly bills.** We need to get most of your monthly bills eliminated once and for all. In its simplest form, if your thirty-year mortgage comes in an envelope in your mailbox each month, let's get it paid off and eliminate it permanently. The day that happens is the day your real financial freedom starts.[179]

No need to win the lottery or get an inheritance. You can have a life of financial freedom without these things. Forensic real estate acquisition, coupled with some solid decisions about your primary residence and how you structure your financing on it, can work wonders.

---

176 The stock market is rigged, make no doubt about it, and YOU are NOT in the know. See here: http://www.huffingtonpost.com/ellen-brown/computerized-front-runnin_b_548148.html. Most important excerpt from article: "*Since then, HFT has quickly come to dominate the exchanges. High frequency trading firms now account for 73% of all U.S. equity trades, although they represent only 2% of the approximately 20,000 firms in operation.*" The word *front running* should send shivers down your spine while you blindly invest your IRA monies with someone you have never met.

177 Then you spend your net pay on items that are also heavily taxed through sales tax and other assorted taxes such as gasoline tax.

178 You buy a highly profitable business at "a song," for example.

179 Paying off other smaller debts also helps tremendously. Remember Dave Ramsey's "snowball" method.

Making $6,500 in One Hour in a Practice Room at The University of Memphis

1776 Sea Isle, Memphis, Tennessee 38117

The great thing about the business of real estate is it can be done anywhere you have a phone that works. Granted, a computer and Internet connection also come into play, but the real brunt of the work can be done over the phone; and with the preparation of one page of simple paperwork, you can get paid within about forty-eight to seventy-two hours. There is no "boss" handing you your paycheck, expecting you to kowtow and be grateful, which makes it even better. This story is one example.

One of my many goals is to get my doctorate in music. I'll probably get one in finance also, just to annoy the bankers, but that is another story. Anyway, while I was a graduate assistant in music at the University of Memphis back in 2000, I never finished my master's degree in guitar. So last year, I decided to rematriculate and continue working on it.

As we get closer to the end of any given semester in the music college, all performance students are required to play for faculty members as a major part of their semester grade. Approaching this day is very stressful, so when I find myself needing to practice and unable to do it at home due to kids, dogs, etc., I go to the university and find a practice room. Out comes the guitar, and the woodshedding begins.

So it was on Tuesday, April 19, 2016, that I got a text message from a local wholesaler who had a house on Sea Isle Road (while I was in a practice room working on guitar-related items). His contract had fallen through, and he (coincidentally) was a loyal radio show listener. This was his second "deal," so to speak, and he needed help. He tried to sell me the house at 48k, and I sent Patrick Burleson out to look at it immediately. Burleson said there was no way we could buy it at 48k, as it needed in excess of 26k in work, so I asked the wholesaler what he was "in" the house at, price-wise, and how much he was trying to make.

He responded, *"I have a contract with the seller at 35k, and at this point, if I made one or two thousand, I would be happy."*

Since I knew he was a radio show listener who was very much a "student" of Robert Feol teachings, I gently suggested to him that he might have locked the house up at a price that was too high for him to resell it. He told me he had a good relationship with the seller, and so I asked him to go back to the seller and tell her he could get the house closed in a few days if she was willing to reduce the price to 30k, which she agreed to. He called me back and said he had obtained a price reduction, and I agreed to pay him a $2,500 finder's fee for the deal.

With the deal now being technically "doable," as it could meet the minimum profit margins I set on every investment opportunity we acquire, whether to keep or to resell to an investor client, I had a few options on how to proceed. However, if we resold to an investor client, we would have to do this large rehab as part of the sale, which I was not really looking forward to doing. Interestingly, I had just happened to get a call that morning from another local investor, who was looking for an off-market deal with a large equity spread in a good area. From the practice room, I called him and asked him to go look at the house. He went and called me back to tell me he would pay 39k for it. I told him it was a deal and called the closing attorney, who had the title work in hand. **Friday of that same week, I went to the attorney's office and picked up my $6,500 paycheck.** How did it work?

a. Wholesaler brings me a deal for 35k. He negotiates down to 30k. **Sales price to me is 30k.**

b. **I agree to pay him a $2,500 assignment fee for the contract. My total cost is $32,500.**

c. **I sell to local investor** (from practice room, on phone, with guitar in my hand) **for 39k, which represents me assigning the contract to him for an additional $6,500.**

Since I assigned the contract, I have no fees as a buyer or seller. I generate $6,500 as a net[180] profit and receive that in the form of a check. But more importantly, I made a new colleague in the novice wholesaler, who knows I can perform and wants to bring me more deals, and my investor friend who purchased the home from me knows I bring him solid, highly discounted and fully deliverable deals,[181] and he is currently waiting for me to bring him the next one.

The best part? **This whole deal happened in a three-hour practice session in a practice room at the University of Memphis as I sat by myself.** I literally got paid to practice for my guitar jury! Not to mention that $6,500 represents to me what was essentially two months of full-time teaching work.

---

180 Pre-tax
181 **Having a "deal" for sale means absolutely nothing if you do not have control of it through a contract or assignment clause** or cannot sell it due to title flaws or other issues known in the industry as a title "cloud." True investors don't have time to buy undeliverable deals. **Make sure you do your homework BEFORE you try to sell or resell a property.** With many moving parts like this transaction had, it can get complicated.

> **Takeaway Lessons:**
>
> a. **If a deal is not priced properly for you to make a profit, do not be afraid to ask the seller for an additional reduction**, even if you already have a contract. The worst they can do is say no.
>
> b. **When you find and lock up a deal, think about the many different strategies you have to make profit**—immediately resell, resell after renovating, keep for a long-term hold as a rental home, or keep for your primary residence using an aggressive payoff. You could also structure the home as an investment property with an aggressive exit like a lease purchase or Contract for Deed—all of these are **great** ways to make money.
>
> **In my world, though, cash IS king,** which is why I resold the property and got my check three days later. And I really wasn't looking forward to doing a large and complicated rehab. **Sometimes there is great value in getting paid a smaller amount and moving on to the next deal without risk**.

Forensic Real Estate Investing in Action

What makes real estate investing so interesting (and so highly profitable when done properly) is the huge number of ways with which you can get a *massive* discount. I often equate it to the experience one has when you notice a car of a specific type or color you have never seen before. Once you do, you see them everywhere and ask yourself, "Why didn't I notice it before?" In a similar vein, most people are simply unaware that you can get houses for a discount, let alone for a song. **And, when realized, this information becomes great power.** So powerful, in fact, it is possible to become financially free by using this information. The key is to have the proper techniques necessary to discern HOW to find these types of discounts, and all these questions start with one simple question: **"Why is the seller selling?"**

Wanted: Modern-Day Sherlock Holmes for Real Estate Investigations

The premise of searching for a property, presumably for financial purposes or gain (i.e., buying your primary at a steep discount with the intention of paying it off in less than thirty years or searching for a deeply discounted property for investment or rental income purposes) all starts with the basic question, Why?

And there are many extensions of this question that also become highly relevant to your search, such as:

- Why is the seller (homeowner) selling?

- Why is the seller (homeowner) behind on payments?

- Why is the seller (homeowner) not paying their taxes?

- Why is the grass overgrown at this property?

- Why is this property in a great neighborhood vacant/boarded up/have its windows smashed out?

- Why does the seller want to move?

- Why is an estate selling the home?

- Why has the home been on the market for so long?

Also, pertinent questions like this become important:

- **Who** is the seller (i.e., private seller, bank, county authority for tax purposes, etc.)?

- Why did the listing expire?

- Why has the home been listed by three different real estate agents and not sold?

- Are there any issues with a home I need to know about that are significant (structural, etc.)?

- What doesn't add up here?

- What is really *going on here?*

It is your goal to figure out the answers to these questions and, in the interest of saving you significant time and resources, realize that you have to become quite adept at aggregating and answering these questions in about two to three minutes when you look at a house to prevent yourself from becoming bogged down in irrelevant minutiae **and using your time UNWISELY**.

Getting started on the path to finding the right property for you, specifically a discounted home that can produce income AND serve as your primary residence, starts with a daily methodical search for prospective properties that not only fit your price range but also tick all the boxes, which make a home potentially desirable for you, financially. A knowledge of basic real estate investing is important here. Remember, evaluating houses comes down to asking the same questions every time. Some houses will NOT fit your criteria, and some may be a partial or total fit.

Basically, it comes down to a simple flowchart, as follows:

Property Price and Condition Evaluation: Quick Guide

1. **Is the property in distressed condition?** Yes/no. If yes, move on to question number 2.

2. **Is the property in a desirable area or location for your purposes?** Yes/no. If yes, move to number 3.

3. **Is the property priced below market value significantly enough to consider it as a prospective property, OR has it been on the market long enough (read: more than six months if listed) for the seller to be willing to entertain an offer far lower than the asking price?** If so, move on to number 4.

4. **Are there any mechanical or maintenance defects with the home that you can ask the seller to pay for?** For example, is the heating and cooling old/outdated/ineffective, and is the seller aware of this and willing to discount the price even further OR pay for new equipment? If so, make sure to ask for a steeper discount and move to number 5. (I usually do this after my personal inspection of the home or after using a home inspector, whatever your preference is.)

5. **Does the property offer any additional features that I may have interest in (other income units,[182] expandability, favorable zoning)?** If so, move to number 6.

6. **Does the seller have any extenuating circumstances that I need to be aware of?** For example, have they been relocated to another city for job purposes and are now paying two mortgages? This is for information purposes to help determine the discounted price you can offer.

7. **Is there any other information I need that I may be able to get from the seller or listing agent?** (Don't be afraid to ask.) **Is seller financing available?**

8. **Once all your information is gathered, use *Feol's Formula* to determine an appropriate asking price on the home,** as follows:

---

182 As you will see in the next chapter, units at a property that produce income in some way are HIGHLY attractive for your purposes of eliminating your housing payment permanently.

> **Feol's Formula**
>
> *(Actual fair market value of home – all needed repairs to get the home to FMV)/2 = asking price*
>
> **Example:** If a home is worth 100k and needs 20k in repairs, that would be 80k/2 = 40k asking price.

Now the thing to consider about **Feol's Formula** is that it is just a guideline for your asking price. You can adjust the divisible number by less than two, or more than two, as you see fit, depending on your market[183]. **However, it gives you a guideline for the types of discounts necessary to make a property investment successful, and a simple benchmark for the type of pricing that you should NOT be afraid to ask for.** Also, don't forget to add your repairs back into the total price, because you will have to do them to get the home up to fair market value, and they will become part of your overall cost. In this simple example, even though you are buying the home for 40k (assuming the seller accepts), you still have 20k in work to do on the house, which makes your cost 60k before you add in closing costs.

And in the world in that I operate in, *40% off is really not that great of a deal.*

If you will recall, in the first chapter of this book, when I was searching for my vacation home, I asked the seller, Emily, why she was selling, and her answer (that they wanted to move to North Carolina and needed 25k to do it) became instrumental in me structuring my entire offer, which consisted of a 60k discount off the 150k asking price PLUS asking for and obtaining seller financing. These two items combined netted me, in the end, a total savings of 107k off the 150k asking price (remember, a 33% all-in cost basis on the home relative to asking price). *More importantly, it clearly illustrates to you how important this information can become in your journey to financial freedom. It can make the difference between getting your home paid off in a few months versus thirty years. When you have the real estate transactional knowledge of HOW to structure a deal properly (and favorably) to you.* It is THAT important.

---

183   **As stated earlier in the book, all markets are NOT suitable for investing or purchasing at a discount as outlined in this book.** While there are discounts available in EVERY market, the exorbitant pricing in some markets may simply preclude you from buying property there for the purposes of financial freedom, even if you are getting a property below fair market value. In this case, you can invest in other markets or find a lower "cost of living" market and set up shop there, applying these ideas. Many Western US coastal markets, for example, are very difficult to buy in and pay off early because of inflated housing prices. And also, remember everyone's income and circumstances vary, so your affordability factors are unique to you as far as what you can and cannot do.

Beware the Real Estate Agent Who Is Unwilling to Ask Questions on Your Behalf

Remember this concept because it bears repeating. **If you are being represented by a realtor, make sure you are using one who is unafraid to ask the questions you need answered from EVERY agent or seller on EVERY prospective home.** Also make sure the agent ALWAYS asks if a seller is willing to consider owner financing, sometimes known in the industry as "owner carryback terms."

I have had a few agents tell me that they think asking these probing questions is "insulting" to the seller. **To be clear, the only thing insulting is the agent's unwillingness to do their job and obtain the necessary information for you as a buyer (investor) to evaluate and consider whether any given property for sale fits your criteria and is worthy of a deeper look.** If you have agents who are unwilling to do this legwork for you, **FIRE THEM AND GO FIND ANOTHER AGENT.** Better yet, become one yourself and keep the commission, which will reduce your cost basis. Plus you can teach other people to do what I am teaching you to do and represent them on their purchases for additional income.[184]

It's a Numbers Game

Robert Kiyosaki's book *Rich Dad, Poor Dad* has a section in which he teaches a friend how to make offers on investment property. His offering advice went like this (I'm paraphrasing here): "Look at one hundred houses, narrow it down to fifty, offer half price on all fifty, twenty will respond, and two or three will probably end up accepting your offer."

This isn't bad advice, truth be told, and certainly has some merit from a sheer numbers perspective. However, asking your agent to make fifty offers on retail-priced homes, in my opinion, is not only a waste of time on their part; it is also a low-probability exercise, which will not get you as many prospective properties as you potentially can find. Why? Because sellers who are listing their homes for retail value, in all likelihood, **are NOT motivated to sell or are BOUND by the amount of debt they have on the property to demand a full-price offer**, or else they will have to bring cash (a "shortage," as it's called) to the table. And as we have discussed, most Americans don't have $500 in a savings account, let alone tens of thousands of dollars to bring to a closing by accepting a "lowball" offer.

---

184 **Can you say, "revenue stream"?** Becoming a licensed real estate agent is relatively easy and carries a tremendous upside potential, incomewise. In many states, licensed agents cannot only sell and list homes; they can rent homes also, which is another viable income stream for a budding real estate entrepreneur like yourself. :)

Remember the seller who "wants" to sell versus the seller who "needs" to sell, as discussed in Chapter 6? **There is no value for us in trying to convince unmotivated sellers to become motivated**. It is simply a waste of time. As such, it is imperative that we focus on finding motivated sellers from the beginning of our search, and in doing so, we preserve our time and spend it wisely on a methodical search for motivated and distressed sellers, **which in all likelihood will give us the best chance of getting a significant discount on a property, which can work with great purpose for us, and in doing so, help us achieve one or more of the following things**:

1. **Stay out of debt** (if we can find a property inexpensive enough that we have the cash to pay for it); or

2. **Be in debt for as short a timeframe as possible** by purchasing a home far below our budget and prepaying each month additional funds toward principal reduction, which will help accelerate our payoff time frame; or

3. **Use other people's funds to aggressively pay down our housing debt** by implementing income-producing units, roommate situations, or favorable and creative property zoning situations to increase our monthly income through an innovative use of our primary housing, which in turn helps us prepay principal aggressively, with the goal of a quick loan retirement (discussed in detail in the next chapter).

Don't Make Offers on Retail Homes

Lots of new investors, when discovering the great real estate mystery that is the potentially massive discounts that are available on property, all make the same mistake: **They assume everyone is a motivated seller.**

Nothing could be further from the truth. Motivated sellers need to be sought out like clues in a mystery investigation. Sometimes things are hidden in plain sight, but more frequently, one has to go digging and searching to find the hidden deals that are, in fact, "out there." And while searching and scouting for discount property may become hard and tedious work, in the end, I promise you it will be worth it.

The flip side of the coin is that some new investors see a "For Sale" sign and believe that, since a home is for sale, there may be a potential to get a huge discount. I had a friend in the teaching profession. She would see "For sale" houses (via a yard sign) and try to get a discount on the home, then come to me and report that a seller was asking 100k and told her he would accept an offer of 99k, as if this was a discount.

Of all the resources we are granted in life, time becomes the most precious. Too few people are in touch with the nature of their life to recognize it, but it is true: ***everyone who seeks to become financially free, in its greatest simplification, in its greatest reduction, are really searching for more time***—time to be with their loved ones, time away from the daily and monthly obligations of incessant debtors, time away from the demands required to barely stay ahead of insolvency, and time to spend freely pursuing what interests us, our passions, and our true joy. When one realizes that we are all simply seeking more free time, one then realizes that making offers on houses where the seller is asking 100k and concedes to 99k is simply not worth our time in any way. In order to get ahead financially, we, by necessity, are required to seek out discounts, which will allow us to pay off our housing quickly, either by our own paycheck or through the paycheck of others.

Remember *Feol's Formula* when you are searching for homes with appropriate pricing for you to consider making a purchase. The discounts have to be steep and also account for any potential work needed, as well as income possibilities. Only in ascertaining this comprehensive picture can one begin to narrow down prospective properties and start to identify what may become potentially ideal candidates for further consideration and due diligence.[185]

When you work to remove your housing payment permanently, you truly are on the path to financial freedom.

Remember, most people starting out, who truly yearn to be free of debt forever, begin with little to no financial means.

This is how I started.

Become intimately familiar with the idea that you are going to pay off your primary residence in just a few years.

See it daily in your mind.

Become one with it.

By applying the necessary steps, you are going to make this a reality.

Make it your destiny.

---

185 A real estate term, ***due diligence*** refers to asking questions and gathering information about a subject property, generally with the intention of evaluating it for purchase consideration.

8

Make Your Biggest Monthly Payment Your Smallest One: Structuring Your Primary Residence for a Lifetime of Financial Success

Let's get one thing straight.

No one can use the **Fannie Mae**[186] **thirty-year lending program and win. Ever. There are NO exceptions to this rule, assuming your goal is to be financially free.**

No one wants to hear this. There are a variety of reasons for this, but primarily, everyone is practically trying to scrape by to meet these Fannie Mae (strict) requirements to obtain a home loan, and therein lies the problem—*most people can barely qualify*. Assuming they are doing the "right" things, generally meaning, they went to college, obtained student loans, have a car payment and a credit card balance, and have a full-time job, which (inevitably) barely covers these expenses. It is extremely difficult to get a home loan, **and this is because Fannie Mae requirements ask for up to 40% of your available net income to be unencumbered and allocated as a house payment.**

I am here to break the stigma for you; you DON'T NEED 40% of your available take-home pay to afford a house.

You can afford a house for a lot less, but for the purposes of this book,[187] **let's agree that your most desirable housing payment is zero.**

---

186 Make no mistake about it, **in the United States, 99% of loans are resold from individual banks to the Federal National Mortgage Association (FNMA), or Fannie Mae, program, and therefore, must meet their requirements. That's you.**
187 Its fundamental premise, actually.

Rafael Lovato's Pressure Passing...for Real Estate?

I train in Brazilian jujitsu four days a week and work with a personal trainer two other days to fill my weekdays. While I have trained and obtained black belts in various martial arts systems over the past twenty years, the three years I have been training in BJJ have been a very punishing and personal struggle for me for a variety of reasons but, primarily, physical and emotional ones. It's hard to motivate yourself to go to a daily training session where you basically get "beat up" by people far more skilled than you and, after that happens, do it again the next day with great eagerness.

Enter my best friend Wilding, who was also the best man at my wedding and, by the way, my best friend since high school, without question. Wilding is a purple belt in BJJ and very skilled. We got together in the Adirondacks recently for what was known as *Feol/Wilding Spring Training,* which consisted of us wrestling on the floor of my vacation home while watching Rafael Lovato videos on pressure passing.

In the video, Lovato (a World BJJ champion) states quite clearly that whenever you are trapped in what is known as full guard, you should *immediately* stand up and begin working to escape the position. That mantra helped me to start passing the guards of fellow students in my own dojo in Memphis, whereas previously, I had little idea on what to do.

More importantly, however, it taught me how effective a simple mantra, which is unequivocally true, can be. Every time I am in full guard, I stand up and start working out of it to prepare to pass the guard.

But when it comes to your financial freedom, your mantra should be **your most desirable housing payment is zero.**

I am no world champion, but I promise you this is true.

If we can't make your housing payment zero dollars a month, let's agree to get it as close as we can to it. As an ancillary idea, we can also speculate on what most people would consider a distant impossibility; that is, **if we can get your housing payment to zero, we can maybe,** *just maybe,* **get you in a position to have NO housing payment and GET PAID TO LIVE IN YOUR HOUSE.**

And now you are starting to understand what The Short-Term Retirement Program is all about.

It All Starts with Tactical Planning

What is tactical planning?

Tactical planning is **short-range planning** that emphasizes the current operations of various parts of the organization. *The organization*, in this particular case, *is you and your family*.

In our case, our tactical plan is to eliminate our organization's (**read: your family, including you if you are single**) largest monthly payment by retiring your principal housing debt, permanently and as soon as possible. Once you do this, you can apply those freed up monies to eliminating other burdensome debts like credit cards, student loans, and auto payments. **Remember, in almost all cases, a family organization's largest payment is their housing payment.**

For the average working person, there are only three ways to achieve this objective:

1. Go the distance, and make 360 payments on a thirty-year loan; **or** purchase a house that can produce income to retire your loan (early) while you live there; **or**

2. Sell your home and rent from a landlord, which theoretically eliminates your principal loan indebtedness but *does not* alleviate your monthly payment of rent, which remains your largest monthly obligation.[188]

For our purposes, our sole interest lies in option 2: *Purchase a house (or similar property), which can produce income to retire your loan while you live there.*

Let's take a look at this *extremely viable and effective* strategy.

What Would It Be Like If You Had No Housing Payment?

I want you to think about this idea.

Imagine if you had no housing payment.

Now, for some people, they have had a housing payment all their life and simply cannot imagine it. They have refinanced their property every few years if rates drop a quarter point to save money when, in fact, while this lowers their monthly payment a few dollars, it ironically *increases* their overall debt by "rolling in" their refinance costs to a new loan and then resets the clock for another thirty years. So they have gotten nowhere and basically committed financial suicide. **Remember, no principal is attacked for the first fourteen years of a loan in any significant way** versus what your payment is each

---

188   There are, of course, other options like marrying into money, etc. This book does not consider those, as they do not apply to the average working-class family.

month (generally, 40% of your take-home pay AND your largest monthly cost) that you are forced to service under threat of foreclosure.

I don't have any help to offer those people. Their destiny is set in stone.

A Sad Eighty-Year-Old Radio Listener

For many years, I have been fortunate to have a popular weekend radio show in Memphis, Tennessee. The world of corporate, monopolized radio is a difficult one to navigate, but fortunately, I have been able to stay on the air for almost a decade with a great listener base that continues to grow. Originally, we started as a thirty-minute radio show designed to give some basic real estate investing tips to fledgling investors, but this eventually morphed into a three-hour show that discusses politics, real estate investing, finance, conspiracy theories, and anything else that is of interest to the safety and security of the average American family.

One of the things I harp on almost weekly is the fact that using a thirty-year mortgage, then refinancing it periodically whenever rates adjust, is financial *suicide*. Most of my listeners are in the middle of their lives and (ironically) in the middle of engaging in this very exercise, so it is hard for them to see the end result of their actions. However, recently we received a call from a long-time, eighty-year-old listener while I was in the middle of a segment discussing the fact that thirty-year loans by themselves—but ESPECIALLY when coupled with a periodic refinance/pull cash out strategy—will keep you in debt for life.

"*Robert, am calling you to let you and the listeners know that you are exactly right*," said the caller. "*I am an eighty-year-old man, and while I bought my house almost five years ago, today I owe more on it than what I paid for it and even far more than what it's worth on today's market. The reason is, I bought it and refinanced it every few years, just like you tell people not to do. Then I took out a second home loan and spent that money. Today, at eighty years old, I know I will die and my children will have to sell my house to pay off the mortgage. It's sad, but it is the result of the choices I made... I hope your listeners will listen to your advice and not make the same mistakes I did.*"

My producer and I looked at each other sadly and paused for a second before continuing the broadcast. What the radio listener had stated was, in fact, true, though **he had succumbed to the thirty-year-mortgage fallacy his whole life, as so many millions of other Americans have**—spending their lives in perpetual debt with nothing tangible to show for it.

> Will you be different?
>
> This story is sad, but if you are listening and paying attention, perhaps you do not have to end up like this caller when you are in your later stages of life. Focus on paying off your mortgage early, and do not get yourself into mortgage debt beyond what you can afford and pay off in a relatively short time[189] *with a fraction of your paycheck*. And ideally, get your mortgage paid by someone else each month while saving and preserving your hard-earned capital for a future day.

But I can help you. **Remember, you can eliminate your housing payment QUICKLY through the strategic acquisition of a primary residence.** And the formula for this is quite simple. There are two major tenets we have to be mindful of to get this plan in motion and make our monthly housing payment actually work for us and begin to eliminate our debt in a short and realistic time frame, as follows:

We need to find a motivated seller who is willing to sell us our desired property for far below market value. We will look at all types of homes, but generally, we want distressed homes or structures that have "good bones," i.e., meaning they are structurally sound. Getting into properties with major structural flaws can be an extremely costly and time-consuming process and, for the purposes of this book, is not suitable for our end goals.

Our subject property, when it is online,[190] needs to generate income for us each month in a recurring and hassle-free way. We don't want income from one-time, "fluky" income arrangements that are a "one off," or short-term temporary arrangement. The property must be set up and comply with all zoning restrictions so you can make money each month without a hassle from local government.

Let's look at what types of properties, specifically income-producing properties, we are discussing.

The Creative Real Estate Mind-Set

I have been able to make a career in real estate investing because of my ability to think creatively and outside the box. This has been great for my competitors who have stolen many of my intellectual property ideas and presented them as their own. **However, my competitors simply cannot out-steal the way in which I think about property or structure my real estate investment deals.[191]** They might take an idea here or there, but at the end of the day, their thinking is still static and immobile, whereas I am so frequently able

---

189   At the very most, twelve years, but preferably seven to ten or shorter.
190   Fixed up and operating optimally.
191   Operationally, they cannot steal my ability to view a property and intrinsically "know" its value. Think *Lovejoy*.

to see things that they are incapable of. That's why they are dinosaurs.

For you, however, you need to have a creative mind-set. You need to see things in plain sight that everyone else has overlooked. Some of this is teachable, and some of it comes from just having a hunger to become financially free that is so deep and profound, it is innate. Readers out there who grew up hungry like I did in a single-parent working home who were forced to work from a young age will clearly understand what I am talking about here. **You have to make the idea of being financially free a central mind-set that you focus on daily, without fail.**

Make no doubt about it: it is a singular focus and a life-changing purpose. More importantly, you have to make this purpose one that is unrelenting and that you work on DAILY.

Your first goal, your first step, is finding the initial property that will change your life path forever.

Types of Creative Properties

Critics of this book will point out I spent seven in-depth chapters to tell you to "go buy a duplex."

Nothing could be further from the truth.

The reality is, I spent seven jam-packed chapters to make you understand that the financial game you are thrust into is essentially unwinnable by the average paycheck-to-paycheck earner. **Radically different investment strategies are needed to (1) get you out of debt permanently, and then (2) begin accumulating assets and cash through the purchase of income-producing businesses and properties**, which you can leave to future generations of your family as inherited assets that produce periodic passive income.

Here is a basic breakdown of the types of homes we need to be looking for. Feel free to be creative, but this is a good list to begin with.

Income-Producing Property Types—Some Examples

1. Multi-unit property—two-, three-, or four-unit small apartments.

2. Single family with upgradable living space for separate living unit or efficiency apartment.

3. Single family with detached guesthouse, sometimes called a carriage house.

4. Commercially zoned multi-unit property, such as five- to six-cabin rental unit.

5. Small mobile home park (read: five to ten units max).

6. Commercially zoned small warehouse or brownstone type, with a commercial vendor

---

leasing space downstairs (think corner grocery) while you live in one (of ideally, several) upstairs apartments.

7. Property with large arable acreage. You live in house and lease land to small, independent micro-farmers, who pay you both in cash and through a portion of their harvest.

8. Small business with residential manager—think tiny self-storage with onsite manager apartment.

9. Small-zoned RV park or private motor club[192]—you live in an RV while collecting the lot rent, then upgrade as your financial situation allows and let the park carry your mortgage on a new primary.

10. Airbnb rental-type property, either renting rooms in your primary residence[193] or renting income units.

11. Commercially zoned flex warehouse-type space where you live in one unit and lease the other four or five

12. Large home with spacious bedrooms to rent to well-screened, suitable roommates.

13. What can you think of?

You Can't Beat the Math

Let's go back to our Timmy the Teacher example. In Timmy's case, he took a thirty-year loan for a principal balance of 100k. Two things are important to note here: Primarily, what is his monthly payment, and **more importantly, how does his monthly payment fit into his overall financial picture on a month-to-month basis?** Also remember that Timmy *violated* two primary rules that we need to adhere to in The Short-Term Retirement Program if we are to be successful, namely:

1. **Timmy paid full retail price for his primary residence,** *and*

2. **Timmy used a thirty-year mortgage.**

---

192 This is more of a mobile, free-living space idea given to me by a radio show listener. **The idea is you buy raw land and improve it to have electrical and water for a variety of RV pads, then you charge a "membership fee," and people who own RVs come and go as they please.** There are no permanent construction fixtures, and it is a "members-only club" on private land, so your operating costs are very low while your potential income is enormous, and you don't have to deal with code enforcement or zoning officials.

193 As you may recall from my example, **roommates are not the most desirable of renters, especially strangers.** Safety precautions are needed for both short-term and long-term tenants, *especially* if you are a single female living alone.

That combination of factors creates a terminal problem for those who are seeking to become financially free. **It becomes untenable to consider financial freedom when you are throwing away years and years of massive payments to bank interest.**

Timmy's Mortgage Payment, Day 1

Recall Figure A, earlier in the book, when we began to dissect the actual amount of principal and interest paid on Timmy's thirty-year home loan, that he elected to pay retail for. Let's just examine year one.

Figure J: Amortization Table of Yearly Interest Paid on a Thirty-Year Loan versus Principal Reduction on a 100k Real Estate Purchase at 7% Fixed

Yearly aggregate amortization schedule—100k loan at 7% fixed interest rate—monthly payment $665.30

Payments	Yearly Total Paid	Principal Paid	Interest Paid	Balance Remaining
Year 1 (1–12)	$7,983.63	$1,016.00	$6,968.00	$98,984.19

Timmy's payment of $665.30 does not reflect his escrow or impound account, which generally collects (in advance each month) prepayments on Timmy's anticipated property tax and insurance obligations. For easy mathematical calculation, we are going to assume that Timmy's total payment is $1,000 per month for his home loan. Remember, while his interest rate is, in fact, fixed, his home's insurance and tax burden generally will rise every two years, on average, **which means his payment will rise continually** and is *another* reason having a home loan for thirty years makes no sense. For right now, however, let's just focus on Timmy's payment of $1,000 on his residence. Also, let's look at Timmy's overall financial picture after he and his wife close the loan on their house.

A few things to focus on:

Timmy the Teacher: Financial Statement

Timmy is a tenured teacher in his local school district. Timmy makes about $50,000 per year as his gross income. Timmy files his W-4 form with the local district to have the appropriate amount of taxes taken out. Timmy also has union dues withheld and some other mandatory things like Social Security tax, state income tax, and so forth withheld from his paycheck. At the end of a pay period, Timmy has cooperated with all government taxation requirements and the mandatory union requirements, and when he gets his paycheck, it looks something like this:

> **Timmy the Teacher—Twelve-Month Pay Period (Twenty-Six Paychecks)**
>
> **Gross pay biweekly:** $1,923.07
>
> **Net take-home pay biweekly:** $968.31[194]

I used a simple online calculator to determine Timmy's net take-home pay.[195] FYI, in this example, Timmy contributes 5% to his 401k savings plan annually and has a state income tax rate of 4%. For clarity, in this example, ***Timmy takes home roughly half of his gross pay***. **Note:** I have not accounted for Timmy's family health insurance premiums, which at the very least, comprise at roughly 10% of his ***net*** take-home pay.

Figure K: Timmy's True Take-Home Pay

Gross Pay ($)		
Pay period:		Biweekly
Gross pay ($):		$50,000.00
Filing Status and Withholding		
Filing status:		Married
Number of withholding allowances (#):		0
Before Tax Adjustments		
Qualified tax deferral plan, such as 401K (%):		5.00%
Other before tax deductions, such as HSA ($):		$0.00
After-Tax Adjustments		
State and local income tax percentage (%):		4.00%
Other after tax deductions ($):		$0.00
After-tax reimbursements ($):		$0.00
Results		
Gross pay:		$50,000.00
Allowance deduction:	$0.00	
Qualified plan deduction:	$2,500.00	$2,500.00
Other before tax deductions:	$0.00	$0.00
Federal taxable wages:	$47,500.00	
Federal tax withholding:		$16,5983.96
FICA Social Security withholding:		$3,100.00
FICA Medicare withholding:		$725.00
State and local income tax withholding:		$1,900.00
Other after tax reductions:		$0.00
Reimbursements:		$0.00
Net pay including any claimed tips:		$25,176.14
Net take-home pay:		**$25,176.14**

---

194 Calculated as his net annual pay/26 pay periods (checks).
195 Taken from http://www.free-online-calculator-use.com/free-online-paycheck-calculator.html

This simple example demonstrates what I have indicated throughout this book. Primarily, **it is difficult, if not impossible, to become financially free when you are forced to give up half of your take-home pay to government taxation. And, because of this, no one can "save" their way to wealth.**

In Timmy's situation, it becomes even MORE difficult to consider the prospect of financial freedom, because while he was working so hard to do the right things, he had unwittingly fallen into a trap that was sucking down the majority of his take-home pay—one which generations of Americans have also been caught in, which has kept them insolvent their entire lives: the thirty-year mortgage.

Let's examine how Timmy pays the bills for a quick primer on how one stays broke their entire life while working in a "safe, secure job with benefits."

Timmy's Take-Home Pay Exercise 1: Paying the Bills

Net take-home pay (first pay period of month): $968.31

Timmy's mortgage: $1,000

Net shortfall: ($31.69)

Uh-oh! Looks like Timmy got sold a bill of goods by Bob the Banker in that he was told he could afford this 100k loan, but he is short! Oh wait, there is another paycheck coming in fifteen days. Let's pretend Timmy pays his bills at the end of the month, after two pay periods. That would look something like this:

Timmy's Take-Home Pay Exercise 2: Paying the Bills—Basic Analysis

Net take-home pay (first and second pay period of month):
$968.31 × 2 = $1,936.62

Less

Timmy's mortgage: $1,000

Timmy's car payment: $250

Timmy's wife's car payment: $250

Timmy's health insurance: $200

Timmy's utility bill: $150

Cell phones: $75

Gasoline for work: $80 (four fill-ups at $20 per month)

Food: $400

Timmy's credit card bill (minimum payment): $125

Timmy's student loans: $200

Net shortfall: ($794.38)

And now the reality of Timmy's situation begins to sink in. As Timmy sits down to pay his bills, **he realizes his job**, which he had to interview for and compete with many other qualified candidates to get, **cannot cover his basic cost of living and debt service.** He was very obedient and did what he was told, i.e., went to college, took out student loans, got married, bought a house...but somehow, somewhere along the way, in doing all the right things, Timmy found himself trapped in a prison, which is, for all intents and purposes, *inescapable*.

Realistically, Timmy himself, and the average American, don't understand why they are short other than the simple admission that they "don't make enough money." **And in Timmy's situation, he needs to start looking for a second job**, or his wife needs to get a job (remember, they are having their first child soon and will have to deal with childcare versus mom staying at home and not working, which is admittedly a hard decision either way) **because, quite simply, there is NO WAY Timmy can cut expenses**.

Why?

Timmy needs a house to live in. He bought one on a thirty-year loan and cannot sell because he will be "short" funds at closing.[196]

Timmy and his wife need vehicles to get around in. They started with no cash, so they bought and financed cars from the dealer and cannot sell, or else they will take a loss AND have no vehicle, so that is not an option.

They need health insurance. A baby is on the way, so they cannot cut that out.

They need gas to get to work and other places, and food. Those cannot be cut.

Student loans need to be paid; they cannot be bankrupted.[197]

They need cell phones for communication and emergency purposes, so this cannot be cut.

---

196 **See previous example of Timmy selling his house in a five-year period with 10% appreciation.** As stated, him getting a full-price offer plus 10% appreciation is unlikely. And even then, he essentially took a loss due to impounds. So there is no feasible way he can sell his 100k house (loan) on day 1 for 100k and break even. He is trapped.

197 As discussed, **recent legislation has made bankrupting student loans impossible**—no doubt because everyone would be declaring bankruptcy simply to get rid of this untenable toxic debt, which is a mortgage in itself for so many millions of Americans.

The credit card minimum needs to be paid, so they have some funds for "emergencies."[198]

What can they cut?

The simple answer is, *nothing*. They cannot remove any of these "essentials" from their life, these obligatory payments, which I think of as "hard" bills—bills that come each month and will in all likelihood NEVER be removed from their balance sheet.

Of course, note that I did not mention other essentials in this equation like clothing, birthdays, eating out, travel, vacations, and so on. And the reason I didn't is because based on Timmy's current situation, he is not going on a vacation anytime soon. Timmy's future, sadly, is predestined—work, work, and more work.

Summary

Timmy is doing "all the right things," but now, Timmy is stuck in a financial prison of his own doing (Bob the Banker did "help" him a bit, to be clear) and cannot escape. **Timmy's greatest mistake was buying a primary residence by paying full retail price and financing it using a thirty-year mortgage.**[199] Because of this life-altering decision, Timmy now has to work two jobs because he is literally THROWING his paycheck into the trash as bank mandated front-load interest each month without reprieve.

Going Down the Rabbit Hole

I can go on and on about how miserable Timmy's life is going to be. Timmy, in all likelihood, is probably going to be facing a bitter divorce at some point down the line because, **as many of you know, monetary problems and financial duress are the primary contributing factors to divorce proceedings**. And based on Timmy's example, this guy is struggling from the date of his first mortgage payment, so we can only imagine how ugly it might get at Timmy's house in months where he needs new tires or an emergency brake replacement.[200]

But now, for the purposes of this book, I am done with Timmy. If you have been paying attention, he has served his purpose here—an illustration of the everyday American who is completely unaware of the nefarious and unscrupulous plot arrayed against him to keep him heavily indebted by the bankers, and hamstrung by the government through

---

198 Better to have no credit card and save cash for emergencies. Credit cards bear interest.

199 Is this lesson sinking in yet?

200 Life and life emergencies happen and need to be planned for (and accounted for financially). Wealthy people understand this and prepare for bad times through smart savings and resource allocation.

taxation and regulation so much so that when he should be waking up in middle age and asking the question "Why can I not get ahead?" **The truth is this: He is too exhausted from working two jobs and the accompanying financial stress to really wonder about anything** and generally just ends up assuming "that's the way it is."

But it does not have to be this way. You CAN be financially free *if* you structure your living needs based on some basic business principles.

Where Is Your Storefront?

Entrepreneurs and business people set up shop and sell products to generate income. Generally speaking, they generate income through the sale of goods, or a service, to a customer. Obviously, the more customers you have, the more revenue you can generate. Have you ever had a resturaunt open in your town that is really, really awesome? Generally, that place is booked for weeks out, and there is a waiting line out the door. That storefront (in this case, restaurant) is generating a significant revenue stream by attracting many customers. Every time a customer pays their bill, the establishment generates revenue and, eventually, profit. And this is great for the establishment's success.

The problem that we face on our quest to financial freedom is as follows: How do we open a "storefront" and get paid by "customers"? Obviously, this is a book on real estate investing—not opening a storefront or marketplace, but the principle remains the same: we need to find a creative way to generate revenue from "customers" and do so periodically—daily, weekly, or monthly. **And the way that we open a storefront and generate customers is through the acquisition of income-producing real estate (through our primary residence), which serves to pay for our housing *and* cost of living and, in an ideal circumstance, also pays *US* in the form of net monthly cash flow.**

I will state this again, as this is the fundamental premise of the whole book:

> **The way that we open a storefront and generate customers is through the acquisition of income-producing real estate (through our primary residence), which serves to pay for our housing *and* cost of living and, in an ideal circumstance, also pays *US* in the form of net monthly cash flow.**

This idea will make you a multi-millionaire, if you apply it methodically first to your own principal residence and then if you carry the idea of someone else paying you (monthly) over to other bills in your life. It goes without saying if you can get your primary residence paid off through the rental payments of others, then you certainly could reapply this technique to other nonprimary residence properties and pay those off quickly, while also generating significant monthly passive income.[201] But for now, let's focus on your primary residence and eliminating your housing payment from day one.

You see, Timmy's problem was multifold. He made some grievous errors that committed him to a lifetime of indentured service through unmanageable debt. ***What were his principal errors?***

1. He paid full retail for a house.

2. He used a thirty-year note.

3. He had no way to generate income to offset his monthly debt, leaving him entirely naked and exposed to the interest payments the lenders require to be paid each month.

So our guidelines become quite straightforward then: **Do the opposite of what Timmy did**.

In this case, this is a simple four-step process as listed below:

1. **Commit to acquiring your primary residence using an aggressive mortgage payoff,** where part or all of your monthly payment is offset by the rental payments of others on the property.[202]

2. **Do NOT pay full retail for a house.** Use Feol's Formula[203] to determine an appropriate asking price for a house you want and only focus on distressed and motivated sellers.

3. **Under NO circumstances do you use a thirty-year note,**[204] Use the ***Mortgage Affordability Calculator*** to figure out what your desired monthly payment is, and make sure it is within a specified period of time you are comfortable with to "retire" your mortgage. Search for properties based on that price criteria.

4. **Make SURE you are able to generate at least 70% of your monthly note each month** through rental payments of others.

---

201 Spendable "money in fist" (MIF).
202 The STR Mortgage Affordability Calculator is a good tool for this.
203 See page 130 for reference.
204 Your lender may force you to use one, which is also fine as long as you are committed to prepaying the loan in full in a specified period of time that YOU set forth. We will discuss this issue shortly.

Aim Small, Miss Small

In the beginning of this chapter, I gave you a large number of creative ideas for income-producing property types, and the reality is, the limit of income you can generate through this approach is only bound by your creativity and imagination. With that being said, however, I have worked extensively in real estate for the past fifteen years and understand how tricky the rental market can be, how much experience and time it takes to learn how to circumnavigate the world that is your local tenant pool, and how to deal with and screen tenants that are an appropriate fit for your income and residential purposes while working with tenants to successfully ensure their happiness and avoid potential problems.

After reflecting on this information, I have narrowed down the viable housing options worth considering as you begin your search to five basic ones, as follows:[205]

1. Single-family residence with guest apartment or carriage house.

2. Duplex, triplex, or quadplex.

3. Two housing structures on one parcel of land suitable for an Airbnb or long-term rental.

4. Roommate placement in your home.

5. RV or fifth-wheel placement, buying in excellent condition but gently used (and HIGHLY discounted) from a private seller.

Let's take a minute and consider each of these housing options, desirability, and what to look for in a prospective property.

The thing to remember is that there is very little difference between a single-family primary residential property with neighbors right next door and a single-family residential property with a discrete separate living unit on a parcel. The difference between your friends who are "too good to deal with" renters and consequently buy a primary residence on a thirty-year mortgage, and you, who buys a property with an income-producing unit and does NOT use a thirty-year mortgage is, well…like night and day. You will have your home paid off in a few years while your "friends" have barely attacked principal in the same amount of time.

---

205 Keep in mind there is no limit to your creativity here, but for simplicity purposes in this book, I am looking at common, affordable housing options that involve a minimum of tenant management.

The Single-Family Residence with Guest Apartment

This is the technique I used after I moved to Memphis, Tennessee, in the year 2000. I rented for a few years while I was a graduate student living on the railroad tracks in a bad part of town; but after I got my teaching position with the Memphis City School District and I was able to qualify for a loan, I knew that I wanted a highly discounted, income-producing property and preferred a single-family house to a duplex because in Memphis, duplexes are hard to find, and I really wanted to focus on residential, owner-occupied areas. **I knew if I could live in a reasonably nice area within my budget, I could attract good renters who would pay my mortgage payment for me through their monthly rent.**

Knowing this, I had to give pretty specific instructions to the buying agent I had retained to help me locate a suitable property for purchase. I made it clear to her that I wanted something discrete, meaning—the income-producing unit had to be discretely located within the property parcel or building so I could still have privacy, **and the income-producing unit had to be upscale enough so I can extract premium rent.** As always, I had no interest in paying retail, so that also had to be a factor. But the day she called me and said she had found what I was looking for, I had no idea it would alter the course of my life forever.

Guest Apartment Plus Single-Family Home Example—Prescott Street, Memphis, Tennessee, 38111

This property was a single-family unit that had been converted to two separate apartments, with an upstairs unit being considered the guest unit and the downstairs unit being considered the main residence. The property was worth about 165k at that time, and while I paid $124,500 for it, it did need only minor and basic renovation—paint and carpet, as well as some updating of appliances on both units.[206]

Once I completed the purchase, I spent some money upgrading the flooring and renovating the upstairs guest unit so that it would really sparkle. I then set out to locate the ideal tenant, which in all honesty took me a few tries since I had very little rental experience at that time. For example, my first tenant, Troy, was drunk half the time and frequently late on rent.[207] But I asked him to leave and he did, and I replaced him with a great female graduate student who was studying botany at a local university called Rhodes College, who always paid the rent on time and kept the place pristine.

In the end, the math looked like this:

Prescott Street—Investor Fundamentals

Property Fundamentals

Purchase price: $124,500

Cash invested, down payment: $4,500

Renovations invested: $2,000, paid cash

Mortgage amount: $120,000

Fair market value after total repairs and improvements: $165,000[208]

Gross Potential Income

Guest apartment: $850 per month

Total aggregate gross income: $10,200

---

206 Note that I was only about 25% below fair market value on this purchase made in 2003. I was just getting started out in real estate, and this place, discounted and with a guest unit, fit my needs perfectly, **especially because the guest apartment made my monthly mortgage payment each month, so I was able to live for "free."** Remember the first sentence of this book, "Equity is dead"? Well, in this case, equity was irrelevant compared to me having my housing payment paid mostly by my tenant and me keeping most of my take-home pay. *That is the opposite of Timmy the Teacher's situation.*

207 I say this not to scare you but to manage your expectations. You may have to ask tenants to leave if they don't behave, but over time, you will gain experience working with tenants and identify good ones before they move in. It does get easier! **Screening is key, as well as verifying they make four times the monthly rent!**

208 At time of purchase in 2003.

Expenses:

Mortgage[209] **(twelve months)** = $552.93 × 12 = $6,635.16

Annual taxes: $2,000 (county AND city tax)

Insurance: $850 per year

Utilities average: $200/split by tenant and myself—$1,200

Total expenses annually: $10,685.16

Less net annual income: $10,200.00

Total net income gain (loss): ($485.16)

So in summary, living in my $165,000 house cost me about $500 per year, including utilities, taxes, insurance, and my mortgage—**all being paid by someone else.** Compare *that* with Timmy's untenable 12k/year payment he is forced to shoulder by himself without relief.

This is the power of The Short-Term Retirement Program. It takes situations like the one Timmy the Teacher finds himself in, where he is trapped for life and exchanges it for one where you as a homeowner can live essentially for free while stockpiling your hard-earned cash for other purposes, presumably paying off and retiring debt permanently *and with impunity*.

Applying Feol's Formula as a Benchmark to Begin Your Search

Things get far more interesting when you apply Feol's Formula to your local market conditions and use this as a compass to locate properties which are suitable for your consideration. Naturally, there are several principles we need to adhere to as prerequisites prior to beginning our search.

Here is a basic list.

Property Search Criteria—"Do Not Do" List

a.   Do not search for homes in a specific price range if it would feel unsafe living in that neighborhood.

---

209 In the interest of full disclosure, I was forced to take a thirty-year mortgage on the property due to me being unable to qualify any other way. (Based on my teaching income and high debt ratios. Remember, I did everything "right," like going to college and taking out massive student loans.) However, I refinanced shortly thereafter on a fifteen-year note. **As of this writing, the home has three and a half years left on the note, then it is paid off.** Value of property at the time of this writing today is about 250k.

b. **Do not even begin a search in areas where you will not feel safe living.**

c. Do not consider homes with major foundation or structural problems, as these tend to be cost prohibitive to our purposes.

d. No fire-damaged houses due to the unseen nature of the damage and extremely costly nature of rebuilding.

e. Do not consider houses with weak or flimsy construction, unlevel structural integrity, and so forth. Crumbling asbestos or rotten T-111 siding should be avoided and most stucco[210] also.

f. **Avoid homes with homeowners associations and condo fees** as these have bylaws that are extremely unfriendly to you generating income and also frequently mismanaged.

g. Don't fall in love with houses.

h. Don't assume that you can add on a rental unit or build an income-producing structure on a property if it does not already have one.

i. Don't be closed minded in your search.

j. **Don't settle for something you don't want or does not provide you with the income requirements** or price points you set forth in your search from the beginning.

Taking *Feol's Formula* and applying it to your local market will allow you to get a benchmark of where to begin your search. Of course, you can always modify the formula based on your expectations and what you are willing to pay or tolerate, depending on your personal financial situation. **The thing to remember is that most Americans are unaware of the types of discounts that are available to diligent seekers of distressed real estate.** I guess that is why most people pay retail simply because they don't know what to do otherwise and also because they have been conditioned to believe that buying a house is a laborious, emotionally intensive process you do generally once or twice in your lifetime.

Realistically, buying a house is no different than purchasing any other commodity. I buy anywhere from 5-10 houses per month for my business, and certainly don't have

---

210 Many types of stucco are an inferior product with high moisture content and many lawsuits. Make sure you consult with a certified home inspector or siding expert if you are considering buying a home with stucco.

the fear or hesitation I had when I was purchasing my first home. Fear is your enemy and can prevent you from seeking a house that can help you achieve your dreams. There is nothing to fear, and **if you are fearful as you begin the search for a property that will help you become financially free, nothing is preventing you from doing the due diligence necessary to get your questions answered so you have all the facts**. Once you have the information necessary to make a decision, you can move forward with a purchase or pass on a property, wherever your comfort level lies. Just make sure (and your realtor should help you with this) you don't start putting down purchase contracts where you cannot get your earnest money back if you find a glaring flaw in your prospective property.

We will talk about offers in the next chapter.

Applying Feol's Formula with The Short-Term Retirement Mortgage Afford- ability Calculator

Remember *Feol's Formula*:

> ### Feol's Formula
>
> *(Actual Fair Market Value of Home – all needed repairs to get the home to FMV)/2 = asking price*
>
> **Example:** If a home is worth 100k and needs 20k in repairs, that would be 80k/2 = 40k asking price.

This is a good benchmark for the types of discounts necessary for you to acquire homes, which can be paid off aggressively. Not surprisingly, you will find motivated sellers in these price ranges, frequently in areas where you would like to live.[211]

However, make sure that you are using the *Mortgage Affordability Calculator* to determine your tolerance for monthly payment amounts and the number of years you are willing to carry the mortgage before it is paid off in full.[212]

Remember, YOU set your own numbers, not some banker.

---

211   Where to search? A realtor setting you up on a housing search based on ZIP codes and your price range is a great start. Also, Craigslist, your local classified ads, placing an ad (you place one) for distressed sellers, bandit signs (you state, "I Buy Houses" with your phone number), your local REIA group, networking with local wholesalers...the list is endless.
212   Known as a full amortization.

Let's use Timmy's payment of $1,000 per month, for easy math. We can use a low interest rate of 5% and assume you want to use a Fannie Mae-type product while qualifying for (and asking for) a shorter payoff term.

STR Mortgage Affordability Calculator

Inputs	Desired Monthy Payment	Desired Interest Rate
	$1,000.00	5.00%
Purchasing Power		
5-Year Payment	$52,990.71	
7-Year Payment	$70,751.83	
10-Year Payment	$94,281.35	

In this example, if we use 100k ARV houses as an example, ***Feol's Formula*** gives us a starting search value of 40k (plus we need to account for 20k in work), for a total needed loan amount of 60k, which we will use for this example. Assuming the borrower (you) wants to shoulder a $1,000-per-month payment until the loan retires, realistically ***he or she can pay off the home and retire the mortgage in about six years***.

Six years? Could you imagine if you had your home paid off in six years? That is probably something you hadn't considered prior to reading this book.

Now, what most people are forgetting is that we don't want to shoulder that $1,000 per month burden for six years; we want someone else to do it for us. Naturally, if we had a rental unit (for example, a discrete guest apartment), which paid rent of $1,000 per month on the property we were purchasing, we would effectively live for free.[213] But for those who are very serious about paying off their home, what happens if we shouldered the $1,000 payment ourself and added in a $1,000 payment from our tenant, prepaying the note by an extra $1,000 each month? How long would it take to pay off the home?

---

213 In this example, I am not counting taxes and insurance, which vary from state to state. **This particular example assumes 100% of the monthly payment goes to principal and interest.** Keep in mind, your loan will generally require escrow, so you will have to determine how much each month is going to principal and interest, and adjust accordingly to see the true timeframe for paying off your mortgage in full.

Loan Payoff—Six-Year Term, 5% Fixed, Prepaying $1,000 per Month Extra Until Mortgage Is Paid

Basic Loan Information					
		Loan Amount			$60,00.00
		Interest Rate			5.00%
		Loan term (in months)			72
		Monthly Payment			$966.30
		# of payments - First year			12
Extra Payments	*Interval*	*Amount*	*Start in Month*	*Duration*	*End in Month*
	Monthly	$1,000.00	1	Until end of Loan	72

Interest Saved and Term Reduction with Extra Payments	*without extra payments*	*with extra payments*
Loan term	72 Months	33 Months
Total Interest Paid	$9,573.28	$4,306.38
Interest Saved Over Monthly Payment Loan		$5,266.90
Loan Term Will Be Shortened By		39 Months

As you can see, paying $2,000 per month on a sixty-year note at 5% fixed interest pays off the loan in about 2.8 years versus 6 years.[214]

The Power of the Two-Year Payoff

Well, now we really have gone down the proverbial rabbit hole. We are talking about paying off homes from the inception of the loan in less than three years. **It really can happen!** And of course, after the loan is paid off, in our example situation here, not only do you NOT have a mortgage payment anymore, you *also* continue to get paid $1,000 per month by your tenant in your guest apartment, assuming you manage it effectively and keep it rented, which is not that difficult to do. That would give you an extra $12,000 per year of income to do with what you please—pay off debt, take a vacation, reinvest the capital on other ventures...the list is endless.

But what is most important to recognize is that YOU HAVE MADE YOUR BIGGEST MONTHLY EXPENSE YOUR SMALLEST ONE. You have eliminated your housing debt permanently.[215] Think of how relieved your family and friends would be if they weren't struggling with their mortgage payments or rent each month. Think of the financial freedom and flexibility that would come with knowing that you and your family have a

---

214 Timmy's payment is $966.30 on a six-year loan payoff (assumes a 60k loan), which is close enough to $1,000/month for this example.

215 Permanently until you decide to keep up with the Joneses. Don't do that.

safe, secure home that no one can take away from you,[216] where you can come and go as you please, and each month you do not have to give away half of your income to a bank in mortgage interest that gets you NOWHERE.

Imagine that kind of freedom, free of financial worry and anxiety. It can be yours. You just have to get the pieces of the puzzle to fit together in a way that works for you and your housing needs. There is a property out there that YOU can afford, right now, somewhere, in your area; you just have to go out and find it!

A Quick Note on Short Loan Amortizations

Some of you may go searching for short, aggressive loan amortizations only to find that your banker looks like a deer in headlights when you ask him for something peculiar like a six-year payoff. They may say to you, "We don't do that. You can only get a thirty-year or fifteen-year term with us." In this case, you can go searching for a different bank (local community banks and credit unions are generally more flexible with their lending guidelines, especially with customers who have a "deposit relationship"[217] with them), or if you are really struggling to find someone who can help you, just take the thirty-year loan, subtract the payment for the thirty-year note from your original planned monthly payment, then pay the balance as a function of your total payment (basically, if you were planning on paying $2,000 per month, pay $2,000 per month and make sure that the required $322.10 minimum monthly payment is designated as the payment, *and the remaining $1,677.90 is designated on the payment coupon as additional principal),* NOT to "advance" your payment schedule (meaning, prepay "x" months of minimum payments). In the end, the math is still the same, as you can see below.

Important! Make sure your loan is NO PREPAYMENT PENALTY.

Basic Loan Information					
		Loan Amount			$60,00.00
		Interest Rate			5.00%
		Loan term (in months)			360
		Monthly Payment			$322.10
		# of payments - First year			12
Extra Payments	*Interval*	*Amount*	*Start in Month*	*Duration*	*End in Month*
	Monthly	$1,677.90	1	Until end of Loan	360

Interest Saved and Term Reduction with Extra Payments	*without extra payments*	*with extra payments*
Loan term	360 Months	33 Months
Total Interest Paid	$55,950.18	$4,228.96
Interest Saved Over Monthly Payment Loan		$51,721.22
Loan Term Will Be Shortened By		327 Months

---

216 Assuming you keep paying your taxes, don't offend the government, local zoning officials, code enforcement, eminent domain people—you get the idea.

217 Meaning, you have money on deposit with them.

156

Other Desirable Housing Types That Can Provide Income

We have discussed the single-family home with a discrete guest apartment. A carriage house is very similar to this idea but is usually a small, cute, detached, home in the rear of a main home. Frequently, this home was used by hired help, or in-laws would stay in this small property. Either way, this additional space is rentable and can provide income for you, and is certainly worth consideration should you come across this type of property in your search.

Let's look at some other viable housing types for your consideration.

Duplex, Triplex, or Quadplex

These are homes that are built to function as multiple units of housing that produce income. **One thing that an investor/buyer has to be aware of is to NOT buy a multifamily unit in a neighborhood of multifamily units**. Why? Simply put, when you have all renters transitioning in and out of a neighborhood where different homeowners maintain their homes with different standards of quality for the tenant base, you (in my experience) tend to have a difficult time maintaining an overall neighborhood standard, which can adversely affect property values, your safety, and your ability to attract a desirable tenant. **Instead, I like to focus on multi-unit housing located in predominantly owner-occupied areas.**

Some things to consider:

Duplex—easy to maintain. You live in one side, and someone lives in the other. You are definitely sharing a wall with someone (unlike a discrete guest apartment, which is frequently adjacent to any shared walls, for privacy purposes).

Triplex—harder to find, generally speaking, smaller per unit living space.

Quadplex—you may share walls and floors; parking may be tight. Off-street parking may be necessary, which subjects you or your tenants to the rules of lawful tow, which vary from municipality to municipality.

With any multi-unit housing, you have to ask many questions, with some basic ones as follows:

☐ What is the heating and cooling situation for each unit? Do the units work, or do I have to replace them due to neglect and poor maintenance?[218]

---

218 This can get costly. Consider replacing the HVAC system in your house and how expensive that is, then multiply by four times in the case of a quadplex—very costly! A home warranty may be indicated in this case prior to purchase.

☐ Are the units on separate meters? **Separate meters are preferable so you do not have utilities in your name for others** where you are forced to collect each month and split the utility bill somehow.

☐ Is the zoning appropriate for these units? Is it lawful?

☐ What is the parking situation?

☐ What is the neighborhood like? Am I safe here? Can I attract good tenants here?

☐ Do all the tenants share the same entryway? (Can be problematic.)

These are some basic precepts to consider prior to making a purchase and when evaluating multi-unit housing. **Remember, at the end of the day, YOU HAVE TO LIVE THERE**, so if something is not meshing with your idea of a blissful existence, DON'T BUY, and move to the next prospect.

On Multifamily Pricing

One of the major issues we run into when purchasing a multi-unit property is appraisal problems. This results from the fact that most appraisers use a "sales comparable" approach to determining value, meaning—they price a home based on square footage by using recent sales in the past six months as a benchmark for what an average home is selling for per foot within a mile radius. Once this is figured out, they extrapolate it to your home.

The problem then becomes that, generally speaking, if you are purchasing a multi-unit home in a residential, predominantly single-family neighborhood, you generally don't have a lot of "comparable" sales. A multifamily home is not comparable with a single-family home, as they differ in a variety of ways. This can make determining the value of a multi-unit very difficult. And, generally speaking, when owners sell multi-units, they ask far higher rates than normal market value for single-family homes of the same square footage.

The point is, you have to be wary of placing too much emphasis on multifamily home pricing. Seek steep discounts and motivated sellers, and don't stray into bad areas. Be careful when you are considering these type of homes as they can be big moneymakers but can also be potentially BIG hassles. You have to do your research to see if a prospective home is suitable for your living needs and if the income it generates is going to be a benefit to you (versus living on top of people, which can also be a major hassle.)

Multifamily Summary

These can make excellent purchases on your journey to financial freedom if you are willing to tolerate people living in (relatively) close proximity and you find a suitable location. Remember John O'Williams, the greatest landlord of all time? He focused on multi-unit apartments in Syracuse, New York, because they were in a predominantly single-family area, and he was able to attract young, vibrant college students—usually who had their parents pay the rents a year in advance.[219]

Keep this in mind as we strive to work on finding a suitable housing prospect for you. Location is the most important thing, as renters and owners all want to be in great, safe locations! Ask yourself one question when considering a multifamily purchase: "If I was looking for an apartment to rent, would I rent here?"

If the answer is NO, then it should be pretty clear that you need to move on.

Two Housing Structures on One Parcel of Land Suitable for an Airbnb

The Airbnb concept has become incredibly popular, much to the chagrin of hotel owners worldwide, but it becomes even more viable when examined in the context of your primary residence, with the purpose of providing significant monthly or even daily income. I personally continue to explore this concept for my own personal investment portfolio and cannot find a downside risk to it other than the onerous and cumbersome pursuit of local municipal authorities trying to find a way to tax it. The truth of the matter is, while most landlords (this will be you if you purchase a property with an income unit as discussed in this book) are used to receiving monthly income, the Airbnb concept provides you with a variety of great financial perks, not the least of which is *daily income.*

Take Memphis, Tennessee, for example. The average rent in Memphis, in my experience, is about $750 per month, which turns out to be $24.19 per day. Now this is fine and certainly a strong rental amount, but what I find fascinating about Airbnb proprietors is that they can get four to ten times that rental amount on a daily basis.

And that is where our interest lies, for the purpose of this exercise.

---

219 It goes without saying that if you are offered a year's worth of rent in advance, **you take it and APPLY IT TOWARD PRINCIPAL.** (This assumes you can carry the payment on your own for a year.) Prepaying a large percentage of your mortgage alters the payoff formula, so each payment you make (after the large prepayment) attacks MORE principal than it was originally designed to, resulting in more aggressive principal reduction and, not surprisingly, a more rapid loan payoff.

Consider the following:

To follow is a random sample of homes in Memphis, Tennessee, taken from the Airbnb website.[220] For purposes of brevity, I selected two homes. But look, a simple two-guest home (which can translate to a one bedroom) rents for $75, and then a carriage house (separate detached guesthouse at a primary residence) rents for $109 per day. This translates into three times and four times the average daily rent respectively.

Because of this phenomenon, researching and prospecting for residential units with rentable, discrete space becomes an extremely viable option then because:

- ☐ You don't have to have your space rented for an entire month to get the same or more income from your rental unit;

- ☐ You have flexibility to NOT rent your unit, if you have family, friends, or guests coming at periodic times in any given month;

- ☐ The wear and tear on your unit is much smaller because people stay there generally to sleep and spend larger amounts of their time visiting the city they have come to; and

---

220   Captured September 22, 2016, from Airbnb.com.

☐ You have the ability through Airbnb to get not only a security deposit but also pet fees, cleaning fees, service and maintenance fees,[221] and more importantly, you can require a tenant to obtain some type of "rental protection plan,"[222] where if they cause damage to your unit, it is covered by this insurance-type product.

All of a sudden, using this type of rental becomes very viable and, more importantly, potentially VERY PROFITABLE.

The flip side of this equation is that you are, essentially, dealing with strangers coming to your home. When you have a long-term tenant, you can pull credit and background checks, criminal history checks, and so forth. With Airbnb, you have to take what you get and hold them accountable through the Airbnb system of deposits and fees. The good news, though, is that most people who stay at Airbnbs are upstanding people who do not want a negative review for them as a renter.

What's Different with an Airbnb Unit?

Lots of things. Unlike a basic rental, with a daily rental through Airbnb.com (or similar site), you have to provide EVERYTHING—furniture, sheets, linens, towels, hand soap, appliances, cooking utensils, utilities, parking...you get the idea.

Now, this will drive up your unit acquisition and renovation price simply because you have to buy furniture for a separate living unit other than your own. However, this easily pays for itself within a few months, and once you have your apartment furnishings paid off, you own them for life until they wear out or need replacing. But remember, you also incur the cost of a utility bill, which needs to be calculated into your monthly cost projections. Many Airbnb-type units don't have separate meters. (Say, for example, you convert a garage in your house and keep it on your main utility meter. Because of that, you have to pay a higher utility bill.)

This isn't the end of the world, obviously, but needs to be factored in.

Location and Access Are Critical

When people are renting an Airbnb, you need them to have a great experience. Most tenants on twelve-month leases will not review private landlords, but Airbnb renters do, and you need to expect feedback (and more importantly, ask for feedback) from each

---

221   Simply put, additional income for you to put in your pocket.
222   Offered through Airbnb.com.

renter. You want positive feedback, so when other people are considering staying at your unit (usually found through the Airbnb site itself), they see that other people have had a great experience and are more comfortable reaching out to you to rent your unit. Seeing negative feedback, generally, will have them immediately move on to other units where the feedback has been more favorable.

Because of this, the type of unit you are offering becomes critical. You need something that has some degree of privacy, is discrete, offers safe and secure parking, and is able to be accessed through a private entryway.[223] And all linens need to be clean. The unit needs to smell fresh, and all appliances need to work and be ready the minute your tenant comes in. Think about times you have traveled long distances and you simply want to check into your hotel room, turn the TV on, and eat or drink something refreshing. The last experience you want your tenants to have is a hassle getting into your place, a hassle parking, a TV that doesn't work, a refrigerator that is off, and no stove.

This is the type of thing that can really be unaccommodating to an Airbnb renter.[224]

Knowing this, one of the most ideal types of properties to consider for this type of rental setup is a single parcel of land with two separate detached houses. And believe it or not, this type of situation exists and is more common than you think, but you may not have seen this simply because you were not searching for it. Think about your daily travels. How many times do you drive by properties that have two buildings on it? All the time. But now when you drive by them, you will think to yourself, "I wonder if that is for sale because I could put a second, independent rental unit there." And when you find the right one, you will not be limited strictly to the Airbnb model because a completely separate, fully furnished home on your property will also appeal to:

- Airline pilots looking for shared "crash pads";[225]

- Business executives who need short-term rental homes for a few months at a time;

- Insurance companies that need to temporarily place families whose homes have been the victims of fire or other natural disaster;[226] and

---

223 **These are guidelines, and your creativity will go a long way to finding a property that can serve this purpose in a suitable way for other travelers.** Use them as a benchmark, but feel free to research and make changes as necessary based on your personal property and its amenities.

224 Full disclosure is the key. Some Airbnb units offer simply beds and baths and no kitchen facilities. If this is the case with your unit, advertise it clearly so there are NO misconceptions.

225 **We talk to FedEx pilots (headquartered in Memphis) all the time about how they constantly seek out this type of arrangement,** as they are sick of staying in hotels and having to pay for hotel food, the rooms, etc.

226 This can bring in HIGH-DOLLAR RENT but is inconsistent.

☐   Other people who need emergency short-term, noncontractually binding housing.

And the best part of this is, **all of these types of renters are willing to pay a premium for the convenience** of having a fully furnished, short-term rental.

Let's consider the 60k home we looked at earlier worth 100k. You buy the home and place it on a six-year mortgage.

Assuming an Airbnb rental at 90% occupancy (as it is unlikely you will ever have 100% occupancy[227]) in this example at a rental of $75 per day, you would net a take-home pay of $2,092.50. Let's see how that stacks up with our six-year rental payoff, assuming you apply it all to your monthly mortgage payment:

Basic Loan Information				
	Loan Amount			$60,000.00
	Interest Rate			5.00%
	Loan term (in months)			72
	Monthly Payment			$966.30
	# of payments - First year			12
Extra Payments	*Interval*	*Amount*	*Start in Month*	*Duration*	*End in Month*
	Monthly	$1,092.50	1	Until end of Loan	

Interest Saved and Term Reduction with Extra Payments	*without extra payments*	*with extra payments*
Loan term	72 Months	32 Months
Total Interest Paid	$9,573.28	$4,101.25
Interest Saved Over Monthly Payment Loan		$5,472.03
Loan Term Will Be Shortened By		40 Months

In this case, the payoff is shaved off by another month and gets you very close to 2.5 years before you retire your mortgage. **Keep in mind this accounts for over $2,000 in rental income that you apply toward your monthly mortgage payment, NONE OF WHICH CAME FROM YOUR OWN POCKET.**

Also remember in our previous example YOU were fronting half (1k) of the $2,000 per month prepayment. In this case, the Airbnb makes the ENTIRE 2k monthly payment for you, and you KEEP your 1k in your pocket for yourself. Oh, and your house STILL gets paid off in three years.

Now that is extremely powerful.

---

227   In the world of real estate investment, this is known as a vacancy factor. You can figure it out by taking your appropriate factor (in this case, let's call it 10%) and multiplying it by your expected rent. For example, if your rental brings in $75/ day, and you have thirty-one days in a month, your expected rent is $2,325; however, when you account for a 10% vacancy factor your expected rent becomes $2,325 – (10% of $2,325 or $232.50) = $2,092.50.

Conclusion

The viability of this model cannot be understated. If you can find a suitable parcel of property that has a fully rentable, independent unit that shares the characteristics recommended, you can get into *the day-to-day short-term rental* business from the comfort of your own home without roommates or tenants on top of you. This income can serve to retire your monthly housing payment in just a few short years. **And then you can continue that stream of income for as long as you like and use that income for other purposes such as retiring debt or reinvestment**. And the renters you will encounter are usually quite professional, independent, and low maintenance.

Roommate Placement in Your Home

This is something that I experienced and is relatively easy to do. I mention this because there are many homeowners who will be trapped in thirty-year mortgages unable to sell, and for many in that particular situation, this may be the only viable option to produce income. Also, as previously discussed, I used this model for several years as a graduate student in Rochester, New York, where I attended the ***National Technical Institute for the Deaf***, and it served me quite successfully.

However, having roommates is an altogether different situation than having tenants in a separate, private, and discrete rental unit.

Some of the factors you need to be aware of are as follows:

- Your roommates, generally speaking, are in fact on top of you.

- You will have to share critical areas like kitchens and bathrooms.

- You are subject to experiencing their personal hygiene habits, and they will elso encounter yours, which can often become a point of contention.

- You will share appliances, food storage areas, refrigerator space, and your food may be subject to their "borrowing."

- Security may become an issue, if your roommates are difficult to deal with.

- Rent can be hard to collect. Also, it can be relatively easy to collect.

- Removing roommates can be difficult, depending on eviction laws in your area.[228]

---

228 Personally, I never had a problem, but it bears mentioning.

- Parking can become an issue.

- Your roommates may want to have friends over, which can be inconvenient for you.

- Your roommates may want to have intimate encounters at your house, which can be uncomfortable and potentially become an issue.

- A litany of other issues not worth mentioning here.

The key to handling renting rooms in your house to potential roommates, in one word, comes down to this: *screening*. Also, setting up inflexible rules for roommate conduct will also help, if it is done from the beginning of the rental relationship.

Of course, it comes down to what you, the owner of the household, will tolerate. In my case, the rules were basic and simple:

1. Your room is where you keep your stuff. Don't leave it anywhere else in the house.

2. No smoking or drug use are tolerated, without exception.

3. Clean up after yourself in the bathroom.

4. No boyfriends or girlfriends stay overnight.

5. Leave my dog alone, and don't let him outside.

6. Don't make me chase the rent or utility bill.

In my case, these rules worked really well. I screened the tenants from the beginning and let them know what the expectations were. In doing so, I ended up collecting a great deal of rent and utility money while making some good friends in the process. Certainly, there were a few awkward times, but in the end it was totally worth it.

However, it bears mentioning that I was single when I owned a single-family house and rented bedrooms to long-term roommates. Today, with a wife and children, this would not be tenable for me, not for the least reason that I do not want any strangers around my children nor my wife, and there are no exceptions to this rule. **Choosing to rent to roommates is a very private decision based on financial need and desire and should not be entered into lightly**. However, with good screening and selection, you can generate significant revenue while providing for others' housing needs and possibly make some great friendships while doing so.

RV or Fifth-Wheel Placement, Buying in Excellent Condition but Gently Used from a Private Seller

I love this idea. This idea has grown on me since I purchased a mobile home park recently and got to see the demand in today's housing market for simple, affordable housing.

You see, since the collapse of the housing market in 2008, the jobs market and the housing market have never really recovered. There are a great deal of economic factors involved in this statement, which are far beyond the scope of this book, but let's just say that it is far more difficult to find jobs today than it was before 2008; and because of this, family incomes and savings are significantly down. The days of renting beautiful, massive houses with exorbitant monthly rental payments for most working-class Americans are gone.

Various people deal with this in a variety of ways. Recently, this article was on the front page of *Drudge Report*, discussing how more and more people are giving up the dreams of owning and renting houses *simply to live in vans*.

The "Van Life"[229]

Imagine paying $120 to live in a studio in Los Angeles, California, where the average rent for a one-bedroom apartment is about $2,300.

Stephen Hutchins, twenty-two, a freelance animation artist and rapper by the name of Lateral, does just that, except he doesn't live in an apartment, or a studio, really. He lives in a van.

A recent graduate of the University of Southern California, Stephen Hutchins is living in a van while he builds his portfolio as a freelance animator.

He's not alone. Last year, 4,600 cars and RVs were used as homes, according to *The Los Angeles Times*. [*Article continued on website*]

The technique for this rental dwelling is pretty simple: buy an RV trailer or fifth-wheel with some slide-out compartments and place it in your driveway. The beauty of this is that used RV trailers can be purchased very inexpensively, and they can be rented for massive rents versus their cost of acquisition. Also, RVs can be placed in your driveway without violating most zoning ordinances[230] and are pretty much self-contained, so they can be used in any residential situation discretely, generally without raising the hackles of local code enforcement or zoning officials.

---

229 Taken from http://circa.com/whoa/the-bizarre/people-are-ditching-apartments-to-live-the-van-life.
230 **If going this route, you would need a plumber and electrician to set you up with an appropriate sewage outlet, direct water line intake to the trailer, and twenty-amp electrical service so your tenant can have air-conditioning**.

166

Here is an example of an RV travel trailer, which is brand-new and very affordable. I am sure this can be financed also, and realistically, this unit could rent for $750 to $850 per month.

Also, remember that you do not have to purchase a new trailer to generate significant income. But even if you paid $15,000 for this trailer,[231] assuming it rents for $850 each month, you would have it paid for in ($15,000/$850) = 17.6 months or about 1.5 years.

☆ **2017 Kingsport Ultra-Lite 238RK with Sofa Slide - $16500**

image 2 of 13

Let's see how the numbers stack up. Pretend you pay 60k for your 100k house, as cited in our previous examples; but in a creative slant on things, let's say you *also* purchase an RV travel trailer for 15k and roll it into your loan for a total encumbrance on your loan of 75k. Let's also pretend you are willing to pay $1,000 per month on the loan. In this case, the extra 15k on your loan makes the monthly payment $1,207.87, and in this case, you also apply the $850 toward your payment, resulting in an additional principal payment of $643 (rounded) each month.

We are assuming a six-year loan in this instance.

Basic Loan Information					
		Loan Amount			$75,000.00
		Interest Rate			5.00%
	Loan term (in months)				72
	Monthly Payment				$1,207.87
	# of payments - First year				12
Extra Payments	*Interval*	*Amount*	*Start in Month*	*Duration*	*End in Month*
	Monthly	$643.00	1	Until end of Loan	

Interest Saved and Term Reduction with Extra Payments	*without extra payments*	*with extra payments*
Loan term	73 Months	45 Months
Total Interest Paid	$11,966.66	$7,320.59
Interest Saved Over Monthly Payment Loan		$4,646.07
Loan Term Will Be Shortened By		28 Months

---

231   Remember, always negotiate the best price, and ***NEVER*** pay retail.

Applying a complete payment of $1,850 per month, **you would have the entire house (and RV) paid in full in less than four years.**

Of course, additionally, you could simply take the $850 per month RV rental payment, apply the difference of $357.87 out of your own pocket each month (making your $1,207 six-year monthly payment), and your 75k mortgage would be paid off in a full six years with your housing payment being about $350 per month—far cheaper than any rent you could find in your local town in a desirable area, most likely.

And this is assuming you don't rent your primary residence in ANY way.

Conclusion of Chapter Concepts

While I use the 60k loan as a basic example, when you apply your income situation and tolerance for monthly mortgage reduction to these examples and geographic location (and economy), your loan amount could be three times to six times the 60k loan I use in this example.[232] **However, it bears noting that 50k/year earners (and lower) get 100k home loans all the time on thirty-year mortgages, so this example is very much applicable to the majority of Americans around the country.**

You can pay off your home in a fraction of the time people normally expect to and have other people do this for you. Remember, however, that without the appropriate type of property, with the potential for discrete, rentable income, it becomes very difficult to do so. **Focus on finding the right property in the right location with the right rentable amenities, and your life can change dramatically** simply by structuring your primary residence to accept the rental payments from others.

> ### Giving Up on Investment Property After Ten Years—a Casualty of the Thirty-Year-Loan Story
>
> A good friend of mine saw me getting into the real estate business ten years ago and decided that he wanted to get into it also. However, he ended up purchasing from a competitor of mine (who is also a good friend). My friend who was getting in to the real estate game ended up purchasing four homes using thirty-year mortgages, and he paid retail for all four properties.
>
> This gave him, *per home*, a $100 per month positive cash flow.

---

232 Assuming you can still effectively offset the payment with proportionate rental income or take-home pay, as discussed in the next chapter.

Now the problem with this math is his payment (with escrow) was, on average, $700 per month (he rented houses for $800ish, in this instance). **However, the issue becomes that when you factor vacancy and maintenance projections into your housing formula, he was actually LOSING money even though he generated $100 per month GROSS positive cash flow, per unit**. Here's why:

My friend's monthly note: $700 per month

Annual total payments: $700 × 12 = $8,400 per year.

Less 10% vacancy factor: $-840

Less 10% maintenance factor: $-840

Total projected loss due to vacancy and maintenance, annually: $-1,680

Divided by twelve months: $-140 loss per month.

Add in positive cash flow: $100 per month

Total net loss per house: $-40 per month.

X 4 houses: $-160 per month

Annual net loss: $-1,920

You see, when my friend purchased the homes, he was so excited to get into real estate that he was blinded to the mathematics involved, which are necessary to make an investment property successful. And after ten years, he called me at my brokerage and asked me to help him sell his homes at a loss (of course). **Why was he looking at a loss? Because after ten years of making payments on a thirty-year note, he was still not very far into reducing any principal.** The transactional costs to sell his homes alone would put him into the negative. But even knowing this, he had thrown his hands in the air and said, "Enough."

My friend, ironically, is a teacher who is a 50k-per-year earner. After ten years of struggling with real estate, he still couldn't make it work, and it wasn't because he isn't smart or business savvy; he is both of those. **However, he simply couldn't beat the math.**

You have to make sure you are approaching purchasing properties with your EYES WIDE OPEN. **If something can go wrong, it probably will.** You need to account for these factors in your projections so you are sure you can generate enough cash flow to cover periodic maintenance and vacancy factors. If you do so, and you use an aggressive mortgage payoff from the start, you will not experience what my friend went through.

9

Analyzing and Finding the Deals: How to Understand and Assess Potentially Undervalued Properties for Income Purposes

The beginning real estate buyer has little or no idea how to find, assess, or analyze properties. As a cardinal rule, let me just begin by saying in the Feol house, "We don't go out and look for properties, **we go out and look for DEALS.**"[233]

Now, there is a stark difference between your average run-of-the mill property that is listed on the multiple listing service and priced at retail, and a motivated or distressed seller who is offering a tremendous discount and value in the process of trying to sell their home. Remember, however, that even though a seller may be motivated, their house for sale may still not be a "deal."

Let's look at examples of motivated sellers we DON'T want to work with.

Motivated Sellers Who Aren't *Really* Motivated: A Short List of Examples

- A seller who is recently divorced but paid retail for their house seven years ago on a thirty-year note and needs a high price to sell the home because they are broke and have a high mortgage payoff.

- A seller who has exorbitant bills and debt and needs all of their equity to pay off seemingly insurmountable debt.

---

233 We often refer to these equally as investment opportunities.

☐ Certain HUD (Housing and Urban Development) houses or similar agencies, who cannot accept a certain percentage below the BPO[234] they received from their representing agent.

☐ Court-mandated sales where a judge sets a minimum price on a home.

☐ Certain types of auctions, which really are designed to drive prices skyward.

As stated earlier in the book, you can find out if a seller is motivated based on asking the simple question, *Why is the seller selling*? This information is crucial to you figuring out if a property is worth investigating.

Determining Home Value

In the world of American real estate, there are three types of ways that people determine what a home's actual market value is:

1. **The Sales Comparison Approach.**[235] This is the most common type of market evaluation a licensed appraiser will perform. Essentially, an appraiser will pull up a list of recent sales within a mile radius of the property that they are evaluating and look at what recently sold and how much per foot the houses were getting, on average. The appraiser will try to identify properties with similar features and amenities as the subject property, which have recently sold retail and, based on that, extrapolate a number per square foot, which represents an "appropriate" value for the home.

2. **The Income Approach.** Here, the appraiser evaluates the property's value based on the income it produces annually minus its expenses, as well as on other types of income-producing properties in the area, which are similar[236] using a local market condition known as a *gross rent multiplier.*

3. **The Cost Approach.** This is used generally by insurance companies to determine value based on estimated cost to rebuild.

Now, there are a myriad of problems with all three of these approaches, and it is important that you understand why **so you don't fall into a trap like so many other investors have**

---

234 **Broker Price Opinion** is used in foreclosed real estate. A bank or holding entity like HUD will frequently ask an agent to give an opinion of value of a foreclosed home, taking the condition and needed repairs of the home into consideration. A home with too high of a BPO can sit on the market for years because no one is willing to buy it.

235 Sometimes known as *The Comparable Approach.*

236 If he or she can find something similar, which can be difficult at times.

done—believing that a home is worth what an appraiser tells you. Appraisals can vary based on what purpose the appraisal is intended to serve. Consider the following:

Scenario 1: You get a home under contract for 100k. You then go to your bank for a loan of 100k on the home. The bank sends an appraiser out to the property.

Appraisal Result: The home appraises for 100k or very, very close to it, +/- about 2%. Why? *Because the bank's interest is not in determining true home value but in determining if the home is worth (minimally) what the bank is considering lending on it.*

Scenario 2: You get the same home under contract for 100k and are going to purchase it because your market analysis shows that you believe it is worth 200k. Your plan is to pay cash for the home, then refinance.[237] You then go to your bank for a refinance loan of 100k on the home after you close on the property. The bank sends an appraiser out to the property.

Appraisal result: The home appraises for 200k or very very close to it, +/- about 2%. Why? *Because the bank's interest IS in determining true home value and having a secure position based on equity,* so the bank needs to know what the actual value of the house is, not just determine minimum value based on a loan amount.

Now take these issues and add in the fact that the ***Sales Comparison Approach*** is based entirely on the value of other homes. This in and of itself becomes quite a challenge in many situations, for example, rural areas. What if the next home sale occurred twenty-five miles away in another state? What does one "compare" its value to?

Also, the ***Sales Comparison Approach*** can be ineffective and erroneous because let's say that you buy a house for 100k, and after you close on the home and move in, everyone else in the neighborhood all work for the same employer, who suddenly and unexpectedly transfers their employees out of town. Every house on your street forecloses for 10k. Well, assuming this happens, your house is also worth 10k, which is a 90% loss of value using the ***Sales Comparison Approach***.

Yet in a miraculous sequence of events, a guy who bought all the houses on the street for 10k fixes them up and sells them all for 200k! Now your house is worth 200k based on the ***Sales Comparison Approach***.

If you have been paying attention, it should be pretty clear to you—the ***Sales Comparison Approach*** to determining home value is a flawed one in so many instances.

Problems with the Income Approach

The problem with the Income Approach is simple: If a tenant is not in a commercial building and no rent is being received, the value of the property is ZERO. This makes

---

237   Known as a rate/term refi.

no sense because if the building burned down today, the insurance company would have to pay out based on the Cost Approach, which is a full retail market value payout. How is a building worth nothing simply because it has no tenants?

Problems with the Cost Approach

This is used in the construction and insurance industry, as well as in new development retail-type sales. Very few people pay for homes based on the Cost Approach.

Between these three appraiser tools of evaluation, most frequently, we are subjected to the **Sales Comparison Approach**. We need to learn how to evaluate homes based on this approach since appraisers will commonly use this, and most people give great credence to this method of determining value. However, before we learn how to analyze value, let me throw in **Feol's Approach for Determining Value**, which is as follows:

Feol's Approach for Determining Value

A house is worth what someone is willing to pay for it and no more.

How to Read and Understand Market Comparables

Inevitably, assuming you are searching for a discounted property to buy for the purposes of applying the principles of The Short-Term Retirement Program, you will end up at some point having a realtor send you what is commonly known as "comps" or sales comparables from their local realtor association. This information can help you determine value but takes a good deal of time to learn how to use. Here is a basic example.

4406 Ferndale: Basic Market Sales Comparables

Physical Data

Source	Date	SqFt	Sty	Rm	BR	Bth	Prk	Construction	Yrblt	Acres	Heat	CAP	LFP	Appr/MLS
Appraiser	08/2016	1683	1.0	9	3	2.0	G1A	Metal, Vinyl/	1951	0.20	Forced Air/Gas	Y N	0	APR71

Comparable Sales

New! Map these Comps!

Address	Dist	Map	Sale Date	Price	Type	Conc	Mtg	Src	Effec	SqFt	$/SF	Sty	Rm	BR	Bth	Prk	Const	CD	Yrblt	Acre	CA	P	H	F
4406 Ferndale Rd	0.00	s753A	6/16/16	48,800	Fore(TT)	-	CU	Apr	5/97	1483	33	1.0	7	3	2.0	C1A	Vm	G	1951	0.20	Y	N		
582 Sandridge St	0.82	753A	8/4/16	120,000	Norm(WD)	-	80CV	Apr	6/16	2137	56	1.0	6	3	2.0	G1D	Br/Wd	G	1947	0.22	Y		F	2
4462 Given Ave	0.14	753A	7/29/16	66,000	Norm(WD)	0	CU	Apr	6/02	1649	40	1.0	7	3	2.0	C1	Br/Wd	A	1951	0.17	N		O	
4467 Ferndale Rd	0.00	753A	7/12/16	20,000	Norm(WD)	-	CU	Apr	6/98	1264	16	1.0	6	3	1.0	0	Wd	G	1951	0.25	N	N		
1572 Russwood Rd	1.05	753A	7/5/16	50,000	Norm(WD)	-	CU	Apr	5/98	1588	31	1.0	6	2	2.0	G2D	Br/Vm	G	1957	0.21	Y	N		1
772 Novarese St	-	753A	7/1/16	43,500	Norm(WD)	4500	80CV	Apr	6/16	1324	33	1.0	7	3	2.0		Ot	A	1950	0.33	Y		F	
4374 Owen Rd	0.22	753A	6/29/16	74,900	Norm(WD)	4494	98FH	Apr	3/01	1671	45	1.0	6	3	2.0	G2D	Vm	A	1950	0.25	Y	N	G	
586 N Foy Cir	0.84	753A	6/16/16	52,000	Bank(WD)	0	CU	Apr	11/10	1430	36	1.0	6	3	1.1	G2A	Br/Wd	A	1955	0.47	Y	N	F	1
4480 Jamerson Ave	0.39	753A	5/31/16	55,000	Norm(WD)	-	CU	Tax	12/14	1657	33	1.0	6	3	2.0		Br		1961	0.16	Y		F	O
4602 Owen Rd	0.48	753A	5/6/16	78,900	Norm(WD)	-	98FH	Apr	10/02	1520	52	1.0	7	3	2.0		Vm	A	1951	0.24	Y	N	0	
964 Novarese St	-	753A	4/1/16	60,100	Norm(WD)	-	CU	Tax	12/14	1500	40	1.0	6	3	2.0	C1A	Br		1959	0.19	Y		F	O
4573 Perkins Grove Cv	0.54	753A	3/29/16	87,200	Bank(WD)	-	CU	Apr	3/06	1316	66	1.0	5	3	2.0	G2A	Br		2005	0.13	Y	N	F	1
4514 Violet Cv	0.21	753A	3/23/16	48,500	Bank(WD)	-	CU	Apr	2/16	1335	36	1.0	7	3	1.0		Br/Wd	F	1959	0.21	Y		F	O

Min Sale Price: $20,000 Max Sale Price: $120,000 Median Sale Price: $55,000

Min Sqft: 1264 Max Sqft: 2137 Avg Sqft: 1528

Avg Sale Price: $61,915 Avg PPSF: 41

In this case, our subject property is 4406 Ferndale. If you look at the headings on this sheet example, you see things like "Dist." (meaning, "distance from home"), construction (meaning, brick or vinyl, etc.) beds and baths, and price per square foot of recently sold homes.

The thing to glean from this example, however, is that other homes are selling for far more per square foot than my little property at 4406 Ferndale. What does that tell me? It tells me that I am buying a property far below its fair market value. Notice the next comparable on Sandridge Street for 120k! This is at $56 per foot, which is not unreasonable when a property is fully fixed up in good rental condition in my local market. **By the way, my purchase price on 4406 Ferndale was 44k**.

A general outline of how I determine value on homes to make sure I am getting a tremendous deal and to make sure I can pay a home off aggressively is as follows:

1. **Locate a suitable property in a good location.** Make sure the home is listed for a price, which is in your general price range, and using *Feol's Formula*, ensure your subject property's asking price is below market price supported by strong sales comparables.

2. **Walk the property, note the work needed, and determine the cost of the renovations necessary to get your home into livable, fully renovated condition.** *It may help to take a licensed contractor or friend who knows construction with you to make sure you see all potential issues.*

3. **Again, review the comparables.** Determine if you are buying an undervalued property using comparables and keeping in mind *Feol's Formula*.

4. **Once you have determined that the home is a good deal, make an offer, which is *"subject to inspection"*[238] and offer lower than the asking price. When you have an accepted contract, confirm the value of the home (after repairs) by obtaining a "pre-appraisal,"** which is an appraisal done in advance of work being completed to estimate fair market value based on sales comparables. Use a third-party licensed appraiser that you trust.

5. **Ensure that you have the home under contract bound by earnest money.**

6. **Based on your pre-appraisal, if the numbers do not work for you purchasing the home at an appropriate discount**, renegotiate the contract *or* move on to the next property. If necessary, exit using your "escape clause." Your realtor can help you with this. **Generally, you will ask in your contract for a period of time (usually numbered in days) to inspect and perform any repair estimates using licensed contractors.** If at the end of this period you do not want to move forward, simply have your agent notify the seller in writing and you get your earnest money back.[239]

Now the important thing to remember is that you need to make sure that you are not spending money needlessly to evaluate homes. **EVALUATING HOMES SHOULD COST YOU NOTHING MORE THAN YOUR TIME.** However, if you have a property that you are confident you want to purchase, a pre-appraisal will help you to solidify your home's true value and, in doing so, consider your financing options more wisely. Plus, they are very inexpensive.

However, it bears noting that when you make an offer on a property, you always need an escape clause. This is something like a line in the purchase contract stating that the offer is "subject to inspection," "subject to partner approval," and so forth. The reasoning for this is that you need to be able to get your earnest money back should you find a glaring issue with the property, which is as it should be and only makes sense. (Outlined above.)

Note, though, that I do not make blind offers on tons of homes. Once I find a home that is in an area suitable for me,[240] I will then look at the home, and **IF THE HOME IS PRICED ALREADY BELOW MARKET VALUE, I WILL THEN MAKE A LOWER OFFER**

---

238 A standard contractual escape clause.

239 Now, unlike most real estate *gurus* (I hate that word), I don't advocate trying to escape from every property. **That is like trying to roll with an opponent in jujitsu by trying to avoid them. It makes no sense.** You need to place homes under contract ONLY if you are serious about buying them, but escape if there is a structural issue or issue with value, etc.

240 And keep in mind, I do this generally for investment purposes, not for my primary residence, but the same skillset applies.

TO TRY TO NEGOTIATE A STEEPER DISCOUNT. And in my experience, this lower offer is usually accepted or, at the very least, countered with an offer priced higher than what I asked to pay but lower than the asking price, in which case I win anyway.

Here is a simple formula for determining value. It may look a bit complicated at first, but once you apply it a few times, it will become very natural to you as you look at various real estate deals.

Basic Property Value Discount Determination Formula

Purchase price + cost of repairs + closing costs (estimated) = acquisition price

Square footage of subject home × (average) sales comparable footage = fair market value of home[241]

Acquisition price/fair market value of home = pennies on dollar you are paying for home

Example: 4406 Ferndale, Memphis, Tennessee 38122
Purchase price (44k) + cost of repairs (20k) + closing costs (1k) = 65k (purchase price)
Square footage of home (1483) × sales comparable footage ($56) = $83,608 (FMV)
Acquisition price (65k) / FMV ($83,608) = 77 cents on the dollar or *a 23% discount*

Now, I got a pre-appraisal for this house—the home has a garage, which helps the value, so the appraiser allotted a 90k value for the home, slightly higher than our estimated per-square-foot value.

Using this formula, the numbers changed slightly, as follows:
Acquisition price/fair market value of home = pennies on dollar you are paying for home
We get this:
65k/90k = 72 cents on the dollar or, a *discount of roughly 30%*

---

241   A pre-appraisal or full appraisal will give you this number also, if you are uncertain.

"But that's not *Feol's Formula*!" you say. "You are paying more!"

Remember, Feol's Formula is simply a benchmark of where to begin your search. In the case of this property, the neighborhood is highly desirable and does, in fact, have rental footage that could generate income while I live there.[242] With repairs, my all-in price of 65k could easily be paid off in seven years or less while generating an $850-per-month income, which would almost offset the note entirely.

Feeling Pressured?

You should never feel trapped into buying real estate. Now, if you are not careful, you can find yourself in situations where you are being bullied and trapped into buying a house you don't want under the threat of suit. I know because I have been there. It was a tremendously uncomfortable place to be, and after the experience I was in, I will never be there again. However, remember two basic rules, and you will be fine:

1. **Do not make an offer on a house unless it really fits your criteria after doing ALL your due diligence.** Make sure you put down the minimum amount of earnest money when you do, and

2. **Make sure you use an escape clause so you can get out of the contract and get your earnest money back** should you have a reason to rescind and withdraw from the contract.

Under no circumstances should you let sellers or agents bully you into making a purchase. **If you find yourself in this situation, WALK AWAY and find a new agent and new seller to work with.** There are millions of them out there.

Multiple Offers and Time Constraints

One of my favorite lessons for my students is to teach them how to say no. **This is the most powerful word in the English language, and we use it too infrequently for fear of offending people or missing opportunity.** Too often today in business dealings are we subjected to unethical tactics designed to pressure us into making a decision immediately without due diligence. My favorite way to deal with this follows a conversation something along these lines:

---

242 Keep in mind, this is a theoretical example. I have already paid off many houses using these techniques and am in a different situation than a new investor just starting out.

> **Unethical, shady property seller:** I got TEN GUYS lined up to buy this property. If you want to buy it, you need to say yes RIGHT NOW.
>
> **Me (calmly, with my car keys in my hand as I prepare to leave):** Well, if you need an answer that quickly, my answer is NO.
>
> **Unethical guy:** Umm, well, what I meant to say was—
>
> **Me (leaving):** Next.

So that brings me to this very famous line I want you to start using in your life, as follows:

> *If you need an answer right now, the answer is* **NO.**

So many times, I end up in multiple-offer situations,[243] and while some of these are legitimate, ***very frequently these multiple-offer situations don't exist at all and are made up by the sales agents who are engaging in the unethical practice of trying to drive a property price higher to get a bigger sales commission.*** Now I have watched this situation unfold so many times, and I have called agents out on it in the past, but these days, for simplicity's sake, I simply move on to the next deal, note who the agent is, and refuse to do business with them in the future.

The point, however, is **DO NOT FEEL BAD IF YOU LOSE A DEAL OR PERCEIVED OPPORTUNITY**. In my experience, when I lose "the deal of a lifetime," another one comes along shortly thereafter (sometimes on the same day!). Because of this phenomenon, we have a saying at my brokerage, which goes like this:

> *The deal of the century usually comes around once a week.*

And over and over again, I find this to be true. You don't have to go running with the crowd in a frenzy to find a good deal. Sometimes they are hidden in plain sight and quite often in the pile of properties everyone has already picked over.

---

243 Situation where more than one purchaser has submitted an offer on a property and then the offering process becomes somewhat auction-like, where all bidders are expected to submit their "highest and best" offer by a specific date and time, it is presumed that the highest bidder is the winner, but this is not always the case.

Deal Analysis: Basics

Generally speaking, properties are priced by square foot. Using sales comparables, you can see what homes are selling for in your desired area per square foot.

When I find a property, I will frequently drive to other homes in the neighborhood that recently sold on the sales comparable sheet and look at them. Are they new? Do they have new features? Do they look like the house I am buying? Are they similar? This information tells my what types of houses are getting the best price in the neighborhood and gives me a roadmap to what I need to do, construction-wise, to my house to get it fixed up and worth its true fair market value.

Once you know this, and assuming your home needs cosmetic work to get it up to fair market condition, **take the price per square foot of similar homes that are fixed up and selling at retail price, and multiply that number by the square footage of your home.** In this case, if your home has 1,500 square feet and you bought it for $30 per foot (purchase price of 45k), but you see other homes that are fixed up with similar square footage selling in the same neighborhood, on average, for $60 per foot, your home is then potentially worth 90k[244], or double its value.

Back in Chapter 1, I outlined some basic construction questions you should ask on every home. Here they are again for your reference. I like to ask the seller these questions personally, but your real estate agent can get this information on your behalf also.

Is there any repair work needed on the home?

The seller is painfully aware (most of the time) of what is wrong with a property. Sometimes they are forthcoming about it, and sometimes they will try to hide maintenance issues for fear of scaring away potential buyers. Asking them directly is the first step to identifying trouble spots within a property.

Does the home have central heat and air?

If it does, what is the condition of it, and how old is it? Have there been any recent repairs to it or any known issues with either of the units (furnace or compressor)? These days, central heat and air are practically a prerequisite for most tenants looking for a rental property. You almost always want to have it in your primary residence, and in a vacation home, assuming you want to be comfortable or you want your potential vacation renters to be, this is a necessity. Look for old exterior units, rust on a/c

---

244 This assumes you do the renovations properly, with quality materials and labor, at a minimum builder-grade construction standard.

housing, flames shooting out of the furnace (indicates a cracked heat exchanger), and so on. HVAC systems are VERY costly, and when in doubt, a licensed heating and air technician will tell you what the actual condition is of the units.

What is the condition of the roof?

The roof is one of the most costly items a homeowner can be forced to replace. As such, look for multiple layers of shingles, old asbestos shingles with a "sheen" (shying and shrunk back from their original form), missing shingles, or a large prevalence of rotten wood on the cornice and fascia, which can indicate improper run off due to moisture entrapment. Exposed rotten wood and decking are all points of concern. Inside, roof problems are often indicated by staining (brownish/yellow in-ceiling sheetrock) mold presence, collapsed sheetrock, insulation, or an overall damp feeling in the house due to rainwater entering the home. When a roof has less than five years of serviceable life, plan on replacing it before a bigger problem occurs, such as sheetrock collapse. Try not to, as most people are convinced to do by unscrupulous roofing companies, make an insurance claim when you need a new roof. Save your insurance claims for large losses, like house fires.

Are there any tax or insurance issues we need to know about?

Outstanding tax liens on a property can cloud title and prevent you from buying a property, which can make you even looking at a property a huge waste of your time (ask me how I know this). Sometimes, due to insurance claims or environmental factors, a property may be uninsurable. You need to ensure that you ask these questions. Also ask if the property is in a flood zone, then verify with your insurance company if you are seriously considering buying.

Do you have title to the property?

This makes sure the person who says they can sell the property actually can.

Is there any seller financing available on the property?

This is the MOST IMPORTANT real estate investor question you can possibly ask. Any time you can get seller financing, you win in many, many ways.

> *If I pay you all cash and can offer a quick close, what is the least you will take for the property?*
>
> This gets to the point, finds the bottom line. It should always be followed up with, "Is that the best you can do?" after the seller names a price.
>
> *Why are you selling?*
>
> This gives you critical information that may help you gain an edge in negotiations.

Always determine the amount of work needed on a home and the cost basis for that work prior to purchase or even before making an offer.

Sometimes Homes Require Too Much Work

Always pass on homes with major structural work or situations where massively costed construction elements are needed to get a home into appraisable, fair market condition. *As a general rule, I try to buy homes that need only cosmetic renovations, like carpet and paint, whenever possible.*

Confirm Zoning and Ensure You Are Legally Compliant

Make sure you and your realtor are researching the zoning on the home you want to purchase. **Get a survey if necessary.** Remember, buying a home for income purposes, only to run into a legal issue with your local zoning or code officials, can be extremely hazardous to your future financial freedom! Don't be afraid to ask for a letter of compliance from your local zoning board. For example, if you are purchasing a duplex, send the zoning board a letter asking for them to send YOU a letter that the home is zoned appropriately for multifamily rental use. When you have this letter in your hand, you know you are in good shape and compliant with all appropriate zoning laws.[245]

Determining Rental Value Prior to Your Purchase

One thing that bears noting is that **no property should be purchased (assuming you are using strategies outlined in The Short-Term Retirement Program for aggressive**

---

245 You can also make this a contractual contingency—i.e., *"subject to an official zoning letter showing property is zoned for multifamily use."*

home payoff) without first determining what the fair market value of rental income you should expect is for the property you are considering.

Let me say this again:

> ### Short-Term Retirement Program's Cardinal Rule of Income
>
> No property should be purchased (assuming you are using strategies outlined in The Short-Term Retirement Program for aggressive home payoff) **without first determining what the fair market value of rental income you should expect** is for the property you are considering.

How do we determine realistic rental income value? There are many ways, all of which are FREE and will COST YOU NOTHING. A basic Internet search for rental units in your ZIP code is a great place to start, but of course, you must make sure you are comparing apples with apples, so to speak. If you have a one-bedroom studio for rent, it would not be comparable with a four-bedroom, two-bath residential home with a two-car garage, for example.

Here are a few ideas to get you started.

1. **Property Management Companies.** No one knows better what rental units can generate, income wise, than property management companies, as this is what they do for a living. If you want to get an idea of what a property management company can get for the rent on your particular income unit, all you have to do is call them, tell them you may be considering letting a management company manage your unit, and ask how much rent and deposit they think they can obtain for your unit. Test this approach with three different companies and go for the median (middle) rent among the three companies as a benchmark of where to start. **Beware!** Some management companies adopt a philosophy of renting below market to make a tenant stay longer and therefore ask significantly lower rents than the market dictates **(this also makes a unit MUCH easier to rent)**. Some companies, alternatively, will ask significantly higher rents to entice you to use their management, then come up short after you have signed the management agreement. When you are looking for rent ranges, you want rent ranges that are considered *conservative* or *appropriate*.[246] *Aggressive* rents are not what we are looking for.

---

246 Real estate financial modeling uses the terms *conservative, appropriate,* **and** *aggressive* to describe income projections for properties. Think low, medium, high.

2. **Rentometer.com**—a simple online tool that aggregates rental information in your selected ZIP code and lets you know—based on bedrooms, baths, and square footage—if your desired rent range is below market, at market, or above market. When Rentometer gets in the red, you are asking too much for your unit.

3. **Zillow.com**—another popular online tool that aggregates data for your easy reference.

4. **Craigslist.com**—under the real estate section, you can find homes offered for rent. Search your desired area and see what types of properties are being offered at what prices. This is your true market comparison.

5. **Your real estate agent** can provide you with rental comparables, using her multiple listing service tools through her local realty association.

6. **Drive your desired neighborhood and call on "For Rent" signs.** See what they are asking, how many beds and baths a property has, and so forth. Also note if appliances are included and what types of heating and cooling systems are in the property. Generally speaking, more modern cooling systems generate higher rent prices than older, more antiquated ones.

7. **Read classified ads in your local paper** assuming you have one.[247]

8. Attend your local ***Real Estate Investor Association***[248] meetings (***known as a REIA***) and ask experienced property owners what they think your home will rent for.

9. **Place an ad on Craigslist or other digital classified sites for your unit, at the rent you feel is appropriate, and see if you get any responses.** You can also place a different ad on a different classified site (at the same time) with a slightly lower rent and compare the response rate for the two ads. This is known as A/B testing.

10. **Use free local real estate magazines, found at your local grocery store** to determine who is asking what dollar amount on properties in your desired area.

Obviously, the list is endless, but once you tap a few of these resources, you will be able to determine what an appropriate market rent is in your area and plan accordingly for your specific unit, using that information to evaluate your financial projections with regard to mortgage payoff, principal prepayment, time reduced through multiple payments, and so forth.

---

247   Newsprint media is dying, partly because people get their news online and from websites, and partially because the media continues to lower its standards for journalistic integrity, as people wake up to the fact that almost all major media conglomerates are monopolized. **The CIA and other agencies also have their hand at work propagandizing the newsrooms. Here is one of many examples:** http://www.mintpressnews.com/u-s-intelligence-infiltrates-news-media-threatening-a-free-press/51243/

248   Your local REIA group can be an invaluable resource for you on your journey, assuming it is run well.

Getting the Deal Done: Finalizing Your Financial Projections

So you have done your research and found your house. You are working on negotiating with the seller or perhaps you have already done so and have the home under contract. You have viewed the property, performed a construction and repair analysis, and all of this fits within your budget. You have gotten a mortgage product, know your interest rate, and have selected a time period in which you can pay the home off or have opted to take an amortization a bank forces upon you with the idea of prepaying the home off in a specific amount of years based on your financial plan.[249] You have obtained a pre-appraisal showing that you are buying undervalued real estate and have a strong equity position in the home you are purchasing. You have identified the rent amount your rental unit on the property will generate. What's left to do before you close?

Finalize your financial projections.

Use this simple calculator to determine your payoff adding in rents, taxes, and insurance costs (which you have identified up front). I am using, in this instance, the property at 4406 Ferndale as an example. Also note, I estimated the taxes and insurance in this example, **whereas YOU need to input the actual numbers, to the penny, of your personal property prospect to get an exact idea of your monthly cost obligation.**

The Short-Term Retirement Program Financial Projections CashCalc	
Property Address	4406 Ferndale
	Memphis, Tennessee 38122
Property Cost	
Purchase price	$44,000.00
Work needed	$20,000.00
Closing costs (estimated)	$1,000.00
Total estimated cash costs	$65,000.00
Fair market value	$100,000.00[255]
Discount off retail market value	35.00%
Rental Unit Income Information—Monthly	
Monthly rent	$850.00

---

249 Ideally, ten years or less until fully paid off.

Management fee (if applicable)	$0.00
City taxes	$25.00
County or school taxes	$75.00
Insurance (estimated)	$50.00
Monthly cash flow	$700.00
Cash-on-cash return	12.92%
Financing Information	
Mortgage amount	$65,000.00
Down payment	$5,000.00
Loan amount	$60,000.00
Interest rate	5.00%
Loan terms (in months)	72 <—Change Amortization Here In Months
Monthly payment (principal and interest)	$966.30
Monthly net positive cash flow (shortage)	-$266.30[256]
Total cash contribution to pay off home	$19,173.31
Six-year amortization, includes all impounds	

Note in this case the calculator does ALL the work for you. You just input your loan terms, rental unit income, amortization schedule and interest rate, and taxes and insurance, and the calculator tells you what your monthly note is and what it becomes less your rental income payment. **Keep in mind, a negative number in red indicates a loss each month, which would dictate that YOU have to pay a difference to make the note on top of the rental income generated from your unit**. Also note, this does not count for utilities, which you would have to pay anyway on your personal unit presumably.

But what if you don't want to carry a negative note each month until your loan pays off? **In this case, simply change the amortization schedule (in months) until you are break even or slightly positive (in this case it took us from six years to nine years).** See below; *the only factor I changed was the loan term in months.* All other variables remained constant.

The Short-Term Retirement Program Financial Projections CashCalc	
Property Address	4406 Ferndale
	Memphis, Tennessee 38122
Property Cost	
Purchase price	$44,000.00
Work needed	$20,000.00
Closing costs (estimated)	$1,000.00
Total estimated cash costs	$65,000.00
Fair market value	$100,000.00
Discount off retail market value	35.00%
Rental Unit Income Information—Monthly	
Monthly rent	$850.00
Management fee (if applicable)	$0.00
City taxes	$25.00
County or school taxes	$75.00
Insurance (estimated)	$50.00
Monthly cash flow	$700.00
Cash-on-cash return	12.92%
Financing Information	
Mortgage amount	$65,000.00
Down payment	$5,000.00
Loan amount	$60,000.00
Interest rate	5.00%
Loan terms (in months)	108 <—Change Amortization Here
Monthly payment (principal and interest)	$691.04
Monthly net positive cash flow (shortage)	$8.96
Total cash contribution to pay off home	-$968.07
Nine-year amortization, includes all impounds	

Now, [250] a nine-year note may seem a bit long to you after reading about six-year note payoffs, but keep in mind, in this situation, the tenant is paying your note and you are, in effect, freerolling[251] until your mortgage is fully retired.

What could be more powerful than that?

Now you are beginning to see that this program truly works, if only you change your mind-set a bit, and instead of paying full retail for homes and shouldering the burden of the monthly payment yourself for thirty years, you purchase at a steep discount and let someone else (who, keep in mind, is going to pay rent somewhere, anyway) pay your note FOR YOU using an aggressive loan term so you do NOT give the banks exorbitant rates of collected monthly interest and instead apply what would be thrown-away interest to reducing your principal balance instead each month resulting in YOU paying down your note in record time.

Finding the Deals—A Guide for New Investors

In my real estate career, I have found that everyone goes through the same cycle as they begin to study the investing process. Essentially, in the beginning, they are so blinded by the fact that you can get amazing discounts on properties that they come to believe that finding discounted properties (hereafter known as "deals") is practically impossible. So frequently in seminars, new investors and fledgling wholesalers inevitably ask me the same question: *"Robert, where (and how) do you find your deals?"*

However, after years of doing this, I remain MORE convinced than ever that **finding the deals is the easiest part** and finding end buyers and investors who are legitimate and liquid enough to purchase properties for your resale purposes is the more difficult of the two endeavors. The good news is, this book deals almost exclusively with buying a specific type of property with a very laser-focused purpose in mind, **so I want to reassure you that finding discounted property opportunities is somewhat easy, simple, and can be done almost every day with little effort.**

First let's review Feol's Formula once more.

---

250 You can always take a thirty-year loan, as we discussed, and then pay monthly based on your rental income and what you can afford. Just use the CashCalc to figure out a loan term that works for you, but know your monthly interest from the thirty-year loan and then ADD your principal payment to stay on schedule. For example, if your monthly interest payment is $200 of your payment and paying $700 toward your note pays your home in seven years, don't send the company a check for $700. You would need to send a check for $900, reflecting your interest obligation plus prepayment to stay on a seven-year schedule.

251 A gambling term.

Again, this is the benchmark that I use to give me a rough idea of where to start looking, pricewise, for my deals. If my fair market value is 200k, I will start looking for houses in the 100k range, less any repairs that need to be performed.

Keep in mind, that doesn't mean I am not willing to pay more for a home, if needed. But *Feol's Formula* gives us a great starting place to work with. Remember, in most cases, your primary residence will be able to generate one source of income monthly on average.[252] Paying *retail* for a home and having one income-producing unit *doesn't really make sense*. Let's assume a 200k house with a rental unit income of $800 per month. As you will see, in this case (keep in mind we aren't even calculating taxes and insurance), carrying the note by ourselves (to the tune of almost $1,100 per month), plus prepaying the $800 still gives us a loan term of almost twelve years. A long time! See this example:

Basic Loan Information				
		Loan Amount		$200,000.00
		Interest Rate		5.00%
	Loan term (in months)			360
	Monthly Payment			$1,073.65
	# of payments - First year			12
Extra Payments	*Interval*	*Amount*	*Start in Month*	*Duration*	*End in Month*
	Monthly	$643.00	1	Until end of Loan	

Interest Saved and Term Reduction with Extra Payments	*without extra payments*	*with extra payments*
Loan term	360 Months	142 Months
Total Interest Paid	$186,508.65	$65,124.55
Interest Saved Over Monthly Payment Loan		$121,384.10
Loan Term Will Be Shortened By		218 Months

---

252 Assumes a mother-in-law wing, rental unit, RV, or roommates, for example.

But what if we paid 100k for the same house worth 200k? *The difference is stark and illustrates why seeking out significant discounts is so critical if your goal is financial freedom.*

Basic Loan Information				
		Loan Amount		$100,000.00
		Interest Rate		5.00%
		Loan term (in months)		360
		Monthly Payment		$536.83
		# of payments—First year		12
Extra Payments	*Interval*	*Amount*	*Start in Month*	*Duration*	*End in Month*
	Monthly	$800.00	1	Until end of Loan	

Interest Saved and Term Reduction with Extra Payments	*without extra payments*	*with extra payments*
Loan term	360 Months	90 Months
Total Interest Paid	$93,251.69	$20,085.01
Interest Saved Over Monthly Payment Loan		$73,166.68
Loan Term Will Be Shortened By		270 Months

And of course, in this case, if you choose to pay the $536 monthly note and prepay the $800 rent from your rental unit, this 100k loan gets retired in ninety months, or 7.5 years. **Again, this is a powerful illustration of why we cannot, and must refuse, to pay retail for a home. Simply put, we cannot beat the math of purchasing a full retail home and then having the bank's front-loaded mortgage algorithm keep us captive to decades of mortgage payments.**

If you have been paying attention throughout this book, you should inevitably be coming to the conclusion that **EVEN THOUGH YOUR BANKER TELLS YOU A THIRTY-YEAR LOAN IS THE MOST "AFFORDABLE" LOAN INSTRUMENT, NOT ONLY IS IT UNAFFORDABLE FOR THE AVERAGE AMERICAN FAMILY, BUT ALSO, IT ALLOWS YOU TO BUY "TOO MUCH HOUSE"** in exchange for thirty years of highly profitable interest payments to the bank.

Simply put, any banker who tells you a thirty-year mortgage is "the most affordable loan product" is uneducated or **IS LYING TO YOU.**

By necessity, we MUST seek out discounted homes in the areas where we want to live.

What Makes a Home Become Discounted?

In a nutshell, there is only one reason why homes become discounted—that reason is SELLER MOTIVATION. However, there are many factors that contribute to seller motivation. Here are a few:

- ☐ Seller is behind on payments.

- ☐ Seller is transferring jobs or has transferred and is carrying two payments (probably two thirty-year mortgage payments).

- ☐ Seller has not paid their taxes and is facing losing the home to tax sale.[253]

- ☐ Seller is divorcing and a court-mandated sale has the seller ***needing*** to sell.

- ☐ Estate sale (or probate court)—property owner passed away and a family inherited the home from far away and want to be rid of it for emotional and economic reasons.

- ☐ Bank has foreclosed on a home and must now pay the taxes on the property.

- ☐ City has abandoned homes that may be for sale under a blight or neighborhood restoration program in an effort to clean up parts of the city that have fallen into disrepair.

- ☐ Seller has fallen behind on payments and bank is willing to accept a short sale.[254]

- ☐ Seller is ill or unable to maintain payments or upkeep on a home.

- ☐ Seller has a home that needs repairs, but they are financially unable to make the needed repairs, so they must accept a discounted sales price.

- ☐ Seller hates weather in local area (long winters, etc.).

- ☐ A natural disaster (tree falling through house) has taken place, and homeowner has no insurance OR took the insurance claim, paid off the mortgage, and is moving on, leaving the existing home there.[255]

---

253 Tax-sale property is beyond the scope of this book, but if you are interested in looking at tax-sale properties, make sure you are familiar with the state's (where the property is located) ***Right of Redemption*** rules for real property. Sometimes you can buy a house at tax sale, and the owner has a right to pay that tax debt off and reclaim the house for several years. **Make sure you do your homework.**

254 Seller owes 100k, and bank is willing to accept 60k to avoid taking the house back—a very profitable way to buy houses but extremely time-consuming both in paperwork and wait time. **For a good primer on short sales, go to DonDerosa.com.**

255 You would be amazed at how much it actually costs to fix a house after a tree falls through it versus what an insurance company pays for these claims. You can buy a house very inexpensively after a homeowner has pocketed an insurance claim and moved on to greener pastures.

☐ Seller had a tragic loss (death of spouse, for example) and cannot bear to continue to live in the same house.

You get the idea. Hardships happen to people every day, and frequently these people own real estate. Remember at the beginning of the book—real estate is illiquid. **Well, now this comes into play.** When you have cash lined up or a mortgage ready to go and people have a problem that needs to be solved through the sale of their property, taking a discount to have whatever headache they are having go away permanently starts to look pretty good.

One Man's Trash Is Another Man's...Income-Producing Real Estate?

Something my director of sales, Patrick Burleson, and I joke about all the time is how "bad" people think houses are that need repair. Everyone is an "expert" on real estate and construction, and they all "know" how much it takes to fix up houses, which, generally speaking, is a great help to me in my business because they really don't know anything at all, and tend to really overprice the cost to repair items, which gives me tremendous discounts when buying distressed property.

The worst house I have ever been in was a home owned on Tutwiler Street in Memphis, Tennessee. Now this home was owned by a motorcycle gang, and it was practically impossible to enter. There was so much hoarding, clothing, chattel, needles, drug paraphernalia, not to mention that there was no electricity, I was literally falling through the subfloor, climbing over unwashed roach-filled rags...I mean, this place more easily could have been bulldozed. For fun, somebody had placed a bunch of lamps on TOP of the roof. How the house wasn't condemned was a total mystery to me.

We didn't bulldoze it; however, we bought it for 10k and spent about 30k fixing it up. Adding on an extra bedroom and bath made the existing structure a four-bedroom, two-bath home with great curb appeal, and during the construction process, we added on a new dimensional roof, new plumbing, mechanical, and everything necessary to ensure a family could live there comfortably and safely. In the end, the home rented for $950 per month. So if a home is *that bad* and can be salvaged, hopefully this gives you an idea of what can be done by seeing past the repairs a house needs and pricing them out with skilled contractors accordingly.

My point in telling you this story is that homes that have needed repairs are often overlooked by other investors due to the nature of these repairs, which can seem unsightly and be an instant turn off. But remember, unless a home has major structural or fire damage, most repairs can be done reasonably by a skilled tradesman. As you get to know homes and repair allotments for standard projects on homes (repainting a 1,000-square-foot home, for example, or placing ceramic tile in a 15x15 kitchen) you will be able to ascertain mentally how much something costs within seconds, for both labor and material. **Always remember, the lower a home's price for purchase, the more you can allocate for construction and repair costs.**

Again, for reference:

> *The lower a home's price for purchase, the more you can allocate for construction and repair costs.*
>
> **Quiz Question:** Suppose you have a house you can buy for 60k, but it needs 30k in work for a total cost basis of 90k. You don't want to be in the house for more than 70k. What do you do?
>
> **Answer:** Renegotiate the 60k purchase price to 40k or move to the next house.
>
> When in doubt, ***ALWAYS*** renegotiate.

Beginning Your Search

Setting out on your search for a suitable residential property that will pay for itself can seem like a daunting task. Perhaps, before you read this book, your focus was doing what most Americans do when it comes to the home ownership process—that is, get qualified for a thirty-year loan and buy as much house as you can "afford," in the nicest area you can "afford."

Now, you may have had your thinking turned upside down. It is impossible, as I have demonstrated, to beat the math of the thirty-year loan, and so now you may be looking at a completely different set of parameters, different locations where you can find either discounted opportunities or locales where "ready to go" income-producing units may be more prevalent. Perhaps you are getting creative and thinking about buying a home with some land for income purposes.[256] But no matter what your strategy is, starting out can be an intimidating and seemingly almost overwhelming task.

---

256 Land, obviously, can be rented to other people with farming interests, who pay you in cash and in produce. You can also grow your own food. **A savvy Short-Term Retirement Program student may look for both land AND property on that land, which can produce rental income.** Show me that person, and I will show you someone who will be financially free in just a few short years.

Remember, You Don't Know Everything

Sometimes, if we are new or inexperienced at something (like real estate), we tend to let our pride get the better of us and become afraid or too intimidated to ask questions or admit to someone that we do not have all the answers. **I have found in my journey, however, that sometimes the most powerful thing you can do is admit that you don't know something and then go to local experts on the subject, pick their brain, read and research as much as you can, and then use your knowledge to achieve what you set out to do.** A very talented sensei of mine once told me that if you read fifty books on any given subject, you are probably one of the top experts on the subject in the United States, relatively speaking. I don't have any data on this, but assuming you read fifty books on a subject, you certainly have a strong command of that particular compartment of knowledge, to be sure.

In the case of your primary residence, however, you need to remember that YOU DON'T KNOW EVERY NEIGHBORHOOD IN TOWN. **Even if you have lived in your municipality for over ten years, you, generally speaking, drive the same streets every day, shop at the same markets every day, and, essentially, have settled into a comfortable niche that serves you well; but it doesn't necessarily expose you to other neighborhoods WITHIN YOUR MUNICIPALITY.**

The thing is, unless you are constantly monitoring your local city's legislation and restorative works for various neighborhoods, you are probably unaware of what parts of the city are scheduled for revitalization or have been undergoing revitalization. And this money invested into the city's infrastructure can create MASSIVE opportunities for you to prosper financially, if you find the right areas with a bit of luck and timing.

For example, when I moved to Memphis, Tennessee, back in 2000, the area known as "midtown" Memphis was a total dump and was frequently considered a "bad" area. Today, however, it is very hard to find quality housing in midtown Memphis because, simply put, everyone wants to live there. The revitalization of midtown by the City of Memphis government has generated dozens of stores, restaurants, major investment from retailers like Whole Foods, and so on. Because of this, housing prices have SOARED.[257]

Now no one knows the future, obviously, but if your local municipality is committed to investing tens of millions of dollars into an area, there may be some undervalued real estate opportunities for you to consider.

---

257 Midtown Memphis also has massive concentration of guest apartments, carriage houses, and Airbnbs. Get the idea?

Where to Begin

The three predominant factors that will dictate your search for a primary residence using *The Short-Term Retirement Program's* guidelines are as follows:

1. How much house you can "afford";

2. What your threshold (tolerance) is for your mortgage payoff, in years; ***and***

3. How much rental income you can generate from your prospective property.

Now, when we discuss how much "house" you can afford, this breaks down into three principal factors, as follows:

1. **Cash—how much do you have (if any)?** Is your plan to pay cash for the property or simply use your cash as a down payment? If you are paying all cash, obviously you would ignore a mortgage payoff threshold and focus on generating (and saving) the monthly rental income you generate. However, most Americans will NOT be paying cash for their primary residence, so a mortgage needs to be considered.

2. **Mortgage qualification—can you qualify for a mortgage?** If so, what has your "banker" told you that you can borrow?[258] If you cannot qualify for a mortgage, don't worry, we will discuss locating and obtaining favorable seller financing in the next chapter.

3. **Projected income from rents**. How much can your residence generate each month in rental income? You then extrapolate this income to your mortgage payoff.

Also, this variable needs to be considered:

> When considering how long you plan on keeping your loan in place (before paying it off), you generally have two choices for payment, as follows:
>
> ☐ **Use the rental income from your unit to pay your mortgage monthly, and in doing so, keep your earnings from your employer** (or other sources of income, whatever they are) for savings, debt reduction, bill payment, or investment purposes. Keep in mind, this results in a longer note term. *Or*
>
> ☐ **Use the rental income from your unit with a supplemental payment from YOUR personal income to accelerate the mortgage payoff.** This results in less disposable cash each month for you, but more time (AND income) without a mortgage down the line.[259]

---

258 Remember, just because your banker tells you that you can borrow "x" amount of dollars does NOT mean you borrow it all. He expects you to use a thirty-year loan, which makes his dollar figure work for him. ***Remember, you have to search for deeply discounted property and REFUSE to pay retail.***

259 Keep in mind, ***several years*** down the line.

Remember the Short-Term Retirement Mortgage Affordability Calculator? It really comes into play as you begin your search.

Let's use a hypothetical girl as an example. We will call her Tennessee. Tennessee has been living at home with her parents, but she wants to move into her own residential house and has read this book, **so she understands how powerful using rental income to offset your mortgage payment can be.** Tennessee just got a nursing job. She starts out at 40k/year. First, let's see how much she takes home each month as a benchmark for what becomes "affordable" when considering her monthly mortgage payment.

Tennessee the Nurse Example: A 40k per Year Earner

See below for Tennessee's take-home pay breakdown, calculated annually.

In summary, she takes home $20,085.14 per year. When we divide that by twenty-six pay periods every two weeks, she brings home $772.50.[260]

For reference, her total take-home pay monthly is $1,545. Let's focus on that number.

Figure L: Tennessee's Take-Home Pay

Gross Pay ($)		
Pay period:		Biweekly
Gross pay ($):		$40,000.00
Filing Status and Withholding		
Filing status:		Single
Number of withholding allowances (#):		0
Before Tax Adjustments		
Qualified tax deferral plan, such as 401K (%):		5.00%
Other before tax deductions, such as HSA ($):		$0.00
After Tax Adjustments		
State and local income tax percentage (%):		4.00%
Other after tax deductions ($):		$0.00
After tax reimbursements ($):		$0.00
Results		
Gross pay:		$40,000.00
Allowance deduction:	$0.00	
Qualified plan deduction:	$2,5000.00	$2,500.00
Other before tax deductions:	$0.00	$0.00
Federal taxable wages:	$38,000.00	
Federal tax withholding:		$13,334.86
FICA Social Security withholding:		$2,480.00
FICA Medicare withholding:		$580.00
State and local income tax withholding:		$1,520.00
Other after tax reductions:		$0.00
Reimbursements:		$0.00
Net pay including any claimed tips:		$20,085.14
Net take home pay:		**$20,085.14**

---

260 It bears mentioning, once again, how the much the US government disfavors the working class by taxing them so heavily. In this case, Tennessee the nurse gives away 50% of her take-home pay to taxation. Yet, if she had an LLC business that generated 40k per year, she would not pay even half that much in taxes.

Using the Short-Term Retirement Mortgage Affordability Calculator: Some Ideas

Now, if our nurse goes to her banker, she will be told that she can afford roughly three times her gross pay as a mortgage note, assuming she uses a thirty-year amortization, which is a mortgage of $120,000.[261] That gives us this mathematical breakdown:

Financing Information—Tennessee's Thirty-Year Loan at 120k	
Mortgage amount	$120,000.00
Down payment	$0.00
Loan amount	$120,000.00
Interest rate	5.00%
Loan terms (in months)	360
Monthly payment (P & I)	$644.19

Now, interestingly enough, let's see what that mortgage payment is for Tennessee *as a percentage of her take-home pay.*

$644.19 (mortgage payment monthly)/$1,545 (take-home pay monthly) = 41.6% of Tennessee's total take-home pay.

That's almost HALF of her take-home pay for thirty years![262] There is no way Tennessee can get by with blindly throwing half of her paycheck in the trash, for half of her life. If she takes this loan, she will be putting herself into a state of financial hardship from DAY ONE!

The math simply doesn't work.

Yet Bob the Banker is giving Tennessee a prequalification letter for 120k, which means she still CAN get a mortgage, if she is ready to make such a terrible, life-altering mistake.

And we will all agree that if Tennessee used a thirty-year loan, the *MOST* she can afford is a 120k house. Let's use 120k as a benchmark for the neighborhood she wants to live in.

---

261 Very general banking rule—remember, lending-industry loan qualifications are constantly in flux and subject to change at any time. **Consult with your lender for qualification information and mortgage rates.**

262 Do you get it yet? **DO YOU SEE IT NOW?** Do you understand why you, and millions of other Americans, can simply NOT get ahead? Do you see how this mortgage hamstrings you and generations of your family for years and years to come?

I think, however, giving away half of your paycheck to ANYTHING is probably a bit too much, and as stated before, Tennessee has read this book, so she is much more informed and wary about taking on a thirty-year mortgage obligation. So let's cut her home's purchase price in half and see what Tennessee can afford if she gives 25% of her monthly paycheck at 5% interest to a home mortgage. How will that stack up?

The Mortgage Affordability Calculator tells us clearly, seen below.

Figure M: Tennessee's Purchase Power with 25% of Her Monthly Take-Home Pay at 5% Fixed Interest

STR Mortgage Affordability Calculator

Inputs	Desired Monthy Payment	Desired Interest Rate
	$386.25	5.00%
Purchasing Power		
	5-Year Payment	$20,467.66
	7-Year Payment	$27,327.90
	10-Year Payment	$36,416.17

Hmmm...even on a ten-year note, Tennessee's meager 25% of her total monthly take-home pay mortgage payment only gets her to a 36k house. That would be a difficult stretch, for someone planning to live in a 120k neighborhood. Is all hope lost?

Oh, but wait, we forgot to add in Tennessee's rental unit income! Now, Tennessee hasn't even begun her house search, but let's say she knows she can get at least $600 in monthly rent from roommates (again, this is the bare minimum). How does the *Mortgage Affordability Calculator* stack up now?

Figure N: Tennessee's Purchase Power with 25% of Her Monthly Take-Home Pay at 5% Fixed Interest Plus Rental Income of $600 per Month.[263]

STR Mortgage Affordability Calculator

Inputs	Desired Monthy Payment	Desired Interest Rate
	$986.25	5.00%
Purchasing Power		
	5-Year Payment	$52,262.08
	7-Year Payment	$69,779.00
	10-Year Payment	$92,984.98

Wow! Now we are getting somewhere. **Tennessee, by adding in rental income of $600 per month, can now afford a 93k house, assuming she is willing to take a ten-year loan.**

Is it realistic to get a 93k home, which needs some inexpensive cosmetic work in a 120k neighborhood? **YES, THIS HAPPENS ALL THE TIME; THEY ARE CALLED FORE-CLOSURES.**[264]

But what if Tennessee does some additional property research and finds a home that has a guest apartment she thinks will rent for $750 per month? The ***Mortgage Affordability Calculator*** should tell us exactly what we need to know.

---

263 Note that in this figure, we take 25% of Tennessee's take-home nursing pay and add $600 to it from roommate income, for a total monthly payment of $986.25.
264 I repeat, **YES, THIS HAPPENS ALL THE TIME; THEY ARE CALLED FORECLOSURES.**

Figure O: Tennessee's Purchase Power with 25% of Her Monthly Take-Home Pay at 5% Fixed Interest Plus Rental Income of $750 per Month

STR Mortgage Affordability Calculator

Inputs	Desired Monthy Payment	Desired Interest Rate
	$1,136.25	5.00%
Purchasing Power		
5-Year Payment		$60,210.69
7-Year Payment		$80,391.77
10-Year Payment		$107,127.18

And it does. It tells is exactly what we need to know—that Tennessee can almost pay "full retail" for her house by giving up 25% of her paycheck for ten years and having someone else help her each month with her mortgage by paying her $750 per month as rental income.

Lastly, for fun, let's say Tennessee really underestimated her guest apartment's rental value and was able to rent it out for $1,000 per month. What do those numbers look like?

[See figure on following page]

Figure P: Tennessee's Purchase Power with 25% of Her Monthly Take-Home Pay at 5% Fixed Interest Plus Rental Income of $1,000 per Month

STR Mortgage Affordability Calculator

Inputs	Desired Monthy Payment	Desired Interest Rate
	$1,386.25	5.00%
Purchasing Power		
	5-Year Payment	$73,458.37
	7-Year Payment	$98,079.73
	10-Year Payment	$130,697.52

Wow! In this case, she can afford MORE than her banker told her she could. **Naturally, her banker will not allow her to "overborrow," as she does not qualify for 130k by her paystubs and she has no rental history on the home that she has yet to purchase and take title to.** But it is an interesting and eye-opening exercise. And, of course, Tennessee could get very close to her desired home's purchase price of 120k simply by using $1,000 per month of income from her rental unit and negotiating her interest rate a bit, as follows:

Figure Q: Tennessee's Purchase Power with 0% of Her Monthly Take-Home Pay at 3% Fixed Interest Plus Rental Income of $1,000 per Month

STR Mortgage Affordability Calculator

Inputs	Desired Monthy Payment	Desired Interest Rate
	$1,000.00	3.00%
Purchasing Power		
5-Year Payment		$55,652.36
7-Year Payment		$75,681.32
10-Year Payment		$103,561.75

Our ideal scenario is shown here. **Our young nurse, Tennessee—just starting out and giving half of her paycheck to various US government entities before she takes home a dime—can still afford her primary residence with NONE of her own money, if she has a renter in the guest apartment at her home paying her $1,000 per month and getting her interest rate lowered by two points.**[265] In doing so, she will have the property paid off in ten years.[266]

So let's summarize what we just learned as some applicable principles for assessing your tolerance regarding mortgage exposure.

---

265 **Remember, rates are ALMOST ALWAYS lower on shorter, more aggressive loan terms.**

266 Now, keep in mind, I do not factor taxes and insurance into the equation here, **but they are very real expenses that need to be accounted for.** In this case, if Tennessee's monthly cost basis was $100 for taxes and insurance, she could ask $1,100 in rental income to offset or run the numbers at $900 per month in principal payment with the other $100 of rent offsetting the tax and insurance burden. **But keep in mind this lowers your purchasing power, so be aware of how this can change your mortgage affordability.**

Short-Term Retirement Rules: Assessing Your Tolerance for Affording and Paying Off Your Mortgage in Ten Years or Less: Some Guidelines

1. Determine 25% of your total take-home pay;

2. Decide if you have projected rental income from your property, and determine the rent range of that income;

3. Decide if you want to subsidize your monthly mortgage with your take-home pay, or if you just want to use the rental income to generate your monthly mortgage payment each month;

4. Use your rental income payment or add your rental income payment with your mortgage subsidy[267] in the Mortgage Affordability Calculator to determine your loan amount in years;

5. Search for suitable properties in that price range with projected rental income that fits your parameters; and

6. When you find a suitable property, always perform your due diligence as stated on page 177.

And of course, always remember:

Never use more than 25% of your take-home pay to make your mortgage payment. DO NOT FORGET, your most desirable housing payment is ZERO! *Use your tenant's monthly rent to make your housing payment.*

Now Back to Finding Deals

The key to finding deals is primarily to know your purchase prerequisites. I have people bring me "deals" all the time that I am simply unable to do anything with; for example, bringing me a house worth 1.6 million that I can buy for 1.3 million. The truth is, the holding costs and repairs on a property like that are extremely cost prohibitive and make no sense for me versus the financial risk I would have to take to acquire and (hopefully) resell something like that profitably.

---

267   i.e., allotment of take-home pay you want to use for additional payment each month on your mortgage coupon.

In the same venue, YOU must be laser focused on finding deals that fit your price range. As you begin your search, keep in mind you will have to dig through many homes to find the right one for you. Something to consider in your search is this: What makes a property "right" for you to live in? Make a list and write down what you need versus want, what you cannot do without, and so on. Married couples with children will have a far more extensive list of requirements, but **the reality is, the house of your dreams, which can also provide you with financial freedom, IS out there; you just have to find it.**

Once you have compiled your list of wants and needs for your home and you have used the *Mortgage Affordability Calculator* to determine your purchasing power and you have your ducks in a row financially (meaning, you have qualified for a home mortgage or have some other source of financing[268] that can help you acquire a property), you can set out to begin the search, keeping in mind your price range and the amount of rental income a unit has to generate in order for you to pay off your home in a specified period of time that **YOU** have set forth.[269]

Seeking a Seller for the End of My Financial Debt Enslavement

That sounds like a silly title, but in reality, that is what you are doing when you are seeking an income-producing property for a quick-term payoff using the ideologies provided by **The Short-Term Retirement Program.** You are looking for a seller who offers one or more of the following:

- [ ] **A significantly discounted price point, far under retail, that allows you to pay off your loan quickly** while providing you with equity, which adds to your net worth and can become liquid cash down the road.[270]

- [ ] **Square footage or a floorplan that allows you to have your personal space as well as income-producing rentable space** to offset your monthly note.

- [ ] **Land to use for income purposes, if desired** (storage, farming, additional rental units that are not on a foundation like an RV, hunting land, etc.).

- [ ] **Seller's terms,** as in a willingness to carry a mortgage each month versus you having to obtain one from a lending institution such as a bank.

---

268 Keep in mind, if you cannot qualify for a loan and need seller financing, this may narrow your search to homes where sellers are willing to carry your mortgage for you. But don't despair! **I bought my dream Adirondack home using this very method, as described in Chapter 1.** So I know you can do it too.

269 And keep in mind, thirty-year terms are NOT an option.

270 **Don't get too excited; remember, net worth is dead. These things are irrelevant for those swimming in debt; only spendable liquid cash, which reduces debt, matters.**

☐ **Other favorable amenities that you are seeking** for income or business purposes.[271]

And when you find this seller, who has a property for you that will fill all your requisite living, housing, and income needs, your life can change permanently. The thing is, you need to be prepared to search deeply and have patience to not only find a property, but to find the *right* property. **Too frequently do buyers get approved for a home loan, and within days, they have found a property**. When you are searching for "the right" property, in all likelihood, your search will not end so successfully, so quickly. Remember my search for a vacation home as told in Chapter 1 of this book? I had to use a lot of creative ideas and kiss a lot of "frogs" before we found the right combination of factors that allowed us to get an income-producing, paid-off vacation home within six months of purchase and within one year of starting our search. Granted that is an exceptional story, and you do not need to hit quite such a "home run" in your journey to be able to pay your home off early with other people's rent money. **But it gives you an idea of what becomes possible when you open your mind to it.**

Casting Your Net: Identifying Your Search Criteria for Your Property

You have identified your price range and your criteria for income production on an ideal property. You have some locations, neighborhoods, and ZIP codes in mind. You have your financing lined up. Now what? You cast your net widely and see what kind of "fish" you catch.

"Casting your net" involves setting up a variety of searches with your parameters. Here is an order I would begin with. **Also, please note that none of these search parameters or services cost any money.** There should be no cost to you to search for a house,[272] even when you are searching for motivated sellers.

1. **Set up appointments with three real estate agents, if you do not have a relationship with one already selected.** Discuss with them what you are looking for, and **MAKE SURE THAT THEY ARE AWARE you want to search for homes that are deeply discounted, as well as investigate all possible seller financing, assuming**

---

271 Many entrepreneurs have found great success by making their primary residence also a place of business. Commercially zoned multi-unit properties certainly carry this type of potential, if that is your inclination.

272 Foreclosure search services and other similar search veins, in my experience, offer nothing special that you cannot find by inquiring with local real estate agents or networking with local investing groups. Save your money.

it is available.[273] Select an agent. Then have them set up a broad search parameter of your entire searching area and send you anything from your minimum to your maximum price range. Remember, you can always offer a lower price. Keep an open mind when things come in. With time, you will learn to quickly dismiss something that is entirely unsuitable for you.

2. **Connect with your local real estate investor association (REIA) group.** Let them know that you are in the market and looking for a specific property. Ask for the names of local wholesalers who are reputable[274] and get their information, then ask them to bring you discounted deals in all areas where you have interest, regardless of condition. Join the REIA group forums if you can and post your needs and desires every few days on the forum.

3. **Use Craigslist and other tools like Trulia.com and Backpage.com**[275] **to post your "Real Estate Wanted" ad.** You can make it extremely specific, but I would keep it broad like I did in placing a real estate wanted ad in the local *Old Forge* newspaper, which will allow more motivated sellers to contact you. Feel free to perform "A/B testing," which is where you run the same ad but with different text to see which is more impactful. Here is a simple example of A/B testing.

Ad A	Ad B:
Buyer looking for home in Maple Street Area	Maple Street Area Home Wanted!
Any condition, will look at all homes	Fixer-uppers okay
Seller financing preferred	Have cash and good credit
Call 123.456.7890	Call 123.456.7890

4. **Place ads in local, inexpensive papers like *Pennysaver* and *Thrifty Nickel*.** Sometimes these ads are free or are very, very cheap. You never know what type of calls you might get.

5. **Place bandit signs on corners with this saying: "*I BUY HOUSES, ALL CASH, ANY AREA OR CONDITION.*"** You can frequently go to rental companies and ask

---

273 **Seller financing is ALWAYS preferable to bank financing, assuming your rates and down payments are comparable, because with seller financing, you have the possibility of a discounted FULL PAYOFF.** A bank will never give you this unless they accept a short sale, which would mean you are behind on payments and are going to lose the house anyway, which is the opposite of what this book is about.

274 The key word here is *reputable*.

275 **All of these sites can be used by creating an account with Zillow Rental Manager at Zillow.com.** I believe you can place your ad for real estate wanted and the software will "spool" your listing out to many sites, which can get you different responses as well as allow for A/B testing. **A great tool for finding tenants also.**

if they have any extra "H stakes" or signs they are going to discard, and if they are, you can take these signs (rental agents change jobs all the time, making their signs obsolete), cross out the number on the sign and use yours.[276] **Make sure the sign does not have a real estate company or logo associated with it.** Alternatively, you can get signs made up for a small cost at a local sign company.

6. **Read your local Sunday real estate classifieds to look for motivated sellers**. With the decline of print journalism, these have really begun to dwindle in size and scope. Nevertheless, if you get your Sunday real estate section, it is worth reading it from cover to cover. You never know what might pop up worth pursuing.

7. **Talk to your bank's REO[277] Department to determine what inventory they have**. I have frequently had banks offer me valuable REO properties then sweeten the already discounted deal by telling me they will finance the note!

8. **Search your local HUD[278] website.** This changes from region to region, so look for the website that applies to the area where you are seeking a property. There are many good deals there.

9. **Courthouse steps.** This is where foreclosed homes are "auctioned off," usually back to the banks, which are the highest bidder. **You can find great deals at the courthouse steps, but in my experience, there is a strong "ol' boy" network in play downtown, and it is hard for you to get a good deal when the rest of the crew doesn't want you there in the first place and will out bid you over and over again to make you go away.** I rarely use this as a source of inventory. However, it may be worth finding a reputable ol' boy down there and offering to pay him (or her) a markup for what you want. Suddenly you might have a strong ally. Again, make sure that you are working with a reputable representative down at the courthouse, which makes the difference between actually buying a home and getting scammed. Also, make sure you get title insurance on ALL homes you buy, including those from the courthouse steps. And remember, you cannot finance courthouse-step properties with bank financing from your local bank, as you need to close on these auctioned homes in twenty-four hours, whereas your bank's lending process usually takes thirty to ninety days to complete. So do your homework before you head down to the courthouse steps!

10. **Estate sale agents, estate attorneys, probate attorneys.** Drop these guys a note

---

276 I'm not a big fan of bandit signs, and I personally don't use them, but many people have great success with them.
277 Real Estate Owned—where properties go when the banks foreclose on homes.
278 Office of **H**ousing and **U**rban **D**evelopment. Where FHA loans (and homes) go when they are foreclosed on.

saying you are looking to buy distressed real estate in specific areas. Some of them will call you back and might even have a house for you.

You get the idea. There are so many ways to find amazing, discounted deals, making a list of ways to find them in and of itself is a daunting task. However, you have to believe they are out there, or else you won't find them.

Remember, there are thresholds to property discounts.

Sometimes, people come to my brokerage at Discount Property Warehouse and ask us for deals that simply don't exist. They might say, "*OH YEAH, I'M A BUYER FOR HOMES IN CENTRAL GARDENS.*[279] *BUT THE THING IS, I NEED A HOME THAT APPRAISES FOR 350K I CAN BUY FOR 50K THAT NEEDS NO WORK AND HAS ALL NEW APPLIANCES, PLUS SELLER FINANCING AT 0%. BRING THAT TO ME AND I WILL BUY.*"

Well, the problem is, that home doesn't exist and, in all likelihood, never will. If you remember *Feol's Formula,* even a completely fixed up house with market value of 300k would have a minimum ask of 150k, and if a home was in pristine condition, *unless a seller was INCREDIBLY MOTIVATED or the market was completely stagnant*, we would probably end up paying close to 200k–220k for a fixed-up house. **Don't forget, discounts happen because work is needed on homes, and because of the work needed, people tend to undervalue their homes**.

Homes in move-in condition are *rarely* laden with steep discounts.

But you must also remember that you cannot get something for nothing. In the case of the buyer wanting to pay 50k mentioned above, their expectations are completely unrealistic. This book is about finding heavily discounted homes that need work, *not* finding unicorns and chasing rainbows.

When property is in distressed condition and needs repairs, whether it is ugly, unsightly, unlivable, etc., the difference between your purchase price plus repairs to fix up the home gives you your total acquisition cost. Consider, however, that once you complete the work on a home, and the home then appraises for fair market value, you have caused the home to adjust from your acquisition cost to market value.

In the world of real estate, this is called *Forced Appreciation*.

Because Forced Appreciation happens when I buy a property at a discount and fix it up for a fraction of its fair market value, it always makes sense for me to purchase properties inexpensively and repair them for as little labor and material possible while generating a high-quality end product.

---

279 Super-upscale area of Memphis, average home price 300k.

When I do this, I create a much more significant market value through **forced appreciation**, and, of course, it gives me more equity down the line.

Understanding **forced appreciation** can give you a greater understanding of how and why investing in distressed and highly undervalued real estate can, over time, make you very wealthy.

Remember, it always begins with finding a deal.

Using Architectural Creativity to Create Income-Producing Units

Below is a picture of a studio apartment in Portland, Oregon, I found on Trulia. com. In this picture, you see the bedroom designed into the space by an effective use of walls, partially lowered ceilings, and various floor coverings. This space isn't really that big but LOOKS very spacious because it has its own bedroom and lots of natural light in the living room area (around the corner).[280]

This is a great example of what a contractor can do with a small budget and BIG ideas. A simple 20x20-square-foot space (400 square feet) can easily be turned in to a discrete, private guest apartment with a full bath, bedroom, kitchen, and living area simply by subdividing the area with walls using lowered ceilings to create the feeling of "space"[281] and having a kitchen and bath share a wall to tap off the same water and drain lines, all within an efficiently designed footprint.[282]

280 https://www.trulia.com/blog/studio-apartment-ideas-with-massive-style/, subtitled Rustic meets real-world efficiency: $1,323 to $3,271/month.
281 For more information on this fascinating subject, see Sarah Susanka's *The Not So Big House* book.
282 If you need assistance with floorplan design, consult an architect, or if you are on a budget, feel free to go to the local college of architecture in your town and ask a professor to designate a student architect to help you design your space, potentially for some extra credit or nominal pay. You would be surprised how masterful young people can be!

10

Acquiring and Using Private Lenders and Private Money Sources: How to Buy Without Banks Using Private Lending and Seller Financing

I hate to admit this, but I when I was a schoolteacher, I always thought my life would consist of me working in my teaching job for thirty years (until I was able to retire and get a pension), and along the way, my plan was to acquire ten duplexes using thirty-year loans, which would coincidentally pay off by the time I was retired.

Presumably, if I was in some semblance of good health at that time (late fifties/early sixties), I would have the benefit of my pension and my rental income, which would double my monthly income. In a case where I had my primary home paid off (this *also* assumed a thirty-year note) and had the school district benefit of my health insurance being paid, I would finally be able to live my life of financial freedom—for what little I had left of it. Even my uncle Davy, who was the head of the Social Security administration in Plattsburgh, New York, for most of his career, would tell me as I got older every Christmas when I would see him at my aunt's house ***that his biggest mistake was "not buying real estate."*** This is a man I have had, and will always have, a deep love and tremendous respect for.

He said to me a quote that I will never forget:

*"**Robbie, if I could do it all over again, I would buy one house a year for the first fifteen years of my career and then sell one house a year for the last fifteen years of my career."***

So I knew that owning income-producing real estate through rental property was definitely part of the financial puzzle for me. But how?

The problem I ran into was twofold—one, primarily, was that I loved teaching but hated working in a school system which rewarded ineptitude and never questioning the status quo, and I knew it would be hard for me to swallow this daily for the rest of my life. I was working hard, getting nowhere, and the long gray line of my future consisted of more of the same if I didn't make a change.

But more importantly, I couldn't solve a pressing question relating to my retirement plan at that time, no matter how many ways I tried to analyze it, which was this: ***How in the world does someone ever buy ten rental properties?***

You see, I had had two experiences buying homes in Memphis—first, my primary residence (remember, this had a guest apartment for income purposes) where at the closing I was berated by the loan officer who was telling me how "lucky" I was to get the loan, how I barely qualified, etc. etc. Then, two years later, I bought my first duplex, where, coincidentally, at the closing I was berated AGAIN by the SAME LOAN OFFICER who was telling me how "lucky" I was to get the loan, how I barely qualified, etc. etc.

For me, I couldn't figure it out. I was paying my bills and barely getting by (sound familiar?), but all my obligations were being met. Yet my credit score was always in the low 600s, which was a product of my massive student loan and credit card debt, which created a terrible **debt-to-income ratio** (DTI). Hence, the loan officers I spoke with basically said, "*I got this done, but there will be no future loans for you.*"

Everyone else I knew who I worked with was struggling too, with massive student loan debt and driving cars that were falling apart. Almost my whole life I had only known people to have thirty-year loans on their primary residence and NEVER had met someone who had actually paid their home off. Certainly, I had heard of people owning a lot of rental properties,[283] but the loan officers told me I wouldn't qualify. I tried and tried but just couldn't get over the pervasive questions of "***How does someone buy ten income properties, let alone twenty? Or even one hundred?***"[284] Basically, I had to resign myself to the fact that, as a public school teacher living paycheck to paycheck, I would never be able to achieve my goal of ten rental properties, and that was ***very*** depressing.[285]

---

283 And, much like unicorns and sea monsters, had also heard legends of people who actually "paid off" their homes but had never seen or met one.

284 I had heard rumors of local Memphis investors who owned three hundred or even FIVE hundred properties. **At the beginning of my investing career, I naturally thought these were just urban legends until I actually started consulting for some of these individuals**. That happened years later, of course.

285 Best thing that happened to me, though, as you will see shortly.

Enter the Fannie Ma(e)trix

Most of the property lending world in the United States is dominated by the Fannie Mae loan system. In a nutshell, Fannie Mae repurchases loans, which meet it's underwriting criteria from banks and lenders nationwide, which allows these banks to make more loans. Remember how we discussed the fractional reserve banking system and Bob the Banker? Well, even Bob has limits of how much fake money he can print and lend before he meets his lending limit versus what he has on total deposit. But, if Bob can sell his mortgages to Fannie Mae (which almost all banks do today), Bob can then make more loans and fees associated with the loans, while selling the loan to Fannie Mae for servicing and back-end payment collection. **Bob the Banker and almost all lenders and bankers in the United States today use the Fannie Mae underwriting system to generate loan approvals.** This is why you generally need a job to get a loan with a "reasonable" interest rate,[286] and having some debt in the eyes of the bank is good for purposes of lending history. However, if you have no credit history and 500k in cash in the bank with no job, you will probably be turned down in a traditional Fannie Mae underwrite scenario.

Strange, I know.

I mean, it makes no sense. People with less financial capacity frequently are given loans, while people who do not have a traditional employer cannot, generally speaking, get Fannie Mae loans! But this system is designed to limit lending exposure and make sure people don't buy "too many" houses, whatever that means. As of this writing, Fannie Mae allows you to have up to ten financed properties, although some lenders who are poorly informed will tell you that you can only get four Fannie Mae loans or sometimes six. Naturally, most lenders are in and out of business with some degree of frequency since the lending rules change on a monthly basis, but **if you are serious about winning the financial game and you start out with nothing like I did, you have to borrow money to get going, and the first step to this is knowing the actual Fannie Mae lending rules.**

But back to my story. My banker had told me that I would no longer qualify for Fannie Mae loans or FHA loans unless I paid off my existing primary residence, cleared out my credit card debt, or paid off my student loans—all of which was nigh impossible as I lived paycheck to paycheck. So how was I going to fund my retirement when at the beginning of my career, fully employed and having done everything I had been "told" to do, I had already been shut down?

---

286 A rate based on the "prime" interest rate, which changes daily, plus usually a point or so. These are the rates your banker gives you when you ask the common question "What are rates today?"

In my heart, I knew there was no way I could remain a teacher forever if I truly wanted to be financially free.

The Radio Show: Beginnings

I had always had a goal of having a radio show on real estate and finance. Back in late 2007, after leaving my teaching job and beginning to work full-time in real estate,[287] I had my publicist at that time put some feelers out for a local station which might be interested in having a local talk show on financial success principles, based specifically in local real estate. And "luckily" I was able to get a thirty-minute spot on a local AM radio station. I say "luckily" because as I found out later, the nature of working in local radio is not as glamorous as it is cracked up to be, and the radio industry is highly unstable, extremely politicized, and constantly changing management. This makes it difficult for local hosts like me to carry on a sustainable show over time, but I was able to do so and was pretty successful at keeping the radio show popular and filled with fresh, relevant content.

The key to my show from the beginning was based on three simple precepts:

1. **I would be relaying, in real time, my personal struggle for financial freedom and the roadblocks I was running into, which I knew my listener base could identfiy with;**

2. **I would bring in financial experts on the show several times a month to assist with various criticial topics (like financing), who would then give away some books and study courses for free to encourage listener participation; and**

3. **I would not sell anything on the show, i.e., try to sell a local real estate deal. The show was to be sales free except for the experts I brought in who could promote their courses and materials.**

This worked smashingly. Over the next year, I was able to take the show from thirty minutes a week to a full two-hour show weekly. And the phone was ringing off the hook, becoming more popular each week.

For me, though, I was still struggling with the issue of obtaining bank financing, with the idea of acquiring more rental properties. Every time a lender would say, *"Hey, Robert, I have a new loan product for you. I just need your tax returns and pay stubs,"* I knew I wouldn't qualify. Because I had such tight debt ratios, I was considered a bad

---

287 We will discuss my transition to full-time investor later in the book, but I left my teaching job in 2006 to work full time in real estate.

lending risk and was turned down. And every time my credit was "pulled" for review, it would drop slightly, making my credit score even worse. It seemed a never-ending cycle of unattainable financing and credit struggles lay ahead of me. Additionally, as I was no longer at my teaching job and was considered "self-employed," in the eyes of lenders, it was even more difficult to obtain loans. The reality of the situation was, I could control houses with contracts and close them with cash *IF* I had it (my resources were very limited at the time), but I had no credit or bank-lending resources available to close the very best deals for myself to keep. It was getting to the point of embarassment.

When the Student Is Ready, the Teacher Will Appear

Right after 2007 ended, I went through a major career transition in that a small but very successful real estate company I had been building with a former business partner in Memphis was unexpectedly dissolved, and I found myself needing to reinvent myself as an investor and, in some ways, as a person. The details of that story are unimportant for the purposes of this book, but basically my income from the real estate company I had built had suddenly stopped completely, and I was almost penniless. **Yet as bleak as it sounds, it was the best thing that ever happened to me professionally, although rebuilding myself after such an adversarial business dissolution was difficult, indeed**.

Somehow, during this rebuilding period, I was invited to speak by another investor to a real estate group in Jackson, Mississippi, which is about three hours away from Memphis. After I was finished speaking to the real estate investment group there, I extended a courtesy invitation to the man who had invited me, named Walter, to come on my radio show in Memphis. He accepted, and this is when my life *really* took an unexpected change for the better. Walter, while a humble man, was actually a very successful investor who had specialized in the art of using **private money lending** for his real estate business funding purposes.

Now, I had never heard of private money lending. I had heard of seller financing, which is where a property seller happens to own a home in the "clear"[288] and may be in a position to let you make payments to them each month on a seller-held mortgage instead of you needing to go to a bank and get a loan, but **private money lending** was a totally different world to me and one which I was completely unfamiliar with.

As Walter and I settled in on the microphones before the show and engaged in small talk that fateful Saturday, I lamented to him about the difficulty I was having obtaining bank loans. And then after quietly listening to my plight, **Walter Woffard gave me one**

---

288 Meaning, they have paid off their mortgages on the house and own it "free and clear."

of the best pieces of advice for financial freedom I have ever received, and it went something like this:

> "Robert, the problem you are having is that you are putting the banks in a position to tell you *no*. **When you remove the banks from the equation, and in doing so, remove the ability for anyone to tell you anything except yes**, your life will change forever."

Then Walter[289] and I spent the next two hours of my radio show with him describing the intricate elements of using private, seller-based financing to fund all your real estate (as well as non-real estate) needs, based on examples he had used in *his* life. Walter spent the majority of that show doing the talking while I, as the host, spent the majority of the time listening, learning, and taking notes because Walter's simple approach to buying real estate had not only given me the key to solving the problem of uncooperative Fannie Mae lenders, but he had also given me a powerful real estate ability I never realized I had—**the ability to buy any property anywhere, anytime, and close it on my terms without a bank ever telling me no again**. And I promise you, this tool can become a *very* powerful utility in your personal journey when using **The Short-Term Retirement Program.**

Flexible Down Payment + Flexible Terms + Negotiable Interest Rate = ☺

Remember in an earlier chapter when we discussed your grandmother? Or more specifically, when we discussed your grandmother who had a CD maturing at a very low rate of return, and you might be in a position to offer her a much higher rate of return if she lent that money to you instead to buy real estate?

That is the basic premise of private money lending.

But the world of private lending spans transactions far greater than you borrowing from your grandmother. You see, if you can change your mind-set and how you think about borrowing money, then the world of financial freedom becomes opened to you, even if you start (like I did) with NOTHING. You can still acquire income-producing assets and have other people pay for them. **And isn't that what The Short-Term Retirement Program is all about?** But first, you need to understand HOW to find the lenders, HOW to negotiate the terms, and HOW to structure each loan to fit your specific needs.

---

289 I would be remiss if I didn't give Walter great credit for his work and appearance on my radio show that day. For more information, go to WalterWoffard.com.

How Robert Feol Uses Private Lending

Every transaction I use to buy investment property, and many times, *also* when I sell investment property, is funded by private lenders whom I have built relationships with in advance of any transaction.

You see, **here is the key to being successful as a real estate investor**.

> **Robert Feol's Real Estate Investing Basic Success Formula**
>
> **If you can:**
>
> 1. Find the best deals for pennies on the dollar, and;
>
> 2. Establish lending relationships with private lenders who are monetarily liquid and committed to your lending relationship, making funds available within twenty-four hours' notice for a closing,
>
> **Then you can:**
>
> 1. Buy any home[290] you want;
>
> 2. Keep the best investment properties for yourself, using highly favorable financing terms and short-term payoffs **with payments made by your tenants,**[291] not you;
>
> 3. Sell the other deals *profitably* to investors to generate revenue in your pocket for cash flow today; and
>
> 4. Repeat the process over and over, ad infinitum, until you are financially free, at which time you own enough monthly income-producing properties that you do not have to work again (unless you want to).

When I am at work on a daily basis at my brokerage, I am constantly looking for investment opportunities. Naturally, I do not have unlimited funds, but I do have an army of private lenders who love generating passive income from my efforts in the form of higher interest monthly payments, plus loan fees. My private lenders also love the fact that I pay off loans quickly, allowing them to make new loan fees to me on new investment opportunities as they arise.

---

290 This assumes you are only buying the best, most highly discounted and highly desirable deals in great areas.
291 **The fundamental premise of The Short-Term Retirement Program.**

How Does Private Lending Work in The Short-Term Retirement Program?

Again, acquiring investment properties is a secondary idea that is beyond the scope of this book and which I will cover in another volume. **The purpose of this text is to show you how to become financially strong by eliminating your housing payment permanently for life.** It is easy to parlay your paid off home's entire equity and "trade up" to a bigger house that you buy for pennies on the dollar, but first, you have to get to the point of having your primary residence paid off and ideally do that by *not* using a thirty-year loan. So how does private lending come into play for you as a potential homeowner?

First, let's review the basic precepts of private lending.

In Chapter 1, I shared with you the fact that I really didn't want to get an institutional loan for my vacation home, primarily because I was hoping to pay off and settle the seller held mortgage at a discount. **Now, it is important to remember that private financing and seller financing are two slightly different forms of borrowing, although both are radically different from bank financing**. I made a great comparison of seller financing versus bank financing in Chapter 1, but I will list a basic summary here of private financing principles and how one generally works with private lenders. **As a rule, remember that private lenders are investors who are looking for returns on their money through you keeping your word with them**—specifically regarding on-time payments, timely loan payoff, fees, higher than average interest rates, and so on—**and is paramount to having a successful long-term relationship with them over time,** and (hopefully) many transactions.

A General Summary: Private Lenders Are:

- Savvy individuals who want greater returns on their money than they can get, generally speaking, from financial markets.

- Have access to liquid cash from other business ventures and understand business very well.

- Want to avoid risk while growing their money.

- Have specific expectations regarding loan repayment and promptness of your execution regarding anything agreed on.

- Don't like to be "jerked around."

- Will frequently use *self-directed* IRAs, 401ks, lines of credit, or cash to lend—all these carry different rules for lending and borrowing.

- Don't usually require an appraisal to lend money to you for a property purchase.

☐ Interest rate and repayment schedule is negotiable between parties.

☐ Fees are negotiable.

☐ Private lenders CANNOT be asked for a discount, which would represent a capital loss to them and would be highly offensive, it would also ruin your borrowing relationship.

☐ Have the right to foreclose on you like any bank lender.

Why Use Private Lenders Instead of Banks?

For me, I am personally convinced that the future of borrowing and lending is realized in its highest and best form between two individual, private parties who have mutual respect and a mutually beneficial interest in a singular transaction. With banks today, including the International Monetary Fund (as discussed in previous chapters) changing their positions that a depositor is no longer a "customer" in their business model and is now an "investor,"[292] banks are setting themselves up legally to seize depositors' funds should the bank have a liquidity crisis, similar to the one that happened in Cyprus.[293] Now, I don't know about you, but if a bank is telling me that they may seize my funds if their business should fail, suddenly I am not willing to trust the bank the way I used to. And as I had discussed and shown you in depth throughout this book, **the bank is NOT your friend.**

Yet, for some of you, especially those readers who have full-time jobs and reasonably good credit, the bank as your lender may be your best opportunity to get a "good" loan. After all, the bank *does* offer something that we all are seeking—a "low" interest rate. And depending on private lending rates in your area, the bank making a loan may be a less expensive option than a private lender, even after you factor in the appraisal and "junk fees" that a bank usually will charge you.

Private lenders, on the other hand, can fill a a variety of needs an individual borrower may have, whereas a bank lender might typically refuse. Let's look at a few examples of bank lenders versus private lenders in situations where you have found a great property which may have some "curves" the bank is not used to dealing with.

---

292 Aka, involuntarily subject to the "risk'" of the bank becoming insolvent.
293 https://www.ft.com/content/9963b74c-219c-11e5-aa5a-398b2169cf79.

The Fannie Mae Bank Lender versus a Private Lender: Who Will Lend on This Property?[294]

Property Type	Fannie Mae Lender	Private Lender	Notes
Mobile home?	Maybe	Yes	Must be on a permanent foundation
Berm home?	Absolutely Not	Yes	A house in a hill— hobbit style—very efficient thermally.
More than four units?	Absolutely Not	Yes	Fannie Mae will not lend on multi-units, generally speaking: only four units or less, and this can change from lender to lender
Home in flood zone?	Maybe	Yes	Flood insurance required
Foreclosed home that needs work?[304]	Absolutely Not	Yes	Considered "uninhabitable" by Fannie Mae
Vacant home with utilities off or missing HVAC systems?	Absolutely Not	Yes	Considered "uninhabitable" by Fannie Mae
Condemned home?	Absolutely Not	Yes	Great deals can be found here
Mobile home park?	Absolutely Not	Yes	Technically "land"
Off-grid house?	Maybe	Yes	Depends on how "off grid" the home is
Apartment complex?	Absolutely Not	Yes	
Churches	Absolutely Not	Yes	
Office condominiums?	Absolutely Not	Yes	
Gold mines?	Absolutely Not	Yes	
Oil fields?	Absolutely Not	Yes	
Agricultural?	Absolutely Not	Yes	
New construction?	Absolutely Not	Yes	
Log home from package?	Absolutely Not	Yes	*Ask me how I know this
Farm?	Absolutely Not	Yes	
Single-family home?	Maybe	Yes	*IF* subject property meets **ALL** requirements

You get the idea. In this comparison, the great humor can be found in the fact that, even when it comes to single-family homes, Fannie Mae may (no pun intended) or may not offer you financing, and single-family homes are Fannie Mae's specialty!

The greatest power using a private lender gives us is the ability for us to say "yes" to purchasing a property when the bank wants to tell us "no." Remember, as much as the mass media, the Federal Reserve, and the banks themselves would like us to believe, we are ***not*** subjects of the bank. We choose to become subjects of the bank only if we

---

294 For complete Fannie Mae lending guidelines, you can go here: https://www.fanniemae.com/singlefamily/other-web-resources. Naturally, it should be stated these loan guidelines are ***constantly*** subject to change.

295 The majority of your home searches will find property in this category here—notice that Fannie Mae considers these homes "uninhabitable."

allow ourselves to give the banks power over us in this way.

As for me, I am always looking for a way to say "yes" *without* the banks!

Mother May I (Purchase a Property?)

Now, for those readers with less than stellar credit, or for those readers with great credit who are having issues with "capacity" (meaning you are getting stretched thin due to payments and debt ratios even though your credit is good, which makes lenders not want to lend to you), private lending offers us a solution. But how does one get started in working with private lenders or even seeking them out? Sure, it is easy enough to say, *"If you had a lender who was willing to offer you a private loan for 100k at a very favorable interest rate and terms, you could easily buy a 100k house without a bank,"* but the question in most people's minds is quite simply how and where do I find private lenders?

I will give you some basic ideas about finding private lenders and a simple system to get started in your search. But more importantly, it is critical to remember that if you want to become successful in owning real estate beyond your primary residence, **you need to have MANY sources of private lending, and to that end you are ALWAYS seeking private lenders**. And you can easily spot the people who *really* have private lenders versus those who have simply what is known as hard money lenders. Those with private lenders can *easily* get deals closed, whereas people using hard money lenders are always scampering the day before the sale to make sure their hard money lender is committed and willing to fund their deal without some parameter of their lending relationship suddenly changing. You see, hard money lenders are like loan sharks, whereas private lenders who are relationship based are more like people who give you lines of credit to build your real estate business and do deals while enjoying the benefit of passive monthly income through periodic payments (from YOU).

Let's examine the two types of lenders in a side-by-side comparison.

Hard Money Lenders versus Private Money Lenders, a Comparison

Lending Parameter	Hard-Money Lender[305]	Private Lender	Notes
Interest rate?	THEY tell YOU what it is	Negotiable	Hard money lender usually has 12% minimum.
Down payment?	THEY tell YOU what it is	Negotiable	Can be none.
Lending term?	Usually 180 days or less	Negotiable	
Loan fee?	Five to ten points minimum	Negotiable	Can be none.
Prepayment penalty?	Sometimes	No	
Lots of hoops to jump through?	Yes	No	
Says no to some loans for no reason?	Frequently	No	

Now, I have known lots of people who use hard money lenders when no other lending sources are available, and the investors I have known who have used them have had a great deal of success. But with that being said, it is very difficult to get by with a 12% payment due each month and points and fees on top of that, all while working under a strict timeline. *The nature of a private lending relationship just makes things a lot easier and a lot less adversarial.* Hard money lenders NEED to re-originate those loans every short period of time (**read: three to six months**) to make the large fees necessary to be profitable as a hard money lender; this is how many of them live. So they have to "crack the whip" and make sure loans pay off timely, even when real estate, at times, can have delays and be somewhat untimely. For me, when I started dictating my own loan terms and fees, my life simply became a lot easier, and I kept MORE of what I made on each deal because I was giving less in fees and interest to the lenders each month. **This idea becomes ESPECIALLY important when you are applying the principles of The Short-Term Retirement Program to acquiring and paying off your primary residence. The less you pay in interest and fees, the better, obviously.**

Approaching Private Money Lenders

Now, as a standard disclaimer, there are SEC[297] rules associated with the solicitation of private money lenders for the purposes of investment. I share this information with you

---

296 **Don't get me wrong, hard money lenders certainly have their place and can be very useful for your real estate purchase needs.** But over time, I have found private lenders to establish relationships with, where you can negotiate favorable lending terms for yourself, that tend to be a better, and more efficient, resource.

297 Security and Exchange Commission, for those of you who are unfamiliar with the term.

freely but with the understanding that **it is YOUR responsibility to ensure that you are one hundred percent SEC compliant when you are approaching potential private lending sources**. I also took several classes on this before I really got into seeking out private lenders for funding on my personal real estate deals, **and I would encourage you to invest the time and money into doing the proper research and getting the education necessary to ensure that you are not violating the SEC rules regarding private lending in any way**. The best course I took was with a speaker named Alan Cowgill. I would encourage you to get his home-study course from his website; just mention that you read about him in my book.[298]

The compliance side of SEC rules for private lending refer, generally, to a solicitor needing a number of "touches" (**read:** formal interactions) with a potential private investor before one actually engages in a discussion or solicitation of an individual for private lending purposes. As a simple rule, if you have had lunch with someone three or more times, you have had enough "touches" to begin a discussion on private lending, but if you have had less than that, you are in violation of SEC rules by trying to solicit someone who you have not had these interactions with for private lending purposes. Naturally, your grandmother or a family member/close friend could be solicited immediately, as you have known these people for a duration, which far surpasses any SEC regulations.[299] **Mailing a blanket postcard to a mailing list saying that you are seeking private money secured by real estate and with guaranteed certain percentage returns would be a clear violation of SEC rules, as (a) you do not know these people on the mailing list, and (b) you cannot offer or "guarantee" returns.** So make sure you do your homework to see how private investors and you can establish relationships without you incurring a civil penalty. (**Alan Cowgill course, buy it!**)

For the purposes of our discussion, we will assume you have had the appropriate number of "touches" with a prospective investor and can legally speak freely with them about your lending needs and have ensured your necessary SEC compliance.[300]

Wanted: Private Lenders!

I will admit that I do borrow from a few members of my family and in-laws for real estate purposes, but I do so only to help them out by providing fees and interest much higher

---

298 **Alan's courses are available here, and I cannot recommend them enough:** http://www.PrivateLendingMadeEasy. com/.

299 Please understand I am NOT trying to encourage you to "hit up" your family and friends for private money loans. It is simply to illustrate SEC compliance examples. **And secondly, it is YOUR responsibility to research what SEC rules apply to you as they are subject to change, and this is not a rulebook on SEC regulation.** We take NO responsibility for you complying with SEC or any infractions you may obtain from trying to apply this material improperly. This book is for educational purposes only. (See all disclaimers for reference.)

300 For your reference, SEC website is here: https://www.sec.gov/.

than they can get from any financial market and by offering them (usually) an additional rate of return, which surpasses what I pay my normal private lenders to help them out financially, although this affects my bottom-line profitability.

With that being said, I am at a point in my career where I have the resources to pay them back in full if something went wrong, and I also have their respect as someone who has done this type of borrowing so frequently that their experience will be very smooth. However, I would encourage you to borrow only from your family or friends in a case where everything is set up in advance and agreed to by both parties, drawn up by an attorney, with very specific outlines for repayment schedules, fees, and so forth. **What you DON'T want to do is lose family and friends through unscrupulous or inexperienced borrowing practices.**

The Dialogue: A Simple Example

A basic dialogue for setting up private money lending scenarios can happen frequently in the course of daily conversation. People like to discuss money in very general ways (i.e., "*These stock markets are killing my retirement*") and often speak to their fantasies and desires (i.e., "*If only I hit tonight's Powerball, I will be able to put a new roof on my house*") in the course of friendly, general dialogue. This is where you can insert a feeler to see if someone is a potential lending candidate.

Consider the following (theoretical) conversation at work one day. You need a 50k loan for six months to purchase, renovate, and refinance a property you are thinking of buying as an income-producing primary residence using **Short-Term Retirement** guidelines. You have a loan approval for a refinance once the house is totally ready for appraisal, but it needs work first, so you are seeking out a six-month bridge[301] loan.

Private Lending: An Introductory Conversation Example[302]

> **Work Colleague**: I'm getting tired of my stock broker. I have had my money with him over four years, but with the ups and downs of the market, he has barely kept it positive at about 1% return a year! It's really frustrating.
>
> **You**: It's funny you should say that. I've been working on a real estate deal, and I need some short-term financing for it. I've been talking to a few guys who

---

301 A temporary loan, which funds the purchase and construction needed on a property.

302 Remember, it is up to YOU to learn about what SEC compliance measures you are required to have accomplished before having these types of conversations.

> specialize in private lending, and those guys seem to be making some pretty solid interest secured by real estate. Most people have no idea that investment opportunities like that exist.
>
> **Work Colleague:** What's private lending?
>
> **You:** It's simple, I'll give you an example. I have been working on buying my primary residence, but I am using some pretty aggressive search methods and parameters to find something that is way below market value. I have found it, but it needs some work. The bank has given me a refinance letter saying once the work is done, they will give me a permanent loan, but the bank generally doesn't lend purchase and fix-up money at the same time. So I need a private lender to make that loan to me in first position, secured by a deed of trust and full hazard insurance, for about six months. And for that short-term loan, I am willing to pay about six or seven times what your broker is generating for you annually return-wise, plus a small origination fee.
>
> **Work Colleague:** Tell me more. It sounds intriguing...

Now, in this case, you have given a basic description to your colleague of what private lending is and outlined how it is used and for what time frame you need monies. Your goal is not to get a *yes* or *no* answer in this first conversation. For many inexperienced lending prospects, it may take months or years for you to get someone onboard with your lending and borrowing vision. **But fear not, lenders who will say yes far more quickly ARE out there.** And for many new borrowers, they will find themselves fielding questions about the variety of risks involved and having to explain themselves out of "what if the sky falls?" scenarios. **Surprisingly, many readers, however, do not understand how safe and secure private lending really is for the lender!** You see, the lender has the benefit of many perks that can ensure their money is "safe" in a potential private lending–based real estate investment and can choose to make loans or NOT make loans based on if a property-lending opportunity meets their criteria.

Private Lender Fail-Safes: Risk Management 101

As a private lender, you are set up to structure a transaction to your liking. Now, while I like to discuss how favorable private lending can be for the borrower, **it is important that you understand how secure it can be for the lender** and, in doing so, extol to them the virtues of control that they have over the transaction. Plus, someday you may become a private lender yourself.[303]

Basic Lender Fail-Safes

As a lender, you can:

☐ Lend on property and secure it by a deed of trust in first position on the home;[304]

☐ Require full hazard insurance prepaid for the life of the loan with your beneficial interest as the primary named insured;

☐ Require a pre-signed and notarized quitclaim deed at the closing, held in escrow by the closing attorney and executed only when and if your borrower defaults, preventing you from having to engage in a lengthy and costly foreclosure process to reclaim the home so you can resell it;

☐ Require an escrow account set up so you collect monthly prepaid taxes and insurance, ensuring that you have the borrower funds necessary to keep taxes and insurance paid and in force, as necessary;

☐ Obtain the right of first refusal on rents for the subject property, ensuring that YOU as the lender get the rents directly, NOT the borrower, which ensures you receive your monthly payment. This assumes the property has a tenant in it, which some do;

☐ You can have all the closing paperwork prepared by YOUR attorney of choice;

☐ You can require a down payment, interest rate, and loan fees of your choosing; and

☐ You can establish the maximum loan to value that you will lend on ensuring you can resell a house profitably should a transaction go wrong.

When I created The Short-Term Retirement Program many years ago, I was pitching it to a local private lender, who then "stole" the idea and turned it into a smashing success

---

303 They say the natural flow of the real estate investor who starts out with nothing is they begin with low-cost homes in rough areas of town, slowly move their way up as their financial situation allows, eventually get burnt out on land lording after years of being a landlord, and when they have made their fortune, they lend it as a private lender through "paper," which is interest-bearing deeds of trust on homes for other borrowers.

304 Meaning, if you foreclose on the house, you get the house; you don't fight over it like a lender in second or third position. The only thing that is superior to your interest at a foreclosure sale is unpaid property taxes, which you can prevent from happening by paying the taxes yourself after you set up and collect monthly escrow.

as a full-time lending entity under a different name. I say, "stole," because I shared the information freely with him; but as a friend, I felt that if he were to do anything with it, I deserved remuneration, which never showed up. And, while I don't hold a grudge,[305] I do remember a very valuable insight I shared with him about being a private lender, which was as follows:

> **Private Lending: Words of Wisdom**
>
> If someone brings you a good enough deal and you make a loan to them structured properly, *your WORST scenario is actually your BEST scenario;* meaning, if you have to foreclose, you will make far MORE money than if you had simply lent on the property and been paid back as agreed!

And this is the reality of the situation: If private lenders structure their loans properly and minimize their lending risk, they can do very well and create, in essence, a situation where their "disaster" scenario actually allows them to flourish the most financially versus the basic transaction just working out. Let's consider an example of a lender making a loan, which pays off as agreed versus that same loan defaulting, which for the purpose of this example, we will consider a private lending disaster scenario.

> **Private Lending Example 1: A 60k Loan Pays Off as Agreed**
>
> **Scenario:** Borrower fixes up home using 55k as purchase and repair money, then sells home after six months and pays back lender.
>
> **After repair value:** 100k
>
> **Home purchase price:** 40k
>
> **Estimated repairs:** 15k
>
> **Borrower loan request:** 60k
>
> **Lending fee (origination fee):** 5k
>
> **Total liquid monetary amount lent to borrower:** 55k
>
> **Interest rate:** 12%

---

305 I do hold a VERY deep grudge, however, to a very well-known local Memphis guy who asked me to introduce him to this lender, which I did, and he agreed to pay me for each transaction he completed with this lender, which he did, until he was doing so much business that he owed me so much in referral fees he stopped taking my phone call. **If you are reading this, you know who you are. Pay up, you scumbag!**

Loan term: six months

Total number of payments made (1% per month interest only): $600 × 6 months = $3,600 interest received

Loan fee repaid: $5,000

Total fees and interest collected over life of loan: $8,600

Semiannual yield: $8,600 (received) / $55,000 (money lent): 15.6% yield after six months

Annualized return: 31.2%

So, as we can see in this case, the nature of private lending can be a very lucrative practice. I am using rates and fees that I have actually paid in the past on many loans (5k loan fee/12% annualized rate), although as we will discuss momentarily, I don't set up relationships with lenders paying such high fees anymore, **and I try to negotiate very favorable rates and fees for myself with the private lending relationships I establish at this point in my career**. However, it is important to remember that if you have a great deal but no money with which to fund it, you have nothing, whereas there may be times you have to pay high fees to secure an investment opportunity which is highly lucrative. The level of discretion and judgment necessary to analyze these scenarios will come with the time and experience of doing several "deals" and will be discussed in another volume.

Now, since we have just established that it is very possible for a private lender to make an annualized return of 30% simply by making real estate loans to private individuals like yourself, let's look at a private lender's worst-case scenario, where the borrower defaults (meaning, stops making payments) and the lender is forced to take the house back.

Private Lending Example 2: A 60k Loan Defaults

Scenario: *Borrower fixes up home using 55k as purchase and repair money, then dies.*[306] He does not make any payments, and the lender is forced to reclaim the house. Fortunately, the lender got a notarized Quitclaim Deed at the closing where he lent the money and asked the attorney to hold the deed in escrow, just in case something like this happened. Now he gets the house back without having to go through a messy foreclosure process.

---

306 I mean, worst-case scenario, right?

After-repair value: 100k

Total liquid monetary amount lent to borrower: 55k

Private Lender Markets Fixed Up Home, Lists with Realtor, Home Sells and Closes After Six Months

Listing price: 100k

Offer price: 90k

Less 6% realtor commission: ($5,400)

Less closing costs: ($1,000)

Gross sale proceeds: $83,600

Less funds lent: $55,000

Net proceeds over life of loan (six months): $28,600

Semiannual yield: $28,600 (received)/$55,000 (money lent): 52% yield after six months

Annualized return: 104%

What? A whopping 104% annualized return on the money lent if the borrower dies and makes NO payments?

How is this possible?

You see, the key to winning in real estate is to always find tremendously under-valued property. When you do, so many great things can happen to you, such as money being easier to obtain (if you need it); insurance and taxes are less expensive; you become wealthier by improving your net worth (but don't forget, **equity and net worth are really dead; what matters is being debt free and having lots of spendable cash flow each month**) and usually, when you buy a house far below market value and fix it up, you have a nice cash flow, which generates spendable money in hand each month.[307]

For a private lender, making a loan to a borrower who has found a far below market value deal is an even easier no-brainer, if you understand the two examples I just gave you above. **When you are making loans at 40% or more below market value, you are**

307　Remember, cash flow is key. **Calling yourself a millionaire because you have 10 million in assets but 9 million in thirty-year debt is asinine**, and by the way, you will never be financially free unless you service that debt for thirty years, which to me sounds like slavery.

very safe. Consider this type of safe lending scenario for a private borrower versus banks, which, at times (like in the days preceding the 2008 credit crisis and housing collapse), were forced to make 100% loans to nonqualifying borrowers. Remember the days of loans known as "no doc" loans, sometimes called "liar loans" or "stated income loans?" The bank knew these borrowers couldn't repay, and even today, unqualified borrowers still get loans made to them, which will inevitably default. **Institutional lenders struggle all the time with zero-down, non-performing loans and even encounter what they sometimes call thirty-day nonpays—meaning, a family buys a house using no money down, pays full market value, and then proceeds to miss their very first mortgage payment and every subsequent one thereafter.** The types of people who can only buy for "zero down," generally speaking, shouldn't be buying houses; they should be working on saving money for a rainy day and paying down (and avoiding) unsecured debt. Yet the bank makes these loans anyway. These people default, and voilà, you can now repurchase these homes via foreclosure for pennies on the dollar using private lenders who can make very safe loans while generating unbeatable returns and while being fully insured and in a safe first position on the deed of trust.

> Additionally, never forget the cardinal rule of private lending:
>
> **You are free as a private lender to say NO to any loan request you do not like or do not feel good about AT ANY TIME and WITHOUT HAVING TO GIVE ANY REASON.**

Private Lenders: Loans versus Credit Lines

If you really have a good relationship with a lender and you have a pristine reputation as a borrower, you can—instead of approaching a lender for an individual loan—ask a private lender for a line of credit secured by the houses you purchase. What this does for you is give you the power to purchase several deals at one time or in the span of a short period of time (like I do), as opportunities arise, and then you can resell the deals you don't want to keep for small profitable margins of several thousands of dollars per transaction.

We will cover this idea of reselling for profit[308] in the next volume.

---

308   Also called wholesaling.

Utilizing Seller Financing versus Private Financing: A Guide

Having private lenders lined up in advance of you purchasing a property, presumably for the purposes of implementing a **Short-Term Retirement Program-like** strategy, will certainly make your life easier as you head toward closing your purchase. **But even before I knew about private lending, I knew about seller financing**, and the great power it entails through the ability to ask for a discounted mortgage payoff down the line (**remember me settling my vacation home's mortgage for a 47k discount as retold in Chapter 1?**). And of course, you cannot ask private lenders for a discount the way you can people holding seller-financed notes. Remember, those who hold seller-financed notes generally would prefer the cash but for whatever reason have been unable to get it.

This brings us to a **critical real estate** rule I cannot stress to you enough:

Feol's Rule on Seller Financing

Whenever you are preparing to make an offer on a property, *ALWAYS* ask the seller or seller's agent if seller financing is an option on your subject property.

Now, when I say "always," please understand what I mean by that. What I mean is **ALWAYS**, as in **EVERY TIME YOU MAKE AN OFFER ON A PROPERTY, ASK IF SELLER FINANCING IS AVAILABLE OR IS SOMETHING THE SELLER IS WILLING TO CONSIDER. If it is, you may be able to negotiate an even more favorable set of lending terms on the property purchase versus using a private lender or a bank institutional lender, with the added bonus of possibly paying off the mortgage at a HUGE discount down the line**.

If you are lucky enough to get a seller who is willing to "carry the paper," so to speak, make sure you or your agent outline the seller-financed terms in the purchase contract. When you go to closing, your closing attorney or escrow agent will set up your deed of trust and promissory note using the exact terms you and the seller agreed to. Once you have closed with the seller, you now have a seller-financed property, and remember, **these can almost always be settled for a discount later on!**

Understanding Private Lending and Seller Financing Terms and Fees

When people are negotiating real estate as we discussed in the beginning of this book, most people focus on PRICE. *But unless one is paying cash, PRICE becomes somewhat arbitrary unless one also understands clearly the underlying TERMS accompanying*

the PRICE. Remember, price is meaningless without terms,[309] and as a general rule, the less favorable the price is, it can be improved through generous and favorable terms for the buyer, who in this case is YOU.

Favorable or Unfavorable? A Loan-Term Summary Guide

Whether you are using private financing, seller financing, or hard money lenders, this guide is a good benchmark of what is fair and equitable and what you can expect in your negotiations with private lenders (or sellers, in the case of seller financing) and ***what is generally favorable to you is in GREEN***. The further you go to the right on the scale, ***what is more favorable to the lender is in RED***. Naturally, you would want everything on the greener side of the chart, but private lending is about creating "win-win" scenarios, and in order to do that, you have to be willing to negotiate, and at times, offer concessions of some sort strictly to get the deal done. **As always, remember, if you found an amazing property but you do not have the funds necessary to take possession of it through secure title, you have NOTHING.**[310]

Here is a general summary of terms in private and seller financing and how they fall on a scale of favorable to unfavorable with you as a buyer.

Loan-Term Favorability Chart

Loan Terms	More Favorable			Less Favorable		
Down payment?	0%	5%	10%	15%	20%	More than 20%
Origination fee?	1%	2%	3%	4%	5%	More than 5%
Interest Rate (Fixed)[320]?	2%	4%	6%	8%	10%	More than 10%
Length of loan?	5 Years	10 Years	15 Years	20 Years	25 Years	30 Years
Prepayment Penalty?	No	No	No	Yes	Yes	Yes

Sealing the Deal: Setting Up and Negotiating Your Terms with a Private Lender

As a rule, I always tell prospective private lenders what I am willing to pay, and they can take it or leave it. With that being said and in all fairness, I have been quite frequently on the ***other*** side of the table, being told by many private lenders what ***their*** lending terms

---

309 Assuming you plan to implement some type of financing.
310 **Of course, you could always resell the deal for an instant profit. This is called wholesaling and will be covered in depth in the next book.**

were, and I could "take it or leave it" (in most cases, I took it!). But a simple dialogue, once you and a lender have found that you have a common synergy and there may be a fruitful relationship for you both in the future, might look like this:

> **You (to prospective lender):** Mr. Lender, when I work with private money lenders, I pay 6% annualized interest and a one-point origination fee at the time of the loan origination. Generally, I repay all loans after six months but may ask for a penalty-free six-month extension if I need one. This is if you do not require monthly payments, whereas all interest will accrue and be paid off at the time I pay the loan in full. If you require a monthly payment, I will need an interest rate of 5%, with all other terms to remain the same. Does that work for you? If it does, I can get an attorney we are mutually comfortable with to draw up a simple lending agreement so we both have our lending relationship in writing and to make sure there is no confusion.

Let's summarize your offer. You basically gave the private lender two loan options, and he can select one or the other or offer a counterproposal.

Loan Term 1	Loan Term 2
Interest rate: 6%	Interest rate: 5%
Required monthly payments?: No	Required monthly payments?: Yes
Origination fee: 1%	Origination fee: 1%
Loan term: Six months, one extension possible	Loan term: Six months, one extension possible

Focusing on Creativity as a Key to Success

You will notice in the dialogue above I offered the lender a LOWER interest rate if he needed monthly payments but a higher interest rate if he did NOT require monthly payments. Why? Because monthly payments are annoying and a hassle. **The reality is, if you have a loan on the books for just a few months, it is easier to have interest accrue as a per diem fee paid at the back-end closing[311] than to write a check for an interest payment each month.** Keep in mind, these private loans are for acquiring and fixing up property

---

311 You will close twice with a private money lender—once when he lends you the money and you close on the property, and a second one when you pay him back and he releases your deed of trust from the county registrar by signing a notarized document indicating that he has been paid back in full and is releasing his first-position lien interest on your property. You will do this when you refinance, sell, or pay him back with cash on or before the end of the loan term.

before you institute a long-term, fully amortized loan product, so you pay interest-only payments each month on your short-term (private) loan. These loans (unless you structure one purposefully for a longer, multiyear repayment period, which you CAN do) are generally meant to be short-term loans that generate interest for the private lender and are paid back in full over a short period of time in one lump sum, which is often called a balloon note in general lending terms.

But did you notice how I gave the lender the option of receiving payments in a situation where their interest rate would be penalized? This type of creativity with the lending terms encourages a higher rate of return for them if you DON'T have to make monthly payments, and in doing so, helps you manage your cash flow effectively, keep your monthly debt service to a minimum, and allows you to focus on the task at hand—acquiring your property and getting the needed renovations completed so you can live in your home and rent out a unit (or area) of your property for income purposes, presumably, to help pay down your mortgage debt as quickly as possible and eliminate your monthly housing payment forever.

At the Closing Table with Your Private Lender

In advance of the closing, you will have set up your terms and conditions with your private lender and will have agreed to all the nuances necessary to ensure that you have created a win-win scenario. Your attorney will have drawn up a letter of memorandum indicating your lending relationship and the terms any loan will take. You will have notified your private lender in advance of the closing date and when the money is needed, and make sure to have told him to have the funds at the closing office twenty-four hours in advance of the closing to ensure a smooth close. The pre-closer at the closing office will have prepared the HUD-1 settlement sheet with your loan terms on it, closing costs, and inform you of any cash you need to bring to closing. Your pre-closer will also have obtained any insurance information your lender required and placed the insurance premiums on the HUD-1 so you will have insurance from day 1.

Usually when you close with a private lender, if you have "overborrowed" on the home (meaning, borrowed money beyond the purchase price of the home for repairs), you will pick up a check for the repairs as a lump sum. **PUT THIS IN A SEPARATE ACCOUNT FOR YOUR REAL ESTATE PURPOSES ONLY**! And ONLY use this money for the purposes it was intended.

Periodically, call the lender and keep them informed of your progress. Offer to let them visit the property with you as your construction is under way. This will instill them with confidence and strengthen your relationship, so that after you have fulfilled your obligation to your private lender and paid him back in full, you always have a lending resource to do future deals with.

Seller Financing: How to Settle Seller-Held Mortgages

Finally, I would be remiss in my work here on teaching you about private and seller financing if I did not give you some guidance on how to approach a seller about releasing a seller-financed mortgage to you at a substantial discount.

Basically, if you have a seller-financed note, your seller, who is holding your mortgage paper, will generally fall into one of three categories, as follows:

1. Someone who is okay holding the paper and may be willing to settle the mortgage for a discount;

2. Someone who is DESPERATE and needs money immediately and would LOVE to settle the mortgage for a discount in exchange for cash;

3. Someone who doesn't need the money, loves the monthly payments, and generally has little interest in releasing you from mortgage servitude.

Now I have dealt with all three types of sellers in these situations of paying on seller-held mortgages, but the people we are most interested in dealing with are Sellers 1 and 2. Seller 3 is most likely a lost cause, although approaching them periodically never hurts.

Approaching the Seller to Ask for Discount

The easiest way to do this is by phone call or letter. If you are doing it by phone, it should be short and to the point, as follows:

> **You:** Hello, Mr. Seller? Hi, it's (***insert your name here***). Yes, well, I just wanted you to know that I mailed you this month's payment, and interestingly enough, I got a call[312] from my mom yesterday who told me my grandmother, who recently passed away, might have left me a small amount of money. As you know, I have been paying the property note every month like we agreed, but I have been saving up some money, and with this money my grandmother is leaving me, I might be able to do something interesting, if we could work something out. Namely, I was wondering if you might be willing to let me pay the mortgage off, and in doing so, I thought perhaps you could give me a discount on the payoff for

---

312   Feel free to make up your own story, which reflects more truthful circumstances. This is just an example.

> paying you early and with ALL CASH? I don't have ALL of the money to pay you in full, but I thought if we could come to an arrangement, I could pay you a lot more than this monthly payment each month, and in return, I could get the home paid off once and for all.
>
> **Mr. Seller:** Well, that sounds interesting enough. How much money do you have?

Now, recall Chapter 1, where Emily asked me how much money I had as we were discussing me paying off my vacation home? ***DO NOT answer that question from the seller!*** Instead, ask them this question:

> **You:** Well, I don't have anywhere near the mortgage amount, but Mr. Seller, let me ask you this question. **If I gave you my entire life savings plus my inheritance from my grand-mother in all cash next week, what is the least you would be willing to take for the mortgage to let me pay off the property in full** and thus conclude our business?
>
> **Seller (thinks for a minute):** Well, I guess I would be willing to take "x."
>
> **You (count to ten before speaking):** *Is that the best you can do?*
>
> **Seller (thinks for a minute):** Well, I guess I could take "y" (which is lower than "x").

Sometimes sellers can't offer you enough of a discount at a given time to justify you paying off your mortgage. If that is the case, don't get discouraged. Remember, people's circumstances change ALL THE TIME financially, and just make a mental note to yourself to call them in another six months or so and ask if anything has changed: Are they willing to consider letting you pay off the mortgage in full for a discount? I have had to ask sellers over a period of years, sometimes before we came to an arrangement. If that's the case, just be persistent.

But What If I Don't Have the Money to Pay Off My Seller Held Mortgage, Even if He or She Offers Me a Steep Discount?

What a killer, your seller-held mortgagor has just told you they will accept a whopping 50% discount on your mortgage to pay it off in full, ***and you don't have the money***! What do you do before pulling your hair out?

Simple, Call Your Private Lender!

While I use private lenders for lots of short-term lending needs, I have paid off MANY homes by using private lenders for slightly longer-term, fully amortized loans. Consider a scenario where you have been paying a 100k, fifteen-year mortgage at 4% for a few months when the seller offers you a steep 50% discount:

Financing Information—100k Mortgage, 4% Fixed, Fifteen-Year Term	
Mortgage amount	$100,000.00
Down payment	$0.00
Loan amount	$100,000.00
Interest rate	4.00%
Loan terms (in months)	180
Monthly payment (P and I)	$739.69
Monthly net positive cash flow	N/A

That's a monthly payment of $739.69. Certainly favorable as a "no money down" purchase, and the interest rate is good. But how do we take advantage of our seller-financed 50% discount? Could our private lender come and save us, helping us to pay our seller-financed note holder in full? How about on a seven-year loan? **Remember, the shorter the loan term, the more aggressive the monthly principal reduction is, while the interest monthly is far less expensive.**

Financing Information—50k Mortgage, 6% Fixed, Seven-Year Term	
Mortgage amount	$50,000.00
Down payment	$0.00
Loan amount	$50,000.00
Interest rate	6.00%
Loan terms (in months)	84
Monthly payment (P and I)	$730.43
Monthly net positive cash flow	N/A

Yes! They CAN save us while slashing our borrowing time in more than half, while our interest rate increases by 50%! **You see, even with my interest rate going from 4% to 6% and my loan term going to seven years from fifteen years, my payment is STILL $9 cheaper,** and I have gained the most important thing—*the most precious asset*: I have instantly saved myself eight years of payments and, in doing so, saved myself eight years of TIME.

Asking for a Discounted Mortgage Payoff by Letter

Usually, I will send my monthly mortgage note and enclose a letter periodically asking for a mortgage discount or inquiring into whether the seller has ever considered this unique proposal. I do this once a year for all seller financed mortgages or sometimes every six months if I sense there is a possible opportunity about to unfold. Your letter might look something like this. Again, keep it short and sweet.

March 19, 2017

Holder of My Mortgage

123 Maple Street

Memphis, TN 38111

Re: Mortgage Payoff?

Dear Mr. Seller:

I pray this letter finds you well. Please find my enclosed mortgage payment for the month of "x."

I am writing to you to see if you would be willing to consider allowing me to pay my mortgage off early, at a discount. **The reason I ask is because I have been saving some money up, and due to some unexpected circumstances that recently put some money in my hands, I believe I may be in a position of paying off my mortgage in full with you, if you were willing to accept a discounted amount for ALL CASH.**

Assuming you find it convenient, could you please call me at *[insert your number here]* to discuss?

I greatly appreciate your help in this matter and am looking forward to concluding our business dealings satisfactorily.

Hope you and your family are well.

All my very best,

[Your Name HERE]

[Insert your company name HERE]

Conclusion

The use of seller financing and/or private financing in your real estate approach are invaluable tools at your disposal when you broach the world of creative real estate investing. To try to become financially free only by using "Fannie Mae-type" thirty-year mortgages as a benchmark for your financing platform is not only a tremendously weak approach, which does little to help you become free financially at best. It is most certainly foolhardy and heavily risk laden at worst. Remember the thirty-year race? Are you willing to run it and see if you succeed when so many others have failed?

Pay off your houses in ten years or less, and begin to embrace a vision of financial freedom not only for you and your family but also for generations to come. This is the ultimate purpose of **The Short-Term Retirement Program**—not only that you can live unencumbered by debt and stress obligations, but also that your children and children's children might have the same fate through your strategic acquisition and payoff of housing debt, ensuring that THEY DO NOT HAVE TO REPEAT THE THIRTY-YEAR (or) LIFE-BASED CYCLE OF HOUSING DEBT.

Are you the one who begins to FINALLY change your family's legacy?

Winchester Office Plaza: A Valuable Study in Real Estate Tools and Techniques

This investment property was one of the most stressful and traumatic deals that I had ever done. There are many valuable lessons in this study, especially on what NOT to do and how critical it is that you are careful to not partner with the WRONG people on a high-dollar, high-stress real estate deal.

There is a forty-four-unit office complex in a part of Memphis known as Hickory Hill on Winchester Road. When twenty-five of the forty-four units came up for sale as a block of foreclosed properties after the 2008 credit collapse, I immediately sensed an opportunity because I had some "inside" information, which was simply this: A very close friend of mine had owned these exact twenty-five units a few years before and had rented them out completely, then sold them to a doctor, who was an investor, for 1.2 million dollars.

In doing so, my friend had made over 500k on the deal as a net profit.

This made the property even more desirable because I was able to purchase the block of twenty-five properties for 315k, which was HALF of what my friend paid.

Now, in commercial negotiation, while everything is "negotiable," these negotiations are a lot firmer and more demanding than buying a small single-family house. **Earnest money frequently becomes nonrefundable after a very short period of time for inspection**. Financing is often far more difficult to obtain for commercial properties as well, and right after 2008, it was nearly impossible to get the funding for this type of transaction. Also, earnest money allotments are far higher than in single-family purchases, whereas in most cases, $500 earnest money is considered sufficient to bind a contract on a single-family home. In commercial property, the amounts are often 5% to 10%, and in this case, the required 10% was $31,500 of earnest money to take the twenty-five units to contract. A steep requirement for many investors, to be sure, and I was no exception.

In fact, I didn't have the earnest money.

The projections on the deal were so good, though, I had to find a way to make it work. I mean, twenty-five units at 315k led to a purchase price of $12,600 per unit, and each unit would rent for $750 on a three-year lease. The cash flow, when fully occupied, would be HUGE, and the resell margins would be much higher as well. But first I had to obtain some take-down money for the whole deal, and THEN I would need to work out a way to come up with the almost 32k of nonrefundable earnest money.

It just so happened at that time that I was working with a few "gurus," one of whom was allegedly a specialist in financing. Now in real estate, you will find that when you have done as many transactions as I have,[313] not many people are able to get things past you that are not based in reality, although it can happen from time to time. In this case, my guru "friend" told me that he had the financing lined up. He was willing to become a partner on the deal and provide the $31,500 in nonrefundable earnest money. Obviously, this was great news for me, as I could purchase the properties and renovate them and we could resell them for a great profit down the line after all of the units were back online.[314] My finance partner and I shook hands on the deal, he put up the earnest money, and I sent the contract to my closing attorney to prepare for the transaction settlement. The timing of this was great also because the twenty-five units were scheduled to close the day before my wife and I left for Disney World in Orlando on a family reunion-type vacation that had been planned over a

---

313 As of this writing, I personally have bought, sold, or acted as a consultant on over 1,700 purchase and sale transactions in my lifetime at the age of forty-three.

314 At the time of purchase, only four of the twenty-five units were rented. Through poor management and huge office condo fees, the previous owner was made insolvent and lost the properties and, through mismanagement, the majority of the tenants also. Keep in mind, commercial property has very little value when it is vacant and not producing income.

year in advance and paid for. Now I am not a huge fan of Disney, but my wife and her family are, so we were looking forward to some rest and relaxation in a place my wife was absolutely thrilled to go.

Sounds great, right?

Well, in the world of real estate closings, I have a saying, which is quite simply this:

"Nothing is done until it is done."

And this transaction is the perfect example of why I use this saying. Two days before the closing, my guru "partner" called me and basically said, *"Hey...bad news...my lender who said he would fund the deal has backed out, and I have no other financing sources to consider. I need you to get my earnest money back."*

This was an issue for a variety of reasons as follows: **(a)** the earnest money was clearly nonrefundable, and **(b)** the transaction was scheduled to close in less than forty-eight hours (which is an almost impossible time frame to get 315k together, even with private lending relationships), and **(c)** the listing agent on the transaction had been acting very strange and aggressively, almost as if he wanted the deal to fall through. Basically, I called the agent, and he said that if we weren't able to close the deal as scheduled, the deal was "dead."

Beware of the Commercial Listing Agent Who Moonlights on the Side

Now, I couldn't figure out what was going on with the selling agent, but I tend to have a great investigative "nose," **and I knew something fishy was going on**. But before I had time to delve into the mystery that might end up shedding some light on the situation, I called the agent's broker and spoke frankly with him, telling him that the financing had fallen through and made him a proposal, which indicated I was fully committed to the closing, as follows:

In exchange for a one-month closing extension (meaning, I have an additional thirty days to close the property), I will put up ANOTHER 10% of NONRE-FUNDABLE EARNEST MONEY. The broker agreed to the proposal, and I went hunting for earnest money while informing my wife that I would be unable to attend our family's Disney World vacation.[315]

Now, there were two major problems that I had to solve and fast. One was coming up with an additional $31,500 earnest money in twenty-four hours to keep the deal

---

315 **And by the way, she was PISSED.**

alive. While that might sound like an extremely difficult task (it was), I had an even bigger issue to solve, which was coming up with the balance of 315k on a commercial property within thirty days, when banks were not lending, and I had no private money resources who had that kind of capacity, let alone tolerance for risk. On a tertiary note, I had to perform some investigative work into why the listing agent was so committed to seeing the deal die and, in doing so, get some type of relief.

Solving Problems: A Guide

Freaking out and crying over missing my Disney vacation or lamenting how terrible my "guru financing partner" was at sticking me in this situation would not help me at all. **I had a lot of money and my word on the line, and I intended to keep it.** So I got to work and began addressing the roadblocks in my way to getting the twenty-five units closed.

1. **Earnest Money Issue.** I needed $31,500 and fast. Nobody in their right mind was interested in lending $31,500 in exchange for nothing and in such an unsecure and risky position. I had to figure out a way to make it worth their while. **Then I remembered the condos were titled as "fee simple," meaning, I was buying twenty-five office units that were each titled individually.** I could sell twenty-five units as one package or twenty-five units as twenty-five single-unit, individual package or any permutation thereof. **So when I meditated on this, I called a friend in California and offered him a rented office condo for free if he would lend me $31,500 as earnest money for thirty days**. He agreed and wired the money to the listing broker the next day. In doing so, I had bought my thirty-day extension. *Problem 1 = solved.*

2. **Funding Issue.** Believe it or not, this was a far bigger obstacle to tackle. I spent a week going from bank to bank[316] asking for a 315k loan and just got turned down *every time*. So, frustrated, I went home and spent some time meditating on my problem, and then it hit me: **Why bother asking for such a large sum of money when I could solicit smaller sums of money, per condo, and investors could lend as much or as little as they wanted!** Remember, in the previous paragraph, how I told you the condos were titled in fee simple? Well, when I concluded that I should stop trying to get twenty-five condos financed all at once and get them

---

316 **Admitting this to you is painful for me because I was SO desperate I started to go to the banks asking for the money and was told NO by all of them**. There is a lesson here.

financed in blocks of four or five at a time, with a minimum loan per unit of 25k, my life suddenly became a lot easier.

Consider the following loan request dialogues:

Loan request A: Excuse me, Mr. Banker or Private Lender, I need 315k for twenty-five office condos that are foreclosed and need to close in less than three weeks or lose my 63k in earnest money. I'm pretty desperate.

Answer: No.

Loan request B: Excuse me, Mr. Private Lender, I am purchasing twenty-five office condos that are foreclosed, and they are closing in three weeks. You can lend as much or as little as you want to, with a minimum loan of 25k per unit at 5% origination fee per loan unit and 12% annual interest for each loan.[317] If you loan on a minimum of four condo units (loan amount of 100k), I will give you a free "fee simple" condo titled to you at the closing. All loans will be paid back in six months.

Answer: Can I lend 200k and get two free condos?

Obviously, the creative aspect of getting free condos plus 12% interest and five points of fees on a six-month loan term makes lending on office condos far more attractive. The 25k-per-unit lending minimum also helped me in that for every 25k lent on one condo, I was actually financing two condos (remember our purchase price per office condo was $12,600[318]). Basically, I needed three 100k lenders and one 25k lender, and my 315k purchase price plus my closing costs and twenty-five units would be paid for, while I could give back the earnest money my "guru friend" and California investor had put up. If I could achieve this, all would be well, and I would have pulled off a seemingly impossible feat.

And I did. I lined up the lenders, got their commitments in advance of the closing, and instead of funding one large 315k-transaction with a single lender, I financed twenty-five units with several smaller lenders, all of whom had their loans secured by a number of condo units. Oh, and by the way, I got three condo units for "free" in the deal, because there were some unencumbered units left after all the financing was secured that I kept personally. **I call that "parting out" real estate, where you buy units in bulk so cheaply that you have the ability to fix up and resell the majority of the units while you have some left over (ideally the best ones) for yourself.**

---

317 Note: These are very high rates and fees, but I wasn't in a position to negotiate.
318 Twenty-five units at 315k total for the package = $12,600 per unit, as discussed.

Let's take a look at how this worked with the twenty-five units at Winchester Office Plaza.

Winchester Office Plaza: Lending and Per Unit Financing Analysis

Total loan needed: 315k

Closing costs: 10k

Total cash required: 325k

Total units: 25

Lending breakdown:

Units 1–4: Loan amount from Lender A, 100k. 100k total financed so far.

Unit 5: Free condo to Lender A.

Units 5–8: Loan amount from Lender B, 100k. 200k total financed so far.

Unit 9: Free condo to Lender B.

Units 10–13: Loan amount from Lender C, 100k. 300k total financed so far.

Unit 14: Free condo to Lender C.

Unit 15: Loan amount from Lender D, 25k (**325k total financed so far, and we have met our financing requirements to close the transaction).**

Unit 16: Free condo to California investor for wiring in $31,500 in earnest money.

Units 17–22: Unassigned and unencumbered (meaning, no loan on these units) units titled to me for resale purposes to help pay off the 325k in loans and generate profit beyond loan repayment.

Units 23–25: A three-unit condo I leased to a church for $1,000 per month. I kept this for my portfolio at no cost to me.[319]

As you can see, by thinking creatively and "parting out" the twenty-five units into easily financeable blocks (made even easier with creative incentives like giving away free condos), I was able to get the units financed. *Problem 2 = solved.*

What About the Listing Agent Who Was Trying to Sabotage the Deal?

I did some deep investigating because I simply, for the life of me, was unable to

---

319   Again, "parting out" real estate. Also, a market value of about 150k worth of real estate.

figure out why this listing agent was so interested in sabotaging the deal. When you think about the earnest money involved, it makes even LESS sense to try, as a listing agent, to "kill" a deal simply because when someone has such a large amount of nonrefundable earnest money down, they clearly are working diligently on trying to close, guaranteeing you as an agent a payday. Yet even during the extension period, the agent was involved in all kinds of unscrupulous things, like speaking to the sellers and telling them to "pull the contract," etc.

After doing some research, I found out the issue: The agent wasn't really an "agent" at all. He was, in fact, a drug dealer with multiple recent "possession with intent to distribute" arrests and was awaiting court dates and sentencing! And he had previous felony convictions for distributing drugs, so suddenly the picture became clear (and I heard this from another inside source). He needed money so badly he was promised part of the earnest money IF the deal fell through!

So I called up the listing agent and told him what I had found out, and we had words on the phone. When I say "words," let me tell you the discussion I had with him was unfit for print in this book. And after I got off the phone with him, I called his agent and put him on notice that he had a drug dealer working in his office and trying to sabotage my deal, which I DIDN'T appreciate when so much money was on the line. **Well, let me tell you the broker's attitude suddenly changed. He became VERY interested in my deal closing and started being VERY nice to me,** and as for his drug-dealing "agent," well, let's just say that guy disappeared very quickly.

All's Well That Ends Well

When all the pieces were assembled and all of the "detective" work done, which gave me insight into the path necessary to obtain financing and get the deal closed while eliminating any existing roadblocks, it suddenly seemed that the closing was possible, and after all the difficulties, it seemed somewhat surreal as we approached the day before closing. In fact, I called my wife, who was at Disney, and told her these exact words: "*I swear if I get this deal closed, I am going to dance a jig.*"

But the day that the closing came, while I expected potentially more problems, I found that things went relatively smoothly. I don't dress up for closings anymore, but I dressed up for this one, and after spending two hours with my closing attorney going over plat numbers of individual parcels, parting out the condos as promised, ensuring the financing was secured by the correct units, and making sure the seller got every penny they were promised, I owned twenty-two units at Winchester Office

Plaza (remember I had to give three away) and had kept my promise to everyone involved, even when I had been thrown under the bus by about everybody but the seller himself, because I had

1. **Arranged for favorable private financing on the property, one condo at a time;**

2. **Eliminated the obstacles that were impeding me from closing, such as the drug-dealing listing agent and his highly uncooperative broker;**

3. **I returned 63k in earnest money to its rightful owners, as promised;**

4. **I paid the seller in full, as agreed, within my thirty-day extension period; and**

5. **In closing the transaction, I gained three free units from "parting out" the condos, plus generated a 10k commission to the brokerage I owned since my brokerage represented me as a buyer, which entitled me to a commission (gravy on top).**

Conclusion

No real estate investment opportunity is "unbuyable" or "uncloseable" when you put enough due diligence and work into it.[320] In the case of this particular transaction, **I had to mentally figure out that there was a BIG difference between financing one (large) twenty-five-unit package for 315k versus financing twenty-five (small) one-unit packages at 25k each** until I arrived at my goal, which happened around unit 15. Once I made this mental connection, approaching lenders was a much simpler process, and they were much more inclined to say *yes* due to smaller loan amounts, high loan fees and interest, plus free condo incentives I was able to offer *only* by thinking outside of the box, in a creative way.

The neatest part, as I recollect, was not getting the transaction done; it was being able to recreate a scene in my attorney's office from Bruce Willis's ***The Last Boy Scout***, where after overcoming a tremendous series of challenging and terrible events as a private detective, Bruce Willis's character finally thwarts a major disaster at a football stadium and, in doing so, dances a jig in the rafters high above the stadium, having solved the case and saved the day.

And you should have seen me dance.

---

320 Barring unresolvable title issues.

11

The Holy Grail of Personal Finance—Total Debt Freedom and Unimpeded Passive Monthly Cash Flow: Sample Portfolio Structures

The thing I find about most people through my radio show and speaking engagements is NOT that they are unwilling to make changes in their life financially to improve their situation. The reality is, in fact, that most "bread winners" within families or those charged with the financial responsibility of supporting their family, who seem to end up in this never-ending vortex of living paycheck to paycheck yet falling more deeply into debt, want *desperately* to do whatever is necessary to change and improve their financial circumstances.

The truth is, they simply don't know how.

Do you remember the game Monopoly we all played as kids? Personally, I am not a big fan of Monopoly as an entertainment venue. I prefer different types of games with far deeper strategy concepts, such as collectible card games and digital role-playing games for my gaming leisure time. However, Monopoly gives us a great and simple real estate blueprint that allows us to discover a recipe that leads us to financial freedom.

In Monopoly, for those of you who are unfamiliar, you take your game piece around a square board filled with real estate "land." If you arrive on an unbought space, you have the option of purchasing the land, and then when you do and other players land on your land, you collect fees in the form of "rent." This rent grows higher when you choose to improve the land with green plastic houses (which you can upgrade up to four times), or you can collect the ultimate rent premium by upgrading your land to a red hotel, thereby guaranteeing yourself the highest possible income per land square. Usually, those who have the most squares of land, which contain the most improvements, generally win through their opponents' financial attrition. Their opponents are forced to pay continual rent premiums from their limited cash reserves as they travel around the board, supplemented by a meager cash infusion of $200[321] each time they pass "Go," which is simply unable to sustain their rent debt obligations over the course of the game.

Now most real estate *gurus* (again, hating on that word) who speak on the real estate lecture circuit[322] will discuss the game of Monopoly as a metaphor for how a real estate investor succeeds in the game-of-life-based real estate investing, mainly that:

1. **Owning single-family homes can generate your income;**

2. **Owning multiple single-family homes can help you generate even MORE income; and**

3. **Owning multi-unit commercial property in desirable areas of your municipality (like Boardwalk in Monopoly) can get you the highest rents and, in doing so, make you wealthy.**

Personally, I can't dispute these simple teachings from a metaphorical standpoint. Yes, the basic premise of these ideas is true: If you own real estate, you can collect rent. If you own premium rental real estate at a commercial location and you are receiving rent from a commercial tenant, you are (potentially) generating "a lot"[323] of gross income.[324]

But my interest in this Monopoly metaphor lies in two entirely different places, as follows:

1. How long does it take you to pay off that real estate debt the gurus extol upon you as being so desirable since the game of Monopoly allows you to purchase and upgrade your properties for a one-time fee of small petty cash, and life isn't like that AT ALL,[325] *and more importantly*;

2. What happens to the people who play Monopoly and never buy real estate?

---

321 Meant to simulate a paycheck.
322 At local REIA groups, real estate symposiums, etc.
323 Extremely relative term.
324 Not to be confused with Net Operating Income (NOI) or "take-home pay" in real estate terms.
325 Remember, most people take thirty years or MORE to pay off a property, if at all. **Statistically, the number of people who ever "pay off" their home is low compared to those who choose to sell their house and upgrade to a larger house (and debt) or simply refinance periodically**. They might "pay off" their mortgage when they sell their home, but they aren't retiring the debt, so to speak, *just simply "kicking the can" down the road with larger payments and taxes, which is a wealth-LOSING proposition*.

Monopoly as a Metaphor for YOUR Life

For the purposes of this discussion, my interest lies solely in Number 2 stated above. What happens to those who "play Monopoly" in real life simply by "traveling around the board,"[326] collecting $200 when they pass "go" and spend all of their "paycheck" on random events they have no control over, such as paying rent, having to "get out of jail," pay for "parking," and so on?[327] **In the game of Monopoly, no player could ever hope to win by simply going around the board again and again collecting their meager paycheck and giving it away in rent and other fees without acquiring land or real estate, with no other sources of earned or passive income.**[328]

Is real life any different for the average person?

The truth is, the world of financial freedom breaks down quite simply into a few basic elements. Let's look at those elements and define those for the sake of this discussion while looking at a few formulae you need to remember.

Cash flow. The amount of money you personally generate from all your income sources, usually gauged in months.

Debt service. The total amount of bills you are required to pay each month. Remember, you arrived at most of these monthly bills either through necessity (like a utility bill) or by signing on the dotted line of a contractually binding credit agreement, or accepting someone else's obligation as your own.[329]

Principal debt. The amount of total debt you have on a particular item, which generates for you monthly bill payments, which you are required to pay. For example, you have 80k in total student loan debt, so you get a bill each month from your student loan servicer and are required to pay it or you go into default.

Essential services. Bills you are required to have to live comfortably and cannot live without (for example, health insurance, a payment on a dwelling like your residential house, a utility bill, food, etc.).

Knowing these definitions, let's define *Financial Freedom* for the purposes of this book:

---

326 Meaning, go through life without direction.
327 i.e., living paycheck to paycheck.
328 **Real life = same way.**
329 Paying your mother's rent, for example.

> **Feol's Simple Financial Freedom Formula**
>
> **A total absence of monthly credit obligations from principal debt, with a monthly positive (and ideally passive) cash flow that exceeds comfortably the total amount of monthly debt service you have from essential services—services that cannot be retired through debt repayment or be realistically removed.**[330]

That sounds complicated. Let's make it simple.

Absence of monthly credit obligations—your total debt is paid off, i.e., you have paid off your house, student loans, credit cards, and vehicles. *You have NO debt*.

Positive cash flow—income from all monthly sources that exceeds any bills you may have, specifically:

Essential services—bills which you will NEVER get rid of (utilities, health insurance, property taxes, property insurance, food, and so on[331]).

So, our financial freedom formula looks something like this:

Absence of monthly credit obligations (bills) + monthly income – all essential service payments = positive cash flow left over

And therein lies the key to never having to worry about money again.

With that said, let's look at a couple of sample portfolio structures (using Timmy as our guide) from beginning to end, which allow our families in these examples to become financially independent and debt free as well, over a period of short years, which they would have to endure anyway, whether they were planning for financial freedom or not.[332]

Trading Equity versus Debt: A Primer for Improving Cash Flow

Obviously, everyone's personal financial situation is different, and as such, it would be far too intensive to try to cover anything except a few common examples in this book. However, it is important to realize that a common theme in most people's financial statements is significant amounts of unsecured debt that they are unable to easily pay off due to a lack of liquidity or a lack of financial resources.

With that being said, in some of these portfolio assessments, I will recommend trading debt for some equity in a house you find, often through the use of private financing,

---

330 The day you arrive here, you should have peace of mind.

331 **Naturally, there are workarounds for these also. Grow your own food, go solar, drill a well, pay your property taxes in a one-time sum so you gain alloidal title, and so forth.** But we are all constrained by the twenty-four hours we each have in a day, so one has to pick and choose their battles!

332 Remember, five years in the future is going to come anyway. Would you rather be financially free in five years or in the exact same situation you are now or possibly worse?

which will in essence immediately improve your monthly cash flow while reducing your monthly debt obligations. This technique, however, brings up a fundamental argument most financial planners and money managers tell you to avoid, which is *"trading short-term debt for long-term debt."*

Consider the following example.

Timmy the Teacher: Short-Term Debt Swap for Long-Term Debt

Timmy the Teacher has accumulated a credit card debt of $10,000. Using his monthly take-home pay as outlined in previous chapters, he does not have enough discretionary, disposable income to pay off the credit card in full or even make aggressive monthly payments that allow him to attack the principal debt each month, which would create a short-term payoff time frame in which he can realistically expect to retire the credit card debt in a matter of months or a few years, depending on how aggressive he was able to pay.[333]

Additionally, the credit line is "open," and Timmy uses the credit card to make necessary and discretionary additional purchases on a monthly basis when his cash flow is short, which is, of course, each month. As such, his debt is unsustainable, but to avoid a credit (or life) issue, he makes the minimum payment every month and hopes for a financial windfall somewhere down the road. He senses deep down that this situation is somewhat hopeless, but he doesn't share this with his wife.

One day, as Timmy goes to deposit his biweekly paycheck, Bob the Banker mentions to Timmy that the bank is offering a low-interest thirty-year mortgage refinance promotion. If Timmy were to refinance, he could *"pull out some cash"*[334] from the equity of his home and *"use it for whatever he wants to."* Timmy starts the refinance process, and Bob calls him a week later to tell him the *"great news"* that based on the equity in his home from Timmy's bank appraisal, at closing (and after $5,000 of "rolled in" closing costs), Timmy will receive a check for $10,000 as the proceeds from the refinance.

Timmy goes to the bank a few days later, signs the requisite paperwork, and walks out with a check for $10,000. He uses this to pay off his credit card then goes home and tells his wife exuberantly that he has "paid off his credit card."

His wife believes that Timmy is, in fact, a financial hero.

---

333 Making the "minimum payment" each month also does create a terminal payoff time frame, albeit one which is long and filled with unnecessary, super-high interest. But this assumes one STOPS using their credit card for purchases *permanently*.

334 Remember, Timmy is NOT making any money here. He is simply borrowing it from the bank based on his home's estimated value through an appraisal.

Timmy the Teacher: Financial Hero or Zero?

Timmy didn't really pay off his credit card in this situation, and many people reading this example don't like the sound of that. But the reality of the matter is **TIMMY SIMPLY TRADED HIS SHORT-TERM CREDIT CARD DEBT FOR LONG-TERM MORTGAGE DEBT.**

Now, financial planners tell you not to do this, simply because of the math involved. Quite simply, refinancing an additional 10k of credit card debt, when added to your mortgage, results in an extra thirty years of $10,000 in interest-bearing debt, at whatever your refinance rate is. The "financial gurus" tell you not to do this because while you might have given yourself short-term relief, you are paying far more interest in a debt that you voluntarily created and, in doing so, kicking the can down the road while destroying the equity in your house.

And I agree with them, conditionally.

Here is modification of that strategy, which is far more impactful, powerful, and realistic for the average person who is working full time and still struggling to make ends meet:[335]

> **Feol's Short-Term versus Long-Term Debt Elimination Strategy**
>
> 1. It is undesirable to trade short-term unsecured debt for long-term secure mortgage debt, or make any type of short-term debt swap for long-term, interest-bearing debt even if the rate is "lower."
>
> However, If you are *really struggling* and have to find a way to trade short-term debt for long-term debt:
>
> 2. Find a piece of real estate that is so undervalued that you can trade ALL your unsecured debt against it through private lending, and then
>
> 3. "Over borrow" against the property using a lender or private lender, such that your total debt owed on the subject property after paying off ALL your unsecure debt is still far below market value, then
>
> 4. Sell that asset at market value IMMEDIATELY (thereby eliminating your debt permanently), or
>
> 5. Use a ten-year mortgage loan (or less) and apply tenant payments from that residence to help you eliminate your debt in one-third of the time a thirty-year-mortgage debt refinance would take.[336]

---

335 This assumes your spending is in order. If you have a shopping problem, until the day comes where you cut the credit cards up and get rid of your unsecured credit lines, I can't help you, and neither will these strategies.

336 This assumes you are living in the property as your primary residence and renting out some portion of it.

Timmy the Teacher Redux: Zero to Hero

Let's pretend Timmy has taken a different tack, mainly that he has been reading this book.

Using the principles we just reviewed and defined, **Timmy goes out and finds an amazing real estate deal.** His wife LOVES their current house, so she is refusing to consider moving to a different house. Timmy understands that he can still pay off his unsecured debt without needing to purchase a new primary residence, although he also understands from absorbing the knowledge in this tome that he is destined to live paycheck to paycheck, for most of his life, while choosing to service his existing thirty-year mortgage with no additional income sources from tenants. Timmy is okay with that; he knows that he needs to demonstrate to his wife that the principles in this book actually work, and paying off their credit card[337] would be an amazing first step.

Knowing this, **Timmy takes his amazing real estate deal to contract.** He found a house needing some fix-up worth 100k (after repairs), which he could buy for 40k, and he is able to get the 15k in needed repairs from a willing private lender, as well as the 40k for the purchase price of the home. The lender is going to charge him a 5k origination fee on the loan, which is almost 10%—substantial. However, Timmy knows that his property is in an area where homes are selling quickly, and he knows this because he has consulted with separate, successful realtors who are BOTH begging to list the house once it is fixed up.

So while his original borrowing plan looked like this:

Private Lending Example 3: A 60k Loan Request

Scenario: Timmy has found a home worth 100k and wants to fix it up and sell it for a profit, which he will make after he successfully closes the house, fixes it up, resells it at market value, pays his closing costs and associated expenses, and pays off the lender as agreed.

After repair value: 100k

Home purchase price: 40k

Estimated repairs: 15k

Borrower loan request: 60k

Lending fee (origination fee): 5k

Total liquid monetary amount lent to borrower: 55k

---

337 Actually, paying it off, not just trading the short-term debt for long-term mortgage debt through a refinance.

Timmy Markets Fixed-Up Home, Lists with Realtor, Home Sells and Closes After Six Months

> **Listing price:** 100k
>
> **Offer price:** 90k
>
> **Less 6% realtor commission:** ($5,400)
>
> **Less closing costs:** ($1,000)
>
> **Gross sale proceeds:** $83,600
>
> **Less funds lent:** $55,000
>
> **Net yield (after six months):** $28,600

He realizes that by finding such a discounted deal, he can make some money AND pay off his credit card debt, eliminating a large monthly principal debt he is obligated to and the associated monthly interest expenses that accompany it. In his heart, Timmy ALSO suspects that he only has to do this a few times to eliminate any toxic, unsecure debt he has (other than his primary house payment) permanently.

So *his revised borrowing plan looks like this:*

Private Lending Example 4: A 70k Loan Request

Scenario: Timmy has found a home worth 100k and wants to fix it up and sell it for a profit *BUT ALSO WANTS TO ROLL HIS CREDIT CARD DEBT INTO THE PRIVATE MONEY LOAN AGAINST THE EQUITY OF HIS PROPERTY BEFORE RESELLING IT ON THE RETAIL MARKET*, which he will make after he successfully closes the house, fixes it up, resells it at market value, pays his closing costs and associated expenses, and pays off the lender as agreed because this allows him to get out of his credit card debt IMMEDIATELY and stop the constant monthly revolving interest, which is killing him.

After repair value: 100k

Home purchase price: 40k

Estimated repairs: 15k

Total credit card payoff: 10k

Borrower loan request: 70k

Lending fee (origination fee): 5k

Total liquid monetary amount lent to borrower: 65k[338]

Timmy Markets Fixed Up Home, Lists with Realtor, Home Sells and Closes After Six Months

Listing price: 100k

Offer price: 90k

Less 6% realtor commission: ($5,400)

Less closing costs: ($1,000)

Gross sale proceeds: $83,600

Less funds lent: $56,000

Net yield after six months: $18,600[339]

And as per his revised borrowing and business plan, Timmy sells the deal he finds for a stout $18,600 profit **but ALSO paid off his credit card and closed the account using the massive equity cushion he had using some creative borrowing from his private lending source.** Also, remember Timmy could take up to an $18,600 discount from the sale of his home AND STILL HAVE PAID OFF HIS CREDIT CARD. The cushion of equity (**read**: profit margin) was so substantial that Timmy had lots of options to pursue if the home didn't sell for full price, which in this example, it did. **This is an example of where an individual was able to successfully swap short-term debt for long-term debt, although that long-term debt became *someone else's* long-term debt.**[340] Timmy went into this with the right idea though he knew he would only have the house (and underlying loan) for a short time, so he swapped his debt against it, and **it was removed permanently from his balance sheet when he divested himself of the asset** (which carried his paid off credit card balance with it).

---

338 Timmy adds 10k to his loan request, and at the first closing where he closes and takes title to the loan using a private money lender, *he instantly sends a check to the credit card company and requests to close his credit line permanently, thus eliminating his credit card debt FOREVER.*

339 Keep in mind, Timmy still generates a great profit here from finding and reselling his "deal," but he did something even MORE important, which is paying off his credit card in the process.

340 **Remember, getting other people to pay your bills can make you wealthy**. This can also eliminate large amounts of debt you have by applying your unsecured debts to an equity-based loan, then selling the property to someone else who is willing to pay retail (*and obviously hasn't read this book*).

Money as a Mental Construct—Changing Your Thinking Paradigm

Now, before we get to looking at a few examples of portfolio structuring with financial freedom in mind, it is important to review the idea of money as simply being a mental construct.

I talk about this with a great degree of frequency on my radio show, and over the years, it has really proven to be "matrix shattering," so to speak, when listeners really connect with some of the examples I give, **and then money goes from being something with intrinsic value in their minds to simply being something that is essentially symbolic in their consciousness and nothing more than a tool, which is at their financial disposal.**

Consider this example.

Amy gets called by her brother, who is encouraging her to tithe. While her brother has Amy's best interests in mind when he is encouraging her to part with 10% of her monthly income for spiritual or charitable purposes,[341] he is stonewalled by his sister, who flatly states to him, *"When I am done paying the bills each month, no money is left over"* and then hangs up the phone. And Amy *IS* telling her brother the truth, she spends every dime she makes and is living paycheck to paycheck.

Her financial picture looks something like this:

Amy's Take-Home Pay: $3,600 per month

Less her thirty-year mortgage (with impounds): $1,000

Less her Lexus payment: $550

Less her student loan payments: $450

Less her credit card payments: $400

Less her utility payment: $300

Less her health insurance payment to her employer: $250

Less gasoline: $150

Less food: $500

Less clothing and entertainment: She has no money left over and is forced to use her credit card because she has expended her monthly paycheck at this time. This probably why she has a minimum credit card payment of $400.

---

341 **Because he tithes himself and understands how powerful tithing can be,** not only from a giving standpoint but also from a wealth building standpoint. See Robert Kiyosaki's **Rich Dad, Poor Dad** for a simple explanation of why tithing, for lack of a better word, can help you become stronger financially.

Again, Amy told her brother the truth. ***In her present financial situation, she has leveraged herself out so heavily between a thirty-year house (that she really couldn't afford) and her new Lexus payment ("Gotta let people know you are successful," she counsels her brother) that she simply could not afford to give away any money, let alone 10% of her paycheck.*** To be clear, Amy believes that to generate $360 more than she makes from her full-time monthly salary is a huge sum of money, almost untenable. In her mind, for her to make an extra $360 per month, she would need a 10% raise, which is unlikely to happen anytime soon.[342]

Now, like all people, Amy is going through life and hoping things will get better, but suddenly, BAM, Amy's brakes need to be replaced, and they are NOT covered under her vehicle's warranty because they are considered a "wear and tear" item. Amy's mechanic gives her the bad news: It will cost $360 to fix her brakes or her car is inoperable. Amy has to get to work to keep the paycheck coming in or she will be homeless, so NOT paying for the brake replacement is NOT an option. And Amy's credit card is maxed out, so she cannot pay for the repairs that way. Fortunately, Amy's workplace is shut down for the next four days (a long-weekend holiday), so Amy leaves her car with the mechanic to fix, gets a ride home, and then works on a realistic plan to come up with the $360, and this is what she comes up with: She is going to rake her neighbors' leaves for twelve hours a day for the next three days (it is fall leaf season, luckily, and she has a rake and some lawn and leaf bags in her garage) at $10 per hour and come up with the $360 she needs to get her brakes fixed and reclaim her car in working condition.

Now, over the next three days, Amy isn't able to work twelve hours a day due to it getting darker than she expected, so she only worked ten hours a day (thirty hours instead of thirty-six), so she only generated $300 in income, but she got $50 in tips, so she made a total of $350 and is only $10 short of her brake total.

Amy, intelligently, calls the mechanical and asks, "I have $350 in cash. If I can bring this to you today in cash, can we call it even?"

The mechanic says *yes*, and Amy gets her car back. All seems well.

Let's Analyze Amy's Performance

Well, how did Amy do? Most people would say "great" because she worked her way out of a disaster. But whether you think Amy did a good job or feel some other way, what I really want you to notice is how Amy addressed her problem, **specifically since after she got**

---

342   As is the case with most employed people who do ***NOT*** realize 10% yearly raises.

off the phone with her brother, where she was convinced that coming up with $360 was pretty much untenable.

Consider that:

- Amy's brakes failed, and she was told she needed $360 to make the necessary repairs, which she did NOT have;

- Amy found a creative solution by working in her off hours to generate (barely) enough income to pay for the needed repairs; and

- When all was said and done, Amy came very close to her target of $360 by generating $350.

The key to consider here is that Amy's performance generating money was clearly linked to how Amy views money in her conscious and subconscious.[343] Specifically, $360, in her mind, is an almost unreachable goal for her, and it takes her three days of significant exertion to generate this revenue.

Notice, never did Amy say to herself:

- I need $360, but I should set a goal for myself of $1,000 so I have a small cushion in case something like this happens again; *or*

- I need $360. I wonder if instead of earning that in three days, can I earn it in one day and do it for three days in a row, generating more cash than I need for other purposes; *or*

- I wonder if I can just ask $360 for one leaf job? How close can I get to $360 for one job instead of doing five or six jobs over three days? Is there a better way to invest my time while simultaneously generating revenue?

In a nutshell, Amy views herself as a $10-per-hour employee through her mental construct. *Never did she think for a second she was worth $50 per hour. That thought didn't even come close to crossing her mind*. Amy views the $360 additional capital she needs to raise to reclaim her car as a massive sum of money, one in which if she works VERY HARD for THREE FULL DAYS (and gets lucky), she may be able to get.

---

343   i.e., *money as a mental construct* is illustrated succinctly here.

Keep in mind also that Amy has NO money for tithing,[344] but she can come up with $360 when she is suddenly threatened with homelessness by losing her paycheck-to-paycheck existence[345] by exerting MAXIMUM effort under MAXIMUM stress when she is FORCED TO.

Meditate on this.

What Is Your Mental Construct?

So here is the key to unlocking your financial prison, mainly, people who earn a certain living in a given year rarely deviate from that living, salary-wise, with very few statistically small exceptions.

Why is this?

Because of how you view money as a mental construct.

For example, pretend you have a friend who earns $25,000 per year as an administrative assistant. Your friend has worked at that position for a few years, then their workplace closes. Now your friend has to begin looking for another job, which is generally a stress-laden nightmare. They scour newspaper classified ads, online ads for job openings, ask friends, and subscribe to job listing sites, and after a few months, they call you and give you the "good news" that they found a job, and, in fact, they are making "more" than they were before! They share with you that they are now making $26,500 versus 25k and couldn't be happier. Your friend, for all intents and purposes, has continued her full-time pursuit of a meager salary and paycheck-to-paycheck existence.[346]

Notice, your friend never did, nor did they ask themselves, any of the following things in their job-seeking process:

1. Consider looking for a job that offered a six-figure salary (**read:** 100k/annually, considered to be a "wealthy" job salary).

2. Ask for 50k versus somewhere in the ballpark of 25k in their job interviews when salary was discussed.

3. Consider changing careers—i.e., "my sister-in-law has been working as a real estate agent generating 3% commissions on a few 100k sales each month, which is more than I make working 160 hours a month full-time. Maybe I could do that?"

---

344 Or any discretionary expenditures, really.
345 If she cannot pay for her brake repair and thus cannot get to work, for example.
346 I am in no way trying to be pejorative or negative or judgmental here, just realistic. I have been in the same position many times.

4. Question the status quo—i.e., "I have been renting a $695 apartment all my life. How do people afford 200k homes in really nice suburbs? How can someone have $2,000 per month to throw at a thirty-year mortgage[347]? I know, not everyone living in, "that," subdivision are doctors and lawyers."

5. Ask, "How can I get a job making twice as much as I have been making?"

But why? Why did your friend (we all have friends like this, or maybe it is the person we see in the mirror every day) not ask any of these questions? Is your friend not motivated? Are they not intelligent?

No, of course not. **They simply have fallen into a routine where their financial circumstances have been somewhat shaped by (most likely) their youth and growing up with parents who had similar financial circumstances**. Maybe their parents lived paycheck to paycheck (very common in the United States) or had money issues, and they grew up thinking this was the norm.[348] Maybe your friend, for whatever reason, did not go to college and has been conditioned that "without a degree," she is an "unskilled laborer" and can only expect to generate a 25k type of salary range, since every time she has looked at jobs in her field, these are the types of salaries offered. Maybe she is conditioned to a subconscious predetermination to seek out what she knows and what she is comfortable with, and this is why her "new job" is really quite similar to her "old job," and her circumstances haven't changed.

No Job Can Make You Wealthy

As we have discussed before, there is no way you can "save" your way to becoming wealthy and financially independent. In fact, if you think about it, most of the retirement commercials you hear on TV and radio today by local financial planners and financial-planning firms focus on the fact that most working-class people using 401k and IRA vehicles WILL NOT have enough money for retirement. If they did, there would not be a massive onslaught of these commercials in every city and every town in the USA currently. But the question becomes, "Why do you work all your life, and most people, even by making the maximum contribution and company contribution match[349] will not, once they are retired, have a comfortable enough sum saved (keep in mind this is their whole life savings) to make it through ten to thirty years of retirement without worry?"

---

347 Basic assumption of payment on a thirty-year amortized mortgage with principal balance of 200k, includes impounds.
348 I had this experience. It was hard to "un-condition" myself from it, and I am not sure I totally have or ever will.
349 If they are lucky enough to have one.

Quite Simply, There Are a Few Reasons:[350]

1. Inability to save a significant amount each month due to overspending;

2. Lack of saving—i.e., many individuals choose not to save and exhibit terrible cash-preservation habits;

3. Overleverage of debt on major, avoidable expenses like thirty-year loans and seven-year car debt; and

4. Inflation

Even ***TheMotleyFool.com*** has this scary statistic, which should make all Americans shudder in fear:

How much do you need to retire comfortably?[351]

It depends. According to many financial experts, you should plan on needing about 80% of your preretirement salary once you retire, including income from Social Security, pensions, and any other savings. And you may need this income for longer than you think:

☐ **The average American retires at age sixty-three.**

☐ **The average retirement lasts eighteen years, but many last much longer.** Plus, who knows what the retirement life expectancy will be by the time you get there? The recommendation is that you err on the side of caution and plan on a thirty-year retirement.

☐ **You'll need $1,060,751 in savings if you expect to draw $5,000 per month for thirty years, assuming 6% annual investment returns and 2% inflation.** Depending on how much income you expect from your savings, adjust this amount higher or lower to come up with your retirement "number."

Did you read this last statistic? Mainly, that for a thirty-year retirement, to draw $5,000 per month, and ASSUMING you continue to make 6% annualized market returns through equity vehicles or similar, **you need a retirement nest egg at age sixty-three of over ONE MILLION DOLLARS.**[352]

---

350 This list is by no means all-inclusive
351 Taken from http://www.fool.com/retirement/general/2016/01/26/20-retirement-stats-that-will-blow-you-away.aspx.
352 Keep in mind this does not include Social Security, assuming you are eligible, and should be considered a "supplement," NOT your main source of retirement income.

Now think of yourself right now as you read this. How old are you, and how much money do you have saved up in your IRA or 401k retirement vehicles when you add them all up? Well, statistically, 35% of Americans REFUSE to save for retirement,[353] and 56% of Americans have ten thousand dollars or LESS saved for retirement, so using these numbers, let's assume that you are forty-two (my age at the time of this writing) and you have saved $10,000 (this is me being generous).

Using The Motley Fool's suggested number of $1,060,751 less your 10k saved, you have twenty-one years to generate $1,050,751, or $50,035.76 per year to make your retirement of 5k a month a reality.

Can you do it, starting today? Can you save 50k per year, post-tax, for the next twenty-one years?

Let's look at one more statistic that helps us determine the likelihood of you generating 50k per month to have a "comfortable" retirement.

From CNNMoney.com[354]

Typical American family earned $53,657 last year

Americans didn't get a raise last year. In fact, they haven't gotten one in years.

The typical American family income was $53,657 in 2014, barely changed from $54,462 a year earlier, the U.S. Census Bureau reported Wednesday.

This was the third year in a row that median household incomes stagnated, following two years of declines.

So assuming you are the "typical" American family (this counts two-income households, believe it or not), you make about 53k per year, and it is going DOWN year by year. In order to meet our "goal" of saving for retirement over the next twenty-one years, you would have to put almost 100% of your *gross salary* into a retirement account each year, which is somewhat problematic and filled with obstacles because:

1. The government limits your maximum annual contribution in tax-deferred retirement vehicles, and you can't just "put" 50k per year into a 401k or IRA, tax deferred or free; and

---

353 http://time.com/money/4258451/retirement-savings-survey/.
354 http://money.cnn.com/2015/09/16/news/economy/census-poverty-income/.

2. The government takes 50% of your annual income, as we have discussed extensively, meaning you wouldn't even have 50k to "put" anywhere; and

3. Even if you could do this, you cannot "live" on $2,000 per year as an American family (the remainder of your take-home pay), which makes this analysis a complete notion of fantasy.

Also, if you were just setting aside 10% of your income each month as a savings initiative to "save" 50k per year, you would need to be generating a 500k annualized income to do it, which statistically is unlikely in most jobs and would definitely place you in the "1%" of American earners, which, realistically, are NOT the readers of this book and only a fractional percentage of Americans to begin with.[355]

Summary:

One cannot "save" their way to wealth. It is unlikely and extremely unrealistic, statistically speaking, that you can "save" your way to a million-dollar retirement nest egg.

How Can We Get There?

I am not trying to discourage you by pointing out that you cannot "save" your way to a million-dollar retirement. Rather, I am trying to show you the futility of the thinking paradigm that leads us to believe that such a thing is possible, or at the minimum, a realistic plan with a high probability of success. Granted, some people[356] do "save" their way to million-dollar retirements, and a fractionally small percentage are able to do so by starting young, being extremely thrifty with their savings, paying off their house early, and so on. Occasionally, life throws other things at you that help sometimes, like life-insurance policies, inheritances, work bonuses, and so on, that when saved and invested properly, they can grow into a seven-figure next egg. **BUT FOR THE MAJORITY OF THE READERS OF THIS BOOK, YOU WILL NEVER "SAVE" YOUR WAY TO A MILLION-DOLLAR NEST EGG**.

Let's identify the problem with trying to save your way to retirement. Here is a multiple-choice question for you; see if you can get it right.

Q: Why is it extremely difficult to "save" one's way to a million-dollar retirement nest egg in one's lifetime through working for an employer by a median retirement age of sixty-three?

---

355 Also, keep in mind that a 500k earner takes home about 250k post-tax, so a 50k annualized liquid savings would be about 20% of their net take-home pay.

356 A statistically small percentage of single-income earners.

Select one of the following answers that *best* fits the question.

a. Because it takes a long time.

b. Because people don't like to save money.

c. Because the US government and dollar inflation are constantly diminishing your only source of income,[357] leaving you very little to work with at the end of each pay period, and what little is left—even when invested—is subject to future dollar inflation, which makes those dollars even **MORE** worthless.

d. Because not everybody makes a million dollars a year for their salary.

The answer, by the way, is c.

Besides, why would you want to when there are other ways to get to a million dollars in cash that are far more fun, lucrative, and time efficient?

Deconstructing What Was Constructed "for Us"

One of the things I always find really "funny" is how financial planners and stock brokers are always discouraging you from buying real estate. We have had countless clients come to our brokerage, get excited about purchasing real estate, then go and check with their financial planner and always come back with the same reason for not moving forward with the purchase, which is, *"My financial planner told me that they don't think it is a good idea."*

Now let me translate that for the uninitiated in the world of financial planning, what the financial planner meant to say was, *"I don't think you buying investment real estate is a good idea...because I cannot make a commission off it."* **And if the financial planner was being even more candid, they would add,** *"And also, I want to mention that if you withdraw money from your account, not only do I have less capital to generate commissions for myself, but it also makes me look bad to my broker dealer boss, so I will repeat myself: **You purchasing investment real estate is definitely a bad idea...for ME AND MY BROKER!!!"***

We have discussed this earlier in the book, but throughout our whole lives, we are conditioned to think that the solution to our financial freedom lies within other people, who "know" more than us in the realm of "finance and investment."

But the reality is, nothing could be further from the truth.

---

357 Assuming your primary employment is your sole source of income

An important rule that I always try to remember when it comes to making money is, if it seems straightforward, and it seems to make sense in a simple way, there is a good probability it will work and is duplicable.

Consider:

Q: I want to make an additional $10k per year buying an investment property around the corner from my house which generates $1,000 per month in rent. How long will it take until the property makes me 10k per year?

A: Assume you purchase the house for 70k, using a 4% interest rate and the gross rent is $1,000 per month, let's use the ***Short-Term Retirement Mortgage Affordability Calculator*** to find the answer.

STR Mortgage Affordability Calculator

Inputs	Desired Monthy Payment	Desired Interest Rate
	$1,000.00	4.00%
Purchasing Power		
	5-Year Payment	$54,299.07
	7-Year Payment	$73,159.28
	10-Year Payment	$98,770.17

Realistically, after about seven years, you could have the property paid off. If you gross 12k per year and set aside $2,000 annually for taxes, insurance, vacancy, and maintenance,[358] when your house is paid off seven years from now, you can count on 10k per year in net income from the subject property. It's totally doable, and after a seven-year period, you have an investment that is tangible and real (no pun intended).

Simple, right? Basically, buy a house and pay it off in seven years, and you can plan on making 10k per year in supplemental income from your paid-off investment, as long as you own it and have it rented in good operating condition, which assumes normal wear and tear.

Let's compare this with a more difficult-to-understand investment concept.

The inverse of this idea would be something like this: **If an investment idea is extremely complex and I do not understand how it works, it may be fraudulent and probably not for me.**

---

358 Roughly a 20% vacancy, maintenance, and expense rate based on 12k gross income, which may be high or low, depending on where you live.

For example:

Q: I want to make money from a credit default swap like the big banks do, because I want to be like them and roll in cash. How do I get on that train?

A: First, let's analyze what a credit default swap is.

Credit Default Swap Definition (from Wikipedia)[359]

A CDS is linked to a "reference entity" or "reference obligor," usually a corporation or government. The reference entity is not a party to the contract. The buyer makes regular premium payments to the seller, the premium amounts constituting the "spread" charged by the seller to insure against a credit event. If the reference entity defaults, the protection seller pays the buyer the par value of the bond in exchange for physical delivery of the bond, although settlement may also be by cash or auction.

A default is often referred to as a "credit event" and includes such events as failure to pay, restructuring and bankruptcy, or even a drop in the borrower's credit rating. CDS contracts on sovereign obligations also usually include as credit events repudiation, moratorium, and acceleration. Most CDSs are in the $10–$20 million range with maturities between one and ten years. Five years is the most typical maturity.

An investor or speculator may "buy protection" to hedge the risk of default on a bond or other debt instrument, regardless of whether such investor or speculator holds an interest in or bears any risk of loss relating to such bond or debt instrument. In this way, a CDS is similar to credit insurance, although CDSs are not subject to regulations governing traditional insurance. Also, investors can buy and sell protection without owning debt of the reference entity. These "naked credit default swaps" allow traders to speculate on the creditworthiness of reference entities. CDSs can be used to create synthetic long and short positions in the reference entity.[9] Naked CDSs constitute most of the market in CDS.[16][17] In addition, CDSs can also be used in capital structure arbitrage.

A "credit default swap" (CDS) is a credit derivative contract between two counterparties. The buyer makes periodic payments to the seller, and in return receives a payoff if an underlying financial instrument defaults or experiences a similar credit event. The CDS may refer to a specified loan or bond obligation of a "reference entity," usually a corporation or government.

---

359 https://en.wikipedia.org/wiki/Credit_default_swap.

Umm...what just happened?

Summary: You or I understanding what a credit default swap is, let alone making money from it = totally NOT doable, unless we are insiders "in the know" who work for the banks themselves. Keep in mind, banks make BILLIONS in insider trading schemes such as front-running, but rarely does anyone go to jail for these treacherous activities. Mostly, banks just pay fines in the "millions of dollars," which is far less than the BILLIONS they make through these totally illegal schemes.

The media tells us what the bad guys are doing, and no one seems to care.

Consider:

Barclays and Credit Suisse Pay Biggest Ever Fines for Dark Pool Trading[360]

Barclays fined $154m as New York attorney general vows to "continue to take fight to those who aim to rig the system"

Sunday 31 January 2016 14.58 EST

Barclays and Credit Suisse has been fined $154m (£108m) following an investigation into the banks' "dark pools" private trading exchanges exploited by "predatory, high-frequency traders" at the expense of the bank's traditional customers.

Eric Schneiderman, attorney general of New York state, said the fines were a "major victory in the fight to combat fraud in dark pool trading" and would help protect investors from "the most aggressive and...

Dark pools are private exchanges for trading stocks and bonds, but unlike traditional markets there are no public prices and trades can be carried out in secret which can favor high-speed traders.

Schneiderman said Barclays had told its dark pool clients that it monitored for high-speed trading, but it didn't, and it actually favored high-speed traders. This meant that traditional players thought they were only up against other traditional traders when actually they were facing "the most aggressive and predatory high-speed traders," he said.

---

360 https://www.theguardian.com/business/2016/jan/31/barclays-and-credit-suisse-to-pay-biggest-ever-fines-for-dark-pool-trading.

> **Credit Suisse was fined $60m fine split between the SEC and NY attorney general's office,**[361] as well as a further $24.3m in disgorgement—which is designed to make it pay back ill-gotten gains—in relation to its dark pool called "Crossfinder."

This Is How the Game Is Rigged

So trying to understand things like credit default swaps gives us valuable insight into how the US housing market collapsed in 2008 and so many people lost not only their homes, but their entire underlying fortunes (**read:** life savings, retirement, and so forth) in the aftermath. You see, when you have banks and other institutional entities setting up specialized investments that very few people know about and are guaranteed to win (for them), someone else generally has to "lose," and in this case, it was the American people.

For example, the subprime loan crisis was not a "crisis" at all. The banks made loans to unqualified borrowers through "subprime" loans, which we have discussed, **and the banks KNEW these would fail**.

The banks KNEW that the subprime borrowers, especially those with "fixed adjustable mortgages" would default as rates "adjusted" upward, and their monthly mortgage payments became unmanageable. **It was not a matter of IF but WHEN.**

Do you understand? *The banks got paid to offer unsustainable mortgages to the unsuspecting public.*

Then they took insurance out on this little-known but extremely likely event horizon (**read:** the mortgages made to unqualified borrowers failing), and when the cards started to fall,[362] BAM, banks that were smart enough to insure themselves or buy investment vehicles that "bet" against the housing market[363] got paid handsomely in the process, and those that didn't (like Bank of America) got bailed out by the government anyway, being touted as *"too big to fail."*

I'm sure your investments in the equity markets when the markets were collapsing weren't quite as lucky, were they?

---

361 One might ask how the SEC and New York attorney general's office get to "split" these bank fines. Are these not publicly funded institutions for the benefit of taxpayers? How exactly do these taxpayer offices get to "keep" these fines from the banks? Should these funds not be remunerated to the taxpayers directly, specifically, the investors injured from these devious practices?

362 i.e., mortgages began to default.

363 Again, outlined in the movie *The Big Short.*

266

For many readers, they will struggle to believe the game is so badly rigged against them. They cannot believe that, with all of the government oversight of banks and corporations and civic offices like the SEC tasked with keeping things in line, the taxpayers as individuals—as well as group-based investors (such as teachers' unions investing their entire pension fund with these banks for retirement fund growth)—would consistently get burned so badly, time after time, with each crisis taking a new and different name and reason for weakness and unexpected volatility?

But example after example of this type of corruption exists, and when you really begin to look at the picture clearly, the only logical conclusion that a sane person would draw is that **in order for an average working-class person to become financially independent, they have to AVOID the game of working with investment planners, equity markets, and securities forever.**[364]

Consider the following article on how many US cities' pension funding has been mismanaged by their fund managers (basically) lying about their annualized returns, and then using that false information to indicate that their pension obligations are "fully funded," when in fact, there are shortfalls so massive that cities like Detroit are forced into bankruptcy. Notably, the fraud here is so blatant that people should be going to prison in droves, yet they aren't, while those who have faithfully paid into these systems their entire lives are facing their retirement being completely eliminated in the name of "municipal solvency."

I would like to rename this article **"The Ineptitude of Teacher's Unions and Municipal Retirement Planners Regarding the Investment and Management of Their Pension Funds, Which Has Created a Systemic and Unsolvable Problem for the Future of Pension Sustainability, Which Will Destroy Many People's Retirements,"** but I won't.

---

364 And now you are officially "outside the box."

Coming Pension Meltdown: The 10 Most Troubled City Systems[365]

By Jennifer G. Hickey | Monday, 11 Nov 2013 04:21 PM

Voters in Cincinnati last week soundly defeated a ballot initiative which would have "overhauled"[366] the pension system for public workers, leaving the city without a plan to deal with $872 million in unfunded liabilities.

The Cincinnati initiative would have turned the public pension system into a 401(k) style-plan and require the city to pay off its unfunded liabilities in ten years.

But here's the real rub: **experts are warning that many pension systems, those claiming they are well funded and those who say they aren't, have all been using rosy projections about future investment returns.**

In a recent editorial in Barron's, Thomas Donlan writes that pension funds have "**hidden the results with dubious financial reporting.**"

He cites as just one example Detroit, which claimed as late as 2011 that their pension funds were 80% fully funded. New auditors found a $3.5 billion shortfall, a hole that pushed the city into bankruptcy.

Detroit, he says, was using the standard 8% return on assets, widely used by other funds. Donlan argues that it is foolhardy to claim an 8% rate of return.

Instead, Donlan suggests pension funds use a 4% rate, the blended rate for no-risk treasuries or a 5.5% rate, consistent with current corporate bond payouts. But if pension funds were to be honest and use such numbers, real unfunded liabilities would jump by a third or more.

Here are the top 10 cities with the lowest percentage of funding for pension liabilities:		
City	**Total Liability**	**% Funded**
Charleston, W. Va.	$270 million	24
Omaha, Neb.	$1.43 billion	43
Portland, Ore.	$5.46 billion	50
Chicago, Ill.	$24.97 billion	52
Little Rock, Ark.	$498 million	59

---

365 http://www.newsmax.com/Newsfront/city-pension-shortfall-underfunded/2013/11/11/id/536027/
366 Meaning, destroyed. [My edit.]

City	Total Liability	% Funded
Wilmington, Del.	$364 million	59
Boston, Mass.	$2.54 billion	60
Atlanta, Ga.	$3.17 billion	60
Manchester, NH	$436 million	60
New Orleans, La.	$1.99 billion	61

Equally startling, **Pew found numerous cities were woefully unprepared to finance healthcare benefit obligations.**

The *Chicago Sun-Times* **reported** that an analysis of pension reform scenarios under consideration by the Illinois legislature "make clear that no matter what legislators do, including major pension cutting, a significant portion of the state's budget for the next twenty to twenty-five years will go toward paying pension bills, consuming 16% to 24% of the state's general revenue fund annually."

So to summarize, these pension funds—massive amounts of money that are given to major banking and growth-fund-type firms for investment oversight and allocation—cannot return even 8% per year, but everyone is acting like the fund in their municipality IS doing that.

That's fraud, right?

But the bigger and even more juicy question is this: How is it that Barclays and other banks not reviewed in this book are openly admitting to engaging in daily, *high yield*, illegal trading practices[367] like front-running and "dark pools," but they keep doing it—just hoping not to get caught—**while on the other hand, these major retirement pension funds in cities across the United States cannot even return a paltry 4% when these funds are entrusted to "the best of the best" financial growth planners that are allegedly available?**

Surely, the pension funds must be some of these banks or "growth fund's" biggest clients, right?

My guess? **I would bet lots of money IS being generated from these massive pension funds, but it simply is not being "returned" to the investor as yields, if you get my meaning.**

367 And keep in mind, these high-yield trades happen daily—twenty-four hours a day—in market indexes across all countries, whenever the markets are open.

Conclusion

When the pension shortfalls begin to come to light in cities across the United States, that's a big clue that even YOUR financial planner may not be able to return what you are promised when you entrust your investment funds into their hands—which, for most people, is the promise of a financially secure future, including retirement. And the reality is, a "purchase and pray for growth" strategy in the stock market, unless you hit a major stock like Apple Computer in its infancy, simply is untenable because of dollar attrition.

Critics of this book will say, "*Feol says the stock market doesn't work, but I have tons of examples of people retiring after working their whole life and investing ONLY in stocks.*" To be clear, I am not saying that you can't make money in the stock market; you certainly can. **But as I discuss in this book, for the average person who lives paycheck to paycheck, investing your retirement in the stock market is a highly volatile and risky strategy that I simply cannot endorse in any way.** Through many examples, I have demonstrated clearly that you simply cannot wholeheartedly trust your money into the hands of other people, assuming you want your money to grow with as little risk as possible.

I will agree, you CAN make money in the stock market, but you have to do it the right way. **There is only one guy I know and trust when it comes to trading the stock market, and that is Tim Sykes**. Sykes, who appeared on my radio show once (it was a tremendous honor), taught my listeners and I about how the ONLY real way to stay safe and make money in the stock market is to make surgically precise trades using highly volatile stocks and get into and out of these stocks on a daily basis. **And Sykes should know—he has grown his account from 12k as a teenager into the millions while documenting EVERY trade publicly—to show how it can be done**. Trading stocks is far beyond the scope of this book, but I will advise you that if you want to grow your retirement using the securities and equities markets, start by studying and working with a trader who has a proven track record and is an EXCELLENT teacher. Go to TimSkyes.com[368] for more details.

Tell him I sent you; he is a true champion of and exposer of Wall Street's blatant fraud.

Back to "No Job Can Make You Wealthy"

So we used some extensive analysis to draw a simple conclusion: Basically, one cannot save their way to wealth. After all, that million-dollars nest egg is a pretty unobtainable goal when you are forced involuntarily to capitulate half of your take-home pay to the government.

---

368 http://TimSykes.com/

But in the good American fashion of our forefathers, a little bit of outside-the-box thinking and American ingenuity can get us where we need to be—decades earlier than retirement age and with far less capital than your broker requires to "give" you a $5,000 monthly allotment until you die, taking fees each time along the way.

Getting Outside the Box

A quick review of The Motley Fool article tells us this:

> You'll need $1,060,751 in savings if you expect to draw $5,000 per month for thirty years, assuming 6% annual investment returns and 2% inflation

Broken down simply, that means if you are sixty-three and retired, each month (from your nest egg), you will draw:

Monthly: 5k (distributed)
Annually: 60k (distributed)
Ten years: 600k (distributed)

Even though that's more than half your retirement nest egg from ten years previously,[369] your financial planners are hoping to miraculously grow that account by 6% annually (highly unlikely, as the municipal financial "planners" have demonstrated and as discussed in the previous article) while fighting dollar inflation of (minimally) 2%, courtesy of the Federal Reserve's destructive monetary policies. Along the way, you might die (as your financial planners breathe a sigh of relief, being no longer "obliged" to try to deliver a 6% annual return for the next twenty years[370]), or you might live and outgrow your nest egg.

Either way, those are bad outcomes.

What if you could get 5k per month without working your whole life and trying to save your way to, well, a "savings"?

What if your retirement could start a few short years from now?

---

369   This assumes you actually "saved" $1,060,751 at the time of your retirement.
370   Statistically, an extremely unlikely event.

The REAL Problem

Let's analyze the *real* problem. The real problem is that the traditional retirement game is *totally flawed* and depends on you choosing to participate in two intellectual and societal fallacies, as follows:

1. You need to work for thirty years in order to retire comfortably; and

2. Your whole retirement plan is predicated on you taking what little money you have left over, after taxes[371], and entrusting it to a financial planner through annual-fee-laden retirement contributions.

Now, I have demonstrated to you that these are both horrible, ghastly, losing situations—having a single employer for life while giving up 50% of your income to payroll-type taxes and giving your money to financial planners you will never meet, "hoping" you will win. Why not start your retirement plan today and complete a huge phase of it in five to ten years while you CHOOSE to work?

Consider the following two retirement plans. Which of these would you choose?

Plan A

Work thirty years and defy all odds by "saving" your way to a million-dollar retirement nest egg, which gives you $5,000 per month during your retirement years while financial planners squander your proceeds with risky trades and fees, depending on the volatility of market conditions;[372] or

Plan B

Generate $5,000 a month in passive income with little or no money out of your pocket starting TODAY. When you achieve this, you get to live just like those who have one million dollars in savings at age sixty-three, though you may be thirty years younger or more.[373]

---

371 Or pre-tax depending on your IRA plan, which is even WORSE. Would you rather be taxed on the seed or the harvest? That's the difference between a Roth IRA and traditional IRA.

372 For example, the 2008 "credit crisis," which many banks—as well as institutional entities—knew was coming from the subprime mortgages issued, most people's wealth in equities dropped significantly because of "the market." As if stocks purchased the day before the start of the crisis, using good company fundamentals, suddenly had "lost value." **What a joke [expletives omitted]**.

373 Depending on what your age is when you read this book and if you decide to implement these strategies immediately.

Which plan would you select? I'm guessing Plan B sounds better because, well, for every reason possible. Is there a way you can do it without trying to save your way to retirement using the real estate principles in this book?

Remember Feol's Simple Rule for Financial Freedom

> **Feol's Simple Financial Freedom Formula**
>
> **A total absence of monthly credit obligations from principal debt, with a monthly positive (and ideally passive) cash flow, that exceeds comfortably the total amount of monthly debt service you have from essential—services that cannot be retired through debt repayment or be realistically removed.**[374]

Keep in mind, it's critical that your financial action plan starts FIRST with you retiring your housing payment permanently. We have discussed this extensively, as eliminating that payment gives you so much more disposable income for other debt reduction and savings purposes.

Now let's look at generating income from real estate as a long-term wealth-building and retirement strategy.

There are two ways to generate passive monthly income from real estate investments as a property owner, as follows:

1. Positive monthly cash flow after expenses and your monthly mortgage payment; or

2. Positive monthly cash flow after expenses and WITHOUT you being required to pay a monthly mortgage payment.

Simple math here illustrates what we need to see and make a decision on how to proceed structuring one's portfolio.

Timmy's First Investment House

Suppose Timmy the Teacher reads this book. He doesn't want to wait thirty years to generate $5,000 (gross) per month, as he currently makes less than that monthly. He checks in with Bob the Banker, who offers him some mortgage loans for investment homes. Timmy gets excited and finds his first home. It costs him $100,000 and rents for

---

374 The day you arrive here, you should have peace of mind.

$1,000 gross per month. **In the real estate industry, we say that Timmy's investment generates him 1% per month, or rather 1% of his purchase price is returned to him as gross rent each month.**[375]

Timmy's operating income breaks down like this:

Timmy's $100,000 Mortgage at 4% (via Bob the Banker)

Property Cost	
Purchase price	$100,000.00
Closing costs (estimated)	$1,000.00
Total estimated cash costs	$101,000.00
Tax appraisal	$84,100.00
Income Information—Monthly	
Monthly rent	$1,000.00
Management fee (10%)[386]	$100.00
City taxes	$56.00
County taxes	$70.43
Insurance (estimated)	$45.00
Monthly cash flow	$728.57
Cash-on-cash return	8.66%
Financing Information	
Mortgage amount	$100,000.00
Down payment	$0.00
Loan amount	$100,000.00
Interest rate	4.00%
Loan terms (in months)	360
Monthly payment (P and I)	$477.42
Monthly net positive cash flow	$251.16
Cash-on-cash return—Ten Years	Error

So, to summarize, Timmy nets $251.16 each month from his rental property. Let's round it down to $250 per month for simple math. **If Timmy wants to make a $5,000 monthly passive cash flow, he has to purchase twenty homes like this to have his passive income.**

However, Timmy unknowingly has several roadblocks:

---

375 The savviest of investors look for 2% per month, but that isn't always achievable, depending on your market, rent conditions, and market temperature. It's more likely during a buyer's market. And we know Timmy isn't that savvy. **This is frequently a benchmark for investment property "quality" grading.**

376 Timmy also has the option of self-managing, improving his monthly cash flow as well.

1. Timmy doesn't "really" make $250 per month, because he will have vacancy and maintenance expenses, which need to be factored into this equation;

2. In this example, Timmy put no cash down to get his thirty-year note from Bob the Banker, which is also a highly unrealistic institutional lending scenario; and

3. There is NO WAY Bob is giving Timmy, twenty "no money down" mortgages using standard banking and lending practices at the time of this writing.

But even IF Timmy could get these loans, I am not sure he would want them.
Why?

Because owning houses creates tax, maintenance, and repair liabilities that cannot be easily handled without being flush with cash, having sufficient monthly positive cash flow, or having a strategic plan. Think about how hard Timmy has to work to manage twenty houses—that's like a second job. And more importantly, his "hassle factor" is multiplied by twenty, as in if you think owning one house with marginal cash flow is a headache (and as discussed, he really does NOT earn even $250 per month due to vacancy and maintenance factors), **imagine multiplying that headache by twenty then trying to hold on for thirty years!**

Timmy is weak financially as he is...that race is one Timmy will not win.

If Timmy was really smart, though, he would realize that he doesn't need to own twenty-five houses to reach his goal. He can do it with a fraction of the houses he thinks he needs to.

Getting It Done with Five Houses

If Timmy was really smart, he would realize that he could achieve his same goal with 25% of the houses he thinks he needs—*five, to be exact.* There are only two modifications he needs to make to his plan, which are as follows:

1. He needs to purchase the houses for half of what he was planning to pay with all other assumptions being the same, and

2. He needs to use seven-year amortizations.

Consider how Timmy's treatment of his rental house varies when he finds a foreclosure, which allows him to purchase at a 50% discount, and he chooses a seven-year payoff.

Timmy's $50,000 Mortgage at 4% (via Bob the Banker)

Property Cost	
Purchase price	$50,000.00
Closing costs (estimated)	$1,000.00
Total estimated cash costs	$51,000.00
Tax appraisal	$84,100.00
Income Information—Monthly	
Monthly rent	$1,000.00
Management fee (10%)	$100.00
City taxes	$56
County taxes	$70.43
Insurance (estimated)	$45.00
Monthly cash flow	$728.57
Cash-on-cash return	8.66%
Financing Information	
Mortgage amount	$50,000.00
Down payment	$0.00
Loan amount	$50,000.00
Interest rate	4.00%
Loan terms (in months)	84
Monthly payment (P and I)	$683.44
Monthly net positive cash flow	$45.13
Cash-on-cash return—ten years	Error

In this case, Timmy has cleverly eliminated his several roadblocks because he has done the following:

3. Timmy generates a nominal cash flow monthly, which is positive, but his goal focuses on a short-term payoff while sacrificing significant monthly cash flow, making the investment far more sustainable with a short-term finish line;

4. Bob the Banker is FAR more likely to give these loans to Timmy based on the equity position in the house, requiring far less of a down payment under Fannie Mae guidelines, if any;[377] and

---

377 Remember, Fannie Mae allows you to refinance for 75% of your appraisal. In this case, Timmy would be zero out of pocket, assuming he took title BEFORE he refinanced using a hard money loan, discussed previously.

5. Timmy cannot get twenty loans from Bob the Banker, but he can most certainly get five loans from Bob, especially if his houses are no-brainer loans, which are 50% of fair market value and, in doing so, be far under the Fannie Mae loan limit of ten financed properties.

It cannot be clearer how damning and damaging the thirty-year mortgage can be versus something like a simple seven-year payoff! The only difference lies in the price you elect to pay. Most people blindly choose to pay retail for a house and put it on a thirty-year mortgage, which as we have identified, is the ***ultimate*** losing strategy.

Don't be like them.

In the words of the immortal Bruce Springsteen:

> ***And I had some victory that was just failure in deceit***
> Now the joke's comin' up through the soles of my feet
> I been a long-time walking on fortune's cane
> Tonight I'm steppin' lightly and I'm feelin' no pain
> (From Bruce Springsteen's ***"Lucky Town"***)

For me, the victory Bruce sings of is such an accurate metaphor for what so many American families go through when they leave their attorney's office after purchasing their primary residence, paying full retail, and using a thirty-year mortgage. They are ecstatic that they have finally purchased the "American dream," when what they really have purchased is thirty years of **bank-sanctioned slavery**.

Ripping the Box Apart versus Thinking Outside of It

Let's go back to our "traditional" retirement scenario we discussed earlier. Hoping to receive a $5,000 monthly retirement allotment "x" years from now, based on saving one million dollars or more, post-tax over your working lifetime, seems a pretty disheartening task.

I mean, let's be frank, if you manage to save a million dollars in the bank from your take-home pay[378] by the time you hit retirement, you would think that you could live like a "millionaire," but the reality is this: ***You are simply living like you always have while you were working with roughly the same allotment of monthly take-home pay given to you each month*** by your financial "planners."

Who wants that if we actually get to choose?

---

378 Again, statistically speaking, the odds are stacked heavily against you.

Does a lifestyle with potentially limitless income actually exist?

Let's examine some rules and the type of mental preparation Timmy needs to have on his seven-year journey to five paid off houses.

A Concrete Plan for a Recurring Base Income

So Timmy makes an executive family decision that he wants to acquire investment properties for residual income purposes. He is committed to it. He has seen the power of **The Short-Term Retirement Program,** and he wants to take the plunge, buying investment properties with aggressive payoffs for future income and growth purposes. How does he go about it, and what exactly can he expect?

A few rules based on my not-so-inconsiderable experience:

a. **The ebb and flow of time passes far more quickly than we realize, and as such, while you may be age "x" at the time you read this, the reality is your age of "x" PLUS seven years is not that far off, and more importantly, IT IS COMING ANYWAY.** I cannot tell you how many times I speak with people about this basic precept of human existence, that whether or not you own paid-off properties when you reach a certain age milestone—let's say age forty, for example—you still are going to reach that age milestone. And it is much better to reach that milestone FINISHING your journey of acquiring properties rather than just starting it.

   Consider:

   Two thirty-five-year-old men, both of whom read this book. One begins to purchase homes using a five-year payoff, and one does nothing. At age forty, the one who chose to invest and have his properties pay for themselves through tenant rent is far better off than the one who has acquired no assets and turns forty with no passive income or increase in net worth.

b. **Timmy may be able to find homes that can be paid off in seven years and acquire the financing to do so; however, he needs to be prepared for a nominal or breakeven cash flow each month**. This would be fine if the tenant stays for seven consecutive years, which is unlikely. Therefore, Timmy has to be prepared to shoulder the expenses of maintenance, vacancy, and transitional "rent-ready expenses" (when one tenant moves out due to a lease expiration before another one can move in), and these will need to come out of Timmy's pocket. Even if Timmy finances the property for no money down using such an aggressive mortgage payoff, he MUST be prepared to shoulder some expenses to see the journey of the property payoff to completion.

Consider:

Timmy buys a home for 70k and places it on a seven-year payoff. With his rental income of $1,000 per month, he can cover his payment. Let's say he gets $1,100 per month, which helps cover his tax and insurance liability, so he makes his payment and covers his expenses. However, his first tenant stays for one year (then leaves), then he places another tenant who stays for three years (paying faithfully, then leaves), and Timmy places one more tenant who stays until the eighty-fourth payment is made. In month eighty-five, Timmy gets to keep his rental income, less taxes and insurance.

Sounds great, but remember, Timmy placed three tenants. As such, he had to get the house rent ready for the first tenant, the second tenant, and the third tenant. Let's assume the cost was $2,500 per incident, for a total cost of $7,500. Timmy would have a rent-ready cost over a seven-year period of $7,500 plus whatever maintenance expenses he encountered, which could easily be $1,000 per year or more. **So Timmy would have to be facing a possibility of almost $15,000 in carry costs over a seven-year loan period, all of which he would have to pay out of pocket.** The flip side of this is that Timmy would only pay $15,000 for a house which we stated is well worth 100k, with his tenants paying the entirety of his loan balance, *assuming all eighty-four payments were made by tenants.* If tenants did NOT pay for any given reason, Timmy would have to be prepared to shoulder this expense also. This is why it is critical to screen tenants and only buy houses in good areas where income is stable.

c. **The selection of the properties is paramount.** Buying C-grade or D-grade, subpar investment homes are NOT an ideal way for Timmy to get to where he needs to be, especially when he has little to no experience. In addition to paying specific attention to foreclosed homes and distressed selling situations, which offer him the price points he needs to begin his journey, A-grade and B-grade homes are where Timmy needs to begin his search, in neighborhoods he knows, and which offer certain attractions such as a high density of college housing needed, etc.

d. **Once Timmy begins the race, he CANNOT stop.** There is no quitting or giving up. The payments must be made, and tenants *must* be placed and properly managed. Any other mission plan will result in critical failure. And to be direct, Timmy needs to be fully prepared for the unexpected to happen, i.e., if a tenant stops making payments (reason is irrelevant), Timmy has to be prepared to make the missed mortgage payments to his bank out of his take-home pay and possibly do so for a few months while an eviction of the tenant is taking place. While a small probability, this COULD happen, and Timmy needs to be fully prepared for it versus jumping ship at the first sight of a storm cloud.

Accumulating a $5,000-per-Month Nest Egg the Easy Way and WITHOUT Waiting Until Age Sixty-Three

If we want to make Timmy's journey really simple and realistic, Timmy has to achieve two basic things to become financially free and live like a retired person, as follows:

1. **He needs to eliminate all his debt, so he has as few monthly payments as possible.**

2. **He needs five paid-off houses, each of which generate $1,000 per month[379] in gross rental income.**

How does this make him able to live the life of a retired person? It's simple. Consider the following:

1. **Timmy currently makes $3,600 a month as a teacher.** Five thousand dollars per month in income would be a significant increase and is the average assumed retirement income (monthly) for a sustainable existence in the United States, at the time of this writing, according to many financial experts.

2. **Timmy currently pays taxes on his earned income through federal taxes and Social Security tax.** Structured properly, he would not be subjected to these taxes, but he would simply pay tax on business income (remember, business income is NOT subject to Social Security tax[380]), which would make his take-home pay significantly higher and save him tens of thousands annually, which he would ALSO take home as income.

---

379 Or, eleven hundred dollars per house monthly, if you want to use a basic scenario where $100 per month cover's Timmy's tax and insurance obligation, creating a NET income of 1k per month. Your personal expenses may vary.
380 Consult your CPA for details.

3. **Timmy works and pays taxes and handles his debts now.** If he didn't have to work, and his income became passive, assuming he had no debt obligations each month (payments), he effectively would BE retired though he would be far younger than most retired people.

And working as a teacher, Timmy gets health insurance, but if he left his job he would lose his insurance. However, his $1,400 increase in income would certainly be enough to handle his premiums should he have to self-pay, which would be the equivalent to him having Medicaid and supplemental insurance should he be of retirement age in an equivalent retirement scenario, though ostensibly his take-home pay would be much less through a teaching pension.

Getting to Five Houses: The Easy Way

The thing about owning rental houses, and this really IS the thing, is that you have to remember **Feol's Cardinal Rule of Owning Rental Property**, as follows:

> **Feol's Cardinal Rule of Owning Rental Property:** Vacancy is YOUR enemy.

And mainly, this comes down to a few simple precepts. If you plan on buying property, you need to close on it, renovate it and place a qualified tenant as quickly as you possibly can. **Notice I said a "qualified" tenant.** Placing a tenant who is qualified is important, not just so you can get your rent in a timely fashion each month, but also to avoid getting into a situation where a tenant wants to pay but is unable to due to insufficient income, so they keep trying to "buy time" and take advantage of your kindness, making promises to pay rent, which never materializes, and leaving YOU to chase options, all of which are bad and undesirable.

I can't tell you the number of landlords who have come to me in bad situations asking for advice, where their tenant is behind rent for over a year! Naturally, the tenant promised to pay, etc., and days turned into months, which turned into years—you get the idea. **Be prepared to manage houses firmly, or do NOT get into the business of owning property.** This is a good lesson for Timmy too. We will talk about property management later in the book.

Portfolio Structure 1: Timmy Goes for the Gold in Seven Years

Let's say Timmy hates his job. He sees value in acquiring properties, and he is vested in his job at the highest pay scale he can be as a teacher of his experience level, plus he gets summers off, so he knows he needs to stay until he replaces his income through passive rental streams. Nonetheless, Timmy is ready to "get the ball rolling," so to speak, and start buying the investment properties that will eventually allow him to bid "farewell" to his job.

Reviewing our analysis of Timmy's search for a house he can pay off in seven years, let's examine his purchasing power one more time, which assumes rent of $1,000 per month.

STR Mortgage Affordability Calculator

Inputs	Desired Monthy Payment	Desired Interest Rate
	$1,000.00	4.00%
Purchasing Power		
	5-Year Payment	$54,299.07
	7-Year Payment	$73,159.28
	10-Year Payment	$98,770.17

So we see that Timmy needs to be looking to be ALL IN to his home price for the low 70k range to make this thing work and be mindful of his taxes and insurance also. The mortgage affordability calculator does NOT calculate excess fees like condo or HOA fees (if you have one, which you should try to avoid) or taxes and insurance.[381] If you find that your total monthly "nut" is way off from your initial expectations, you need to obtain a higher monthly rent to accommodate for the additional expenses or use a longer amortization to make the payments "work."

But in this case, let's assume Timmy's taxes and insurance are enough to make his $1,000 monthly rent payment from his tenant "work," meaning break even.[382]

Now it is time for Timmy to focus on purchasing his first house; to repeat, buying his FIRST house is his focus.

NOTE: TIMMY WILL NOT BUY FIVE HOUSES AT ONCE! He does not have the experience, cash resources, or credit capacity to undergo such a daunting task; and even if did, he would probably go bankrupt trying to figure out how to rent five houses while suffering through five mortgage payments a month waiting for his vacancies to be filled. MANAGE YOUR EXPECTATIONS APPROPRIATELY!

---

381   Nor vacancy and maintenance allotments, which are REAL expenses. It is up to you to factor these in based on your locality and reasonable expectations.

382   **You do NOT need to try to be break even**, but in this case, Timmy is "going for the gold," meaning, looking to pay off his investment property as FAST as possible.

His acquisition time frame probably looks like this.

T – 30/60 days. Timmy gets preapproved for his loan or lines up a private lender and goes shopping for a foreclosed house, a distressed seller, or a unique opportunity. Timmy finds his first house that works for him and puts it under contract, gathering all the inspections necessary (and using a qualified agent) to help him navigate this process. Timmy's accepted contract is sent to his lender, who initiates the appraisal and underwriting process.

T – 30 days. Timmy's appraisal comes back, and the underwriter begins processing his loan. If, as a borrower, Timmy is using private money to "take down" the property (or YOU are), this step and the next two would be skipped.

T – 15 days. Underwriting finishes preliminary work and issues loan "conditions," which Timmy must meet.

T – 7 days. Lender verifies Timmy's cash to close and sends the package to the closing attorney or escrow company. Insurance is set up and verified.

T – 0 days. Timmy signs all documents and brings a check to closing.

T + 5 days. Timmy begins the rehab or rent-ready process.

T + 30 days. Home is rent-ready, management company in place, sign in yard[383] advertising "Home for Rent."

T + 45/75 days. Qualified, paying tenant is in, and Timmy's first investment property is now online.

What Does Timmy's Roadmap and Time Frame for Acquiring Five Houses Look Like?

It would look something like this:

0–6 months: First property acquired.

6–12 months: Second property acquired

12–24 months: Properties 3–5 acquired, each within a 120-day period.

NOTE: If a property is not "online," meaning a renter is absent or is present but not paying, the process immediately STOPS, until ALL homes are online and functioning as designed.

Again, it is important to note that if Timmy is using a seven-year payoff for all homes, his journey to five paid off homes completes around year NINE, not year seven, due to the time needed to start the acquisition process and ensure the continuity of rental income streams.

---

383 This assumes Timmy elects to use a management company.

Portfolio Structure 2: Timmy Likes His Job and Is Risk Averse: A Ten-Year Plan

This is a more common direction I tend to see with investors who come to us, and truthfully, it is one that makes more sense logistically. In this case, Timmy recognizes that while going to work may not be his favorite pastime,[384] he understands that if he is vested in his job, salary, retirement, and insurance plans, and he doesn't DREAD getting out of bed every day, then acquiring properties over a longer, more conservative period of time can be an ideal way to diversify his income streams while adding multiple streams of income, which as we have discussed in previous chapters, is an excellent way to build long-term wealth while insulating yourself against the possibility of financial ruin, i.e., you get fired from your job and cannot find another one, and so on.

The Same Rules Apply

In this case, Timmy will start buying houses in year one but take a bit more time to acquire each one, letting each investment come online and "season" appropriately to Timmy's comfort level. Again, keep in mind that the rules of **The Short-Term Retirement Program** all still apply—short, aggressive amortizations, high rents per square foot or multiple-income units, and low purchase prices relative to fair market value. However, in this particular case, Timmy may start with some ten-year amortizations while finishing up his portfolio acquisitions with five-year or seven-year amortizations to meet or come close to his goal of ten years of acquisitions resulting in five fully paid off houses.

In this case, his roadmap would look something like this:

> **Zero to six months:** First property acquired, placed on *ten-year note*.[385]
>
> **Twelve to eighteen months:** Second property acquired, placed on *ten-year note*.
>
> **Twenty-four months:** Third property acquired, placed on *seven-year note*.
>
> **Thirty-six months:** Fourth property acquired, placed on *seven-year note*.
>
> **Forty-eight months**: Fifth and final property acquired, placed on *five-year note*.

It is critical to note that Timmy is able to meet his ten-year goal (actually about eleven years, given the second property is on a ten-year note, but finishing the journey

---

384 He could love his job too. This is also a possibility. Basically, someone who is employed, secure, and has no immediate plans to leave their job fits this description.

385 For this discussion (and as discussed throughout most of the book), all notes are *fully amortized*.

is the most important part) and use increasingly aggressive mortgages for two reasons, as follows:

1. He should have a small cash flow, which accrues from his first few houses on a ten-year term.
2. He is still purchasing these homes inexpensively and well below market value.

Let's look at how this portfolio stacks up and whether we are setting Timmy up for success over a ten-year period. To remain constant, let's use Timmy's aforementioned sample property, a discounted 50k purchase that rents for $1,000 per month as a benchmark for all five properties, while applying the appropriate amortizations.

Properties 1 and 2: Analysis

Property Cost	
Purchase price	$50,000
Closing costs (estimated)	$1,000.00
Total estimated cash costs	$51,000.00
Tax appraisal	$84,100.00
Income Information—Monthly	
Monthly rent	$1,000.00
Management fee (10%)	$100.00
City taxes	$56.00
County taxes	$70.43
Insurance (estimated)	$45.00
Monthly cash flow	$728.57
Cash-on-cash return	8.66%
Financing Information	
Mortgage amount	$50,000.00
Down payment	$0.00
Loan amount	$50,000.00
Interest rate	4.00%
Loan terms (in months)	120
Monthly payment (P and I)	$506.23
Monthly net positive cash flow	$222.35
Cash-on-cash return—ten years	Error

Summary: Timmy uses ten-year amortizations and generates a $222.35 monthly positive cash flow, which helps him handle maintenance and vacancy costs, which will invariably arise through the ownership of these properties.

Properties 3 and 4: Analysis

Property Cost	
Purchase price	$50,000
Closing costs (estimated)	$1,000.00
Total estimated cash costs	$51,000.00
Tax appraisal	$84,100.00
Income Information—Monthly	
Monthly rent	$1,000.00
Management fee (10%)	$100.00
City taxes	$56.00
County taxes	$70.43
Insurance (estimated)	$45.00
Monthly cash flow	$728.57
Cash-on-cash return	8.66%
Financing Information	
Mortgage amount	$50,000.00
Down payment	$0.00
Loan amount	$50,000.00
Interest rate	4.00%
Loan terms (in months)	84
Monthly payment (P and I)	$683.44
Monthly net positive cash flow	$45.13
Cash-on-cash return—ten years	Error

Summary: Timmy uses seven-year amortizations and generates a $45.13 monthly positive cash flow, which helps him handle maintenance and vacancy costs, which will invariably arise through the ownership of these properties. While these loans are more aggressive, they have much smaller time frames in which Timmy will retire his debt, so assuming he purchased homes in good condition simply, needing a bit of cosmetic "sweat equity," and assuming he insulates himself against major expenses,[386] he should be able to pay off these homes in seven years without a major cash flow incident.

Property 5: Analysis

Property Cost	
Purchase price	$50,000
Closing costs (estimated)	$1,000.00
Total estimated cash costs	$51,000.00
Tax appraisal	$84,100.00
Income information—monthly	
Monthly rent	$1,000.00
Management fee (10%)	$100.00
City taxes	$56.00
County taxes	$70.43
Insurance (estimated)	$45.00
Monthly cash flow	$728.57
Cash-on-cash return	8.66%
Financing Information	
Mortgage amount	$50,000.00
Down payment	$0.00
Loan amount	$50,000.00
Interest rate	4.00%
Loan terms (in months)	60
Monthly payment (P and I)	$920.83
Monthly net positive cash flow	-$192.25
Cash-on-cash return—ten years	Error

Summary: Timmy uses a very aggressive five-year amortization and generates a significant $192.25 **monthly loss**. He does this as a trade-off against his monthly positive cash flows, knowing that this loss is one he has to carry for sixty payments only.

Here is his (monthly) cash flow after his five houses are online:

---

386 Purchasing a home warranty yearly is a great way to do this, and is incredibly cost effective.

House 1: $222.35

House 2: $222.35

House 3: $45.13

House 4: $45.13

House 5: ($192.25)

Total aggregate monthly cash flow: $342.71

The thing to remember, however, is that **by the time he institutes a five-year payoff on house 5, he is halfway to paying off houses 1 and 2 in full and houses 3 and 4 have four and five years left on the mortgages, respectively**. Basically, by the time he takes a negative-cash-flow property, he is more than halfway there on his wealth-building plan, which would effectively more than DOUBLE his monthly income.

This is a race that Timmy is set up to win.

How Does This Investment Stack Up?

While I am loath to compare paid off real estate returns[387] versus some arbitrary returns in the equities market, this is a great time to compare Timmy's investment versus his colleagues (noninvestment), who teach by his side each and every day. It is reasonable to assume that Timmy reading this book AND applying these principles in action would be an exception, while the majority of his colleagues would continue to do what they have done every day, i.e., live paycheck to paycheck and do nothing except relegate part of their paycheck to their mandatory monthly pension and 401k contributions.

Let's assume we are comparing Timmy versus his colleagues over a ten-year period where Timmy has started to purchase real estate AND finish paying it off all within the same ten-year period.

---

387   And the oft-missed "real estate paying itself off" returns, which is a form of forced savings.

START of Ten-Year Period: Timmy versus His Colleagues

Timmy versus His Colleagues: Year One	
Timmy	His colleagues
Has negative net worth	Have negative net worth
Contributes involuntarily to his 401k and/or pension each month through payroll deduction	Contributes involuntarily to his 401k and/or pension each month through payroll deduction
Lives paycheck to paycheck	Lives paycheck to paycheck

END of Ten-Year Period: Timmy versus His Colleagues

Timmy versus His Colleagues: Year Ten	
Timmy	His Colleagues
~~Has negative net worth~~	Have negative net worth
Contributes involuntarily to his 401k and/or pension each month through payroll deduction	Contributes involuntarily to his 401k and/or pension each month through payroll deduction
~~Lives paycheck to paycheck~~	Lives paycheck to paycheck
Has $500k net worth from paid off housing equity	Net worth remains negative
Makes his salary PLUS $5,000 per month additional gross	Makes teaching salary ONLY
CAN retire	CANNOT retire

What is notable in this crude example is that, through a simple action plan and by leveraging the power of investment real estate, Timmy has generated a net worth and passive income that far surpasses his colleagues, and more importantly, he did so BY INVESTING LITTLE TO NONE OF HIS OWN MONEY because he chose to purchase undervalued, foreclosed real estate and did so in such a way that his lender found making these loans EXTREMELY favorable.

His colleagues, on the other hand, continued to do what has taken from them so much yet gotten them SO little simply by doing the same thing over and over again without making any alterations to their work habits or outside investing strategy.

And in a great twist of irony, our good friend Timmy has gone quite literally from zero to hero while his colleagues were waiting for their fortune to change.

If we wanted to draw this down to a numbers comparison, let's just say that Timmy and his colleagues, at the start of year one, each have 100k in their 401k accounts. When ten years go by, what have those accounts grown to? Maybe 110k? **That would be a 10% return over a ten-year period, which REALISTICALLY IS EXTREMELY UNLIKELY DUE TO DOLLAR INFLATION AND MARKET VOLATILITY.** However, in Timmy's case, he has his 401k worth 110k (as do his colleagues), but he has an ADDITIONAL 500k by investing almost NO money of his own through smartly leveraged investment real estate.

And the real question here is, do YOU have a financial advisor in the securities markets who can take zero dollars and turn it into half a million over a ten-year period, with you making little or NO contributions and almost NO downside risk?

I didn't think you did.[388]

In the beginning of this book, I stressed to you that equity and net worth are really not focal points of The Short-Term Retirement Program. Yes, having tons of paid-off homes that create a significant net worth looks great on paper and is certainly favorable to your banker, but remember, **what people REALLY want is spendable "money in fist," which they can use to pursue their passions each month, whether it is eating, traveling, a secondary profession or business, or simply paying the bills while having enough money left over each month to save it while enjoying something that is so fleeting for so many millions of Americans—peace of mind.**

Remember! Passive income from paid-off properties can help you achieve this goal.

Success Tips for Timmy's Five-Year and Ten-Year Plans

1. Buy undervalued real estate. **Never pay retail**.

2. Make sure you have all deferred maintenance addressed as a condition of sale or at the time of sale, ensuring you won't have any surprise expenses early on down the road.

3. Make sure you have a home warranty on each property, and renew it every year. The cost of a home warranty is pennies compared to the maintenance expenses you will pay over time, and frequently, you can get used equipment upgraded with brand-new items, if your repair qualifies.[389]

4. Never let your insurance lapse, and make sure you have enough coverage. Don't be underinsured!

---

388 AND IF you say you do, you are a LIAR.
389 Speak with your home warranty vendor for details on coverages and exceptions (meaning, what is NOT covered).

5. A million-dollar liability umbrella is an inexpensive investment that can protect you—get one! See your insurance agent for details.

6. Screen your tenants and pull credit and background on each one.

7. Collect full security deposits on each tenant and get the first month, last month, and one-month security deposit if you can.

8. Use a good lease, and make sure your lease states you are not liable for auto damage, glass breakage, or acts of God.

9. Deal with trees that are dying, dead, or diseased as quickly as you can to avoid liability.

10. Once you start with your investment plan, DON'T QUIT! Cross the finish line; you will be glad you did.

The Importance of Selling Properties "As Is"

I've been buying and selling properties for a long time. And I have owned, worked for, and consulted for brokerages that sell properties to investors in all states of condition and repair, offering properties for sale from "as is, where is" condition to a completely renovated "turnkey" condition offering all kinds of warranties, expressed and implied. Through countless buy-and-sell transactions, however, whether on the outside or whether I am a party to a contract, I have come to one infallible conclusion that cannot be denied: **You must ALWAYS strive to make sure you sell your properties "as is"—and make sure you have the legal framework in place with which to do so—so that, once you leave a closing table, you have total peace of mind.**

Why?

As cutthroat as it sounds, in business, you have to protect yourself first, and this is a good rule no matter how ethical or honest of a business you are running. Suppose you sell a property to a buyer and you tell him or her the furnace works, and the day after you close the home, it DOESN'T work. Pretend the buyer calls you up and says, "*You told me this furnace works, but it doesn't, and I have a bill on my hands now when I paid you $x dollars in good faith.*"

Then let's suppose you go and fix the furnace and foot a $500 repair bill because you feel badly for the new owner, even though it wasn't your fault.

Well, legally, you have provided a framework now implicating yourself in a conspiracy where the buyer could claim, "*He told me everything worked, Your Honor, and when I called him after the closing and told him the furnace did NOT work, he came and fixed it and admitted that he KNEW it didn't work*. And here is a laundry list of items that ALSO don't work that I need repaired plus my attorney fees."

All of a sudden, you, as an innocent seller of property, are obligated for all kinds of fees and repairs due to your actions trying to be a "nice" guy while being accused of fraud or breach of contract at the same time.

The reality is, there are no nice guys in real estate. There are only buyers, sellers, and amendments to contracts that obligate buyers and sellers to perform tasks beyond the simple conveyance of a property. Do not give a buyer or seller a reason to believe that you have improved a property's condition beyond what they see at the moment of sale, and ensure that your contract states that everything is sold in "as is" condition. **When you do this, you let the perils and pitfalls of owning property fall directly where it should—on the property owner—and not on you**, as someone who owned the property at one time in the past but are held accountable for modern-day Newton's Third Law-types of wear, tear, and mechanical failure through the ambiguity and casino-like nature of today's legal system.

PART 3

PUTTING IT ALL TOGETHER

12

Growing Your Real Estate Holdings: To Manage or NOT to Manage?

Property management is NOT fun.

I am telling you right now. It is hard to do correctly, and when done properly, at BEST it is boring, and it only gets worse from there.

Beyond that basic and rather unsavory introduction, the reality of property management is that it is inherently conflict based, and there is NO avoiding this. Most people are seasoned to avoid conflict at all costs, which makes them weak in confrontations (which is bad and unsafe for them, should any conflict escalate), and in many property management situations, you have to tackle conflicts HEAD ON, **and I am speaking so seriously when I say this because if you show tenants weakness, then they will walk ALL over you**. If you cannot handle property management or engaging in direct conflict with people, verbally and emotionally,[390] either find a *GREAT* management company[391] or do NOT buy property.

It is that simple.

My colleagues at the Brazilian Jujitsu Dojo where I train (most of whom are in the military or law enforcement) and I joke about the fact that the police officers at the dojo have the worst job, but as a property manager, I have the second worst one; when we have this discussion, there is very little laughing. Managing properties involves dealing with the worst side of people—the money side—and generally, **any tenant's rent payment is their highest bill, so when things go wrong financially in a tenant's life, the rent is**

---

390 I would add physically also, but really, you just need to be confident and assertive in confrontations, and this is a good standard for handling yourself. This book is not about handling yourself in self-defense situations. Find a good martial arts self-defense instructor if you need to sharpen your personal defense skills.

391 This would be like finding a unicorn.

usually the first thing to be missed. To add to this, housing laws tend to give tenants time before they are evicted even though they are in default, and in many states, throwing tenants out is an involved legal process, which can be time consuming and monetarily draining. Even worse, once you get through this process, you generally get the house back in a poor condition—which requires time, money, material, and labor to rectify—all while you are NOT getting paid by a tenant and STILL responsible for your mortgage payment.

The flip side of this negative discourse is the following: **IF** you select properties in good areas, and **IF** you screen tenants properly, and **IF** you maintain your rental residence in a way where it places the tenants' safety and well-being first, and **IF** you have a good lease in place that is amenable to your needs as a landlord backed by an attorney who is extremely competent, and **IF** you have laid down the law for your tenants as a condition of renting with effective systems in place should they default, then you PROBABLY will have a very boring experience of getting paid by the fifth of each month and only needing to respond to an occasional maintenance call, with little variance.

Now, boring is good. Boring is what you need. Owning a successful real estate investment portfolio should have as little drama as possible, and **in a happy tenant-landlord relationship, you will find that you should (generally speaking) have little to no contact with the tenant**. If you follow the guidelines I set in this book, your life, regarding owning rental properties, should be very uneventful and boring.

Assuming it is, you are doing things properly.

Setting Expectations Appropriately

Thanks to the advent of modern-day reality television, however, new investors or people considering investing in real estate are under the assumption that investing in real estate is just like these modern reality shows or late-night infomercials showing fledgling investors "living on the edge" (of bankruptcy) only to have a massive windfall payday, which allows them to leave their jobs. Throw in a few cursing contractors, angry tenants, squatters, and local code enforcement, you have a recipe for a hit show.

But to be clear, that would be a hit show, which is highly dramatized, and **probably not based in reality**.

Real investors[392] in the real estate "vertical" are generally not larger than life. There is a guy in my town who is knocking it out of the park selling real estate, and if you saw him, you would have no idea because he looks like the kid from next door. But he is smashing it. Watching him do it inspires me to be better in real estate. However, his demure nature

---

392 The actual ones who have little debt and a very high net worth and massive monthly cash flow from paid-off homes.

belies the reminder, which I need daily and which I share with you now, which is this: Real estate investing is a lot of hard work, a lot of time invested, and frequently that time does NOT always lead to a payday. It can be a daily grind, but you HAVE to put in the work.

Property management and finding the right tenants can be a bit like that also.

If you want to manage your own properties, you need to set out with a strong foundation of base expectations. I will give you a basic summary of my experiences shortly, and you would do well to remember them because they will help you sleep at night after you have acquired your first (or hundredth!) rental property.

The Humblest of Beginnings: How I Became a Successful Real Estate Investor

When I give real estate seminars, I cite two basic reasons for why I am a successful real estate investor today. Most seminar attendees think it has to do with doing a great "deal" and making a lot of money or something along that tack, but the reality couldn't be further from the truth. The reason I have had *any* success as a real estate investor in my life is because of two dramatic, life-changing real estate experiences. One was me failing terribly (in my very first investment "flip"), and one was the experience of me leaving my tenured teaching position with the Memphis City School District to take a job as a rental agent for half of the pay and no benefits.

Let's discuss what happened when I became a rental agent, because I am convinced this experience was what gave me the ammunition to be successful in a lifetime career of real estate investing.

I will never forget the day that I asked a local investor to lunch, and at the time, to me, he was a BIG deal. On the board of the local REIA group, I had seen him give seminars, and obviously, he was in the game. I had met him by wholesaling him a few properties, as well as at the monthly REIA gathering, and I had felt like maybe I had some talent in real estate and wanted to explore that further and more deeply, which heralded me asking him to a lunch meeting.

At lunch, he confirmed what I was thinking, and while speaking very positively about what he felt was my "potential" in real estate, he then offered me a position in his office as a full-time rental agent, but the stakes were VERY high, as follows: a $500 per week salary, no benefits, and a six-week probationary period where if I had not rented a sufficient number of houses for his company, I would be terminated without recourse.

Compare this with my current teaching position at the time: I was well-respected, making $3,600 per month, summers off, health insurance, and a retirement plan! I had a GREAT teaching assignment teaching K–fourth grade music and really liked it. But I felt like I was capable of doing something more. Talk about a difficult decision!

But the decision wasn't difficult for me, to be honest. I went in to my principal the next day and resigned my teaching position, which started a long and fruitful career path, which has allowed me to write this book and share this knowledge with you.

However, being a rental agent, now, that was a journey in itself.

My first day of work was pretty intimidating, to say the least. I was asked to come to a nine-o'clock Monday morning meeting with my new boss, his business partner, a coterie of staff, and the guy who was resigning the rental agent position—all of whom, in a very suspicious fashion, wished me "luck." To this day, I remember that rental agent sliding the "rental cell phone" and charger toward me as if to say, *What have you gotten yourself into?* And, after the fact, I found out he had been asked to resign because he was TERRIBLE at renting houses. I am sure that part of it, in retrospect, however, was that he probably found renting houses just as distasteful as trying to find success at it, and it was probably a mix of him hating the job and the job being punishing that made him, for very obvious reasons, want to move on to greener pastures.

My situation was a bit different, however, as I was "in" the greener pasture since I had left my teaching job and had NO retirement or health insurance!

It was time to get to work.

When the Student Is Ready, the Teacher Will Appear (Redux)

I was the only rental agent in that office for almost three years.

It was punishing, to say the least. I remember showing up for work at 7:30 or 8:00 a.m. and leaving at 10:00 or 11:00 p.m., only to come back the next day and start again, and this happened for months on end. Days and weeks started to blend together. There were no days off, to say the least. And I remember trying to ask my boss for time off to go to the Adirondack Mountains in July of one year, only to be met with an hour-long lecture to answer his question, which was, "***Do you really have time to go with so much work to do here in this office?***" which resulted in me canceling the trip. I barely got time off for my wedding. The work environment was unfair and rewarded other rental agents and real estate agents who engaged in theft. I recall one day coming into my office to see someone had ransacked my pile of investment housing offers, only for us to find out we were in multiple-offer situations, and we would be beat by other agents in our office by a dollar.[393]

---

393 Basically, other real estate agents in my office knew I had a talent for finding discounted deals, so they would look through my offers, see what price I had offered, offer on the same houses, and add a dollar more to their offers, **which would result in me losing to another agent in my office BY A DOLLAR.** When I told my boss they were stealing intellectual property, he refused to punish them and instead blamed ME for not locking my papers securely!

It seems bleak, but all those people who were desperately stealing from me in the office struggled to maintain their careers in real estate, where as I have been fortunate to stay in the industry and see my race to completion.[394] Some people might cite ethics or karma as being in my favor, but I know differently what helped me grow stronger and gain the knowledge necessary to succeed. While others in the office were out conniving and stealing my work, I was fortunate to have my own personal, private real estate mentor with me daily, showing me how to effectively screen and manage rental property—**the rental phone**.

How Many Missed Calls Will YOUR Cell Phone Accept?

To give you an idea of how much the rental phone rang each day, I was asked on an occasion to speak at a lunch meeting for new real estate investors. Since I was still the property rental agent at the time, and the phone did ring a lot, I placed it on silent when the meeting began. The whole luncheon, including my speaking part of the engagement, took about an hour. When I took the phone out of my suitcoat pocket after the meeting, I glanced down to see if I missed any calls, and to my amazement, the phone said, "*YOU HAVE 99 MISSED CALLS*."

Why ninety-nine calls? Because the cheap rental phone wasn't capable of "flipping over" to one hundred missed calls! That means I missed over one hundred phone calls in an hour, all inquiring about separate rental properties! I am not sure a human can field one hundred rental inquiries in a sixty-minute period, but it made me realize just how hard I was working and the demand that had been put upon me by my boss.

While I have long since resigned from his company to form my own, I have had several separate occasions where I have spoken with his current rental agents, and they all say the same thing: **"We HEARD about you! Our boss says you were the best rental agent he ever had, and no one compares to your ability to hustle and rent houses!"**

To be honest, hearing that swells my heart with pride, but there is nothing super-natural about me; I was just a broke kid who was hungry and desperately wanted to become somebody, and the rental phone—as strangely as it sounds—became my teacher and gave me the opportunity I had been looking for in the strangest of places.

---

394 Or thereabouts.

You see, the rental phone was an incomparable teacher when it came to me learning the inner workings of real estate. People generally make a living "trading" real estate one of four ways, as follows:

1. They are licensed agents or brokers who act as middlemen, generating commissions.

2. They buy and sell property, known as wholesaling (unrenovated) and flipping (renovated for retail sale).

3. They make loans on real estate to qualified borrowers (known in the industry as "trading paper").

4. They own income-producing real estate (residential or commercial).

But of these four income streams, only two are truly passive and residual in nature—trading paper and owning rental property.

The Rental Phone as a Merciless Instructor

The reason the rental phone was such an awesome teacher was that it let me step into the shoes of the investor/owner without paying a heavy price to have the experience of real estate ownership. This manifested itself in a variety of forms, but even before I spoke to a single tenant, I was getting an invaluable and priceless education into the following things:

1. Where actual[395] investors were buying property;

2. The floorplans and layouts of property that investors and tenants were attracted to;

3. The floorplans and layouts of property that investors and tenants were ***NOT*** attracted to;

4. Kitchens, bedrooms, and baths which tenants liked versus hated;

5. Good areas, which were easy to rent versus sketchy or "bad" areas, which were far more difficult to rent, let alone find qualified tenants, and often potentially unsafe;

6. Homes banks would lend on versus NOT lend on;

---

395 Not fake/pretend investors.

7. Construction costs for many items related to owning a home;[396]

8. Insurance issues related to fire, flood, and acts of God, plus liability and mold;[397]

9. Areas I didn't feel safe in and would NEVER own a rental property in; and

10. Many intricacies far too broad to list here.

Keep in mind, this was all BEFORE I took the first phone call. Getting on the phone with actual tenant prospects was an entirely different game in itself and gave me instruction into

1. Who was running a game;

2. Who was a professional renter;

3. Who just got out of jail or was facing jail time;

4. Who just declared bankruptcy or was evicted;

5. Who was a criminal or leans toward criminal behavior;

6. Who was related to a criminal or undesirable;

7. Who could not be trusted;

8. Who was not reliable and does not pay their bills; and

9. Who was not responsible and was financially weak.

10. Once you get through the first nine points, you might have a tenant worth screening.

Dealing with Actual People

I have never rented properties in a city other than Memphis, Tennessee, and I want to be clear: I love Memphis, Tennessee, and this has been my home for almost twenty years. But with that being said, Memphis has often been referred to as "the bankruptcy capital of the world" and carries one of the highest crime rates in the United States,[398] generally leading in violent crime. The upside of this is you will probably have a far easier task of

---

396 Everything from HVAC install to refinishing hardwood floors, I was forced to take notes and count costs on. As a company employee, I knew what actual construction and material cost was vs. marked-up client cost, **which helped me know how much I should be paying as a property owner** vs. what was excessive.

397 I am a certified mold inspector, though I don't practice it in any capacity beyond my personal homes. **You should become one also.** Pete Youngs' has a great course on this, see here: http://peteyoungs.com/

398 https://en.wikipedia.org/wiki/Memphis,_Tennessee#Crime

property management than I have faced in Memphis. Also, we have done well in Memphis using simple systems, which I will share with you. So my point is, if I can own property in Memphis and not pull my hair out, how much easier will it be for you?

Assuming you follow basic systems and have a well-thought-out plan, that is.

Self-Managing Your Rental Properties: A Breakdown

I will summarize my property management philosophies with you, and you can add or delete what you feel works for you. **Some of this may seem harsh, but I am not going to apologize for encouraging you to run a business like, well, a business.** If your goal is to give away months of free rent to people while your net worth dwindles and the assets you have worked for are ransacked, that is up to you. But I cannot encourage that in my students, so I will tell you the rental philosophies that have helped me succeed in owning investment property. Let's begin with tenant screening.

Tenant Screening: On the Phone

1. **Grammar and manners rule the day** and are an indication of what you can expect from the tenant prospect in the future. A lack of both = disqualification.

2. **NEVER do same-day showings**; always schedule for the next day.

3. **Always have a tenant prospect call you at a pre-arranged time the next day to schedule a showing** (if you want them to actually *see* a house. Some people will be disqualified before this step on your first phone call). This will ensure that they can follow instructions and are serious about renting the house. My call time is 10:00 a.m. each day.

4. **If a tenant is more than five minutes late at a scheduled showing, LEAVE,** and they are disqualified. If they will not respect your time for a showing, they will not respect you as a manager.

5. **When people ask you "what are the qualifications to get the home as a rental," say this:** NO EVICTIONS, NO CONVICTIONS, and NO JUDGMENTS. You must make four times the rent and demonstrate proof of income. No recent bankruptcies or foreclosures. Must have a good rental history and at least two landlord references. I need first month, last month, and one-month security deposit PLUS application fee of $100. House is ready on day "x," and you need to be ready to move on day "x," or this won't work.

6. **If a tenant's car is a mess, DO NOT RENT TO THEM.** Look inside their car. Don't be afraid to ask and come visit their house if you are unsure about a tenant being a good fit for you.

Tenant Screening: In Person

1. **Always pull credit, background, and criminal history.** Charge the tenant a $100 application fee and let them know it is **NONREFUNDABLE.** Charging them $100 will keep all but the most serious applicants from applying, and no one is going to spend that money without first giving you questions and information, which will let you know that a tenant has a questionable background (such as, "*What are the qualifications you look for?*").

2. **NEVER take an application without a FULL DEPOSIT.** Remember, anyone can come up with an application fee, but SERIOUS tenant prospects will come up with a deposit also. Get the application in full along with a copy of their driver's license and Social Security card.

3. **Assuming a tenant qualifies, set a date for the lease closing and make sure they come to YOUR office,** not the house and not a Starbucks.[399]

4. **NO SHORT PAYS.[400] NO PERSONAL CHECKS. MONEY ORDERS OR CERTIFIED CASHIER'S CHECKS ONLY. NO EXCEPTIONS.**

5. **Do NOT be alone with a tenant prospect, whenever possible. Always have a buddy or an independent witness to monitor your transactions with the tenant. DO NOT GET PERSONALLY INVOLVED WITH TENANTS IN ANY WAY. TREAT THEM AS CUSTOMERS. DO NOT GO TO A TENANT'S HOUSE ALONE, IF POSSIBLE.**

Tenant Screening: Safety and Showings

1. **Carry a personal firearm at all times and be trained in how to use it.** Keep "one in the chamber" at ALL showings.

2. **NEVER CARRY CASH** and DO NOT ACCEPT RENT PAYMENTS AS CASH.

---

399 **Even a virtual office will work, but NEVER your home and NEVER at the home.** Have an independent setting where they realize it is like coming to a house closing. Treat it as such.

400 Meaning, don't accept rent that is less than what is owed, ESPECIALLY AT A LEASE SIGNING. That is a bad harbinger of things to come.

3. **Always keep your office door locked** and security cameras on.

4. **Do not go to house showings alone.**

5. **If you feel unsafe for any reason, ask the tenant to excuse you for a minute, THEN LEAVE.**[401] **Call the police if necessary.**

6. **Always check the back door on vacant houses BEFORE you open the front door, and make sure an exterior inspection of a home shows it is secure BEFORE you enter it.**

Keep in mind, all these items are the basic rules to simply try to identify a qualified tenant to place into your home. While it may seem daunting at first, I cannot stress to you how much easier it becomes when you have the right property in the right location, which draws the right tenant. Remember John O'Williams, the greatest landlord in the world we discussed in an earlier chapter? His rental world was much easier than the average property owner because he owned higher-income-producing rental homes in nicer areas, specifically near Syracuse University. This drew a main base of college kids, many of whom had their parents pay their rent for them and frequently a year in advance.[402] **John O'Williams was a landlord who thought about things from a different perspective, and this variation in perspective led to great profitability.**

Conversely, when landlords do not do their research or buy in marginal areas, they can end up with a lot of problems, which cannot necessarily be ameliorated by good property management. Owning homes in dangerous, rough areas of town and having to go to their property to deal with issues is not only unsafe, but it is also unwise and unprofitable.

Do so at your own peril.

Post Move-In: Once a Tenant Is Placed in a House Management Strategies

Once you have a tenant placed in the home, you will still have a bit of legwork to get to what I call the "boring" part of owning real estate, which is simply where your tenant routinely pays monthly rent to you and you respond to an occasional (and I do mean "occasional") maintenance call.

---

401 **I used this self-defense technique to avoid a carjacking once, and it proved incredibly effective.** A crazy guy came up to my window at a Popeye's chicken in Memphis and was banging on it and cursing me out to let him in the car and open the door. I calmly held up my index finger, looked him in the eye and said, "Hold on a second," at which point he relaxed and paused, and I peeled out. He was in a rage, shaking his fist as I sped off to the interstate. But you would be surprised at how many people actually are willing to "wait a second." :)

402 If you think about it from a strategic standpoint, what parent is going to NOT pay their kid's rent and let their college kid be homeless? **Not many.** Would you?

Primarily, it is important to understand that no matter how much work you have done to a property or how thorough of a renovation you think you have done, a tenant will find some issues with a property when they move in. Whether it is the shower head spraying sideways, an undiscovered leak under the sink, or some pest issue, a tenant will find some problems and want them to be fixed. **As a rule, I let my leases reflect that I will fix all items, WITHIN REASON, in the first thirty days.** After thirty days, the tenants themselves are responsible for all items less than $100, and **the following things will NEVER be covered by the landlord, and there are NO EXCEPTIONS to this rule.**

These items are:

1. **Glass breakage:** The landlord is NOT responsible for any glass breakage, including break-ins or acts of God.

2. **Pest control**: This is the tenant's responsibility, unless it is termite related.

3. **Auto damage:** The landlord has NO liability for any auto damage, including but not limited to theft, break-ins, or acts of God.

4. **Break-ins/theft:** We have found this is usually done by friends or family, and almost 100% of the time thefts are performed by someone the person knows, who has been in their home.

I will cover major repair issues such as roof leaks, heating and air, and electrical problems (plus major plumbing) throughout the lease term, assuming it is not due to tenant negligence. Tenants are informed at lease signings that they MUST change their air filters in the furnace every thirty days, or THEY will be responsible for AC unit damage and freeze-ups, plus associated service calls.

Are YOU Living in Reality as a Landlord and Property Manager?

At times (and these have been very unpleasant times), I have had to consult for landlords and property owners who, quite simply, shouldn't be property owners, and most of these came from my radio show listener base. Most of the time this takes the form of landlords who are unable or unwilling to pay for appropriate and periodic maintenance and upkeep of homes but want premium rent while the tenant takes care of all problems at his or her expense while paying promptly every month. Ultimately, the landlord tries to blame the tenant for all problems and uses a confrontational technique to try to avoid taking responsibility for genuine issues within their rental property. It can be a mess.

The short answer is, this never works and ends up having you lose a tenant and have a great deal of difficulty in re-renting a home by doing NO work to it. I do not recommend using this type of strategy in any way, as it is a losing tactic. Do the work and repairs necessary to get your home in rentable condition, and do not let problems fester. You will be glad that you did.

I should state, for the record, that there is a way you can get your tenant to cover all the maintenance on your home at their expense; **it is called a LEASE OPTION**. But lease options are beyond the scope of this book, and when you do have a lease option about to begin, it is imperative that you and the tenant have a mutual understanding of tenant and landlord responsibilities, or you will end up with confusion or, worse, an ambiguous situation that could result in legal action from the tenant due to a misunderstanding.[403]

It is important that you set your expectations realistically and be prepared to handle your tenant's maintenance requests promptly and thoroughly. Remember, happy tenants tend to pay promptly each month without an issue.

Using The Short-Term Retirement Program with a Single Tenant for Income Purposes

Most of the time, if you are using STR principles to buy and pay off your primary residence, you might end up just working with one tenant. In this situation, especially if a tenant is renting your home, some footage within your home, or an accessory unit, your tenant will generally be single (due to small footage allotments in rental units and accessory units, in my experience). In this case, it is even MORE imperative that you address your tenant's concerns and requests IMMEDIATELY to avoid any feelings of neglect or creating a situation that harbors malcontent. **And it goes without saying, do NOT get personally involved with tenants, EVER!** It is good business sense and helps you to avoid a sticky legal situation sometime down the road. However, remember that ALL safety and screening rules apply to ALL tenants. Just because someone looks like they would be responsible does NOT make them a good tenant! Always perform a full screening.

When a Tenant Moves Out

Inevitably, tenants will leave. My first advice to you is this: **ACCEPT THAT YOUR TENANTS WILL LEAVE, AND THIS IS A NATURAL PART OF OWNING RENTAL PROPERTY.** Don't get hung up in a state of depression because your amazing tenant of three years is moving

---

403 For a thorough education on lease options, if you are interested in using this highly profitable technique, learn from the best. Go to http://wendypatton.com/. Tell her I sent you.

on to someplace else. Understand that no tenant stays forever. You will have many tenants over the years if you own rental property successfully. Then, once you know a tenant is leaving, initiate a business plan that allows you to get the unit ready as quickly as possible and get a new tenant with as little of an interruption in income as possible.

Here is a good basic checklist for your review:

Tenant Move Out: The Plan

T – 30 days. Tenant gives you notice. You immediately start marketing the property as "For Rent," with the unit ready in forty-five days.

T – 15 days. Show the property to qualified tenants. Begin to ask for (and take) applications, and when you have an approved applicant, let the deposit go "hard" (meaning nonrefundable until the end of the new lease term). Lock in the tenant. Confirm their move in for up to fifteen days (two weeks) after the first tenant has left.

T – 5 days. Confirm with existing tenant their move-out date, a walk-through inspection with the tenant (when their stuff is out to confirm that the home is left in "broom-clean" condition). Arrange for a key swap, getting the key back (and legal possession) from the tenant. Always tell the tenant you will MAIL them their deposit, if any is left, within thirty days of their move out.[404]

T – 0 days. Tenant leaves. Make sure no trash or debris is left in the unit. Make sure utility services are ON in your name, if necessary.

T + 1 days. Install your rehab crew to do the necessary cleaning, painting, and repairs. Change AC filters, rinse the AC compressor outside (if you have one), and check high-maintenance areas like around tubs and toilets and under kitchen sinks, for any sign of wood rot. Fix immediately if you have some as to prevent further damage or a falling hazard for the tenant.

T + 5 days. Re-key locks to your master key, using a qualified locksmith.

T + 6–14 days. Have new tenant come to your office, sign lease and other documents, provide evidence of insurance, and write a receipt for payment. Give new tenant keys.

T + 3 days (after tenant move in): Cut off utility services, if needed.

Reminder:

DON'T DO EMERGENCY MOVE-INS!

---

404 **You do this because you may not find hidden issues until you start getting the unit ready for the next tenant.** It is surprising what problems a tenant caused and is living with without informing you. Not reporting leaks, breaking appliances, etc., is ALL the responsibility of the tenant (if your lease allows for this). **Hold the deposit until you are SURE there is no damage.** As a matter of record, very few of our tenants get their deposit back due to wear and tear, issues, late rents and fees accumulated, not giving proper notice, and so on.

Emergency move-ins are where a tenant calls you and says they need to move in today. Why such a rush? Generally, because they are about to be evicted (thrown on the street literally), or they are having some domestic abuse situation where thy HAVE to leave. Usually there are financial issues, or drugs can frequently be involved. **Whatever the case, do NOT make their problems your problems**. DON'T DO SAME-DAY MOVE-INS!

What to Do When Things Go Wrong

Every state has different laws governing tenants' rights, and it is YOUR responsibility to know what laws pertain to your state. I would recommend buying an hour of time with a well-recommended attorney who does eviction and collection work for a living and ask him or her what the procedures are, time scales, and for a copy of a lease, which is in full compliance with your local landlord housing requirements, specifically one that will hold up in a court of law against an adversarial tenant.

With that being said, if you are in ownership of real estate for investment purposes and plan on doing it for the "long haul," you WILL have a tenant relationship go south on you and turn into a non-pay delinquency. Even with the best screening, this still can happen (I have seen it and watched it happen to friends of mine who own excellent property management companies). Prepare yourself in advance for this eventuality and you will find your preparedness will create a much smoother transition for you and add some degree of peace of mind to an otherwise unpleasant situation.

Degrees of Tenant Delinquency

The great catch-22 isn't that a tenant is late on their rent; **rather, it is IF they will pay, and then assuming they are paying (assuming), WHEN will the money materialize?**

Consider the following example:

Timmy the Teacher owns a rental property and the tenant (paying rent of $1,000 per month) has not paid by the fifth. The tenant is late.

Choose your own adventure here.

Timmy can:

- ☐ Call the tenant and ask what's up, or
- ☐ Wait for the payment to show up.

Let's say Timmy chooses number two. Choice number two is bad for many reasons. What if the tenant has moved in the night, for example, and Timmy doesn't follow up? You get the idea. Timmy will be in the dark for a long time, and **EACH DAY HE DOESN'T PROACTIVELY TRY TO COLLECT RENT OR REMOVE A NONPAYING TENANT FROM HIS HOME DELAYS HIS NEXT PAYDAY A DAY FURTHER, WHILE (POTENTIALLY) OBLIGATING HIM TO MAKING HIS MORTGAGE PAYMENT OUT OF HIS OWN POCKET.**

So suppose Timmy chooses choice number one. He calls the tenant, who had "a death in the family"[405] and the tenant says they will pay on the fourteenth.

Timmy says okay and waives the late fee.

MONTH ONE ON THE FOURTEENTH

The fourteenth shows up, but the tenant's rent does not. Timmy gives it a few days, but it was the weekend when Timmy was going to call, and he didn't want to deal with the issue before the weekend started, so by the time Timmy calls, it is the twentieth. Timmy calls the tenant, and the tenant doesn't answer.

Finally, the tenant calls back on the twenty-second and says they are really having a financial problem, but they can pay next month on the fourteenth. Timmy reluctantly agrees.

MONTH TWO ON THE FOURTEENTH

(A month later) on the fourteenth, no payment arrives. Timmy calls the tenant, and the tenant dodges the call and taps it. Timmy texts the tenant, no response. Timmy goes to the house, and the tenant is (obviously) still living there. The tenant tells Timmy he is *so* sorry but will have all the money on the twenty-fourth and is simply waiting for a "big check." Timmy breathes a sigh of relief and waits until the twenty-fourth, where—you guessed it—payment does not materialize.

MONTH THREE, DAY FIVE

So Timmy finally calls his attorney, who needs a week to get documents together. Timmy gets the documents together and files on the third month of delinquency, when his attorney is back from golfing in Aruba. Timmy is out 3k so far in rent PLUS his attorney fees and filing fees, and while the tenant is obligated for these fees, **OWING versus COLLECTING**

---

405   This is one of a bucket list of excuses tenants use. Yes, family members die, but responsible people do not let it affect their responsibilities, or **if a death is going to affect their ability to pay on time, GOOD tenants will call and MAKE ARRANGEMENTS BEFORE THE RENT IS LATE**. I have had many people die in the past twenty years while I have owned rental property that I have been close to. How many mortgage payments have I missed? ***NONE.***

the money are two different things entirely. Realistically, Timmy just want's his house back. But now he has to wait for the court system.

His court date is set for the last week of the month.

AT COURT, MONTH THREE, WEEK FOUR

The tenant shows up and asks for a "continuance," and they are entitled to one (Timmy's attorney says this somewhat jovially), so the judge gives the tenant three more weeks and resets the court date.

AT COURT AGAIN, MONTH FOUR, WEEK THREE

The tenant no-shows, and Timmy gets a monetary judgment that he is extremely unlikely to collect and a possession judgment, but is required to give the tenant ten business days to get out (two more weeks) before he can forcibly remove the tenant. Timmy is starting to really feel sick to his stomach.

MONTH FIVE, WEEK TWO

Timmy needs a Federal Entry and Detainer Warrant filed (known as an FED) and calls his attorney to do so. This costs him more money in fees and filing surcharges. His attorney says, "It will take a few days."

MONTH FIVE, WEEK THREE

The FED comes through. Timmy hires a process server and crew to put the tenant out. This costs $600. The crew shows up, but the tenant is gone. By the way, the house is trashed, and the tenant left a lot of damage to the infrastructure of the home.

Calculating Timmy's Total Damage

Timmy lost six months[406] **of rent.** $6 × 1000 = $6,000

Timmy has $1,000 in court costs and attorney fees: $1,000

Timmy paid the "put-out crew" $600: $600

Tenant caused $5,000 worth of damage, as their utilities were cut off and this wreaked havoc on their living situation, plus they vandalized things and stole the

---

406　**Minimally six months of rent. He regains possession at the end of month 5, but the home's condition is so poor there is no way Timmy can "turn" the house back to rent-ready condition, let alone show it or rent it in a week.** So he loses month six of rent also.

mechanical equipment: $5,000

Timmy's estimated total loss: $12,600.

Side note (IMPORTANT): Assuming Timmy makes the obligatory "$300 per month in positive cash flow" after paying his mortgage, this tenant put Timmy back FOUR YEARS from being profitable—assuming Timmy had 12k accessible to throw at the problem. Some investors would be bankrupted by this tenant and FORCED to sell due to illiquidity.

A Better Way to Deal with Nonpaying Tenants

Let's agree that the way Timmy handled this was suboptimal, mainly, in that he let the tenant do whatever he or she wanted for three months before starting the legal process, which created a situation of hopelessness and expense.

Remember, when a tenant stops paying you, time is NOT on your side!

Here is the simplest way to deal with nonpaying tenants—it is the most methodical but does carry some cost you probably will not recoup. Charging higher security deposits can help offset this expense.

Consider the following example:

Timmy the Teacher owns a rental property and the tenant (paying rent of $1,000 per month) has not paid by the fifth. The tenant is late.

Solution: Timmy calls his attorney and asks him to file on the tenant, submitting the necessary digital copies of leases and personal information needed to get on the court docket IMMEDIATELY. A court date gets set the next day, generally two weeks out due to court backlog.

Probable Outcomes:

1. **The tenant does NOT pay—tenant gets evicted in court at the first setting, and usually doesn't even show up**. This puts the tenant out within the first month, only resulting in a loss of one month of rent and some attorney fees, which should be covered by the forfeited security deposit of one month's rent.

2. **The tenant shows up and PAYS**. You require the tenant to pay the legal fees that you paid to the attorney, and the tenant pays the court costs also. **However (IMPORTANT), even though the tenant has made right with you, continue your proceedings in court on the same day as scheduled, and ensure you get A POSSESSION JUDGMENT**. This allows you to file the FED WITHOUT HAVING TO TAKE THE TENANT TO COURT AGAIN IF THEY ARE LATE ON RENT OR DO

NOT PAY—YOU HAVE THE RIGHT TO EVICT THEM ANY TIME IN THE NEXT SEVEN YEARS WITHOUT RETURNING TO COURT.

Since you were forced to set the court date due to a tenant non-pay, **DO NOT DISMISS THE COURT DATE EVEN IF THE TENANT SHOWS UP AND PAYS!** Get the judgment for possession. Then, if they do not pay timely again, file on the tenant, and disclose this to them that the process-serving crew will be coming in a few days to place them on the street[407]. Generally, this ensures prompt payment, and at the very least, communication if rent is going to be late.

Delinquent Tenants: Three Generic Reasons You Will Be Given

Remember, delinquent tenants who have not paid their rent will give you one of three general answers about IF and WHEN they will pay their rent when you contact them, as follows:

1. They give you a "firm" date for payment based on an incoming paycheck or benefit check. These dates will usually fall around the third, fourteenth, seventeenth, or twenty-fourth of the month

   YOUR RESPONSE: You can choose to file on them for eviction or wait until the alleged payday, whatever your threshold of tolerance is.[408]

2. They tell you to go f——k yourself.

   YOUR RESPONSE: File on the tenant immediately or try one of the bluffing strategies listed below.

3. They tell you they have "no earthly idea" when they will be able to pay you.

   YOUR RESPONSE: FILE IMMEDIATELY WITHOUT QUESTION.

It is important to note that, in the first two examples, I am okay with the tenant either giving me a firm date or telling me to go pound sand. **Either is okay because I know EXACTLY where I stand.** The third example is NOT okay because when a tenant expresses total ambiguity about their financial situation, their life is probably falling apart, nothing else is getting paid, and them moving out of your property is the best thing you

---

407 Keep in mind, I am outlining the process as we observe it in Memphis, Tennessee. **Your state and municipality may be different, so consult with a good eviction attorney to make sure YOU understand the rules, and FOLLOW THEM!**

408 As stated previously, systematically filing will get tenants out but sometimes alienate good-paying tenants also, so a certain level of discretion is involved on your part.

can do for yourself, as they will never get back on track, and (IMPORTANT) their plan is to probably try to stay as LONG as possible because they have no financial resources and nowhere else to go.[409]

Good Quote to Remember

Do you know the hardest game to win at?

The "catch up" game.

I've never seen anyone win at that game.

—Anonymous

Other Techniques You Can Add to Your "Toolbox"

Now, I don't like to spend money I can't recover, so the attorney and filing option, while the most sound for average landlords, is not the best for me before I try a few other "tried and true" tactics. Some of these may or may not be legal in your state, but I have used these, and generally (if you are a good poker player) you can often "bluff" delinquent tenants into moving, without a controversy developing.[410]

The easiest way for me to illustrate is through dialogue. In each of these examples, let's assume the tenant has not paid, it's the sixth of the month (suppose it is a Wednesday) and you call them, and they basically tell you that they have no idea when they will have the money.

NOTE: ANY TIME YOU GET A DELINQUENT TENANT TO MOVE OUT OF YOUR INVESTMENT PROPERTY WITHOUT A CONFRONTATION, LEAVE YOUR HOUSE IN BROOM-CLEAN CONDITION WITHOUT DAMAGE, AND FORFEIT THEIR SECURITY DEPOSIT, YOU WIN.

Bluff 1: The Tale of the Moving Truck and The Locksmith

You (*calling*): Hey, tenant, I haven't gotten your rent this month and was calling to see when you were planning on paying.

Tenant: Um, actually, I just lost my job and am planning on moving back with my mom.

---

409   Tenants with drug habits often find themselves in this situation, so be wary.
410   Like Bruce Lee, "The art of fighting without fighting."

You: When are you planning on moving?

Tenant: Two months from now, when my mom is back from Europe.

You: And you are not planning on paying rent anymore, am I understanding you correctly?

Tenant: Yes

You: Okay, listen to the words that are about to come out of my mouth. You are in default, and that means after I get off this phone, the next call I am making is to my attorney who will file to evict you in court, and you will probably be in court in a few days, with the sheriff coming to the throw you out after. An eviction stays on your credit report for seven years. You won't be able to rent a house ever again, and I will garnish your wages and sue you for the entire lease term.

Now, I won't do that if you work with me, as follows...I want you to go out immediately, rent a moving truck, get some friends to help load you up, and be out in the next forty-eight hours. My next call is to the locksmith, and I will be telling him to come change the locks Friday at 5:00 p.m. Is that something you can do? I don't want to see you homeless, but you are about to be.

Tenant: Um, well, I...

You (*interrupting*): What time should I tell the locksmith to come? Five? Or would four be better for you? Do you think you could be out by noon?

Tenant: I, umm...think I can be out by three.

You: Okay, so you will be out by three, Friday, but at 3:01 you will not be able to get back in the house because the locks will be changed. So you need to be out right away. Make sure you leave the house in broom-clean condition and mow the lawn also.

Tenant: Um, well, I think I could—

You (*forcefully*): LAWN MOWED ALSO. I'm calling the locksmith right now. So 3:00 p.m. Friday or the sheriff will put you out.[411] Thanks.

IMPORTANT! Go put a "For Rent" sign in the yard IMMEDIATELY, then TEXT the tenant and tell them the locksmith is confirmed for Friday. You can tell them you have tenants wanting to see the house asap also, which adds pressure.

Probability of success: 5/10

---

411 Notice how I throw the sheriff coming back into the mix at the end just to make sure the tenant has a few extra things to think about.

Bluff 2: I Have a Tenant Ready to Take Over Your Lease

You (*calling*): Hey, tenant, I haven't gotten your rent this month and was calling to see when you were planning on paying.

Tenant: Um, actually, I just lost my job and am planning on moving back with my mom.

You: When are you planning on moving?

Tenant: Two months from now, when my mom is back from Europe.

You: And you are not planning on paying rent anymore, am I understanding you correctly?

Tenant: Yes.

You: Actually, the timing of this is pretty good. I have a tenant who is willing to take over your lease and loves the house. They want to be in by this weekend. If you can be out by this weekend, I can let you out of your lease and NOT evict you or garnish your wages. When do you think you can be out?

Tenant: Um, well, I…

You: I need you to be out Friday by five. What time should I tell the locksmith to come? Five? Or would four be better for you? Do you think you could be out by noon?

(Continue with the locksmith dialogue as outlined in the first example. Tell them they forfeit their security deposit due to breaking their lease, but you will give them a good recommendation if they leave the house in broom-clean condition and mow the lawn.[412])

Probability of success: 6/10

Bluff 3: You Qualify for Our "Hardship Program"[413]

You (*calling*): Hey, tenant, I haven't gotten your rent this month and was calling to see when you were planning on paying.

Tenant: Um, actually, I just lost my job and am planning on moving back with my mom.

You: When are you planning on moving?

Tenant: Two months from now, when my mom is back from Europe.

You: And you are not planning on paying rent anymore, am I understanding you correctly?

---

412 If a tenant was exceptionally good, you can give them back their security deposit (or part of it) as a condition of being out within your timeframe. This is an additional "carrot" you can use as you see fit.

413 Sometimes in the industry known as "cash for keys."

Tenant: Yes.

You: Okay, listen, I don't usually tell people about this, but we have a hardship program for good tenants who fall on hard times like you are right now. And the good news is, we can avoid a messy eviction with you being thrown out by the sheriff and having your credit ruined and all that. Here is how it works. If you are out this Friday at 5:00 p.m., and you leave the house in broom-clean condition and the lawn mowed, I will bring $200 cash to the house, and when you give me the keys to the home, I will give you the cash, and you drive your moving truck away. We can part as friends, and I will give you a good recommendation for your next landlord. But I need you to do this Friday by five or else you will not qualify for the program. What do you think?

Tenant: Sounds great, I can be out Friday at five.

You: Okay, I am going to schedule the locksmith for 5:00 p.m., Friday, and meet you at the home and give you the cash. If ANYTHING is left in the home, you won't qualify. See you at five.

Next step: Take $200 cash from their security deposit, give it back to them, and wave goodbye as their truck rolls down the road, placing a "For Rent" sign in the yard and getting the place ready for the next tenant.

Probability of success: 8/10

Fear Turns to Greed at Breakeven

Now, the problem with this third strategy is that many readers will be appalled and repulsed at the idea of giving money to a tenant who is behind on rent money to move. **But the reality of the situation is, you are running a business, the investment house is your "storefront," and when a nonpaying tenant is in your "store," it is essentially "closed" for business.** Consider Timmy the Teacher's debacle we discussed previously, where he completely mismanaged his house, let the tenant have *carte blanche,* and in doing so, racked up a $12,600 loss. Do you think, if Timmy could reverse the flow of time, he would LOVE to go back, throw $200 of the tenant's security deposit at the problem, and move on with his life, getting a new tenant in his house the same month without an interruption in cash flow?

You bet he would.

In all of business, this is the best quote that defines the human existence, in my opinion:

> *Fear Turns to Greed at Breakeven.*

For example, think about when your tenant stops paying. You are freaking out, Will he pay? When? What if he or she NEVER pays?

Then you start to think to yourself, *"At this point, if I can just get the tenant out, I will be happy. When will the tenant be out*?"

Then suddenly, unexpectedly, the tenant shows up with the rent.

What's the first thing you do? You ask for a LATE FEE!

The point is, late fees are the last thing on your mind when rent isn't being paid, but the first thing on your mind when a tenant pays rent. **This is an example of fear turning to greed at breakeven.**[414]

And by the way, I am NOT saying don't collect late fees. I am simply illustrating my point.

Using Management Companies Effectively: A Primer

Now that I have outlined a general management strategy for you if you elect to manage your own properties, let's discuss using a management company. A few things to remember from the outset of this discussion:

1. Management companies are absolutely FOR PROFIT.

2. Management companies make profits in one of three ways—renting houses, collecting rents, and marking up maintenance.

3. Markups (maintenance) can be as high as 100% and usually a minimum of 30%.

4. Management companies will NEVER do as good of a job managing your home as you do.[415]

5. Most rental agents and employees at management companies are usually non-real estate professionals who do not own rental property and have never considered it.

6. Your rents, if/when collected, are usually disbursed on the last business day of the month, forcing you to wait an additional thirty days to get paid, essentially.

7. You do not keep late fees.

---

414 This is something to be aware of, emotionally, in your business dealings.
415 Unless you are terrible.

8. If a tenant does not pay the rent on time, the management company, depending on the size of their management portfolio and workload, may not immediately check the status of your home to see if it is vacant, which could put you into a second month of nonpayment and deeper into a financial hole if you do not manage them properly.

The trade-off with using a management company, essentially, is that you have to let them become your "eyes and ears," and to be realistic, the more work intensive your property is, the less astute those "eyes and ears" become. With a limited number of staff managing a variety of "spinning plates" at the company and always having to attend to emergency situations first, your property, especially if you have a singular holding or tiny number of holdings, may not be a priority for the management company versus their biggest clients. And it is hard to get in touch with tenants as the owner of the property if the management company has an established relationship in place with your tenant, even if the management company is not doing an acceptable job in your eyes.

With that being said, most people do NOT have the temperament to manage houses, and, as such, using a management company becomes a necessity. It is good to ask a prospective management company for a few references of other owners who have a similar number of homes in the same area that you do. When you do, ask the references the following questions:[416]

1. Is the tenant screening effective? Meaning, does the management company place tenants that are reliable and pay on time?

2. How long do the tenants stay, on average?

3. What are the maintenance costs and response times to fix problems?

4. Has the reference had any unusual issues with the management company? Is the rent disbursed promptly each month as agreed?

5. What is the minimum contract time you have to keep a house with a company?

6. Does the management company take your phone calls? Do they actually answer the phone?

---

416 You can ask the management company these questions, but realistically, they will probably tell you what you want to hear versus the reality, which is usually different. **Make sure you read the management contract BEFORE you sign.**

You get the idea. Try to get a solid footing of what you can expect from the management company; that way you are not caught "unawares."

The Goal

Lots of people who choose to invest in real estate lose sight of the goal. They think it is about buying the best house, the "prettiest" house, the "best deal," the "best" return, and so on. The reality is, **no investment property is operating appropriately unless it is giving you consistent monthly income, year after year, with little or no interruption in monetary flow.**

Let's repeat that:

> **NO investment property is operating appropriately unless it is giving you consistent monthly income, year after year, with little or no interruption in monetary flow.**

Consider the following example:

> Timmy the Teacher collects $15,000 per month in rents, and his rents come in twelve months a year without interruption, on average.
>
> **OR**
>
> Timmy's friend collects $20,000 in rent and gets this about two-thirds of the year or about eight months of the year.

Which would you choose? Timmy's friend's income or Timmy's income?

Basic math tells us that that Timmy's friend has an annual income of about $160,000 per year, which is eight months × 20k per month. Timmy, however, while having a smaller monthly rental income of $15k per month, gets that twelve times a year for a total gross of 180k per year—a 20k net increase over his friend.

I cannot illustrate or emphasize more clearly the fact that, when engaging in investment real estate, the goal is not simply to "buy houses" or to "buy good deals." The fundamental nature of purchasing real estate for investment purposes is to establish a long-term passive income stream which is designed to come in monthly, with as little investment of time and effort on your behalf as possible. All homes purchased need to serve this function or, for those starting out, be (at the very least) a stepping stone to this function. For example, suppose you buy a rental house at a deep discount, get it rented and online, however, the property is ***extremely*** management intensive. You have a lot of equity in it—what do you do? You would sell this property at market value when the timing was correct,[417] and use the equity to "level up" to a house that would be a long-term, more stable asset in your investment portfolio—which could provide a headache-free source of income for you for the medium and long-term ranges. **And, keep in mind, once you have a property operating optimally and paying you cash each month, it becomes a simple exercise to extrapolate HOW MANY of those particular homes you need to meet your monthly income or retirement goals.**

Consider: A simple formula illustrates the number of homes you would need to meet your goal. Suppose you require 10k per month net passive income and you can get $1,000 per month net rent.

How many houses do you need? Simple math tells us what we need to know.

> $10,000 (net monthly income goal)/$1,000(per month house net rent) = 10 paid-off houses total (needed for goal to be met).

Conclusion

The singular goal of financial freedom can be met through acquiring and paying off investment properties. If your goal is to develop and grow a full-time business surrounding this idea, you can read about that in my next book. The building of a turnkey real estate brokerage with the goal of acquiring paid-off rental real estate is a complex endeavor, however, and far beyond the scope of this book.

Simple financial independence can also be found, though, in the noble accomplishment of paying off your primary residence and, afterward, continuing to have an income stream from someone else, other than you, through an accessory unit, for example.

I have been on both sides of the money equation in my lifetime, the broke side and the non-broke side, and while money helps in many ways, in and of itself it cannot and never will be able to provide you with a sense of peace. Just like the very first example I gave in this book, **having a million dollars in equity (making you a "millionaire") while having nine million dollars in debt obligations is NOT a financial peace proposition.**

Having no bills and a paid-off home can give you far more peace than millions of dollars in cash and an equal or greater number of debt obligations. Remember that.

---

417   Remember, DO NOT "fall in love" with houses.

It occurred to me the other day, as I was taking my neighbor's trash to the road (they were on vacation), that **buying and paying off a primary residence really is an exceptional value, especially if your plan is to buy your house and LIVE in it** versus many people who keep trying to upgrade to larger houses they may or may not be able to afford due to low interest rates in an effort to put on a veneer of financial success. I realized, as I was taking my neighbor's trash to the curb, that buying and paying off a primary residence is a fantastic deal, especially if you do it the following way:

1. Buy a house in a good, safe area, big enough for you, your family, and your dreams.[418]

2. Make sure you have an income unit to pay off your mortgage.

3. Use an aggressive amortization to pay off your home quickly and (ideally) you bought your home tremendously under value.

4. Live in your house for ten or fifteen years, and bankroll your paid-off mortgage payments when you retire your mortgage. Let your kids and animals grow up and live in the house, and let the wear and tear accrue.

5. When you finally decide to upgrade, use a reasonable contractor to repaint, carpet, re-tile, and do what is necessary to get the home into prime, salable condition. Use a realtor to help you with this before you list it if you need help.[419]

6. Sell the house at market value, and bankroll a HUGE sum of money, far more than you paid, while you essentially lived free the whole time, and someone else paid off your house for you.

7. Now THAT's what I call a great housing investment!

Sadly, the reality is, **most people who never read this book will always use thirty-year mortgages,** refinance every few years, and move every five years,[420] while the dream of owning a paid-off house will always be just such—a dream that disappears in the waking hours of morning, right before the alarm clock goes off and the "homeowner" is forced to go back to work and make the next, seemingly never-ending mortgage payment.

---

418 Whatever they may be.
419 I certainly would.
420 Again, statistical average in US at the time of this writing.

Closing Story

The other day, a guy I work with in Memphis (he is from Honduras but has been in Memphis for almost thirty years) came to my office and asked if he could speak with me privately. Basically, he told me he had a house in Memphis rented for $650 and he wanted to sell it. I asked him why he wanted to sell, and he stated that he had owned it for a long time, and it wasn't really going anywhere.

I asked him how much he owed on the house, and he said 49k was his payoff, and he had twenty-eight years left in the mortgage. The house is worth 50k in today's market at the time of this writing.

Then I asked him how long he had owned it, and he said 1995 (that would be twenty-two years as of this writing in 2017).

Then I asked him how much he paid for it, and he told me he paid 37k in 1995 for the house and rented it immediately.

Astute readers of this book would instinctively know that there is only ONE way a homeowner can buy a house twenty-two years ago and owe 12k more on it than he paid (twenty-two years ago). This is by using a cash out, thirty-year refinance.

Disaster!

Can you see how disastrously my friend managed his rental house? Consider it made $650 a month for all twenty-two years, and he paid 37k in 1995. How long would it take for him to pay it off if he managed it himself and applied $550 of the $650 monthly payment to principal and interest, escrowing $100 for taxes and insurance monthly?

STR Mortgage Affordability Calculator

Inputs	Desired Monthy Payment	Desired Interest Rate
	$550.00	45.00%
Purchasing Power		
	5-Year Payment	$29,144.89
	7-Year Payment	$38,913.51
	10-Year Payment	$51,854.74

As you can see, if my friend had simply placed his 37k home on a seven-year payment, he could have had his home paid off by 2002. **This would have given him FIFTEEN ADDITIONAL YEARS of unencumbered cash flow, and assuming he "nets" $550 per month, he would have made ($550 × 180 payments) $99,000 over the past fifteen years of his life, passively through monthly income, if he paid the loan off in a seven-year time from the date of his purchase.**

Contrast that with his refinance two years ago. He probably "pulled out" $7,000 after "rolling in" about $5,000 in closing costs (a total of 12k), which reset his thirty-year mortgage at 49k, and other than his $7,000 cash "pullout" in the last twenty-four years, he has had a nominal cash flow, and, after paying for twenty-two years, has another twenty-eight to go. By the way, that's a FIFTY-YEAR PAYOFF ON A 37K HOME.[421]

Can you see it now? **Are you able to see it now? The thirty-year mortgage game is a death trap designed to enslave you and hundreds of millions of others into keeping the banks and fractional reserve banking system wealthy and in business, all at YOUR expense.**

Have your eyes opened yet?

I told my friend I couldn't help him, as I can't sell a house for him where he is so highly leveraged. I recommended an agent in my office to help him, but he would have to pay a commission; however, I told him the agent in my office WOULD get it sold quickly. At that point, my friend said, "But then, I would have to pay a commission, right? I guess I will just sell it myself."[422]

He has a hard sell on his hands. In all likelihood, he will have to hold on to it for TWENTY-EIGHT MORE years or sell it at a loss.

That's how devastating thirty-year loans and mortgage refinances can be.

A death sentence.

A commitment to NEVER paying off your house before you die.

Remember that before you go to the closing table.

The R. Thompson Way of Doing Things

Recently, I had to take a tenant to eviction court. She was three months behind on her rent. Normally, we don't let tenants get behind even a month, but I own two houses across from one another on a small four-house street, and the tenant in the house across the street (who has been with me over three years) had recommended her best friend when a vacancy arose, so in good faith, we took her on.

---

421 UGLY.
422 This is another great example of fear turning to greed at breakeven.

Fast-forward, her friend (named R. Thompson) started paying on the last day of the month (a common tactic for professional renters), and while she made multiple promises to pay (and we gave her the benefit of the doubt), finally I gave in and filed for eviction on her.

The day of her court appearance, she failed to show, and I proceeded to get the monetary judgment (which goes on her credit report) as well as the possession judgment on her residence. Once this happens in the State of Tennessee, a tenant has ten days before the sheriff shows up and throws all their personal belongings, including furniture, clothing, and electronics, on the street. Basically, they empty the house at gunpoint. When that happens, passers-by go into a frenzy and start grabbing flat-screen TVs and the tenant's personal effects from the curb. *It's an ugly side of humanity, to be honest, and we hate seeing it.*

Our solution is to call the tenant the day of the court appearance (assuming they have not showed) and advise them that the sheriff is coming. We offer a clean slate with them and some moving cash to help them on their way.

In the case of R. Thompson, however, her solution was to get nasty on the phone when we told her the sheriff was coming and begin arguing about what day of the week the tenth day was. I told her the sheriff was coming and that she needed to get her things out before she even got close to the deadline.

She ignored me…to her peril.

At the end of the day, dejected and saddened, I came home and asked my wife, *"How can someone so close to the most devastating, catastrophic housing event you can be in just bury their head in the sand and argue about what date it is going to happen on?"* I guess that is the way it goes for some people; they have never had good role models, so they don't learn good decision-making skills. **Example: Should you do the right thing and pay your rent as agreed, or not pay and blame your landlord?**

I place this example in here not to be critical of my former tenant but as a call to action to all readers who see their creditors as the enemy. **No one who starts with nothing can become financially free without risk or borrowing money and taking on financial obligation, period.**[423] Part of that borrowing is an obligation to

---

423 Assuming you have no cash (*as most people start out with*)**,** you cannot go to college without taking on student loans; you cannot buy a house without taking a loan; you cannot purchase a vehicle without taking a loan. You get the idea.

repay your creditors, even if the terms become unfavorable. Recently I had a hard money lender DOUBLE my monthly interest rate because the note I had with him expired after six months. ***The 12% rate for six months was hard to handle, but the 24% rate was unbearable!***[424] Yet I had given my word I would repay him, so what did I do? I repaid him in full with a degree of difficulty and inconvenience and told him I was closing business ties with him, as his greed had become untenable for my small company. I didn't shirk my responsibility with him nor did I vilify him. I just recognized that our multiyear-long business relationship[425] had become unsuitable for me and closed it out on good terms.

And that is what life is all about.

---

424 I promise you...imagine if your mortgage payment suddenly doubled until your lender was "paid in full." Difficult, yes?
425 Where I had borrowed and paid back over one million dollars.

13

Living Small to Live BIG

Using Short-Term Retirement Concepts
in Your Daily Life and Other Musings

The Short-Term Retirement Program, conceptually, really isn't about buying houses or investing in real estate. It is more of a mind-set of frugality and applying basic finance principles like cash versus credit, interest rate versus time, and so forth in an effort to allow one to operate in a free market governed by fractional reserve banking and excessive taxation through government overreach, and still, at the end of the day, be able to carve out an existence that bears fruit for yourself and coming generations of your family.

To that end, we have gone over some basic principles in this book that hopefully you have internalized. **For example, NEVER pay retail.** Always price match and shop for the best deal. These basic ideas and precepts go without saying.

Beyond this, recognize that there is most certainly a war for your mind, and the never-ending nature of "interruption advertising" coupled with modern social media ad integration has us constantly being given messages, many of which are not necessarily in our best interest.

First, let's do an experiment.

The next time you go grocery shopping (for your weekly haul, not just a few things), cash your weekly paycheck and take $200–$300 cash with you. Try to do the following things over the span of a weekend, and the best day to start is on a Friday after work. Instead of putting everything on a credit or debit card, think about your weekend, estimate how much money you will need, cash your paycheck, deposit what you need, and put enough cash (up to $300) in your wallet or purse to do the following things over the course of a weekend:

1. Get takeout Friday night or go out to dinner.

2. Get Starbucks (or your equivalent) for church on Sunday.[426]

3. Go grocery shopping.

4. Fill your and your spouse's gas tank to full.

5. Get a treat (fast food, ice cream, whatever).

6. Go to a movie or rent one.

7. Take your kids (if you have them) to the toy store and buy a gift for an upcoming birthday party.[427]

8. Tithe cash at church.[428]

9. Finish a small project that requires you to run to a hardware store or equivalent.

Now what I have outlined is a typical family's weekend. Yours may be different, but lots of families go to church, go grocery shopping, get gas, etc.

The thing I want you to notice is how lean you start to feel when that stack of cash you estimated you would need for the weekend gets wound down to, well, little or nothing. And in doing this exercise, what you are learning is, essentially, how to become reacquainted with the value of a dollar.

Once you do this, you really will start to be hesitant to make unnecessary large purchases, and that is GOOD. In my personal case, I HATE credit cards. Hate them. I carried a large balance for many years on credit cards, and when I finally paid them off, it was one of the best experiences of my life (sad, I know).

But the freedom and liberty that I was empowered with was unparalleled.

Naturally, this led to me having to allocate cash on debit cards and REALLY try to estimate weekly budgets, which change, of course, with doctor's appointments, insurance copays, and other random events that occur when you have a family. Sometimes we came up short and had to figure out a solution. But the most important thing that happened to us is this: **WE STOPPED BUYING THINGS WHEN WE DIDN'T HAVE THE MONEY FOR THEM AND WERE FORCED TO WAIT FOR THEM UNTIL WE HAD THE CASH RESOURCES NECESSARY TO MOVE FORWARD WITH A PURCHASE.** When we wanted something that was not in our budget, we had to plan for it to allocate money conscientiously to it.

---

426 Or whatever, on a Saturday afternoon, etc.
427 Assuming you have one upcoming, we are at a stage where we do lots of these.
428 Assuming you go.

That is a principle of **The Short-Term Retirement Program**.

You have to be able to feel the pain of spending money because checks, credit cards, lines of credit, and mortgages have allowed us to detach from what money really feels like and what having money REALLY feels like. Maybe that is by design—to encourage overspending. But as I have discussed before, one of the greatest issues that people who have never experienced financial freedom run into is how to act when they have a lump sum of cash in their hand,[429] and most of them have it spent within hours, IF IT WASN'T SPENT IN ANTICIPATION OF THE CHECK ARRIVING.

This type of impulsive, poorly planned spending will end a person exactly back where they were before and sometimes (even worse)—*in even MORE debt.*

Buying an RV as an Illustration of an STR Mind-set

My wife and I like to do BBQ contests. The contests themselves are great fun, but lots of pressure, especially if you are exacting chefs, like my wife and I tend to be. We like to win.

It isn't easy.

The logistics of traveling to a BBQ contest, on the other hand, is a very precise study and meditation in the art of packing as lightly as possible while bringing everything you can (and need) to cook outside, as a professional, for two to three days, while being judged by professionals and when you are competing AGAINST world-class pros.

When we started to get serious about BBQ contests, I began to look at RV solutions that could allow the family to travel safely and conveniently to out-of-state locations. One of the primary factors was that I did not want to sell my paid-off Ford F150, so we had to use the towing capacity of my vehicle as a benchmark for what we could get. Then we had to find an appropriate model which could haul all our gear, known as a "toy hauler." After that was discerned, we needed specific amenities that would make us independent at these contests if power and water were not provided. The model we were looking for had to have a bathroom and tub, plus bunks for the kids. A generator was also needed and unavailable on many models. The list went on.

I started this search almost FOUR MONTHS before I finally decided on a vehicle. I checked with my Ford dealer TWICE to confirm my towing capacity, recommendations, and specifications. I had to educate myself on trailer hitches that mitigate the "sway" of the vehicle you are towing. I was operating in a very exact budget and did NOT want to overpay. On top of that, I had to find a dealer who actually had something that had ALL of the features that I wanted in a wholesale package direct from the factory.

---

429 I'm talking, like, IRS tax refund size or greater here.

My point here is not to expound upon the art of RV buying (although I feel educated enough at this point on the subject where I could write a book!) but rather **to illustrate the comprehensive, methodical nature of analysis that is needed and required to go into major purchases, especially if you are serious about financial freedom.**

I ended up buying an RV from a dealer in Texas, and while I could have paid cash, I chose to finance. This preserved my working capital and allowed the lender to assume the risk[430] while I paid the vehicle off. But the interesting thing I found out is that RVs are financed on fifteen-year terms (180 months)! Meaning, if you buy a car for 30k, they will give you (generally) a five-year loan; but if you buy an RV for 30k, they will ask you to take a fifteen-year loan! This all comes back to what the banks think you can "afford," but **the reality is taking fifteen years to pay off an RV loan of 30k is craziness**, the same way you would laugh if your auto dealer offered you a fifteen-year term on a 30k auto loan!

As you have hopefully learned by now, beware of the terms any lender is "offering" you. Only take loan terms that fit YOUR financial and freedom goals. All loan terms are negotiable; otherwise, walk away from the lending table and seek out another lender.

I took a fifteen-year loan, but as always, I set up a payment plan that was affordable in my head prior to the purchase. In this case, I was going to pay off the RV in thirty payments (versus 180) by paying $1,000 per month on the RV. **Keep in mind, I was able to do this from having the discretionary cash flow from paid-off homes to make this type of plan**. If you are starting out and you are taking home $2,000 per month (for example), sending half of your take-home pay to an RV payment would be irresponsible. As always, do not buy items that you do not need, and if you are starting out in the world of financial "awareness" by reading this book, always **focus on eliminating unnecessary payments FIRST,** and then focus your efforts on eliminating your housing payment using one of the many strategies I have outlined in this book.

These Days

These days, especially now that I have young kids, I have become very sensitive and wary to how "on the radar" the American people have become and the consequences that accompany that "on the radar" information bombardment, both digitally and civically, to unsavory economic ends. For example, owning property in the City of Memphis makes you a prime target for the city's nonstop and ever-changing "social" programs, which are directed at homeowners in the name of beautification but really are just designed

---

430 If a tragedy happened, for example, and insurance didn't cover a claim (unlikely), the lender would take the loss versus me.

to generate revenue due to the city's insolvency. For example, if you own a house in Memphis and the city deems the grass to be "too long," they will cut it "for you" (without your knowledge, approval, or consent), and send you a $63 bill. Now, on the surface, that doesn't seem too harsh,[431] but these bills can apply to a variety of "imperfections" with houses, which can result in a myriad of fines. Worse, any citizen can call and complain about any other citizen's house, prompting a visit from local code enforcement, which can result in an additional variety of fines and other citations that could end you up in the city's version of housing court, called Environmental Court.

Big Brother, it would seem, is ALWAYS watching you.

The thing to note here is that the City of Memphis (and I am sure there are many other cities nationwide that do this) understands that homeowners being forced to pay involuntary bills is a good source of revenue for the city. Now, in Memphis, half of the population owns homes and half rents. But the city does not focus on innovative programs like a consumption tax, which would apply to 100% of the citizens who shop at stores to buy food, for example.[432] Instead, they just add programs designed to harass homeowners for an easy payday. This type of shortsightedness, I believe, is unsustainable because many homeowners are getting tired of the harassment, and what happens then? They are moving ten minutes down the road—to Mississippi! There, their property tax rate is a fraction of what they pay in Memphis, with far less intrusion from financially starved authorities. Losing citizens is bad for any city, which results in higher taxes, which results in more citizens leaving...you get the idea.

Interestingly, the City of Memphis has two taxing authorities, which, when combined, levy the highest property taxes in the State of Tennessee. However, if you travel to various cities in the great state of Tennessee, you will find that Memphis, even among all of the other larger ones (Nashville, Knoxville, Chattanooga, etc.) carries the highest rates of crime, violent crime...the list is endless. **This, of course, is a prime example that reinforces the notion that you cannot overtax those who choose to work or elect to own houses and then try to redistribute those funds through entitlement benefits and ineffective social programs and hope to solve overwhelming social problems.** Redistributing wealth, regardless of intention, simply doesn't work as a long-term solution for economic insolvency, neither for the city NOR the citizen.

It only serves to bankrupt communities.

---

431 Although there is a more in-depth debate to be had here about whether any city's employees belong on your property without your consent.

432 And if implemented and properly managed would probably solve the city's insolvency issues.

And beyond the scope of this book lies the eternal question *"What happens when the entitlement monies run out?"* This doesn't just apply to entitlement programs, it applies to pensions also.[433]

Consider this article from ZeroHedge.com.[434]

Kentucky Public Employee Retirements Surge as Fears of Pension Collapse Mount

Sep 6, 2017

Slowly but surely it is becoming increasingly clear to public workers in states with massively underfunded pensions that they've been lied to for the past several decades as their states can't possibly afford to pay for the retirement they've all been promised. As a local radio station in Bowling Green points out today, fears over potential pension changes in Kentucky have resulted in a surge of early retirements as workers move to lock in payouts before any potential cuts go into effect.

An independent consultant recommended sweeping changes Monday to the pension systems that cover most of Kentucky's public workers, creating the possibility that lawmakers will **cut payments to existing retirees and force most current and future hires into 401(k)-style retirement plans.**

PFM also recommended **increasing the retirement age to 65 for most workers.**

For those already retired, the consultant recommended **taking away all cost of living benefits that state and local government retirees received between 1996 and 2012, a move that could significantly reduce the monthly checks that many retirees receive.** For example, **a government worker who retired in 2001 or before could see their benefit rolled back by 25% or more, PFM calculated.**

The consultant also recommended **eliminating the use of unused sick days and compensatory leave to increase pension benefits.**

Even if all of that is accomplished, State Budget Director John Chilton said Kentucky would still need to find an extra $1 billion a year just to keep its frozen pension systems afloat. Moreover, absent tax hikes the state will ultimately be forced to cut

---

433 And Medicare and Social Security and...any long-term payout program you have been promised, which has been financially managed by others!

434 Taken from http://www.zerohedge.com/news/2017-09-05/kentucky-public-employee-retirements-surge-fears-pension-collapse-mount. Edited by author.

funding for K-12 schools by $510 million and slash spending at most other agencies by nearly 17% to make up the difference.

"The PFM had some pretty drastic recommendations that **we think are not what's in the best interest of public school employees** and public school students," Winkler said.

So, in conclusion (and I hate to be the bearer of bad news here), your pension or future pension, assuming you have one, is probably in jeopardy, whether you are in Kentucky or not. There will be no pensions in the future, unless you are somehow able to privately negotiate one, as money managers of these pension funds[435] have not only shown that they are incapable of providing the returns they promised when these funds were considering the managers in the first place! Also, as the government discusses "publicizing" your IRA, i.e., forcing you to buy government securities with your IRA in exchange for worthless IOUs, **you may begin to realize that you, and your family, are the very last people to be considered when it comes to the governments so-called "solvency," which was sold a long time ago to private corporations and foreign entities**.

The government of the United States, both at the executive level and the so-called deep-state level, will do ANYTHING to keep the current economic system in place, including seizing your IRA, bank accounts, and pension monies to ensure solvency and stave off civil unrest for whatever period of time they can buy.

That's pretty bleak, I know, and harder to swallow even if you are a patriot who grew up loving the United States and the principles of freedom it stands for.

There is a silver lining to this, however: **You can take solace in the fact that the derailment of the US economy was planned long before you were born, and the reality is, there is *nothing* you or I can do to stop it.**

Which brings me to the most important part of this chapter—living small to live BIG.

Living Small to Live BIG

Tim Ferris says it best in his best-selling book *The 4-Hour Workweek.* Basically, he says you don't need to be a millionaire to LIVE like one. You just need to have the income necessary to pursue your dreams and NOT be tied down by a dead-end job, which pays you meager wages while sucking down your time and the life from your body indefinitely.

---

435 **Keep in mind, these are some of the largest funds in the world**—teaching associations, police and firefighter associations, and so forth. If these financial planners cannot come up with simple single-digit returns for such large amounts of capital, are they truly skilled at managing money?

And he is TOTALLY right.

The key to living The Short-Term Retirement way is to understand that we voluntarily signed up for (or were thrust into) the stress and hassle of all of these debt obligations, some of which are necessary (like housing), and some of which are unnecessary (insert bill you hate and thing you wish you hadn't bought *here*). I remember, for me, it was my senior year of high school. I would work at a tuxedo shop and get paid on Friday, put my check in the bank, and it stayed there until I spent it on something.

Pretty cool!

Then my first few years of college at Syracuse flew by, and suddenly I had rent I had to pay, a car payment, tuition, gas, books, food, a credit card payment, fees, and I remember working full time, going to school full time, and realizing that I was in way over my head with my next week's paycheck spent LAST WEEK!

Then I finished college and my student loan repayment started, at which point I realized the truth: I was in waaaaaaay over my head, having done everything "they" told me I should do.

Does this sound familiar?

How could something so well-intentioned go so wrong?

Somewhere along the line, in each of our lives, we became trapped in a cycle of debt obligations, which became inescapable. You leave your parents' house and need somewhere to live, and so you pay rent. Rent is expensive, so you get a job. You need a car for a job, but you don't have the money, so you take a car note. You need insurance on the car and gas for the car. You have to maintain the car, or the engine will seize. Soon, your paycheck at your first job doesn't cover it; you get second job, but such a large amount of tax and FICA are withheld that you don't have *that* much more take-home pay. Even with the second job, you barely get by. However, at the end, you live paycheck to paycheck, and as the years go by, at some point, you take out a credit card—which is now maxed—and now you are stuck paying the minimum because that is all you can afford.

No paltry raise at your company will change this.

Suddenly you realize that you are just like your parents and friends—struggling. And, even worse, we are bombarded by the idea that our true happiness lies in having shiny new things, like cars and big houses. **We are indoctrinated into the idea that we have to keep up with the Joneses, when no one thought of disclosing to us that the Joneses are functionally bankrupt and we really don't want to be like them at all.**

The key to "Short-Term Retirement"-type living is understanding that we need to think differently about paying bills and taking on debt. Sometimes, we may have to accept the reality that we have to tackle a debt for years in order to "slay" it or retire it permanently.

Housing payments are a great example.

Quick Quiz:

Regarding Making a Housing Payment

Which of these investment techniques best fits the ideal strategy for financial independence, assuming you want to be debt free? Choose one:

1. **Rent a house that you love that takes about 40% of your take-home pay. Sign a five-year lease so your rent doesn't go up for five years.**

2. **Rent a different house each year and keep moving if you can't make your rent payment.**

3. **Buy a foreclosed house and rent bedrooms to roommates, putting your home on a seven-year mortgage so you know in seven years you won't have to hassle with a housing payment anymore.**

The answer, if you haven't read this book, is number three—neither of the other two techniques do anything except place you in a paycheck-to-paycheck cycle, **which is almost impossible to break**.

Obviously, the key is to think about what debt you are willing to take on and for how long, and then once you decide, use the factors outlined in this book to take on a housing payment as inexpensively as possible while having other people (tenants/roommates) make your payments for you whenever possible until you have your house paid off in the shortest period of time you can tolerate.

That doesn't mean it will be easy. You might have to take roommates on for years (like I did). Some readers are appalled at the idea of having roommates. **But if having roommates means you will be financially free in a few years, why wouldn't you have them?** Sometimes the power of financial freedom means that you have to humble yourself to the situation you are in and realize that you may not be able to do it without help, even if that help is as simple as a roommate paying you rent and utilities each month, easing the financial burden on *both* of you. And who knows? You might make a new friend out of it. Having a roommate and applying Short-Term Retirement strategies to getting your financial situation in order **is not the end of the world; it is the beginning of your**

idealized future and realizing your hopes and dreams. Remember, no one is realizing their dreams or purpose when they are starving and homeless. You need financial security to pursue what you were sent here do to, whatever that is. People can try to sell you lines that they "don't care about money," but the fabric of reality is this: **You control money or the lack of it controls you, and it's just that simple in our current financial system**.

The Importance of Recognizing Control Loci: Knowing When You Have Control and When You Don't

At the end of the day, some things are in our control, and there are many more things that are outside our control. We need to accept this as fact lest we spend a great deal of time worrying about things that may never affect us and will take place regardless of the consequences of our actions.

US foreign policy is an awesome example of this. One might mull over a question like *"**Why did we invade Iraq if Saddam Hussein had nothing to do with 9/11? That seems strange**."* You ask around but can't find an answer that satisfies you. Then you see on the television that the president is thinking of sending more troops back to Afghanistan, where it THEN occurs to you that we have had troops in Afghanistan since 2001, and nothing notable seems to be happening except lots of our soldiers are getting hurt, and other than in the name of democracy, most Americans aren't quite sure why we are even there. Then you worry about Afghanistan and more troops being sent there, and you really start getting worked up.

The reality is, the US is sending troops where it wants to send troops, and you can't really do anything about it. There is no point of getting worked up.

It's happening whether you like it or not, as ugly as that sounds.

Learning to relinquish control or an illusion of control is part of disengaging from the matrix that certain people WANT you engaged in. You control your life and have some impact on the life of your other family members, friends, and colleagues. Beyond that, if you can get your life in order and become financially stable, you are making a great contribution to society in a variety of ways because you are paying your taxes,[436] and once you get out of "survival mode," you might start to want to give back in some way—maybe help the homeless guy down the street or do some community service, volunteering, or whatever appeals to you—helping your

---

436 **Again, I have very mixed feelings on income taxation, but for the sake of this discussion, let's say you being financially free and happy, paying your "fair share" of taxes is better than you being unhappy, insolvent, and needing an entitlement that adds a societal burden, which, at some point, cannot be met**. One hundred percent of the population of the US cannot be on entitlements. Any economist is free to debate me and prove otherwise.

community and giving your time, whereas previously, you had never even thought about doing that because you were so busy stressing about money and working to pay interest on bills (like minimum credit card payments) while years of your life passed by. Service to others is tremendously rewarding, positive, and helpful. Getting to a point where you are able to give back freely of your time or other resources is wonderful and rewarding.

And it is important.

But it is also important to realize that part of getting to financial freedom involves a certain sense of peace, and coming to this very basic understanding that **there are some things in life you can control, and many things in your life you simply cannot control**. And to be ultrarealistic, it has been this way since the inception of humanity.

The sooner you have a realization of what *is* in your control and what *is beyond* your control, you will become much better at managing your time AND your emotions. And these types of self-management are critical if you want to become successful.

After buying and selling thousands of homes and managing hundreds of properties in my lifetime, I have come up with a simple, five-step blueprint for general happiness in the current incarnation of our time period of living. **Keep in mind this is a simple plan for financially free living and focusing on what makes you happy, with the goal of eliminating monetary stress permanently.**[437] Zen Buddhist monks, gurus on mountains, and other "masters" with far more knowledge and wisdom may disagree with me, and I will defer to them, certainly because I do not claim to know all. I think this is just a basic blueprint for Americans who would like to spend more time doing what they love with their families and less time going to endless, meaningless jobs that they hate while keeping them from the ones they love, all the while being bombarded with interruption-style ads extoling the virtues of the material world and political conflicts, which may or may not be real.

It also assumes most people do NOT want to be solicited by phone for phishing scams, junk mail, vehicle warranties, credit card offers, etc.

It is as follows:

---

437 For a robust primer on mini-vacations, finding your "muse," and realizing your dreams, read *The 4-Hour Workweek* by Tim Ferriss.

Feol's Five (or Six) Step Plan for Happiness and Prosperity—Very Basic Blueprint

1. **Be anonymous, OR as anonymous as you can be.** Use a phone with an unlisted number and use caller ID mask for your phone when making outgoing calls. Develop a stance where solicitation on your phone or at your home is unacceptable.[438] Avoid engaging with city officials regarding your properties whenever possible.[439] Think of this as "risk avoidance."

2. **Have no bills or debt OR as few monthly bills as you can have.** Use a PO box to receive mail so no one is able to molest you at home with junk mail or "mailers."

3. **Have a paid-off primary residence, and keep your taxes paid.** Always contest your property tax increases.

4. **Have monthly passive income from paid-off sources, which allows you to spend your time doing what you want, WHEN you want.** Pay cash for everything and get to a point where you take on NO debt. *If you love your work and want to, then work.* If you HAVE to work, get to the point where you DON'T have to. Then do what you love.

5. **Answer to no one except your family and God.** God and family come first.

6. (*Bonus Points/Optional*) **If you can, try to unplug as much as you can from mass-media-based TV and social media.** Many of these media outlets have specific agendas to influence your thought processes and mind, and at the time of this writing, some are currently engaged (based on my observation) in trying to foment extreme hate-based agendas. If you walk around thinking everyone hates you and is out to get you, well, it's hard to be happy, right? Read some good books instead; watch some instructional videos. Work on improving at something daily.

If you get to this point and have realized these five or six steps in your daily life, then you have won.

---

438 Keep in mind, if you are using your phone for business, then maybe having two phones is the answer. You want your business phone to ring, right?

439 **Once the City of Memphis figured out we were transacting a lot of business in Memphis and found out my PO boxes, they inundated me with TONS of certified letters, random weed bills (for homes I didn't even own), tax bills (for homes I didn't even own), code enforcement notices, etc.** None of this would show up if they hadn't found my PO box number and would have been a non-issue. City authorities seek out people they can find and spend little to no time on those they can't.

Well, you have won the battle that so many people will never win, which is the battle for financial freedom. You see, so many people are born into this financial system, which reinforces the idea of financial scarcity and despair, and the idea of living paycheck to paycheck becomes such an entrenched reality for so many of us that it is hard to shake off. We saw our grandparents struggle. We saw our parents work and struggle and never pay off their house. We struggle. We bear children and do everything we can to prevent them from struggling, but staggering inflation and monetary policies fomented by all-powerful, ungovernable organizations like the Federal Reserve, along with specifically engineered social issues, keep us focused on everything EXCEPT what is important (God, ourselves, and our families) and prevents us from asking the most basic questions, such as "**If The United States is the greatest and wealthiest country on Earth, why are so many people struggling so badly? Why are so many people hungry and homeless? Why did I go to college and I am barely getting by? Why do we send off billions of tax dollars in foreign aid when our own civic infrastructure and schools are crumbling?**"

And beyond a lack of simple financial aptitude, which could certainly help a person begin to achieve (at the very least) some financial stability, we have ideas reinforced to us that have no basis in reality—i.e., "*If you want to be wealthy, you have to be a movie star or a professional athlete, etc. These are the people I see on TV all the time. They have everything, I'm swimming in debt, etc. The odds must be against me.*"

Financial success and stability is something that is available to everyone, but so few will achieve it because breaking out of the financial matrix, which we have been conditioned to think inside of, is, well, very, very hard. It requires work, not just taking the time to read books like this one, but to then go out and try to find properties and fail—and try again and fail—and to keep trying until you get it right…it's a daunting task, to say the least. Failing is something we are taught should be avoided, and the additional reality is that if you are working a forty-hour-a-week job now as you read this, the thought of working weekends and evenings to try to get your financial "ship" righted when you are already exhausted is, well…exhausting.

To keep myself motivated at times I have told myself that I am the first of my family lineage to actually begin thinking about what I am going to leave, not only to my children, but to their children as well. **And the only way I could have done this was to go through the hardships and excruciating financial agony that my parents and their forebears were unwilling to go through.** You have to be serious about getting on the path and then actively seek the path. The path, by the way, doesn't go in a straight line. It goes in a myriad of directions, with all kinds of twists and curves. So be prepared.

When I was starting to wake up to the long journey that is the path to financial freedom about twenty years ago, my mentor Al Plumb told me something that has been emblazoned in my mind since I first heard it, and I will now share it with you. I was in a particularly bad place at that time, really just sad and down, and Al had seen how hard I was working as a teacher and, in my off hours, in a network marketing group he had introduced me to, but I wasn't really getting anywhere. One night on the phone, Al said this statement, which I will never forget, and I hope it inspires you also:

Robert, the path to financial success...well, I will be honest with you...it really runs straight through the garbage dump [of life]. But when you get there...and someday, Robert, you WILL get there...it will wash away so clean, you won't even remember how bad the struggle was. All you will think about is how clean it feels to have worked so hard to finally arrive in a place where you never have to go back to what you were before or how you struggled. It's out there waiting for you, but you have to get back up on your feet and go search for it. Then once you get there, go out and teach others how to get there, like I am showing you.

—Al Plumb, Alpco Recycling, 2001

I truly believe that Al Plumb's words of inspiration for me also ring true for you as the reader. **There is a future for you of financial freedom, and little to no worry, but you have to seek the path that takes you there**. Your path will not necessarily be an easy one nor a simple one. And it will be different from everyone else's journey because you are unique and have your own set of resources and issues to contend with, as do all others. But the path to financial success is there for you, and it is up to you to begin the journey that ultimately ends in your success.

If money is truly a mental construct, **then the idea of you being financially free starts with you having a vision for that financial freedom and meditating on it each and every day**, thinking about it, praying on it, realizing that YOU are the traveler that has to take the journey if you want to get there, and the journey will be long. **The one guarantee that I can give you is if you pursue it properly, with the right tools and the right motivation, given enough time and unwavering persistence, you WILL get there**.

Some Essential Short-Term Retirement Concepts: A Recap

1. **Pay off your house as soon as you can**. Don't use thirty-year loans. Use the STR mortgage affordability calculator to figure out an optimal cost basis for your home based on your needs and current situation. If you are borrowing, be VERY careful about loan terms and your threshold of tolerance for interest rate and repayment terms. Get yourself on a finite clock for having your house paid off. Remember, once you have your house paid off, you can always sell for cash and "trade up" if you are so inclined. Never forget, make your biggest payment your smallest one!

2. **Always try to have tenants' income or other people pay your bills**, and ultimately, pay off your debt.

3. **Be anonymous and keep a low profile. Follow all laws and always treat law enforcement with great respect**. Pay your taxes and stay current with the IRS and all legal authorities. Follow the rules, and don't expend energy into trying to fight city hall. It's hard to try to change or improve corrupt systems that so many people have an entrenched financial interest in. Remove yourself from interacting in these systems as much as possible to preserve peace of mind and avoid unnecessary expense.

4. **Pay cash for everything you can, and always negotiate costs when you can**. This means using actual capital you have to pay for things versus using credit.

5. **Don't make unnecessary purchases**. Question the necessity of large purchases and always try to seek discounts. When saddled with large or emergency purchases, always try to get multiple estimates and pricing from a variety of sources. Fixing things properly versus totally replacing them is a good rule of thumb, whenever possible (roof, plumbing, cars, etc.).

6. **Reject unnecessary bills**. Don't just pay a bill you receive; look at the bill for unnecessary charges and other items, which you would not pay. Ideally, eliminate such a bill permanently. *Some bills, like health insurance, car insurance, home insurance, and property taxes, you can only try to minimize and cannot eliminate*. Once you have eliminated your bills to the simplest and smallest amount you possibly can, you will feel a great sense of peace and financial stability.

7. **Go solar and stop being a member of the energy matrix**. Going solar removes you from the energy/fossil fuel matrix, which is driven by money and corruption,

and hurts the planet. Pay once and use the sun's energy for a lifetime with little or no cost to you. Have you ever been on vacation with your power totally off and you still get a $60 power bill for taxes and fees from your energy provider? That's money that just "feeds" the corruption; it has nothing to do with you getting energy. Eliminate that bill if you can, and in general, if you sense your money is being used to "feed" any corrupt system, be conscious of it and try to eliminate it.

8. **Be wary of taxing authorities.** The power to tax is one that is wielded with a heavy hand, and the nature of Short-Term Retirement living is to be very discerning with what you are taxed for when, where, and why. Pay attention to where your money goes. The mismanagement of civic infrastructure and use of illegal kickbacks runs wantonly through what is known as city hall, which drives up your costs, drains the ability of a city to maintain its infrastructure for the benefit of the taxpayers, and—as we all know—taxes don't really go down; they only go up. Be careful and monitor where your money goes and to whom. Try not to "feed the beast" whenever possible.

9. **Make decisions for yourself**. The media and other large for-profit entities have a vested interest in getting you to feel one way or another about certain situations, which may be real or may be of a more fictional nature. From swaying public opinion to selling you items that represent a specific political stance or vision, people in media are very interested in "helping" you feel one way or another. Start to realize this and be slower to make decisions, and form opinions for yourself. If this takes you time, even better. Don't be quick to judge or get polarized about something you see on TV, because the reality is...well, it's TV, and **the majority of programming on TV is fictional. They aren't always transparent about what is real and what is fiction**, so you need to figure it out yourself.

10. **Understand that being financially free is a right that you have and it is attainable**. Seeking financial freedom or achieving financial freedom does not make you a "member of the 1%" or some other such nonsense. Remember everyone's path is different. Yours may not lie in investment real estate, but having your primary residence paid off and becoming debt free will certainly help you on your way, wherever your path may take you, and strengthen you for the journey.

Meditation

Zen Koan—Empty Your Cup

Nan-in, a Japanese master during the Meiji era, received a university professor who came to inquire about Zen.

Nan-in served tea. He poured his visitor's cup full and then kept on pouring.

The professor watched the overflow until he no longer could restrain himself. "The teacup is full! No more will go in!"

"Like this cup," Nan-in said, "you are full of your own opinions and speculations.

How can I show you Zen—unless you first empty your cup?"

14

Things in Life Worth Loving

Using Your Two Greatest Resources: Time and Time Management

Giving School a Grain of Salt

At the end of the day, while we are taught to respect authority—our bosses, our teachers in high school and college, and so forth—the reality of the situation is this: If we could glimpse into the personal lives of most of these people we are taught to put on a pedestal, we would be shocked and lose great respect for them because they are frail and struggling financially, just like so many of us. They aren't perfect. They have personal issues too—addictions, drugs, alcohol. You name it.

In a nutshell, they are human too.

I remember in college at Syracuse at the end of my sophomore year, in the school of music education, you had to go for an interview to see if you were "eligible" to be admitted to the upper-class curriculum. I put on a suit, went for my interview, and answered their questions. Yet even though my grades were fine, I had far more experience working with kids than my other school peers did, and I was well recommended, they still decided to put me on "probation"—that is, conditionally accepted with the possibility of being removed because, in the interview, I dared to voice my ideas on education, which was beyond what they wanted to hear from the upcoming students. What they really just wanted you to say was *yes* to this (somewhat unspoken) question, ***Are you willing to do what we tell you to and keep your mouth shut?***

I just wasn't that guy. And the old, tenured professors (who hadn't had an inkling of what it was like working with actual kids in a classroom, having been at the university for several decades) didn't like it. They didn't like me being brazen enough to have ideas on how to teach people at age twenty. So I was punished for it.[440]

---

440 Don't worry about me, though; that probation was removed the next semester when they realized they had no grounds to keep me out of the program and I graduated just fine, going on to have a great, tenured, and award-winning teaching and coaching career.

But what I also didn't realize at that time was, if I could glance and look into their lives, their financial pictures were—in all likelihood—the same as so many struggling American families today. Yes, some professors do very well at college, salary-wise, but the music (or education) department is not generally known for being one of them. And recall, many people who make great salaries also struggle financially due to a lack of understanding financial principles, like we have discussed in this book. **Remember, it isn't about how much money you make, it is about how much you keep.**

The truth of the situation is, at almost any general labor or entry-level position you work in, just from a statistical standpoint, your colleagues and your bosses are also struggling financially and just trying to hang on. **You simply can't beat the math that points to this inevitability or deny these factors that create this causality.**

We are all in the same financial matrix, so to speak.

This became even more shocking and apparent to me when I got into the world of education as a teacher myself. I was young and fresh faced, ready to change the world, **but I was shocked to see that so many of my teaching colleagues were angry and hated—I mean HATED—their jobs.** They were just there to get a paycheck, and so many of them really didn't care about the kids. Many were mean and demeaning to the students. I watched school principals who could—get this—barely read and spell engage in what you could describe as anything but ethical behavior with both the kids and with their colleagues. Tons of teachers were forced to work second jobs. It was unlike anything I had been taught to expect in college, that's for sure.

At that point, I came to realize that my love of teaching and learning could not be satisfied within the framework of a municipal school system, and I also realized that the nature of school itself is changing from when I was a student, with many teachers these days **complaining that their teaching positions are less about "teaching" and more about "babysitting."** A lot of this stems from the chaos and disarray of so many students' home life today, whereas out of necessity (parents working multiple jobs) or circumstance (parents in absentia, single-parent homes, and so on), students' lack structure, which is then carried over into a chaotic learning environment, with teachers woefully unprepared and lacking the type of classroom management skills necessary even to calm the classroom, let alone begin to educate. As it sits, the overall general level of educational competency in the US is on the decline, with a shocking 19% of students who are graduating from high school being unable to read.[441]

---

441 http://www.statisticbrain.com/number-of-american-adults-who-cant-read/.

Now, maybe that's why you can count on one hand the number of teachers and coaches you encountered in your scholastic journey whom you felt really loved you and took an active interest in you. I'm talking about the teachers that *really* inspired you. For most readers, there simply weren't that many. **What is far more prevalent, however, is the memory of mean teachers, who were verbally or physically abusive.** These types of stories are much more common. And beyond this common thread is that when the scholastic journey ends and students get out into the "real world," the question becomes "Where do I go? What do I do? How do I get there? Why do I feel so unprepared?"

And, of course, the ultimate question "How exactly am I going to pay all my bills?"

Back to "No Job Can Make You Wealthy": Part 3

After I read *Rich Dad, Poor Dad* by Robert Kiyosaki, I was haunted by his idea that "*it's not your boss's job to make you wealthy.*" It sounded weird to me. I thought people sought out careers for financial reasons and personal growth? It kind of nullified all my ideas about working and doing my best every day. Kiyosaki made points that really bothered me and forced me to start thinking and opening my eyes. **He pointed out that, at most jobs, the paycheck for a job well done and a job poorly or mediocrely done was identical when a pay period concluded.** Things I was so proud of, like my first year of teaching's perfect attendance, suddenly morphed into me thinking that maybe my colleagues were using their benefits more wisely by using (and getting paid for) their sick days. And you would get a small raise each year for staying on and teaching the following year, but it had nothing to do with performance. It was just based on the number of years you put in. Good teachers, bad teachers, it really didn't matter; getting a pay increase was rewarding tenacity, not competency. It started to occur to me that maybe I couldn't stick around for thirty years waiting for retirement.

I realized Kiyosaki was right. It isn't your boss's job to make you wealthy. Becoming wealthy or financially independent falls squarely on YOUR shoulders.

It is something that inevitably has to be pursued in your "off time."

Waking Up on a Weekend

As I discussed previously in this book, when I attended a class on wholesaling homes with Scott Rister, I suddenly had my eyes opened to what my financial future might look like, and it was relieving to know that there might be an alternative future other than thirty years of public school service. Within a week, I had sold and closed my first wholesale home and made $3,700, which was over a MONTH of take-home pay, for just a few hours of work. **This experience started to make me think about time and the nature of time.** It forced me (again) to think about what Kiyosaki was saying, and then what Tim Ferriss spoke about in *The 4-Hour Workweek* that these standards of time used by modern-day institutions (like public schools) or corporations are all based on the Industrial Age, the idea of what was a "fair" amount of time traded for a "fair" day's wages **with the ultimate conclusion being that forty hours a week are NOT needed to accomplish most tasks assigned to a forty-hour worker within that week**. A worker works as inefficiently as possible to try to accomplish what he or she needs to based on arbitrary deadlines—and when the corporate culture reflects this, you have a lot of people spending most of their life doing makeshift tasks that end up producing nothing—and accomplishes very little, going nowhere.

Conversely, I came to the realization that **people who are highly efficient with their time tend to be MASSIVELY productive,** and economically, are generating more revenue than thousands of day workers combined.

Take Warren Buffet, for example.

Buffet has been well written about, but his methods of investing and acquisition of companies WORK. He has made himself and many of his fellow investors, very, very wealthy.

But the thing I am reminded of (humbled by) is that people like Buffet (and so many other stories of entrepreneurial success) still have the same twenty-four hours a day that each human on Earth is afforded. Ergo, we must conclude that Buffet is far more efficient with his time than the average worker, and therein lies this moment's priceless lesson:

Feol's Time Theorem

If we do not structure the use of our time for maximum efficiency (and eliminate wasteful, time-consuming tasks), we are doomed to be inefficient and struggle to find blocks of free time where we can be productive, with the goal of that productivity bearing fruit for us monetarily (or to some great end). The more accepting we are of our inefficient use of time (complacency), the more likely we are to remain static with our inefficient use of time and remain economically unproductive.

Put simply, if we don't consciously work to use our free time as efficiently as possible in the pursuit of financial independence, we are doomed to waste time spinning our wheels, locked in a financial struggle where we are FORCED to work inefficiently (i.e., a forty-hour work schedule).

Consider the following idea—that all time is NOT alike. We know that time can pass more quickly or slowly based on how pleasant the tasks are that we are engaging in within that time space. Your day flies by. Your day when the state auditors come to your office, well, not so much. ☹

The state of your body also disposes itself to being naturally productive or unproductive in time spaces, depending on its condition.

Here are some general outlines.

Body State Productive	Body State Unproductive
Refreshed	Tired
Well rested	Exhausted, sleepy
Well fed and nourished	Hungry, eating nutrient-deficient foods
Exercised	Sedentary
Hydrated	Thirsty, dry

Your mental or emotional state can ALSO impact your level of productivity and performance. Consider the following chart:

Mental State Productive	Mental State Unproductive
Relaxed	Stressed out
Confident financially	Worried about money or bills
Well fed and nourished (brain fats[452])	Hungry, eating nutrient-deficient foods
At peace	Emotionally upset, upheaval
Happy, enthusiastic	Dreading
Zen	Yin-yang out of balance

These factors are things that we tend not to think about, but they really help us get a feel for the type of mind-set you need to have if you are seeking to be productive with your time, especially with learning or performance-based tasks.[443] You simply cannot approach them effectively if you are tired, hungry, out of balance, or facing a million other inhibiting factors that we encounter in our day-to-day lives. **And ultimately, YOU have to be in control of setting yourself up properly to maximize your use of time.** Getting enough sleep, blocking out time for performance or learning tasks (not rote working, like

---

442 Mental work demands significant energy, nutrition, and calories. The brain requires good fat for optimal performance. Speak to a nutritionist on this if you have questions.

443 Or financial freedom-type work, with which we are concerned in this text.

at your job), and so forth, all come from you giving yourself the discipline and direction necessary to be ready to use your time as wisely as possible.[444]

What Now? Monitoring and Distributing Your Time Resources Effectively

I am a simple guy. For me, making progress in any venture I wish to pursue (martial arts, classical guitar, real estate, etc.) involves setting realistic and attainable action steps, and then implementing those steps on a daily, weekly, or monthly basis and holding myself accountable to those action steps via progress monitoring and realistic, objective feedback. **The pursuit of financial freedom is the same way and should be pursued using the same realistic ideas.** These action steps you set for yourself are similar to the overused term "goal setting."

However, be warned: setting unattainable goals in overwhelming circumstances may lead to ineffective or backward progress. This is especially true in financial crisis situations.

Here are a few examples of massive goals and trouble spots with unrealistic outcomes versus appropriate actions in crisis situations.

Crisis Example 1

Issue: My landlord is evicting me, and the trash-out crew is coming tomorrow, and my car is scheduled to be towed tomorrow as well. I need $10,000 to catch up. I have no money and resources and was fired from my job.

Unrealistic action step: It's 5:00 p.m. now, and the police are coming at 8:00 a.m. tomorrow to remove me from my home, so I still have a few hours. Maybe I should start calling my friends and asking for a 10k loan? I'll just let them know I am not sure when, or if, I can ever pay it back.

Realistic action step: Move back in with your parents or a friend. Focus on regrouping and see where you went wrong financially. Learn from the situation. Focus on finding a job that you can support yourself with, get back on your feet, and then use the principles introduced here in **The Short-Term Retirement Program** to ensure that you are never underwater again with your housing situation. Get your payments and monthly liabilities under control.

Crisis Example 2

Issue: My credit card is maxed out. I just tried to buy groceries with my credit card, and it was declined.

---

444 I learned this from playing poker. When online poker was legal, I used to play a lot of tournament poker and did fairly well. As I began studying with poker pros, they were ALL ABOUT body rest and mind-set. There was a huge list of "do not play poker if(s)..." And when I was tired (a *do not do*) or doing something else simultaneously (again a *no-no*), my game would really suffer. **The truth is, there is no such thing as effective multitasking.** Singularly focusing on a task is the best way to get it done.

Personal Finance Statement for Joe the Plumber, a Normal, Hard-Working American

Assets

	Cash in Bank		$100.00
	Job total take home net pay (monthly)		$4,000.00
Total Cash in Bank			**$100.00**
Real Estate Location	*Starting Balance*	*Current Balance*	*Payment*
123 Maple Street	$1,000,000.00	$99,000.00	$1,000.00

Liabilities

	Credit Cards		*Current Balance*
	Chase		$2,000.00
	Amex		$5,000.00
	Discover		$3,000.00
	Other Card		$0.00
	Other Card 2		$0.00
Total Credit Cards			**$10,000.00**

Notes Payable (excluding monthly)	*Amount Owning*	*Origianl Amount*	*Monthly*
Car #1	$35,000.00	$37,000.00	$700.00
Car #2	$40,000.00	$35,000.00	$800.00
Credit Cards	$10,000.00	$10,000.00	$100.00
Other Item 1	$0.00	$0.00	$0.00
Other Item 2	$0.00	$0.00	$0.00
Other Item 3	$0.00	$0.00	$0.00
Other Item 4	$0.00	$0.00	$0.00
Other Item 5	$0.00	$0.00	$0.00
Total Notes Payable	**$85,000.00**	**$82,000.00**	**$1,600.00**

Mortgage/Real Estate Loans	*Amount Owing*	*Original Amount*	*Monthly*
Bank of America	$99,000.00	$100,000.00	$1,000.00
Bank of America HELOC	$20,000.00	$20,000.00	$200.00
Bank 3	$0.00	$0.00	$0.00
Bank 4	$0.00	$0.00	$0.00
Total Real Estate Payable	**$119,000.00**	**$120,000.00**	**$1,200.00**

Total Aggregate Monthly Payments	Debt as a % of Income
$2,800.00	70.00%

Unrealistic action step: I will call the credit card company and ask for an increase in my limit.

Realistic action step: Call the credit card company and tell them you want to suspend the account. You will make payments on it until it is paid off, but you do not want purchase privileges on it anymore. Your credit cards being maxed out is a sign of financial distress. Cut up the card.

Alternatively, you can get with a credit card company and consider "settling" the debt.[445] I have not had experience with this, but many companies frequently advertise these services, and they may be worth investigating.

The important thing to realize here is that you used credit due to a lack of liquidity. Your issue is a lack of cash flow versus overwhelming debt obligations.

---

445 Bankruptcy could also wipe your unsecured debt. See your financial advisor for details.

You don't make enough money and have too many bills, put quite simply. Your credit cards reaching their limit is simply a visual symptom of this.

This might make you feel better, though most Americans are in a similar situation.

Consider this simple example: The personal financial statement of an average American worker, which assumes $4,000 in take-home pay and the following hard debt obligations:

1. A 100k mortgage, thirty years;

2. A 20k home equity line of credit, which was used on something[446] and now has become a liability;

3. Two vehicles, mid-30k–40k range on five-year notes;

4. A 10k maxed-out credit card; and

5. $100 cash in bank.

As you can see, this particular American (we called him *Joe the Plumber*) has "pledged" 70% of his take-home pay to hard, unyielding liabilities, WHICH, IN ALL LIKELIHOOD, CANNOT BE REMOVED. He needs the cars;[447] he needs his house; and he has no money or equity in the cars or the house with which to negotiate a more favorable trade or reduce his liability for any of his debts.

To wit

a. He cannot sell his house, or he will have to bring money to the table due to a thirty-year note and no equity. He is underwater due to his HELOC, a total encumbrance of 120k on his house versus 100k market value of his home.

b. He cannot sell his cars, and realistically, there is not a viable trade. He bought cars "new," and with "off the lot" depreciation, his cars are underwater too.

As you can see, **Joe is stuck** unless he comes into a massive, surprise sum of spendable cash, which is, statistically speaking, highly improbable.

And beyond being highly unlikely, what is MORE important to realize is that Joe leaves 30% of his take-home pay for other necessities, like food, gas, entertainment, clothing, and so forth. That creates a slim margin for error when unexpected expenses arise, which happens for most families monthly.

Allocation of Time Resources and Action Steps

So in contrast, the flip side of looking at Joe's financial picture and the action steps people

---

446 **"Something" = who knows?** Was it a boat? Go kart? Vacation? Many people cannot remember what they maxed out their HELOCS for and have the same lack of memory when it comes to their credit card spending. Terrible!

447 **Assuming he is married, and his spouse drives also, they have kids who need to go to school, the doctor, etc., and Joe cannot take off work for that with any degree of frequency**. Also, Joe does not have student loans or any other debt, which statistically is unrealistic.

tend to take in crisis situations. Let's discuss how one begins setting up a reasonable action plan for daily accountability and forward financial progress.

Example 1: Your Journey to Financial Freedom

    Bad, unrealistic goal: I want to be SO, SO RICH!

    Realistic goal: The Short-Term Retirement Program recommends making my biggest payment (housing) my smallest one by acquiring a residence that can provide me with a safe, secure stream of monthly rental income.

    This is a great first step toward my financial independence.

    I want to achieve this within the next twelve months. What is a good action plan?

    Use this simple worksheet to track your goals on a daily, weekly, or monthly basis. An editable version of this is available[448] if you want to make alterations to it or add additional steps—whatever works for you is what you need to put in writing. Notice how I have set up and broken down tasks into related columns, i.e., one of (finding a lender), daily, weekly, monthly time frames, etc.

Action Plan: Realistic Steps	Date Completed
Goal: Purchase Income Producing Primary Residence	
Timeframe: 12 Months	
Start Date: January 1st, 2019	
Action Steps: 1st 30 Days	**Date Completed**
Interview Three Realtors and Select One Specializing in Foreclosures	
Private Lender for Takedown Money	
Set Up Home Inspector for Inspection	
Identify Insurance Agent	
Identify Management Company (If Needed)	
Identify Closing Attorney	
Action Steps: Weekly	**Date Completed**
Look at Five Houses	
Make at Least One Offer at 50% Asking Price	
Browse Craigslist® to Look for Seller-Financed Opportunities	
Action Steps: Daily	**Date Completed**
Meditate on Eliminating Your House Payment	
Mediate and Visualize Finding Your "Right House"	
Action Steps: Moving Forward with Purchase	**Date Completed**
Property Contract Accepted and Signed	
Earnest Money Submitted	
Home Inspection Completed	
Money Lined Up to Close	
Closing Date Set	
Document Signed and Title Recorded - Finished!	

---

448   Go to ShortTermRetirement.com/downloads.

Kissing Frogs and Keeping Yourself Accountable

Notice that none of these types of worksheets work if YOU are unwilling. Part of daily goal setting and action steps is holding yourself accountable to what you did or did NOT do. Remember my vacation home that I told you about in the first chapter of this book? **I actually HAD to put an ad in the paper, and then I HAD to take over 100 phone calls from people who had properties I was NOT interested in!** It was only after going through such large numbers that I was able to find what I was looking for by sifting through LOTS of calls and e-mails about houses I was NOT looking for.

Finding the "right" home using Short-Term Retirement principles is pretty much the same way. You have to kiss a lot of "frogs" for one to turn into a prince or princess. **Part of the journey is NOT finding what you are looking for.** For example, you might find a perfect home except it had a water issue in a basement. While this might be frustrating, you can also learn from this by changing your search parameters to include ONLY houses that DO NOT have basements and save yourself some time and the reoccurrence of this issue, which was so frustrating to you in the first place.

But the most important thing is to do the following:

1. Make a plan with concrete, repeatable, achievable action steps.

2. Perform the action steps and hold yourself accountable to ensuring that they took place in the time frame you give yourself,[449] and

3. Reflect on what you learned, what was helpful versus a waste of time, then REVISE the action steps accordingly.

4. Repeat steps 1–4 until you have met and/or satisfied your goal.

Here is one more example of an action plan you might need on your journey to financial freedom using real estate:

Example 2: Finding Private Lenders

Bad, unrealistic goal: I need someone who will lend me as much money as I need RIGHT NOW with no payments and no interest for five years!

Realistic goal: Due to poor/marginal credit or other issues in my financial history, I cannot qualify for a traditional loan. **The Short-Term Retirement Program** recommends that I use private lenders to purchase an income-producing property, which can also serve as my primary residence. I need to interview some lenders and set up some new relationships, tracking how much they will lend to me and for how long. *I want to*

---

449 i.e., if your action plan calls for looking at ten houses a week, well, LOOK AT TEN HOUSES A WEEK!

achieve this within the next three months. What is a good action plan?

Here is another sample worksheet, which outlines a simple tracking and data-keeping plan for your research into private lending relationships. Keep in mind, it is YOUR responsibility to keep with all federal, state, local, and SEC regulations. A lack of knowledge is NOT an excuse to NOT follow the law!

Action Plan: Realistic Steps	Date Completed
Goal: Identify and Establish Relationships with Private Lenders	
Timeframe: 3 - 6 Months	
Start Date: January 1st, 2019	
Action Steps: 1st 30 Days	**Date Completed**
Buy Alan Cowgill Course	
Finish Studying Alan Cowgill Course	
Attend Local REIA Group Meeting and Speak with Private Lenders	
Make List of Lenders	
Interview Lenders	
Identify Terms	
Action Steps: Weekly	**Date Completed**
Have Lunch/Coffee with at Least Two Lenders per Week	
Make at Least One Offer at 50% Asking Price	
Browse Craigslist® to Look for Seller Financed Opportunities	
Action Steps: Daily	**Date Completed**
Continue Looking for Housing	
Bring Sample Properties to Your Lender for Review	
Action Steps: Moving Forward with Purchase	**Date Completed**
Property Contract Accepted and Signed	
Earnest Money Submitted	
Home Inspection Completed	
Money Lined-Up to Close	
Closing Date Set	
Document Signed and Title Recorded - Finished!	

Finding Motivation Even When It Is Eluding You

Let me tell you about a week I had recently. I had been out of town for a month in the summer, and when we returned home to Memphis, in addition to trying to play business "catch up," my wife reported to jury duty only to be sequestered! This put me in a position of having to care for our three children, all under the age of five, and put us even *further* behind in taking care of our business obligations.

When my wife was "released" from jury duty, I had several property vacancies arise and also had several people asking for my counsel in helping them acquire investment homes. The Sunday before the work week started, my wife and I had a hard conversation about the stack of work that lay ahead for both of us. It was a large task, trying to market and rent homes while working on catching up, business-wise, to the things in our brokerage that needed attention. I was kind of dreading it, to tell you the truth. But, realistically, the work had to get done.

So I vowed to do the following things:

1. Get up at 6:00 a.m. every day, leave by 7:30 a.m., work until 6:00 p.m. minimum, more as needed.

2. Take at least three applications on rental homes.

3. Get two new homes under contract.

4. Close at least two sales transactions.

5. Get all our accounts payable completed (an arduous task).

Now, it was a VERY long week, but I accomplished all of my goals. How? BECAUSE I KNEW I HAD TO OR I WOULD FALL FURTHER BEHIND.

Falling further behind would mean I have to work harder the following week or face the possibility of falling behind on my earning schedules and servicing my debt obligations. And in my heart (most importantly), I knew if I applied myself, I could get it done. I KNEW that I needed to DO the work, to benefit FROM the work, and put myself in a position to continue to earn FROM the work.

And, my friends, THAT is the difference between a paycheck-to-paycheck worker and one who has a Short-Term Retirement Program mind-set. Quite simply, the difference between a worker working with a mind-set of earning and getting paid today (dollars for hours, wages earned as a function of time) versus acquiring assets, which will pay you for LIFE, where the real paydays may be days, months, or even years down the line.

Entitlement Mind-set versus Working with a Purpose

Today at my brokerage, we got a call from a girl we will call Kelly. Kelly called to rent a house from us, but the conversation went like this:

Kelly: Hi, I am calling about that house at 123 Maple Street. I wanted to ask about renting the house because I am having a problem. I was evicted a few days ago and am under bankruptcy and was on Section 8 until the inspector said I wasn't taking care of the house, and then my landlord sued me for additional damages and won, but I have retained a lawyer and am about to sue. Will you rent me a house?

Now, Kelly doesn't fit our rental criteria because she is under an open bankruptcy and

THINGS IN LIFE WORTH LOVING

has a raw (very, very recent) eviction. But it was obvious from the phone call that Kelly wasn't great at making good, proactive decisions. Especially since the government was paying her rent via Section 8 and she was thrown off the program for a lack of effort.[450] Kelly's life would have been far better if she had:

a. Taken care of the house the government was paying her rent on, thus ensuring the integrity of her rental payments and guarantee self-preservation, or

b. Moved (as she stated the landlord didn't "fix anything").

But Kelly found herself with a bankruptcy (obviously, she was in over her head on her bills, rent paid by the government notwithstanding) and evicted, and now throwing what little money she had at a lawyer to pursue a lost and futile cause (suing a landlord who evicted her, presumably, for nonpayment).

Kelly's future is looking rather bleak.

Now, people will look at Kelly's situation in many ways. Some will say she is a victim of the system, of poverty. Some will say her case is sad because she lives in a land of such great opportunity and isn't able to take advantage of it, for whatever reason **[insert reason here]**. Some will question her work ethic, and some will praise her work ethic.

But the truth is, no matter which way you look at it, the truth is, Kelly is homeless and insolvent. These circumstances are clearly a consequence of her decisions. People may disagree with me, but I am going to go with the whole "Kelly, a working adult, is responsible for her life" thing.

That's just me.

On the opposite hand, alternatively, people have the option of working with a purpose, or what I call "working smart."

And that starts with this basic understanding of precepts, as follows:

Feol's Real-World Rules

1. Whether we like it or not, we are born into a system that operates around the availability of money.[451] This system does not discriminate and is color blind. You either are "born into" money,[452] meaning your parents are rich and you have a trust fund, so you don't have to work and experience the hardship the rest of us

---

450 Which is pretty hard to do?
451 PS, I didn't create the system, so don't get mad at me. :)
452 The infamous "one percent" of America.

do, or you are born into the 99%, who start out with a net worth of zero or less, and it's you versus the world, if you want to eat.

2. Assuming you like eating, you "scratching up" an existence will sometimes start after you leave your parents' house or, as is the case with many, many people, will start at a much younger age, due to parent abuse or neglect.

3. Starting with nothing means you have two simple choices:

4. **Choice 1:** Work every day (school, a job, attend college, entrepreneurial endeavor, etc.) with the idea of working your way up and believing you are the master of your own destiny; or

5. **Choice 2:** Realize that it is easier to live on government assistance and do so, either blaming the system for dealing you such a bad hand of cards and blaming other people for your circumstances, acknowledging that your destiny was completely out of your control and you have been victimized.

6. Either way, whatever you believe, you are right.

7. See rule number one.

8. Optional (helpful) information—entitlements are unsustainable and will eventually run out, leaving those who subsist on them to starve. The government knows this but avoids it by raising the "debt ceiling." At some point, that will end.

Now, the difference between the person who makes choice number one versus choice number two is simple. In choice number two, they acknowledge that they have a bad hand and feel they can do nothing about it, but in choice number one, they acknowledge that they have a bad hand BUT CAN do something about it.

But to be clear, they both are dealt a bad hand.

What the beautiful people on TV don't tell you is that 99% of the world's population is dealt a bad hand. Yes, that's right, 99% of the world are born without trust funds and, frequently, into poverty and squalor. In fact, being born as a lower-class or middle-class American in the United States at the time of this writing gives you access to education, healthcare, and sanitation, which goes far beyond that of most third-world countries, which gives you an extreme edge in survival odds, if not prosperity.

So, yes, it is true that most people in the world are dealt a horrible hand in the sense of that they are forced to play cards within the framework of the current incarnation of our financial system, which is skewed toward a select few.

It's as if 99% of the world's population is playing Texas Hold 'Em, and they are born looking at their hole cards—2–7 off suit, while the 1% is born looking at A–A.[453]

The only difference is how the cards get played.

Pro tip: Sometimes 2–7 off suit wins BIG pots, though the odds are against it.

The person who makes choice number one in this scenario understands they have a bad hand, but that doesn't mean that they are willing to give up and "fold" the hand. In fact, they will scrape and fight and do almost ANYTHING to prevent the creditors from coming and knocking on their door.

And sometimes this means:

1. Paying creditors before they pay themselves;

2. Providing for their families before they provide for themselves;

3. Working as many hours as it takes to get the funds necessary to stay solvent;

4. Losing sleep;

5. Neglecting their heath and exercise in the interests of everyone else's health and well-being;

6. Going without **[insert necessity *here*]; and**

7. Sacrificing pleasures for today, as they search for a better future.

Which person are you?

Working and Planning for the Future

When I started **The Short-Term Retirement Program,** I realized that life was happening fast.

So fast, in fact, that while I had just gotten married in my early thirties, I couldn't really recall where my twenties had gone. It seemed like just yesterday I was still in high school, then BAM, my college years flew by and my twenties were not far behind it. I am pretty sure, in retrospect, this was due to the sheer number of hours I was working. I remember working as a full-time teacher in Utica by day, then working at The Ground Round restaurant at night, five shifts a week, including a double on Saturday. One night, while returning home to my apartment in Oneida, I remember being so exhausted that I sat on the edge of my bed (it was bitter cold in wintertime), and with my winter coat and boots on, I thought, *I'll just close my eyes for a minute,* only to wake up fourteen hours later

---

453 Double Aces, best starting hand in Texas Hold 'Em.

with my boots on and my coat on. I had slept fourteen hours straight after collapsing on the bed in my winter clothing! Most of my twenties were spent working those kinds of hours.

In my thirties, I realized that my forties would come, and wouldn't those be better if I had five paid off homes to help me, income-wise? After all, my forties *were* coming, and I realized, IF I DON'T START TRYING TO PAY OFF PROPERTY NOW, I WILL HAVE TO START IN MY FORTIES.

So that is how I started—working my regular job but buying houses at the same time and using aggressive mortgage payoffs to accelerate my wealth building. While I went to my day-to-day job, I was always thinking about, and strategizing, for the future. In doing so, I was acquiring assets along the way that were paying themselves off.

In a sense, I was working smart.

Ironically, all my colleagues who bought investment homes about the same time I did, using thirty-year loans, now have (ten years later) almost unchanged mortgage balances and twenty years left to go, but for me, most of my properties are paid off and cash flowing each month.

Am I smarter than my colleagues?

Absolutely not.

But somewhere along the line, I learned that the number one cause of divorce was financial insolvency, and I thought about my mom and dad getting divorced when I was three (which neither of them really ever recovered from) and **realized that I didn't want that for my wife or kids, so maybe working on a stable financial picture was in MY best interest, and that of my family's**. I realized that I would never become financially free if I didn't put in the work and gain the knowledge and understanding of these financial principles I now share with you. **It was about understanding and accepting that I was COMPELLED to do the work and to get the knowledge necessary to start acquiring assets the *right way* and not just do so blindly.**

And I knew real estate was the way for me.

Working and planning for the future, using investment real estate as my base, was the best decision I have ever made.

Why?

Because I knew the future would inevitably come, like my thirties and forties.

And more importantly, I realized that the things in life worth loving were the very same reasons that I wanted to "slay the financial dragon" in the first place: **my wife, my children, and spending time with them and keeping them safe. I realized that maybe putting my single-parent upbringing behind me, once and for all, could be addressed and conquered by giving my wife and children something my parents could NEVER**

give me—a stable home, a stable family, a life, hope, love, and a sense of safety and purpose.

I realized along the way that these things worth loving, these things worth cherishing, they are WORTH working for and, most importantly, WORTH loving, WORTH giving to, WORTH sacrificing for, and even worth dying for, if needed.

I recognized that just because I was a broke kid from a broken home; those circumstances didn't have to define me.

In fact, I have refused to let those circumstances define me.

A lack of financial stability in any family is bound to cause problems at best.

At worst, it will destroy it.

Those are the facts. **If you cherish your family, and you are a provider or parent, it is your RESPONSIBILITY to provide your family with a financially stable environment.** If you cannot do that in this land of opportunity, well, ask yourself if you are really working hard enough. If you feel like you are working hard enough but not getting to where you need to be, change the question **and then ask yourself if you are working smart enough.** With the knowledge you have gained in this book, there is no excuse not to begin your journey to financial freedom. **You will never get there working paycheck to paycheck.** I have shown you through the math; it simply doesn't work, and you have to be smarter about it if you truly wish to become financially free.

That's all I can tell you. Your financial destiny, like your life's destiny, is in YOUR hands.

Accept your fate or change it; it is solely up to you.

The skills and knowledge of how to shatter the financial "matrix" you have been entrapped in is all contained within this book.

The person responsible for where your life is today can always be found in the mirror in your bathroom.

Remember that, then meditate on this wisdom.

THE MYTH OF "REAL" PROPERTY, A "LIFE GUIDE"[454]

You cannot "own"[455] a property until you ACQUIRE it.

You cannot ACQUIRE a property until you have EARNED the money for it.

If you have not invested enough hours[456] to have EARNED the money for a property, you must BORROW it.

If you BORROW money for a property, you are forced to comply with the LENDER'S TERMS.

It is in the LENDER'S BEST INTEREST to KEEP YOU IN DEBT AS LONG AS POSSIBLE. THIS IS WHY THIRTY-YEAR MORTGAGES EXIST.

THEY CREATE AN ILLUSION OF OWNERSHIP WHEN STATISTICALLY VERY FEW PEOPLE EVER SEE THEIR MORTGAGE PAY OFF AFTER A THIRTY-YEAR PERIOD.

IF YOU WANT TO BECOME WEALTHY BY ACQUIRING ASSETS, YOU WILL (GENERALLY) HAVE TO BORROW MONEY AND PAY IT OFF TO SECURE THE ASSET FOR YOUR FAMILY. IF YOU DO SO, SERVICE THE DEBT AS QUICKLY AS POSSIBLE AND USE THE INCOME OF OTHERS TO DO SO (IF POSSIBLE). ONCE YOU DO THIS, YOU CAN KEEP THE ASSET IN YOUR FAMILY FOR MULTIPLE GENERATIONS AND PASS WEALTH ONTO YOUR CHILDREN'S CHILDREN.

BANKS DO NOT LEND REAL MONEY; THEY LEND WORTHLESS PAPER AGAINST REAL ASSETS.

REAL WEALTH DOES NOT LIE IN WORTHLESS PAPER, STOCKS, AND BONDS. IT LIES IN PHYSICAL COMMODITIES, LAND, SEEDS, LIVESTOCK, WATER, REAL ESTATE, AND APPLICABLE HUMAN KNOWLEDGE AND SKILLS.

IT IS IN YOUR FAMILY'S BEST INTEREST TO ACQUIRE THESE ASSETS WHILE YOU CAN.

THE CASINO THAT IS WALL STREET IS DESTINED TO FAIL. IT IS ENTIRELY BASED ON FRAUD AND USURPING THE AMERICAN PEOPLE. IT WILL FAIL

---

454 Assumes you are starting from zero, net worth zero, no family help.
455 Meaning, paid off.
456 A highly arduous task as a day laborer, to be clear, and one which takes an enormous amount of TIME and DISCIPLINE while municipal taxes and governmental taxes work against you.

AGAIN AND FAR WORSE THAN 2008. TAKE YOUR MONEY OUT WHILE YOU CAN AND STOP "FEEDING THE BEAST."

MANY PEOPLE WILL READ THIS MESSAGE, BUT FAR FEWER WILL UNDERSTAND THIS AND PUT IT INTO ACTION. TAKE ACTION TODAY BY PAYING OFF DEBT AND REPOSITIONING YOUR INVESTMENT AND FINANCIAL GOALS INTO ACCUMULATING ITEMS OF VALUE FOR FUTURE ECONOMIC AND PERSONAL STABILITY. DOWNSIZE IF NECESSARY.

PAY OFF YOUR PRIMARY RESIDENCE. IN DOING SO, YOU WILL BE KEEPING YOUR FAMILY SAFE.

LOVE ONE ANOTHER. HELP THE HOMELESS. FORGIVE.

BECOME COLOR BLIND.

ASK FOR THE GIFT OF DISCERNMENT TO LEARN HOW TO AVOID THE LIES BEING TOLD TO YOU FOR SPECIFIC AGENDAS.

TITHE 10% OF YOUR EARNINGS, AND WATCH THE BLESSINGS RAIN.

REMEMBER, GOD'S TAX IS 10%. ANYTHING HIGHER THAN THAT IS USURY.

ON MISSISSIPPI HIGHWAY 302, ONE NIGHT, I WALKED ALONE FOR MILES AND MILES AND WAS GIVEN THIS MESSAGE, BUT IT TOOK ME SEVEN YEARS TO UNDERSTAND IT AND PLACE IT INTO THIS WRITING.

I HAVE BEEN ASKED TO SHARE IT WITH YOU IN THE HOPE THAT IT HELPS YOUR FAMILY.

WE ARE ONE BROTHERHOOD OF HUMANITY.

BE WARY OF ANYONE WHO SEEKS TO SET US AGAINST ONE ANOTHER.

LOVE, FORGIVE, LOVE, FORGIVE, LOVE.

Zen Koan: Flower Shower

Subhuti was Buddha's disciple. He was able to understand the potency of emptiness, the viewpoint that nothing exists except in its relationship of subjectivity and objectivity.

One-day Subhuti, in a mood of sublime emptiness, was sitting under a tree. Flowers began to fall about him.

"We are praising you for your discourse on emptiness," the gods whispered to him.

"But I have not spoken of emptiness," said Subhuti.

"You have not spoken of emptiness. We have not heard emptiness," responded the gods. "This is the true emptiness."

And blossoms showered upon Subhuti as rain.

15

The Man Who Tunneled Through Mountains

Another Zen Meditation

The Tunnel—A Zen Koan

Zenkai, the son of a samurai, journeyed to Edo, and there became the retainer of a high official. He fell in love with the official's wife and was discovered. In self-defense, he slew the official. Then he ran away with the wife.

Both of them later became thieves. But the woman was so greedy that Zenkai grew disgusted. Finally, leaving her, he journeyed far away to the province of Buzen, where he became a wandering mendicant.

To atone for his past, Zenkai resolved to accomplish some good deed in his lifetime. Knowing of a dangerous road over a cliff that had caused death and injury to many persons, he resolved to cut a tunnel through the mountain there.

Begging food in the daytime, Zenkai worked at night digging his tunnel. When thirty years had gone by, the tunnel was 2,280 feet long, 20 feet high, and 30 feet wide.

Two years before the work was completed, the son of the official he had slain, who was a skillful swordsman, found Zenkai out and came to kill him in revenge.

"I will give you my life willingly," said Zenkai. "Only let me finish this work. On the day it is completed, then you may kill me."

So the son awaited the day. Several months passed, and Zenkai kept digging. The son grew tired of doing nothing and began to help with the digging. After he had helped for more than a year, he came to admire Zenkai's strong will and character.

At last, the tunnel was completed, and the people could use it and travel safely.

"Now cut off my head," said Zenkai. "My work is done."

"How can I cut off my own teacher's head?" asked the younger man with tears in his eyes.

16

A Journey of
One Thousand Miles

Begins with a single step.

On the surface, that sounds really easy and simple.

"Just get started," say your friends. "Start today!"

Simple, right?

But if you are like me, life has been filled with a lot of starts, false starts—multi-level marketing companies, jobs, careers, investments, and other endeavors, which I realized were not for me or were too arduous and time-consuming for me to get onboard with. For example, I LOVE multilevel marketing, but it just became too hard for me to start looking at everyone like a prospect. I am not in any way criticizing the world of MLM, but the top performers in that niche, to be honest, have the gift of total persistence and never backing down when someone tells you *no*. It's impressive, to be frank, and many people make a lot of money in multilevel marketing. I am just not one of them.

I joke with myself and tell myself I will make a lot of money in multilevel marketing when I have a platform where I can teach people about a product on a widespread scale versus having to "pitch" them. **But the reality of MLM is you have to be prepared to "pitch" people, and I am not great at doing that.** MLM companies for me, for example, have had a lot of excited but "false" starts. Lots of anticipation at what the income potential was, but when I got into the thick of it, I realized that I didn't have the time or motivation to work the way I needed to obtain the results I wanted. And sometimes I recognized that the investment of time versus the financial recompense was not on equal footing, and in the end, I abandoned one pursuit or another.

Real estate investing, however, and the obsession that I have developed with paying off debt in the wake of it and my pursuit of financial freedom, was never a false start. It was one of the few *real* starts I ever had and one of the most worthwhile.

The best part? When you are transacting real estate, the number of zeroes is so much bigger than when you are selling or engaging in the transaction of other items, it almost makes it so that pursuing other, non-real estate careers almost doesn't make sense.

I have been accused of many things, but no one has ever accused me of forgetting my roots or the life I was forced to live before I came to Memphis as a broke and hungry kid. I understand the value of a dollar, and I learned to recognize that dollars slipped from my hand far too easily when I was younger.

Sometimes today it feels like they do also, but I don't feel that way quite as much, or at least not quite as frequently as I used to.

I didn't really know my dad, but he would say this to me often. He would say, "**Son, a fool and his money are soon parted.**" I think about this saying and have done so my whole life, and ultimately, it ends up with me asking myself the uncomfortable question of "**Am I the fool? In this transaction,**[457] **am I the fool?**" Sometimes the answer is clear, and sometimes, to be honest, the answer isn't quite as forthcoming. It is a question that haunts me.

And this is the nature of money. Things that look attractive on the surface are often worthless. Things that look like junk, well, just might be the best deal you have ever found. What's important is being able to delineate between the two. Foreclosed homes are a perfect example. There is treasure to be found there, certainly, but lots of trash to be dug through on the way there.

Remember what my mentor Al Plumb said?

"**Robert, the path to financial freedom is paved straight through the garbage dump of life.**"

Money corrupts people. Don't ever forget this. People become blinded by money, and frequently, the scarcity of it, in their lives, for whatever reason, will cause them to go insane and do crazy things. I had a contractor steal 130k from me one time over a series of transactions. It was an extremely difficult and embarrassing thing to go through, but it made me realize that the line of moral failure for humans is very thin and VERY gray, and many people, given the temptation, are prepared to go over the precipice without knowing it.

It's a sobering thought.

But money, in the right hands, can be a powerful tool, not only for building wealth but also for helping others. It can be a life-changing tool, not just for yourself, but when you have enough of it, for many, many other people also. And as I have discussed so frequently in this book, you really cannot think about helping others until you save

---

457   Buying or selling...whatever.

yourself from drowning, financially speaking, and from the lodestones and negative consequences that come with that type of financial insolvency so many of us are beset with. The stress. The anxiety. The sleepless nights trying to tell your spouse and/or kids that you cannot do "x" because you don't have the funds, and that the reason you do not have the funds is because you have not made good decisions financially.[458]

So take that first step. That single step. Start your own **Short-Term Retirement Program.**

And I hope that step is the most powerful, life-changing step you can possibly imagine, which changes your life for future generations of your family to come. **Get that mortgage paid off.** Use other people's income to help you make your payments and then EXCEED them. **Don't focus on what you cannot do; focus on a lifetime of LIMITLESS POSSIBILITY and UNBRIDLED JOY.** Make these mantras and the ideas in this book the cornerstone of your brilliant and prosperous future, the one you didn't even know you had until you read this book.

I took the first step, and it was one of the best decisions I ever made.

Now you go do it and run a different race that you set for yourself, NOT the one the bankers want you to run in and fail.

Go. **Go and make your own Short-Term Retirement plan.**

Create your own destiny.

And when you take your first step, let me know about it—robertfeol@gmail.com.

I promise no one will be cheering harder for you on your way to the bank than I will.

Here's to your *brilliant* success.

Robert C. Feol
January 15th, 2019

> **Get a Year or Two of Your Child's College for Free Using Uncle Sam's Money as an Interest-Free Loan**
>
> First, I want to reiterate that college is a bad investment.
>
> It's bad. Period. And designed to keep your kids in debt for a long, long time.
>
> In fact, over 51% of students surveyed in 2017 by the National Association of Realtors reported having 50k or more in student loan debt upon graduation.[459]

---

458   But would you actually tell them that?
459   https://www.nar.realtor/sites/default/files/reports/2017/2017-student-loan-debt-and-housing-09-18-2017.pdf.

When you send your kid to college, while you think you are sending them to get an education, the truth is, you are sending them to get an *almost* worthless piece of paper that will yield them little to no long-term income, but be assured, you are definitely paying for the basketball and football programs and contributing significantly to those coaches' multi-million-dollar salaries.

We can't fault the schools, really. I mean, we worship college athletic stars far more than the most intellectually gifted student in attendance. For example, name your favorite college athlete who was just drafted into a professional career? I am sure you can.

Now name last year's graduating valedictorian and salutatorian from your favorite college or your alma mater.

You can't.

Don't feel bad, your friends can't either.

The schools (colleges) realized long ago that it was far more worthwhile to build stadiums; sell concessions, seats, boxes, sprit wear; and create an athletic celebrity environment while forming contracts with television broadcast networks like ESPN to increase revenue than to pay teachers, give them long-term benefits, invest money in academic programs, and address the needs of young students in a volatile, changing work environment and, in doing so, deliver what is truly needed to make a student employable while give them a fighting chance to earn a living wage. The reality is, most professors these days are adjunct, non-tenure track, part-time babysitters happy to make $2,000 per semester helping all students to "pass" whatever dumbed-down course material they have been charged with.

Think I am joking? Go ask *Professor Doom*.[460]

Of course, I can't blame colleges for wanting to run a business. Colleges, generally, are for profit. The administrators love it that way. They love to get paid, jumping from institution to institution while making terrible investments[461] and *generally* doing nothing for the students, while getting million-dollar raises. It pays to be chancellor, I promise you.

---

460 http://rense.com/general96/profofcol.html.
461 http://professorconfess.blogspot.com/2016/06/the-hierarchy-of-education-fraud.html?q=bankrupt.

Naturally, some of us, ***myself included***, value these worthless pieces of paper[462] and value it for our kids.[463] So let's learn how to go to school for free.

Disclaimer: This example assumes you are planning on sending your child to a 50k-a-year college and have the money to pay for it. If you are broke and hoping to go to college yourself, there are far easier and more cost-effective ways to do it. AP classes (which give you free college credit, honored by most universities, assuming you test well on the exam), college equivalent classes (where you take classes in high school, which give you college credit, accepted by most universities), three-year universities which give you a four-year degree in three years, playing the tuba,[464] etc.

Step One

Determine the price of college annually.

Let's assume it's 50k. This includes room and board, books, miscellaneous expenses (of which there are many), and so forth. It costs you 50k. You have the cash to do it.[465]

Solution 1: Pay the 50k when it comes due in late August. Now your 50k saved nest egg has disappeared, and in doing so, you are unable to invest, lend, or gain interest on savings.

Solution 2: Keep your money. Let your student take out a fully subsidized, interest-deferred "direct loan."[466] While your student is learning, you are busy putting your money to work in real estate.[467] Here are a few ways you can do it. Keep in mind, if we generate 50k in income from our 50k nest egg, we are winning. Anything more is gravy.

1. **Make "hard money loans":** As discussed in previous chapters, these are loans that are secured by real estate with high equity positions. A general baseline for loan fees is five points and 1% per month aggregate interest, with a ninety-day balloon turnaround time. Assuming 50k lent, done four times per year, your yield would look like this:

---

462 For whatever random reason, for ourselves or our children.
463 I have four degrees myself and am currently working on two more.
464 **A little-known secret by high school band directors is that very few players want to play tuba, so there is usually a full scholarship waiting for a competent high school tuba player willing to march in college band.** Very few notes and just three valves; maybe YOUR kid has what it takes and can get a free college degree with it!
465 **If you don't have the funds, you or your kid will end up taking student loans,** which results in 200k of aggregate debt—far more than the average price of an entry-level house.
466 Or equivalent. See here: https://www.studentloans.gov/myDirectLoan/index.action.
467 If you hate real estate, you can also look at other plays, such as this: http://www.simpleoptions.com/.

50k × five origination points (5% – $2,500), + 1% monthly for 3 months: = $4,000 per loan, interest payments and fees.

Generating four loans per year = $16,000 per year revenue on 50k lent.

Lending this scenario over four years of college: 64k profit PLUS your 50k retained funds

Total capital plus profit after four years: $114k

Annual aggregate return: 32%

2. **Decide how you want to pay off your child's college.**

   Choice 1: Apply your 114k accrued nest egg to your child's 200k debt encumbrance, and your child has a loan balance of 86k versus 200k. Not a bad parental contribution.

   OR

   Choice 2: Continue to lend your 114k until it reaches 200k. Assuming 32% on your money, this would be about 2.5 more years, maybe three years total if you want to pay deferred interest. Then when your nest egg reaches 200k, pay off your child's student loans and let them live a life of financial freedom.

   Summary: Buy three years of college, get one free at minimum. Your child spent 200k on college, but you retained 60k from lending interest and fees, which offset a year of college costs minimally.

   OR

   Keep reinvesting your profits into a secure private lending scenario and have your kid's 200k in loans paid off within thirty-six months of their graduation. **Now you are parent of the year!** ☺

Just a Normal Day in the Robert Feol Office[468]

471

468 Uh-oh! Looks like someone is about to get the deal of their life, 200k in equity and a four-acre lake view for one-sixth of what the previous owner paid. Unfortunately, I was a day late and a dollar short on this one, but my loss is someone else's gain. And to pay off the house worth roughly 250k for a purchase price of $43,500, using a five-year payoff, makes their monthly payment $801.12, assuming 4% fixed interest. Cheaper than rent for a 200k net gain? Not to mention a luxury living arrangement for most people using a "beer budget." Foiled again, big banks! **I mean, why should I indebt myself to you for thirty years when I can pay you off in five, assuming I use you at all?** Later, fools!

Epilogue

You understand the nature of a man by his enemies.
—Alex Jones (2017)

The first time I heard this expression, it immediately made sense to me. When I heard it, contextually, Alex Jones[469] was using it to discuss his view on President Trump's initial adversarial days in the Oval Office with the media, but the expression itself is timeless and alludes to this: **If you understand the nature of the people who hate a man, then you must be able, through antagonistic inference, to understand the character and nature of the man so hated**. To use a crude example, if said man is very much in favor of freedom and democracy, his enemies by their nature cannot be in favor of such freedoms; it is because of his nature that they hate him. They cannot ally with him, for he stands for everything they oppose.

I don't know whether this book will succeed or fail, as I write this from my home in Memphis, Tennessee, after a seven-year effort. My guess is that if it does find any success, it will receive a significant amount of criticism and discredit from large financial firms and financial "advisors," as well as major financial media, all of which have a deeply vested interest in you and every American family NOT putting their money into real estate and NOT paying off their mortgages early. They want American families to perpetuate the endless cycle of debt and refinance. The Federal Reserve is complicit in perpetuating this ideology as well.

If the only thing the book achieves is a growing awareness of why thirty-year mortgages are "bad," then I think the book has served a strong purpose of increasing the financial awareness of the American people. If, beyond that, people more deeply understand the importance of debt elimination and/or the value of acquiring real estate for financial stability, then even better.

---

469   Famous radio show host and founder of a website called InfoWars.com.

372

One time (years ago), I consulted for a local Memphis real estate brokerage that was struggling. As I began to turn their business around significantly within a one-year period, I discovered that they were lying about their business model and deceiving their customers. Immediately, I resigned on the grounds of their unethical (and illegal) behavior.

A few weeks later, I silently listened on the phone as one of the principals of the firm I resigned from disparaged me to one of the staff at my personal brokerage. "A LIAR," he said, not knowing I was listening silently. "KNOWS NOTHING ABOUT REAL ESTATE," he went on. "A FRAUD."

I went on to watch him and his partner lose hundreds of properties at tax sale and to foreclosure a few months later. And to be frank, he is a terrible guy. Really disgraceful.

The point is, when I think about that guy from time to time, instead of feeling hatred toward a man I helped so much for taking such a hostile stance and generating such blatant lies against me, I only feel a sense of peace. Peace because he was so mad that I resigned from his brokerage once I saw the fabric of his character. He saw me as an enemy, an enemy because I would not lie for him and collude with him for some monetary gain.

Obviously, he and I were cut from different cloths.

Following different rule sets, it would seem.

Our mamas taught us differently, as they say in the South.

And I'm okay with that, to tell you the truth. **If deceitful, malicious people are my enemy, then I must be doing something right.** I can look my wife, my son, and my daughters in the eye and know that I am heading in the right direction as a husband, father, and man and pray it is acceptable in the eyes of the Lord, too.

It is important to recognize, however, that the same thing applies to the critics of this book. If they find reasons to malign this text and the financial, economic, and mathematical theory behind it, I am okay with it and hold no malice toward them. I just hope the American people see it differently.

But I am guessing that those critics have thirty-year mortgages.

Robert Feol
Memphis, Tennessee
January 15th, 2019

About the Author

International speaker, author, and radio personality, Robert Feol is considered by many to be one of the youngest, most up-and-coming real estate investors and motivational speakers in the real estate industry today. Feol's maverick approach to real estate acquisition and financing, and uncompromising attitude toward integrity and full disclosure-based method of real estate investing has earned him numerous accolades, including having *New York Times* best-selling real estate author Robert Shemin stating that Robert's radio program is "the best real estate investing radio program in the United States."

Considered a "visionary" by many of his clients and radio show listeners, Feol's innate ability to locate highly discounted investing opportunities and get them online has resulted in him being involved in over 2,000 purchase and sale transactions over the past twelve years—a phenomenal accomplishment for someone who is just forty-four years old.

In 2009, Robert created and trademarked through the United States Patent and Trademark Office "The Short-Term Retirement Program" (www.ShortTermRetirement.com), a groundbreaking real estate purchase system that allows any investor, regardless of nationality, to take advantage of private financing and aggressive amortizations to build a strong real estate portfolio and have it paid off in as little as five years.

For over nine years, Robert was the host and founder of *Pieces of the Puzzle: Journeys in Creative Real Estate Investing*, the number one weekend radio talk show on 990 KWAM—"The New Voice of Memphis" with listeners around the world. Its main focus is real estate education and understanding how to meet one's goals of financial freedom.

Robert has also distinguished himself with high accolades and awards across a variety of disciplines, including graduating as a triple major from Syracuse University; obtaining a master's degree from one of two all-deaf colleges in the United States, where all his classes were taught in American Sign Language; having five black belts in various martial arts systems, and currently holds a blue belt in Brazilian jujitsu. Robert is a highly accomplished and award-winning Junior Olympic volleyball coach who coaches both academic and club volleyball; and he is ***also*** considered a highly accomplished guitarist on both classical and steel-string fingerstyle guitar, currently working on his graduate degrees in music at the University of Memphis. He is a former award-winning educator who was tenured in the Memphis City School district and is a published choral composer and arranger.

Robert is also heavily involved in charity work in his hometown of Memphis as well as Rochester, New York. He has saved the lives of hundreds of helpless dogs and cats through his strategic partnership with Save 1 Pet of Memphis and established an endowment for underprivileged youth to attend McQuaid Jesuit High School, his alma mater, considered one of the top schools in New York State.

Robert has been married to his beautiful wife Shannon for the past eleven years, and they share three beautiful and amazing children—Robbie, Kerrigan, and Tennessee. Their family travels routinely and competes in high-level BBQ contests under the name Uncle Feol's Tennessee Style BBQ. Their award-winning BBQ sauce won the Virginia State Championship in 2017, placed 2nd in the Mississippi State Championship in 2018, and they were the Grand Champions of The Hernando, Mississippi Water Tower BBQ Festival in 2018, placing 1st in Ribs and 1st Place overall. They live in Memphis, Tennessee.

Destiny isn't a chance, it's a choice.

—Robert Feol

Winning is not a sometime thing; it's an all-time thing. You don't win once in a while, you don't do things right once in a while, you do them right all the time. Winning is habit. Unfortunately, so is losing.

—Vince Lombardi

Acknowledgments

Here I am—working on, trying to, thank all the people who have sat with me on this journey, bringing this book to readers globally.

I am so proud of the endorsements I have received from authors I truly love and to have *New York Times* bestselling author Robert Shemin, a great inspiration to me, agree to write a foreword? I was over the moon.

In my office, a brilliant real estate prodigy named Stephen Akindona comes into my office everyday and lets me know how I am doing, regarding success or failings, and frequently in song form. Sometime it is hard to hear, if things aren't going right. But these days, I realize the voices in my office and my team, from my close colleagues and friends, are the greatest music I could hope to hear. These true friends refuse to let me down and only want me to do my very best. Bringing this book to market has been a labor of love, but it is a clarion example of how no man is an island. Without a team of people in place who are experts in their successful fields, and committed to *your* success, it becomes extremely difficult for anyone to succeed.

So, it is in that sentiment, though there are so many people that I cannot thank everyone who has been involved in this project, that I want to say thank you to the following people:

<u>Amy Collins at New Shelves Publishing:</u> For the leap of faith, taking me on, your mentorship and coaching, and access to your personal cell phone. This project came to life because of your faith in me.

Steve Harrison – I've been a big fan of Steve Harrison for years. If you don't know, Steve Harrison is the publishing expert who made Robert Kiyosaki famous. The story goes, Robert Kiyosaki's wife somehow found Steve Harrison, called him, asked him to help liquidate the 10,00 copies of *Rich Dad, Poor Dad* which were molding in their garage. And, well, the rest is history. I took the Kool Aid, and subscribed to Steve's channel, his webinars. The guy is a genius.

Keri-Rae Barnum and Conor Rohan at New Shelves Publishing – for your diligent, and daily, work to bring this book to fruition. That's a lot of emails and correspondence! But worth every moment invested.

To Patrick Burleson – We've been together 10 years, and what a ride. I could not be where I am today without your help! I am so excited about our work together and your generous use of your time to help us improve every day, at both Discount Property Warehouse and Rivertown Realty. But the best part is calling you one of my closest friends. Can't wait for what is next to come!

To Stephen Akindona – Your work and faithful countenance is an inspiration to me. I cherish our friendship, and when we are in our element working together on marketing and sales efforts I really feel alive. You truly have the real estate gift in you!

To Suzanne Scott, and all our staff and contractors at Discount Property Warehouse – Construction is the straw that stirs the drink. You guys have the most important job. You ARE the reason.

To Mom and Nana – For working so hard when we had nothing, and teaching me what work really was.

To Hulet Gregory and Eric Linderman of REI Capital – Our private lending relationship and your mentorship has been invaluable to our team at Discount Property Warehouse. Thank You!

To Alex Meadows, Bo Hardy, and ALL my brothers and sisters at Midtown Grappling Academy – for the daily lessons, beatings, and healings over the past five years.

To Pastor Danny Williams of Victory Electric – For being my spiritual advisor in the darkest of times. I love it when we pray together.

To Al Plumb of Alpco Recycling – For your mentorship through the years, and your generous time, starting back 20 years when I was nobody. PS: I am still nobody, don't think I haven't learned that! "The road to financial success is paved through the dump." – Al Plumb

<u>To Shannon Feol</u> – my loving wife, so faithful and steadfast. You are my best friend. I LOVE YOU SO BAD! Nothing I have ever done I could have achieved without you. I told you when we got married it would be worth it. I hope it has been. Don't stop believin'.

<u>To Robbie, Kerrigan, and Tennessee</u> – My precious babies. I love you SO BAD!!!

<u>To people who have stolen from me or have not fulfilled their promises or kept their word</u> – Stop being a disgrace. You know who you are.

<u>To you, the reader</u> – I hope this book brings as much value to you as the system I teach in here has brought to me and my family.

Made in the USA
Monee, IL
11 September 2022

13790306R00221